ESDAILE'S MANUAL
OF BIBLIOGRAPHY

ESDAILE'S MANUAL OF BIBLIOGRAPHY

Fifth revised edition

ROY STOKES

THE SCARECROW PRESS
1981

FIRST PUBLISHED	1931
SECOND EDITION	1932
THIRD REVISED EDITION	1954
FOURTH IMPRESSION	1958
FIFTH IMPRESSION	1963
FOURTH REVISED EDITION	1967
FIFTH REVISED EDITION	1981

Library of Congress Cataloging in Publication Data

Esdaile, Arundell James Kennedy, 1880–1956.
  Esdaile's Manual of bibliography.

  Includes bibliographies and index.
  1. Bibliography.   2.   Library science.
I.   Stokes, Roy Bishop, 1915–   II.   Title.
III.   Title: Manual of bibliography.
Z1001.E75   1981   010'.7   81-9088
ISBN   0-8108-1462-5   AACR2

ACKNOWLEDGMENTS

Grateful acknowledgment is made to Messrs. H. P. Kraus of New York for permission to quote from their catalog No. 108; to Messrs. Bernard Quaritch of London to quote from their centenary catalogue of 1947; to Mr. Richard Sadler to quote from his late father's *XIX Century Fiction;* to the Trustees of the British Museum to quote from the *Catalogue of Books Printed in the XVth Century;* and to the Walters Art Gallery of Baltimore to quote from Dorothy Miner's catalog *The History of Bookbinding 525 to 1950 A.D.*

CONTENTS

FIGURES

PLATES

2. Paper making in Europe in the sixteenth century. The vatman, coucher, and layman are performing their respective duties. The "pistolet," or heating device, may be seen on the extreme left. (Size of original: 22.9cm × 16.5cm.)

Photograph by courtesy of the Institute of Paper Chemistry, Appleton, Wisconsin.

3. English wooden press, early eighteenth century. Popularly known as the "Franklin Press" because Benjamin Franklin worked on it when employed as journeyman printer in London, 1725–1726.

Now in the Smithsonian Institution, Washington, D.C.

Smithsonian Institution Photograph Number 17539c.

4. Engraving by Abraham von Werdt of the interior of a printing office. The print is included in the first volume of Deutsches Leben der Vergangenheit in Bildern, by Eugen Diederichs (Jena, 1908). The date of the original print is 1666. (Size of original: 13.75cm × 20.5cm.)

Photograph by permission of the British Library.

5. The composing room. Frontispiece to C. H. Timperley's The Printer's Manual (London: H. Johnson; Manchester: Banck's and Co., 1838).

6. Wotton binding. Cicero, Les questions Tusculanes. Lyons (n.d.). British Library: C.69.D.17.

Brown calf, tooled in gold with interlacing ribbon, solid and open tools, and with on the upper cover: THOMAE WOTTONI, and on the lower cover: ET AMICORVM. Decorated with black paint. Re-backed. 163 × 110 × 20mm.

Sir Thomas Wotton was an English book collector of the mid–sixteenth century who had many of his books, as this one, bound for him in Paris.

Photograph by permission of the British Library.

7. *Front cover of the St. Cuthbert Gospel, also known as the Stonyhurst Gospel. The earliest known surviving European leather bookbinding. Crimson-stained goatskin over thin wooden boards. Late seventh century, probably shortly after the death of St. Cuthbert in 687. (Size of original: 13.75cm × 9.75cm.)*

   By permission of the English Province of the Society of Jesus. Photograph by permission of the British Library.

8. *St. Cuthbert Gospel, back cover.*

   By permission of the English Province of the Society of Jesus. Photograph by permission of the British Library.

ARUNDELL ESDAILE

1880-1956

Sometime of the British Museum

Sandars Reader in Bibliography in the University of Cambridge 1926/27

Lecturer in Bibliography in the University of London School of Librarianship 1919–1939

This fifth revised edition of Esdaile's *Manual of Bibliography* is published soon after the hundredth anniversary of his birth and exactly half a century after its first appearance. That century has virtually seen the birth and development of bibliography as it is now understood; that half-century has seen a vast expansion of writing on bibliography and a continuing revolution in bibliographical techniques. It is nevertheless to be hoped that this work will continue to serve the same purpose for which Dr. Esdaile originally intended it.

Esdaile's concern was always with the young student, and several of his writings bear testimony to this. His Sandars Lectures were, he wrote, "addressed not to palaeographers or palaeotypographers but to novices, to mere readers of books." Similarly he wrote of his lectures at University College, London, as teaching "the first elements of bibliography." This last phrase seems to be the true subtitle of this *Manual*. Designed for the literary student, the student librarian, the embryo book collector, it assumes nothing at the outset beyond interest. It should take such readers to the point where individual interests begin to develop and more advanced texts can point the way to further reading and investigation. Much of the post–World War II writing on bibliography has been directed toward the literary student, along the lines of McKerrow and Greg. The best of such writing has been outstanding and influential, but this does not cover the whole of the bibliographical field. The historical bibliographer, the conservator of book bindings, the student of plate-books with no text, are equally part of the bibliographical family. In other terms, *The Book Collector* is as essential to a full understanding of bibliography as *Studies in Bibliography*.

The end-of-chapter references have held this intention in mind. Those that provide specific references speak for themselves. Those that provide suggestions for future reading are designed to give as much variety as possible in the hope that something, perhaps something unexpected, will spark a student's interest. To this end the reading of bibliographical journals is of the utmost importance. They are many and varied, but a select list of those that should be scanned regularly includes:

> *The Book Collector*
>
> *Journal of the Printing Historical Society*
>
> *The Library: The Transactions of the Bibliographical Society*
>
> *The Papers of the Bibliographical Society of America* (referred to later as *PBSA*)
>
> *Proof: The Yearbook of American Bibliographical and Textual Studies*
>
> *Studies in Bibliography. Papers of the Bibliographical Society of the University of Virginia*
>
> *Transactions of the Cambridge Bibliographical Society*

The selection of everything listed throughout the book has been strongly influenced by the students to whom I have taught bibliography since 1946. On occasion a book or article has been included not because I have thought it particularly good but because students have commented on its usefulness to them.

Bibliography, said Lawrence Wroth, is the road that leads far. This book is set at the first milestone on the journey.

ESDAILE'S MANUAL
OF BIBLIOGRAPHY

1.

THE NATURE OF BIBLIOGRAPHY

Bibliography is a word that is difficult of exact definition. It can either be briefly defined in a few simple sentences or it can profitably be discussed at considerable length.[1] It is more difficult to reach agreement on an acceptable midway stage of interpretation. At its very simplest there is the now classic definition of Sir Walter Greg in the last of his several important attempts to describe the study adequately.

> To avoid ambiguity I would define "bibliography" to mean the study of books as material objects. The qualification is important. It is a sort of *filioque* clause directed against a particular heresy; one which is or has been widespread, is still popular, but is in my opinion none the less damnable. It seems obvious that I may study the Book of Genesis, or the *Odyssey*, or *The Laws of Ecclesiastical Polity*, or *The Origin of Species*, or *The Bad Child's Book of Beasts*, and never come within a hundred miles of bibliography, because bibliography has nothing whatever to do with the subject or literary content of the book.[2]

In another notable paper, read before the Bibliographical Society in 1932, Greg made the purpose of bibliography clear in two sentences. "At the root of all literary criticism lies the question of transmission, and it is bibliography that enables us to deal with the problem." "Books are the material means by which literature is transmitted; therefore bibliography, the study of books, is essentially the science of the transmission of literary documents."[3] From this it follows that books must be studied in order that their part in the transmission process is understood and that, following such an investigation, their salient features may be recorded. Beyond that analysis and that recording of the data deductions may be made regarding both the status of the physical object itself and the text that it transmits. This, however, is an aspect that lies beyond the initial definition of the field of study. Thus bibliographical method falls into two reasonably distinct halves. The first is *systematic*, the second is *analytical*, or *critical*.

Systematic bibliography

In many respects this is the easiest area of bibliography for the student to understand at the outset. The idea of a bibliography as a list of books and of a bibliographer as the compiler of such lists is well rooted in the public mind. This is in fact the full limitation in the use of the term in the eyes of many people. The need for this kind of work has always been obvious if books were to be findable, with the result that for long it monopolized the word "bibliography," much as one virtue monopolized the word "Virtue."

Clearly the first need is of a general repertory, by means of which the existence of a book may be presumed. A bibliographer is always concerned to discover everything possible about any book that is under examination, and this will entail searches in bibliographies and catalogs of all kinds. The ultimate desirability would be a list of all books that have ever been printed and published. However impossible such a dream may be, it has not prevented attempts from being made. These, even in their incompleteness, are frequently of great value. No matter how selective they may be, they are of interest in recording what was regarded as important at the time of compilation without limitation of language, subject, or time.[4]

Hopeful attempts at world bibliographies began to be made early in the sixteenth century. The father of the craft was Konrad Gesner, physician of Zurich, a man as amiable as he was learned. Although he died before he was fifty, he became a *doctor universalis*, master not only of the natural sciences but also of much of the general learning of his day, by reading and by maintaining friendly relations with scholars of all countries. Modern vernaculars were then despised by the learned, to our great loss, which accounts for the limitation expressed in Gesner's title.

Gesner was contemporary with the foundation of the first of two annual international lists of new books, the *Messkataloge* of the great book fairs of Frankfurt and Leipzig, which ran from 1564 to 1749 and from 1595 to 1860 respectively, and were gathered up and indexed by Gustav Schwetschke. But the fairs were not only (as Schwetschke suggests in his title) chiefly used by German publishers; they were largely confined to the learned works likely to achieve an international sale. Like Gesner, they excluded the vernacular and local works that are now the hardest to trace and in some ways (certainly so far as market value is evidence) the more valuable.

Another important series of listings of the same universal scope are those concerned with "rare books." Even though this term is not very easy of simple and satisfactory definition, it denotes a type of material with which a bibliographer is likely to be closely concerned.[5]

Such listings as these are invaluable in that they record the existence, at least at some time past, of individual books. They do not, however, necessarily give assistance in locating copies. In the long run this is the most important aspect for the bibliographer because there is no alternative to the handling of copies of a work under discussion. One prime source of this nature is the catalogs of great libraries.[6] They are varied in the completeness of their records, the amount and type of bibliographical information given, and, naturally, the biases exhibited by reason of their own geography.

In one form or another most nations now have a law of deposit. In England the Act of 1663, which made deposit in the Royal Library and the university libraries of Oxford (the Bodleian) and Cambridge legally binding, and in itself doubtless an imitation of the French decree of 1617, had been preceded by an arrangement made at the beginning of the seventeenth century between Sir Thomas Bodley and the Company of Stationers in favor of the newly founded Bodleian Library. The Bodleian was for at least a century and a half in effect the national library; and it is correspondingly rich in rare English books. Its published catalog was at the time of its issue in 1843–1851 "the largest presentation of printed literature which had ever been issued." Now as a record of that great library's holdings it is, naturally, very incomplete, but there are several special catalogs. Cambridge University Library, likewise rich in English books, has no published general catalog. The greatest contributions of the other "copyright" libraries and their catalogs are in the literatures of Scotland, Wales, and Ireland respectively. The Act of 1709 gave the right of free deposit to nine libraries: the Royal Library; the university libraries of Oxford, Cambridge, Edinburgh, Glasgow, St. Andrews, and Aberdeen; the Faculty of Advocates at Edinburgh; and Sion College, London. King's Inns and Trinity College, Dublin, were added in 1801, the year of Union. In 1836 the four Scottish universities, King's Inns, and Sion College were bought out for small annual payments, equivalent to the poor use they had made of the right; and in 1911 the National Library of Wales was added. After the separation of the Irish Free State the existing rights were reciprocally continued.

In all these varieties of endeavor the ultimate aim is to record books. It might be thought that all books have been recorded, but this is very far from being the case. When his *Repertorium Bibliographicum ad Annum MD.* was published in 1826–1838, the bibliographer Ludwig Hain recorded some sixteen thousand incunabula, or books printed before the end of the fifteenth century. When the English bibliographer W. A. Copinger published his supplement to Hain in 1895–1902, he added nearly six thousand entries for books not referred to by Hain. Today the number known, though not yet all registered in any single list, must total at least three or four times Hain's original figure. In sale catalogs the word "unrecorded" is of frequent occurrence, and even when a book is recorded the record is often inaccurate or inadequate to fulfilling its main purposes—showing what is in the book and distinguishing it from other books and other copies. The modern solution of some bibliographical problems, to which reference will be made later, provides ample evidence of the need to make the record accurate and complete.

Bibliography as a concept is concerned with writings surviving in manuscript as much as with those that have been multiplied by print. The handwritten book is as much a book as the printed one. The early printers, by their mechanical invention, merely gave book-buyers more cheaply and abundantly a commodity like in all its aspects to that to which they were accustomed; and the principles of examining and recording both are the same in essentials. But the bibliography of manuscripts, and especially of pre-Gutenberg book manuscripts, has unfortunately been in modern practice largely severed from that of print. This separation has become necessary to some extent by the special expertise needed for the study of such material. This specialization must not, however, blind the student to the unity that lies behind the bibliographical interpretation of all recorded forms. The beginning student will find a variety of sound and readable introductions to the long history and elucidation of manuscript materials.[7] Equally there are some outstanding examples of catalogs of manuscript collections that should be studied in order to understand both the similarities and the differences.[8]

It is therefore apparent that the record of books may take many different forms. The first need for all who deal with books is that of a bare registration of their having been printed or produced at a specific place and date, with the author's name and the distinctive title. In modern times—that is, within the last century or less—the organized book trade of each civilized country has produced current lists that do this, though never exhaustively. But all these lists, of every period, are scattered and an entry must be hunted through many volumes. Clearly, if the student is to find a book, which is the aim of such records, there is a need for something simpler. In the seventeenth and eighteenth centuries attempts were made at more or less universal bibliographies. These were, however, at once too universal, in that they aimed at what was then quite impracticable, and not universal enough, in that their selective principle disregarded popular and fugitive literature. The modern historian recognizes the value of what is thought to be, and in fact often is, ephemeral when it is new. G. K. Chesterton observed in his *Heretics* that "good books can tell us the mind of one man; bad books can tell us the mind of many men."

It is difficult to make any estimate of the total number of editions of books actually in existence. In 1911, in the *Bulletin de l'Institut International de Bibliographie*, Iwinski put the figure at twenty-five million at the lowest guess; and fugitive sheets and pieces of all kinds, often of great interest and always of extreme rarity, are innumerable. In the same collection of statistics Iwinski calculated that world book production had doubled in the period between 1858 and 1898.

During the twentieth century the situation has become increasingly complex. Book production has multiplied year by year, and a modern calculation on the lines of Iwinski's would now be virtually impossible. There are over fifty thousand new English-language titles a year, and many languages that had virtually no written literature at the beginning of this century now have vigorous publishing programs. *British Books in Print 1978* recorded over two hundred and eighty-nine thousand titles currently in print, compared with the thirty-five thousand listed in the first edition in 1874. Moreover, a huge quantity of printed matter in modern times, and increasingly from year to year, appears in periodical literature, and much of it is not separately listed or analyzed. New forms of publication, such as microform, have added significantly to the total bulk and complicated the business of control, while a burgeoning reprint trade has kept older titles alive to an extent not previously possible.

In all this enormous accumulation of material the student would lose direction, wasting years before finding even a part of what was needed, were it not for systematic bibliography. It has been absurdly stated that bibliography comprehends all sciences; some bibliographers, and many more who know nothing of the matter, have looked to bibliographers for the criticism and selection of books. But it is obvious that no one but a chemist can assign their relative merits to rival books or papers on chemistry, and that the bibliographer who attempts any such task, even by collating expert criticism, is straying outside the province of bibliography. The bibliographer is concerned with fact and not with judgment since the fundamental concern is to record, as completely and accurately as is humanly possible, whatever has been written. A "bibliography" must not be selective by any qualitative standard. Any limitation to its scope must be on factual grounds, and within that carefully and specifically defined field the record must be a complete one. There is an important distinction between a bibliography and any selective listing of books, graded and organized, which is rightly the prerogative of a subject specialist. The systematic bibliographer does not chafe under this restriction. In the original edition of this manual Esdaile wrote, "He has no need for humility; if he builds honestly, his work is founded on a rock and will endure." Old-fashioned words, but no less true now than half a century ago.[9]

Two terms have been associated with this area of bibliographical work, *enumerative* and *systematic* bibliography. Sometimes they have been used as though interchangeable, and sometimes the different emphasis of each of them has been stressed. The idea behind "enumerative" is clear in that it places its weight upon the listing done, with no consideration of any further problem. Yet a list that is not systematized is well-nigh useless. Order must be made to reveal the relationship among the facts that have been recorded.

Some bibliographers have sorted the titles into a simple alphabetical order of authors; but that is often due to intellectual laziness or want of imagination (perhaps the same thing). Although the alphabet enables the searcher to gain access in a library to a particular book or to refresh the memory as to a title or date, or other detail in the title, it serves no other purpose. The alphabet does nothing to collate material bearing on the same or a closely allied side of the subject. It serves up impartially the prisms and prunes together.

So while the alphabet is reserved for an index to serve the subsidiary purposes mentioned, the main arrangement has to be sought by "fundamental brainwork" in distinguishing the essence of the subject-matter and the point of view of the normal inquirer.

The arrangement of the entries in any bibliographical tool is a matter of considerable importance. In all too few instances will any existing scheme of arrangement be suitable because it will impose a pattern upon the new material that is frequently inappropriate.

For example, the year 1928 was a turning point in the development of author bibliographies in that it saw the publication of Michael Sadleir's *Trollope: A Bibliography*. This bibliography demonstrated more clearly than ever before what kind of background was required of the compiler. The subtitle of the book stated that it was "an analysis of the history and structure of the works of Anthony Trollope, and a general survey of the effect of original publishing conditions on a book's subsequent rarity." In 1928 these were broad and generous outlines in which to conceive the construction of a bibliography, but in the event the subtitle was almost an understatement. The book is a masterly introduction to the bibliographical problems of nineteenth-century fiction and illuminates the whole of it through its approach to the single author. It is a function that one would not expect to be carried out, for example, by the author entry in the

British Museum Catalogue, and the student could usefully compare the two in relation to Trollope. A separately published
bibliography can add a different dimension to bibliographical
research, as Sadleir explained in his Preface.

The only satisfactory way for the student to learn anything
about the problems and solutions in this field is to analyze as
many examples as possible. The lesson will soon be learned that
the main danger is to have preconceived ideas before the collection is complete or nearly so. There is not one right method, and
exactly the same material could be arranged in a fresh manner
with a certain increase in understanding and appreciation.

Analytical, or critical, bibliography

In all sciences laboratory work on the specimen precedes
classification. Before entries of books can be rationally assembled, it is necessary to create the individual entries—in other
words, to describe books. When a volume comes into a bibliographer's hands, certain questions have to be answered. First:
What work, or works, does this volume contain? Second: What
edition of that work is this? Third: Is this copy perfect? The
briefest library catalog entry must answer these questions, and
the difference between it and the description in a full-dress descriptive bibliography is one of degree of detail.

This basic statement of the broadly conceived objectives of
analytical bibliography permits a very simple understanding of
the problem. The actual techniques involved in the solution of
these problems are less simple, although always heading toward a
clear goal. It is often only by much experience and research that
the authorship, order of printing, and date and place of printing
can be satisfactorily established when the book does not bear
these facts on its face. Judgment as to the relevance and importance of bibliographical features within the body of the book and
the significance of any matters pertaining to the perfection of
copy requires constant critical familiarity with the material itself.
The importance of all these features will emerge as the parts of
the book are dealt with in turn and, in the later chapters, when
collation and description are discussed. The techniques of "book
building" must be understood in order to establish the facts re-

quired. Moreover, to establish them for a book and at the same time to record the details of its production in typography, decoration, and so forth, is to lay a secure foundation for placing and dating other books of the same class or period. Each book is a monument, great or small, of the civilization of its time and place: in the aggregate, therefore, an understanding of that generation's mind. It is perhaps a lesser merit, yet not a negligible one, that by assembling such historical book descriptions we help to write the history of all the material means and circumstances surrounding the transmission of ideas. Detailed descriptions of this nature can provide raw material for the illustration and elucidation of areas of art, economic, social, cultural, and technological history. An example will serve to underline this point. Harvard University has published two catalogs of its holdings in French and Italian sixteenth-century books. They include fine descriptions of the library's holdings in these fields, which in themselves are valuable source material for several aspects of sixteenth-century French and Italian history, disassociated from the importance of the books that they record.[10]

The placing and dating of books together with their record is of value not only to the historian of civilization; it is specially valuable to the literary editor, in that it enables the order of editions to be determined and the mysteries shrouding the transmission of the text to be explained. An author's books cannot be properly edited—nor can the author's life, so far as it is in his or her books, be properly written—without our first distinguishing, describing, arranging in their right order, and making available in libraries first the original editions of all the works, then all the later editions in which authentic alterations may have been made. First editions, which are sometimes supposed to be an idle fad of bibliophiles, or mere counters of sordid speculation, have for students the genuine importance of being normally, though not always, the nearest we can get to what the author wrote, and they will be the editor's first care. In fact, behind every editor should stand a bibliographer, ideally in the same person. Comparatively few of our important literary works have been so edited, yet without this sort of editing there is no security that we are reading what the author wished us to read.[11]

The best way in which it can be made clear that a close examination of a book may prove of value in determining the origin, date, and textual authority of a particular edition is by showing how it did so in one very notable instance.

Of the forty or more quarto editions of separate plays by, or once attributed to, Shakespeare, which appeared before the publication of his collected plays in one folio volume in 1623, there are nine, of which, as A. W. Pollard noticed, several sets are known bound or at least till recently bound together. In some cases the bindings are very little later than the date of issue, and there is therefore some reason to suppose that they were put on the market together. But the plays are not all dated in the same year; three are dated 1600, two 1608, three 1619, while one has no date. They have marked typographical similarities that differentiate them all from other Shakespeare quartos, the chief of which is the absence from all of them of a publisher's address showing where the book might be bought, and from most of them of even a publisher's name. There arose, therefore, an *a priori* suspicion that some of them are falsely dated and that they were all not only issued but printed at once. Had they been merely issued together, those dated 1600 and 1608 might have been truly dated. But if some of the dates were false, these could only be the earlier dates, for no publisher would postdate a book by eleven years, still less by nineteen. The presumption was therefore that they were all printed together in 1619 and that the earlier dates were reprinted exactly from known or lost editions of those years, not necessarily with intent to defraud.

While Pollard, the discoverer of the mystery, was wavering between these two solutions and clinging halfheartedly to the more conservative theory of a reissue, Greg took up the hunt. Being at that time Librarian of Trinity College, Cambridge, he had in his charge one of the sets of the nine plays, that in the Capell Collection. He set himself to examine the paper on which those copies were printed, afterward doing the same with the three other available sets: Garrick's in the British Museum, the Bodleian set, and the set in the Huth Library, now dispersed. Pollard gives the following account of the inquiry:

> The greatest work on watermarks ever published, or ever likely to be, is that by M. Charles Briquet, entitled *Les Filigranes*. As a result of the experience gained in compiling this monumental work, M. Briquet is convinced that the device of twisted wire tied

to the paper frame to make a watermark had a life of about two years before it lost its shape altogether, and that it is unusual to find any given "make" of paper still in existence unused after ten years, and very unusual indeed to find it surviving after fifteen. Now, what Mr. Greg demonstrated was that no fewer than five of the watermarks used in the paper of the *Merchant of Venice* or *Midsummer Night's Dream* dated 1600 are found also in identically the same forms in the *Lear* dated 1608 and again in the *Pericles* of 1619, in addition to minor connexions between pairs of plays in different groups. On the theory that the dates 1600 and 1608 are authentic, we have to suppose that Roberts in 1600, in printing two plays for himself and a third for Pavier, used a job lot of paper bearing some fifteen watermarks; and what was left of this job lot was preserved for eight years and then handed over to Jaggard, who added a few other kinds and printed two plays for different publishers; lastly, that the remnants of the job lot were again carefully saved for eleven more years, and then again added to and used to print four more plays. Since the theory that rocks were created with ready-made fossils in them in order to tempt proud geologists to unbelief, so staggering a proposition has hardly been set forth.[12]

Some of these 1619 printings had been accepted as solid first editions, which, if printed in 1600, they might have been. Each of the five supposedly printed in 1600 or 1608, except one that may be accounted for by a lost edition, was rivaling an actual edition bearing the same date. Until these facts came to light it was disputed by editors of Shakespeare which member of each pair could claim priority over the other. Only bibliography, involving an examination of watermarks, has displaced the false first editions of such masterpieces as *A Midsummer Night's Dream* and *King Lear*.

A few years later the research of an American scholar, W. J. Neidig, confirmed the late printing date.[13] He demonstrated, by the superimposition of photographs of the title pages, that all but one were associated by having some areas of standing type in common. No amount of coincidence could permit the belief that type, once dispersed, could be reassembled after various periods of time with certain pieces of the type in precisely the same position. Title-page layouts that exhibited such precise similarities must have been printed at the same time, and consequently all the quartos were printed in 1619.

This was one of the first truly successful demonstrations of the "new bibliography" and did much to convince many of the sceptics of its value. Even among those who were persuaded of the value of bibliographical studies, however, were those who saw the field limited to books of the hand-press age. It took some time for there to be conviction that nineteenth- and twentieth-century books might yield to the same techniques.

A more recent example of the same kind of bibliographical investigation applied to books of a later period can be seen in the uncovering of the "Wise forgeries." The student will find the beginning of the story in John Carter and Graham Pollard's *An Enquiry into the Nature of Certain Nineteenth Century Pamphlets.* [14] The authors used methods that included a minute examination of the material, especially of the types and the papers. By these means they proved that a number of small books by nineteenth-century British writers had been printed many years later than the dates on their title pages and were therefore forgeries. The books had appeared frequently in the rare-book market and on many occasions had realized high prices. For this reason perhaps more public attention was devoted to them than was usual in such cases. The forty or so years since the publication of Carter and Pollard's book have added, literally year by year, bibliographical evidence of increasing scope and importance. The discovery of more confirmed forgeries, the unraveling of the skein of deceit behind their production, the revelation of Wise as a thief of leaves from the British Museum: these have followed each other in one publication after another. The student may occasionally feel that the great classic examples of bibliographical investigation have all been finally determined and filed away. If this viewpoint is accepted, then a faded textbook atmosphere may surround them. The Wise forgeries provide an instance where this cannot be so at present. New evidence is regularly coming to light, and it is a continuing inquiry in which any bibliographer is at liberty to join. The bibliographer, in the seclusion of libraries, is not the dusty and bloodless creature of some popular imagining, but a detective engaged in a thrilling kind of hunt. The methods are now acknowledged universally and practiced widely in the United Kingdom and in the United States of America with results that have been extremely heartening.

Another example, even more recent than the Wise forgeries,

will illustrate the application of ever more sophisticated techniques. In 1954 the Pierpont Morgan Library in New York, one of the truly great rare-book libraries of the world, announced the acquisition of "one of three recorded copies of the earliest surviving printed book." It was the undated Missal of the Use of Constance, first known in modern times in 1880, when discovered by Otto Hupp. Working primarily on typographical evidence, Hupp, a distinguished bibliographer, claimed an earlier date for the Missal than the 42-line Bible.[15] A new round of research began after 1954, with expert opinion ranged on both sides.[16] The problem seemed incapable of resolution by typographical investigation. Later on in the year of the Morgan's acquisition of the Missal Allan Stevenson began his investigation of the paper of the book. In his words, "Although half a million words had been spilt concerning the typography of the Missal, decidedly few had been ventured concerning the paper." For the next few years Stevenson carried out the most detailed study of the paper of one book that had ever been attempted. It involved new and revolutionary methods for the investigation of watermarks and a greatly refined procedure for dating from such evidence. Stevenson's detailed monograph assembled an impressive quantity of evidence and concluded that the Missal could not have been printed much earlier than 1472 and was probably printed in mid-1473.[17] It was a model of bibliographical investigation and the first to base its conclusions primarily on paper evidence.

Historical bibliography

A further stage in the study of the book, commonly called historical bibliography, is beyond the scope of an introductory handbook. It has very close connections with critical bibliography, and some idea must be given of its great importance, of its development, and of the revolution it is working in literary history and in the editing of older authors. As Greg said, "Strictly bibliographical investigation is three-fourths of textual criticism."

Just as the examination of books may be called their anatomy, so the study of books as artifacts may be called their biology. The book is the genus; the country or town is the family, of which all books produced there are members; the printing press is the species; the edition is the subspecies; the copy is the specimen of all this. As the book arts evolve, we can follow them just as biologists follow the evolution of the species of living creatures.

"You may dissect and you may describe," wrote Greg, "but until your anatomy becomes comparative you will never arrive at the principle of evolution. You may name and classify the colours of your sweet pea and produce nothing but a florist's catalogue; it is only when you begin grouping them according to their genetic origin that you will arrive at Mendel's formula."[18]

This fertilizing idea, commonly known as the "natural-history method" of bibliography, is a product of the same development of thought as culminated in Darwinism; it is in fact Darwinism applied by analogy to a human activity. It was first applied to the historical classification of books by Henry Bradshaw, Librarian of Cambridge University (1831–1886), following the lead that had been given by J. W. Holtrop. On 10 May 1866, Bradshaw wrote to Holtrop:

> We cannot afford to lose our master yet; for I always look upon you and speak of you as the chief of my department—the *département des incunables*—for indeed there is no one connected either with any English library, still less in Paris, who has the leisure and inclination to study our subject scientifically.[19]

Bradshaw's work was carried on in Cambridge by Francis Jenkinson (1853–1923), who, being a distinguished entomologist as well as a scholar, was prepared to appreciate the idea.[20] But it was first worked out on a larger scale by a younger bibliographer, Robert Proctor (1868–1903), who examined and arranged under their countries, towns, and prèsses, and in the last resort chronologically, all the incunabula, then numbering some eight thousand, in the British Museum.[21] Very many early printed books give no indication of either place, or printer, or date, and some indicate none of these. By working, as all science must, from the known to the unknown—that is, by classifying the books that did bear these facts on them, and then comparing the types, the ornaments, and the signs of printers' technical development—Proctor succeeded in attributing to their true printers nearly all the unassigned books in this great collection.

Later and more detailed research, culminating in the still incomplete *Catalogue of Books Printed in the XVth Century Now in the British Museum,* has failed to upset his conclusions very materially, though it has largely added to them. All this he achieved by a genius for detail and for fact, aided by a wonderful visual memory.

Though, as we know, analogy is not argument, Bradshaw's analogy has changed the face of historical bibliography. Its influence can be measured by a comparison of the admirable author list of all incunabula then known, Hain's *Repertorium Bibliographicum* (1826–1838), already mentioned, and Proctor's *Index of Early Printed Books,* the fruit of his work at the Museum, or the British Museum's fifteenth-century catalog just mentioned.[22]

A notable example of this method is the establishment of Caxton's claim to be the first printer in England. The first book from his Westminster press that bears a date is the *Dictes or Sayengis of the Philosophres* of 1477, though an indulgence of the previous year has now been identified in the Public Record Office. But there is a book, the *Expositio S. Hieronymi in Symbolum Apostolorum,* from the Oxford press of Theodoric Rood, bearing the date 1468. On its face this gives Oxford and Rood a long priority, and many bibliographers once accepted it. But the natural-history method shows that not only are there no books from Rood's press bearing dates between 1468 and 1479 but that his books of those two years represent exactly the same stage of typographical development. Now anyone who has worked on incunabula by the new method knows that no printer at so early a period remained for eleven years at the same level of accomplishment, since the art was then in the pioneer stage and rapidly advancing. The only possible explanation of the date 1468 (M.CCCC.lxviii.xvij die decembris) is that an x has dropped out of the colophon, and the date is 1478—a misprint for which there are exact parallels.[23] This explanation is now universally accepted, and Caxton is acknowledged as our first printer, though at a painful sacrifice to scientific integrity on the part of patriotic Oxford bibliographers.

A very similar situation developed on the same lines when the so-called "Cracow fragments" were investigated. Here the previously unsatisfactory date accorded to the "1448 calendar" provided misleading origins to early Mainz printing. Now that date is firmly removed and the whole story of early European printing is correspondingly more lucid.[24]

Later periods are not so full of "unassigned" books as the early years of printing, but every period produced books with false imprints and similar problems that need investigation. Once the experimental years of printing are passed and the techniques of printing and the structure of the book trade become more complex, historical bibliography can be seen to assume even greater importance in the whole world of bibliographical studies. It provides a frame of reference within which the other aspects of bibliography operate, but it must be wider than "the book" itself. It must not degenerate into a simple "history of the book" because the book was never an end in itself. It is the sum total of the history of each of the several areas that constitute book making and distribution; paper making, typography, printing, illustration, binding, authorship, publishing, bookselling, reading taste, etc., etc.

In one respect it can be regarded simply as a branch of historical studies in its own right. As such it has an important part to play because it deals with something as fundamental as the communication of ideas. To the bibliographer it has an additional importance beyond the cradle years of the art. The books that will be studied for bibliographical analysis are the products of an age, a town or city, a particular press, and even of individual workers. In order to understand the special problems of a book the bibliographer must be as fully as possible aware of the circumstances surrounding its production: The work habits of the author, particularly insofar as they affect proofreading; the relationship between the author and publisher; the methods of printing at the particular time in that particular town and, if possible, in that particular printing office; the compositorial habits of individual workers in the shop; the methods of distribution and bookselling; an understanding of the reading taste of the period; the economic aspects of the trade. All these, and others, can be vital in providing the kind of background that the bibliographer needs in approaching a book. Historical bibliography is a study that rests like an umbrella over all other areas of bibliography. It affects them by providing some understanding of the society in which and for which the books were produced.

Descriptive bibliography

From some of the above examples it will readily be apparent that one of the chief end-products of the bibliographical examination of the book is the ability to describe it in full bibliographical detail. The catalog or bibliography that results from this kind of activity is quite different in its purpose from the purely enumerative aspect of a systematic bibliography. The latter records, the former describes. Many of the greatest examples of this genre are the products of great bibliographical research libraries, but it is salutary to remember how many are rooted in entirely private collections and owe everything to the enthusiasm of the individual.

It is a common delusion that the aims of the bibliographer, librarian, or student and of the book collector are widely different, that the serious and practical interests of the former are to be contrasted with the frivolity of the latter.[25] It cannot be denied that in book collecting, as in other pursuits, there are people who simply follow fashion; these buy the famous books that everyone else buys and about which everything is known. Books, contrary to a common notion, are very little bought for mere rarity; it is rarity combined with interest that gives them their market value.

The real collector has instincts much more varied than a purely pecuniary one. The concern is usually the building up of a collection within a fairly well-delimited field. The best and largest of them are subject-specialist libraries of rare materials and so have a double-pronged importance. Many collections of this nature have been memorialized through the publication of catalogs so important that they are foundations of the study of those branches of knowledge. Some of the outstanding examples of this kind of activity, both from the standpoint of the collector and the resultant bibliographical tools, have been through the selection of some field of which hitherto little was known. Such collections have included Michael Sadleir's of nineteenth-century fiction, Sir William Osler's of medicine, Paul Hirsch's of music, Rachel Hunt's of botany, Edwin J. Beinecke's of Robert Louis Stevenson, William A. Speck's of Goethe, and Lord Rothschild's of eighteenth-century printed books and manuscripts.

In all too many instances the only monument of a great collection is the sale catalog that records its dispersal. Even in such cases the catalog may become an important tool, as in the example of the Streeter catalog of Americana. In other more fortunate instances collections of this caliber have become part of a great research library where they have retained their own identity as a collection. Indeed it is not too much of an exaggeration to say that the great bibliographical research libraries of the world are in large part the accumulation of private collections.

Descriptive bibliography sets out to record in detail the bibliographical nature of a book. It is rooted in historical bibliography and must be preceded by a full-scale analysis of the work. The catalogs and bibliographies that result from such descriptive work thenceforward provide some of the main tools for further bibliographical analysis.

The application of bibliography to textual problems

This area of bibliographical study is sometimes referred to loosely as textual bibliography. The objection to the term is not a purely pedantic one; it has more to do with the clarification of the type of work involved and the objectives of such study. The objection to the term "textual bibliography" rests on the fact that the bibliographical work itself is not of a peculiar and particular kind. Rather is it that there is an attempt to determine whether the results of analytical bibliography can throw any light on the problems of the text as such. Analysis will reveal with some clarity the processes through which a book has gone from author to reader. The application of this understanding can throw light, and has done so on some notable occasions, on the establishment of the text. It cannot concern itself with a critical evaluation of the text—that is the province of literary criticism. It cannot, moreover, assume the whole role of evidence in textual studies. By long usage the established fields of evidence were historical, literary, and linguistic. They remain of primary concern. All that has happened in the course of the twentieth century is the suggestion that bibliographical evidence has a role also. The occasional comment that may appear to suggest that it has somehow replaced the older three is absurd. It is simply another tool that has been added to the editorial armory.

The text is conveyed on series of physical materials from the time of the author's first holograph to a recorded text in the present day. If one could assume the logical impossibility of a first text that recorded precisely the author's intention and later versions that reproduced that text with such punctilious accuracy that no two versions differed one iota from each other, then no bibliographical problems affecting the text could arise. Bibliographical investigation seeks to reveal any textual variations among the texts and then to use factual bibliographical criteria to assess the authority of the variant readings. A correct understanding of the sequence of editions, impressions, issues, etc., would ideally permit the construction of a stemma of texts. Substantive texts could be separated from derivative editions and the textual authority of the former subjected to more detailed scrutiny. This is admittedly both an oversimplification and a gospel of perfection at the same time. Nevertheless, it is the theoretical structure on which work would proceed. In these days of more sophisticated techniques connecting bibliographical and textual studies it is often difficult to discern this simple outline. It is more readily visible in some of the early work in this field.

The textual aspect of bibliographical work evolved slowly in association with the advance of modern bibliographical method. Certain embryonic signs are visible in the late part of the nineteenth century, but for the most part it has been a major part of the contribution of the twentieth century. If it became desirable to point fairly specifically to works that gave the clearest possible indication of the future direction, there would be three main claimants, all in the first decade of the twentieth century. Pollard's *Shakespeare Folios and Quartos* is as near an opening salvo in the campaign as can be found. Its main impact, as has already been mentioned, was in Shakespearian studies, but it profoundly affected thinking in many other textual studies. McKerrow's edition of Nashe, issued at the end of the decade, is one of the earliest successful attempts at demonstrating exactly how bibliographical considerations can affect the establishment of the text, and it included such evidence in its critical apparatus.[26] The third is less specific, but it recognizes the considerable effect of the reviews of editions of literary works that had no recourse whatsoever to bibliographical methodology. Such reviews were largely the work of McKerrow, Pollard, and Greg, the trio who more than any others laid the foundations of much that is best in modern textual work. Two of the three especially carried the work much farther, McKerrow with Shakespeare and his own seminal work on bibliography[27] and Greg with Marlowe and Jonson.[28] By the time of Greg's death in 1959 there were few responsible textual critics who could reasonably deny the possible advantages in the application of some kind of bibliographical basis. Since that time there have been notable advances in two directions. Several books and many articles have extended the broad theoretical basis of textual studies in bibliography,[29] and there have also been examples of bibliographically based critical editions of literary texts and studies that have not as yet necessarily culminated in a textual edition.

There are still those who are unconvinced by the studies of the past half-century or so and who have expressed their opposition.[30] It is possible that some of the claims made for bibliography have been more enthusiastic than realistic, but sober judgment confirms that an increasing amount of bibliographical work has been witness to its importance in some areas of textual work.

Fashions in instructive writing and textbooks change rapidly. The clear statement of one generation is the cliché of the next, and any kind of moral exhortation is out of fashion today. In spite of this, however, it is difficult to remove or change the words with which Dr. Esdaile concluded the introductory chapter of this manual nearly half a century ago. They still have force, validity, and a certain nostalgic charm.

At the risk of seeming too serious I will add seven commandments to bibliographers:

1. *Be proud, and think highly of your calling.*
2. *Be humble, and do not despise details.*
3. *Be accurate, in small things as in great.*
4. *Be brief.*
5. *Be clear.*
6. *Take nothing on trust, except in necessity, and even then not without saying so. There have been many bad bibliographers, and it is human to err.*
7. *Never guess. You are sure to be found out, and then you will be written down as one of the bad bibliographers, than which there is no more terrible fate.*

It would be easy to write a discourse on each of these heads, enriched with many notable warnings and examples; but their truth will be borne in on the student by experience. They come in the mass to no more than an amplification of our old friend, the copy-book motto, that honesty is the best policy. And indeed the real bibliographer, like the real scholar in whatever field, must be intellectually honest, for their task is to seek truth and ensue it.

REFERENCES

1. Following are the definitions that the student should read:

CHAMBERS'S ENCYCLOPEDIA. Articles on "Bibliography" and "Book Collecting."
ENCYCLOPAEDIA BRITANNICA. Articles on "Bibliography" and "Book-collecting."
GASELEE, Sir Stephen. "The Aims of Bibliography." *The Library.* 4th Series. XIII: 1932–33. pp. 225–258.
GREG, W. W. "Bibliography—A Retrospect." *The Bibliographical Society, 1892–1942.* 1945. pp. 23–31.
GREG, W. W. "Bibliography—An Apologia." *The Library.* 4th Series. XIII: 1932–33. pp. 113–143.
GREG, W. W. *Collected Papers.* 1966.
POLLARD, A. W. "Bibliography and Bibliology." *Encyclopaedia Britannica.* 11th ed. 1911.
STOKES, Roy. *The Function of Bibliography.* 1969. 2nd. ed. in press.

2. Greg, "Bibliography—A Retrospect," p. 24.

3. Greg, "Bibliography—An Apologia," pp. 113 and 115.

4. Some of the more important ones are:

GESNER, Konrad. *Bibliotheca Universalis, sive Catalogus Omnium Scriptorum Locupletissimus, in Tribus Linguis, Latina, Graeca, et Hebraica.* 1545.
SCHWETSCHKE, Gustav, ed. *Codex Nundinarius Germaniae Literatae Bisecularis.* 1850–1897.

In the first half of the eighteenth century two singlehanded attempts were made at a world list:

GEORGI, Gottlieb. *Allgemeines europäisches Bucherlexicon.* 5 parts (covering 1501–1739). 1742–1753. 3 supplements (covering 1739–1757). 1750–1758.
MAITTAIRE, M. *Annales Typographici ab Artis Inventae Origine ad Annum 1664.* 5v. 1719–1741; with 2v. supplement (covering period 1549–1599), by M. Denis. 1789.

5. The following are a few examples of a vast number of tools that broadly cover this field:

BURE, G. F. de. *Bibliographie instructive: ou traité de la connaissance des livres rares et singuliers.* 7v. 1763–1768.

De Bure's book is a large repertory, and is classified, and was once very useful. It was largely superseded in the nineteenth century by the famous

BRUNET, J. C. *Manuel du libraire et de l'amateur de livres.* 5th ed. 6v. 1860–1865. 3v. supplement. 1870–1880.

Brunet gives us, besides the main author list, a subject index, the arrangement of which in its time was a standard and is still used with modifications in some large libraries. The three supplementary volumes include one that is a *Dictionnaire de géographie ancienne et moderne,* being a list of place-names found in imprints. Brunet, first published in 1810, was imitated and supplemented, but has not been superseded, by

GRAESSE, J. G. T. *Trésor de livres rares et précieux.*

A general list of rare books after the manner of Brunet, but less accurate and confined to English authors, is:

LOWNDES, William Thomas. *Bibliographer's Manual of English Literature.* 6v. in 11. 1858–1864.

Although Lowndes was first published in 1834, it is best known through the considerably enlarged edition, edited and published by H. G. Bohn in the middle of the nineteenth century.

Out-of-the-way books will also naturally be traceable by their appearances in the auction-room, often the only evidence of their existence. These can be found recorded in such works as:

Book Auction Records. Annual from 1902.

Book Prices Current. Annual from 1886.

American Book Prices Current. Annual from 1895, which covers American sales only.

Another work that will assist the student in this field is:

BRITISH MUSEUM. *List of Catalogues of English Books Sales, 1676–1900, Now in the British Museum.* 1915.

Mention should also be made of the important part played by the book catalogs issued by the great booksellers. Details given are frequently very full and, in the cases of the best examples, of meticulous accuracy. The student should certainly make a point of seeing and studying catalogs of Bernard Quaritch, W. H. Robinson, Maggs Bros., E. P. Goldschmidt, and Bertram Rota in England and H. P. Kraus, Lathrop C. Harper, Zeitlin & Ver Brugge, and Goodspeed's Book Shop in the United States. No would-be bibliographer can possibly spend too much time in and around the world's great bookshops.

6. There are numerous examples of library catalogs that are important bibliographical tools. Their value will normally depend upon two things: the quality of the collection, and the efficiency of the catalog in recording the necessary bibliographical information. It is an important part of a student's training to begin to recognize the adequacy of different catalogs as general bibliographical tools.

It is most helpful to approach such catalogs in particular categories:

National libraries: such as the British Museum Library, (now the British Library); The Library of Congress, Washington; and the Bibliothèque Nationale in Paris. In certain instances, as with the British Library and the Library of Congress, there are important subject indexes or catalogs as well as the main author catalog. Many such national libraries are, and have been for a long time, legal deposit libraries. The catalogs of a national library make a logical starting place for a search for material connected with the appropriate country. Many also house a wide variety of special bibliographical materials and publish a range of specialized catalogs. An indication of the variety and the specialisation for one institution can be seen in:

ESDAILE, Arundell. *The British Museum Library.* 1946.

The other important category is of research libraries that have published catalogs of special collections of materials. Examples of this kind are:

Early nonconformity 1566–1800. A catalog of books in Dr. Williams's Library, London.
5v. Author catalogue. 1968.
5v. Subject catalogue. 1968.
2v. Chronological catalogue. 1968.
The Mitchell Library, Public Library of New South Wales. *Dictionary Catalogue of Printed Books.* 38v. 1968. 1v. supp.
New York Public Library. *Dictionary Catalog of the Rare Book Division.* 21v. 1971. 1v. supp. 1973.
The Newberry Library, Chicago. *Dictionary Catalogue of the History of Printing from the John M. Wing Foundation.* 6v. 1961.
University of Texas Library, Austin. *Catalog of the Latin American Collection.* 31v. 1969. 16v. supp. 1971–75.

7.   Especially recommended, to cover different aspects, are:

DEUEL, Leo. *Testaments of Time.* 1965.
DIRINGER, David. *The Hand-produced Book.* 1953.
DOBLHOFER, Ernst. *Voices in Stone.* 1961.
MADAN, Falconer. *Books in Manuscript.* 1920.

8.   As examples, see the catalogs of manuscripts in Cambridge College Libraries, by M. R. James. (1862–1936): Jesus (1895); Sidney Sussex (1895); Peterhouse (1899); Christ's (1905); Clare (1905); Pembroke (1905); Queens' (1905); Trinity Hall (1907); Magdalene (1909); and St. John's (1913).

9.   The best account of the development of this area of bibliography is:

BESTERMAN, Theodore. *The Beginnings of Systematic Bibliography*. 1935.

10. HARVARD COLLEGE LIBRARY. Department of Printing and Graphic Arts Catalogue of Books and Manuscripts. *French Sixteenth-Century Books*. 2v. 1964. *Italian Sixteenth-Century Books*. 2v. 1975.

11. The student should watch for discussions on these matters in reviews of texts in scholarly journals.

There is also a growing literature on problems of textual editing, touching on many aspects in addition to the purely bibliographical one. Some of these are referred to throughout this book in specific instances. Others are:

BALD, R. C. "Editorial Problems—A Preliminary Survey." *Studies in Bibliography*. III: 1950-51. pp. 3-17.
BOWERS, Fredson. *On Editing Shakespeare*. 1966.
BOWERS, Fredson. "Remarks on Eclectic Texts." *Proof*. IV: 1975. pp. 31-76.
BOWERS, Fredson. "Scholarship and Editing." *PBSA*. LXX: 1976. pp. 161-188.
BOWERS, Fredson. "Some Relation of Bibliography to Editorial Problems." *Studies in Bibliography*. III: 1950-51. pp. 37-62.
GREG, W. W. *The Editorial Problem in Shakespeare*. 3rd ed. 1954.
LEECH, Clifford. "On Editing One's First Play." *Studies in Bibliography*. XXIII: 1970. pp. 61-70.
McKERROW, R. B. "The Treatment of Shakespeare's Text by His Earlier Editors, 1709-1768." *Proceedings of the British Academy*. XIX: 1934.
PECKHAM, Morse. "Reflections on the Foundations of Modern Textual Editing." *Proof*. I: 1971. pp. 122-155.
TANSELLE, G. T. "The Editing of Historical Documents." *Studies in Bibliography*. XXXI: 1978. pp. 1-56.
TANSELLE, G. T. "The Editorial Problem of Final Authorial Intention." *Studies in Bibliography*. XXIX: 1976. pp. 167-211.
TANSELLE, G. T. "External Fact as an Editorial Problem." *Studies in Bibliography*. XXXII: 1979. pp. 1-47.
TANSELLE, G. T. "Greg's Theory of Copy-text and the Editing of American Literature." *Studies in Bibliography*. XXVIII: 1975. pp. 167-229.

TANSELLE, G. T. "Some Principles for Editorial Apparatus."
Studies in Bibliography. XXV: 1972. pp. 41–88.
TANSELLE, G. T. "Textual Study and Literary Judgement."
PBSA. LXV: 1971. pp. 109–122.
TORONTO UNIVERSITY. Beginning in 1965 Toronto has held
an annual conference on editorial problems, and the University Press has published each set of papers. The topics covered
have included sixteenth-, seventeenth-, eighteenth-,
nineteenth-, twentieth-century texts and also Renaissance
dramatic texts, Romantic period, etc.
ZELLER, Hans. "A New Approach to the Critical Constitution
of Literary Texts." *Studies in Bibliography*. XXVIII: 1975. pp.
232–264.

12. POLLARD, A. W. *Shakespeare Folios and Quartos*. 1909. pp.
93–94.

13. *Modern Philology*. VIII: 1910–11. pp. 145–163.

14. The student should read the following:

CARTER, John, and POLLARD, Graham. "An Enquiry into the
Nature of Certain Nineteenth Century Pamphlets." 1934.
FOXON, David F. *Thomas J. Wise and the Pre-Restoration Drama*.
1959.
TODD, William B., ed. *Thomas J. Wise Centenary Studies*. 1959.

15. Hupp wrote three monographs on the subject:

Ein Missale speciale, Vorläufer des Psalteriums von 1457 (Munich,
1898); *Gutenbergs erste Drucke* (Munich, 1902); *Zum Streit um
das Missale speciale Constantiense* (Munich, 1917).

16. The most important writings on the Missal, to be read in sequence, are:

SCHOLDERER, Victor. *"Missale speciale Constantiense."* *Book
Collector*. IV: 1955. pp. 8–15.
BUHLER, Curt F. "Who Printed the *Missale speciale Constan-
tiense?*" *Book Collector*. VI: 1957. pp. 253–258.
BUHLER, Curt F. "The Constance Missal and Two Documents
from the Constance Diocese." *PBSA*. L: 1956. pp. 370–375.
MASSON, Irvine. "The Dating of the *Missale speciale Constan-
tiense*." *The Library*. 5th Series. XIII: 1958. pp. 81–101.

BUHLER, Curt F. "Another View on the Dating of the *Missale speciale Constantiense.*" *The Library.* 5th Series. XIV: 1959. pp. 1–10.

BUHLER, Curt F. "The *Missale speciale* and the Feast of the Presentation of Blessed Virgin Mary." *PBSA.* LXVI: 1972. pp. 1–11.

17. STEVENSON, Allan. *The Problem of the* "Missale speciale." 1967.

18. GREG, W. W. "What Is Bibliography?" *Transactions of the Bibliographical Society.* XII: 1911–13. pp. 40–53. Reprinted, Greg, *Collected Papers,* pp. 75–88.

19. Bradshaw's life has been written by:

PROTHERO, G. W. *A Memoir of Henry Bradshaw.* 1888.

His papers published as:

Collected Papers of Henry Bradshaw. 1889.

Some of his correspondence has been published:

HELLINGA, Wytze and Lotte. *Henry Bradshaw's Correspondence on Incunabula with J. W. Holtrop and M. F. A. G. Campbell (1864–1884)* 2v. 1966–1978.

20. STEWART, H. F. *Francis Jenkinson . . . A Memoir.* 1926.

21. Apart from the Index there is little published work of Proctor available. Special attention should be paid to:

PROCTOR, Robert. *Bibliographical Essays.* 1905.

which contains a memoir of Proctor by A. W. Pollard.

22. Fuller details regarding these catalogs and bibliographies of incunabula will be found in Reference No. 19 to Chapter 10.

23. A recent study of this Oxford book is:

DE LA MARE, A. C., and HELLINGA, Lotte. "The First Book Printed in Oxford: The *Expositio Symboli* of Rufinus." *Transac-*

tions of the Cambridge Bibliographical Society. VII, Part 2: 1978. pp. 184-244.

Hellinga suggests another possible reason for the error—that "some of the variants introduced by the compositor in other places derived from a different textual authority." That other authority might well have been the first Rome edition of Sweynheym and Pannartz, printed in 1468. If so, the error in the Oxford printing might be a "contamination" from the Rome printing.

If, however, it is simple error, there are many other examples. Notably the Rylands *St. Christopher* print (1423), the earliest extant piece of European block printing, has a rival in the Brussels *Madonna*, of which the date on the block of 1418 is recognized as incorrect. Also among early book printing Jenson's edition of the *Decor Puellarum*, Venice 1461 (for 1471), which was once thought to give Jenson priority in Italian printing.

For further information see:

BUHLER, Curt. "False Information in the Colophons of Incunabula." *Proceedings of the American Philosophical Society.* CXIV: 1970. pp. 398-406.

24. The main account of the Cracow fragments is contained in:

WEHMER, Carl. *Mainzer Probedrucke in der Type des sogenannten Astronomischen Kalenders für 1448.* 1948.

This pamphlet is not, however, widely available. Students are therefore advised to use the chief authoritative reviews of the work. They are:

Times Literary Supplement, 6 May 1949.
The Library. 5th Series. V: 1950-51. pp. 65-68.
Signature. No. 9 (N.S.). pp. 55-58.

25. The student will find help in many of the books about book collecting:

CARTER, John. *ABC for Book-Collectors.* 4th ed. 1966.
CARTER, John. *Books and Book Collectors.* 1956.

CARTER, John. *Taste and Technique in Book Collecting.* 1948.
CHAPMAN, R. W., and others. *Book Collecting: Four Broadcast Talks.* 1950.
MUIR, P. H. *Talks on Book Collecting.* 1952.
PETERS, Jean, ed. *Book Collecting: A Modern Guide.* 1977.
QUAYLE, Eric. *The Collector's Book of Books.* 1971.
SOWERBY, E. Millicent. *Rare People and Rare Books.* 1967.

26. McKERROW, R. B., ed. *The Works of Thomas Nashe.* 1910. Reissued 5v. 1958.

27. McKERROW, R. B. *Prolegomena for the Oxford Shakespeare.* 1939.
McKERROW, R. B. *An Introduction to Bibliography for Literary Students.* 1928.

28. GREG, W. W. *Marlowe's Doctor Faustus, 1604–1616.* 1950.
GREG, W. W. *Jonson's Masque of Gipsies; An Attempt at Reconstruction.* 1952.

29. Of special importance are:

BOWERS, Fredson. *Bibliography and Textual Criticism.* 1964.
BOWERS, Fredson. *Essays in Bibliography, Text and Editing.* 1975.
BOWERS, Fredson. *Textual & Literary Criticism.* 1959.
BRACK, O. M., and BARNES, Warner. *Bibliography and Textual Criticism.* 1969.
GOTTESMAN, Ronald, and BENNETT, Scott. *Art and Error: Modern Textual Editing.* 1970.
THORPE, James. *Principles of Textual Criticism.* 1972.

30. For example:

BATESON, F. W. "Modern Bibliography and the Literary Artifact." *English Studies Today.* 2nd Series, ed. G. A. Bonnard. 1961.
WILSON, Edmund. *The Fruits of the MLA.* 1968.

2.
THE PARTS OF A BOOK

Before very much useful work can be done in studying the book as a material object it is necessary to understand the functions of its parts. Not necessarily every book will contain all the several features, but they are the common elements of books and all of them will be encountered regularly in the course of bibliographical investigations. Variations will be found among books of different kinds and of different periods, and students should become increasingly familiar with all the possible types of usage. It is highly probable that in due course a bibliographer's interest and expertise will become focused on a particular period or place of book production, or a particular type of book or the corpus of a particular writer. In the early days, however, it is important for a student to see and handle as wide a range of material as possible. Later specialization, the cry of so many modern activities, must be broadly and securely founded. A book falls fairly naturally into certain parts: preliminaries, textual matter, and subsidiaries. No hard and fast rules can be laid down governing a strict usage of these terms, and experience will prove the only guide.

One set of definitions is, however, necessary before anything else. A *sheet* refers to the full sheet of paper as laid on the bed of the press for printing. After printing this is folded in a predetermined manner to create the *section, gathering,* or *quire.* Before the book can be read, in all formats other than folio, it is necessary to cut through the folds, or to guillotine them away so that all the text may be easily visible. This is the process of *opening* a book, and it creates the individual units of the book called *leaves.* Each leaf consists of two *pages,* one on the *recto* of the leaf and one on the *verso.* It follows then that a leaf is the smallest element in the book that can have any real identity. For example, it is impossible either to tear a *page* out of a book or to put one back. A page can be written or printed upon, but only a leaf can be repaired. The unit in all instances is the leaf. There is sometimes confusion between the terms *uncut* and *unopened.* The former refers to the binder's practice of trimming or cutting edges of the leaf, an action that reduced the size of the margin on the page. Most primary binders have exercised caution and respect in this connection. It is at the time of rebinding that most harm has been done, with the loss not simply of proportions but more significantly of marginal notes and, in extreme cases, of text. "Unopened" is used to describe a copy where the bolts, folds made when the sheet was folded according to its format, have not been opened or cut. When, as in the manuscript period and that of early printed books, the leaves are numbered in sequence, the book is said to be *foliated;* when the pages are numbered, it is *paginated.*

Preliminaries

These are usually printed last, and on a separate sheet or sheets, except where in a reprint no new prefatory matter is expected.

They are usually paged separately and, most frequently, in a distinguishing font. A common European practice was the use of roman figures for the preliminaries, especially when printed last, and with arabic figures for the body of the text. It is not uncommon to find one sequence of arabic figures, without break, in the case of reprinted works. In any event, whether there are one or two sequences of pagination or foliation, the bibliographer hopes to find that the reckoning has been made from the first recto of the book, whether blank or not. Tipped-in leaves, whether artistic or textual, are always a problem, and they will be discussed in more detail in the chapter on "Collation."

The half-title or bastard title (French, faux-titre)

The title leaf, itself a wrapper to the (often decorated) first page of text, began in the latter half of the sixteenth century to be preceded and protected in its turn by another leaf, which often bore merely the signature letter A on the recto. From the mid-seventeenth century the verso of the half-title was used for the imprimatur, and in the latter part of the century it became common to print the short title on the recto, resembling the early title-page. This is the half-title of today.[1]

The primary purpose of the half-title leaf is this purely protective one, but it has also served to identify the book to which the first sheet belongs, which a blank first leaf would not. From this it follows that the leaf is normally that which immediately precedes the title leaf. If the volume is part of a series, the half-title page is usually the place for the series title. The verso of the leaf may bear the printer's imprint, but this is far from being common practice. It is more usual to find the verso, and therefore the page facing the title page, devoted to a listing of other works within a series or other books by the same author. In German books the series title and the book title frequently and conveniently face each other.

There has arisen a practice of printing the half-title not on the first but on the second or even the third recto, in order to save any page with print from the paste where the end pages of the casing are pasted to the sheets. This produces a situation in which a leaf is provided to protect the half-title, which exists to protect the title page, which exists to protect the text. This elaboration seems as needless as the provision of dust jackets for the protections of casings, which themselves exist in order to protect something else.

The title page

The title of a book can appear in a wide variety of places—on the spine of the binding or casing, on the half-title page, on the title page, and frequently on the running headlines throughout the book. It is not unusual for these titles to vary from each other, occasionally quite radically. The importance of the title on the title page is that this is the "official" title of the work and the one that should always be used in any formal description of the book.[2]

The manuscript and the quite early printed book had no title page; the text, normally with an *incipit* ("here begins"), began on the recto of the first or second leaf, and in the latter case the first leaf was blank. A very short "label" title, like our half-title, began about 1480 to be printed on the blank recto of the first leaf, though the actual first title pages known, to a Bull of Pius II printed at Mainz in 1463 by Fust and Schoeffer, and to a sermon by Rolewinck printed by Arnold ther Hoernen at Cologne in 1470, are wordy. But the Parisian publishers from about 1485 filled the space below the short title with their device and name and address below; the printer's imprint was in the colophon, as in all other books of the period.

Even within the period of book making during which the convention of the explanatory title page has been widely accepted there are still problems to be faced. There are many examples of deceptively worded title pages; one of the best instances gave rise to a story dear to H. B. Wheatley. A Midlothian stockfarmer saw in an Edinburgh bookshop a copy of Richard and Maria Edgeworth's *Essay on Irish Bulls* (1802), which is decorated at the head of the text with a wood engraving of that animal. Having read it through with becoming gravity, he observed that Miss Edgeworth must be "a fule body, to write a book of bulls and no ane word of horned cattle in it a', forbye the bit beastie at the beginning." Fancy titles must be allowed to human weaknesses, but they should be explained by a subtitle.

Other important facts can also be expected on the title leaf, either on the recto or verso. There is usually a clear and succinct statement of (a) the book's title and subject matter, with or without the aid of subtitles; (b) the author's name, and relevant facts as to status in relation to the book's subject—e.g., academic position and authorship of similar works; (c) the name of any translator, editor, introducer, or illustrator; (d) the edition number; (e) the imprint, giving the place, the publisher's name and address—in other words, information as to where copies can be procured—and the date. Some publishers decorate the title page with their device. This, since the time of the almost complete separation of the functions of publisher and printer, is virtually the modern equivalent of the printer's device.

Next to the identification of the work the most important, and frequently the most elusive, piece of title-page information is the date. Undated books were common in the fifteenth century because the manuscript had usually been undated. In many such cases of early printing the date is in the colophon, which always has to be regarded as an "auxiliary" title page since, when it appears, it provides the same kind of information as would be expected on the title page. Beyond the years of early printing the absence of a date from the title page may be indicative of some current practice or outlook. The repressive measures of the mid–sixteenth century, for example, caused many political and religious works to appear undated and without much evidence of identification of those responsible. Many twentieth-century books have appeared without any title-leaf date in the hope that the decreasing contemporaneity may pass unnoticed.

It is also of interest to observe the changing fashions in title-page design and layout. Aside from the binding or casing no part of the book is quite so evocative of the period in which it was produced, or frequently so indicative of the work of the printer, as the title-page opening. It is a part of the book that is subject to design and consequently records the passing fashions and the habits of the contemporary book trade. At a period, for example, when it was a common habit for title pages to be displayed by a bookshop as advertising, it is to be expected that both the design and the wording of the text will bear witness to this usage.

The statement of editions

The verso of the title leaf is a common place to find a piece of vital information, the complete listing of editions and impressions of the work. The forms of this information and the details that are made known have varied over the course of printing history. There is necessarily a correlation between such statements and contemporary reprinting policies. There needs to be fuller discussion on the definitions of edition, issue, impression, etc., and this will follow in a later chapter. Before such statements became detailed and fairly general in the nineteenth century, brief statements were frequently found on the title page itself. It has never been an area of dependable accuracy, but the indications that are given can not be ignored. The tabulation of publishing history that is, one hopes, revealed is one of the pieces of bibliographical detail that the bibliographer is attempting to establish, and the printer's or publisher's own records should be of cardinal importance.

No one book is likely to have all the various kinds of bibliographical listing, but the following items are commonly found:

(a) record of previous publication of the material or any part of it, in periodical or other form;

(b) details of original version in the case of translations with notes of completeness or otherwise of translation;

(c) photographic reprints record the printing that was used and, in instances of important literary or bibliographical texts, the identification of the copy or copies that were reproduced. The vast increase in the number of facsimile reprints makes such identification of great importance.

Care must be exercised in the event of a book that has been transferred from one printer or publisher to another. The latter will sometimes, while setting out an apparently full table of editions, ignore any not published by that house.

Another statement relating to the edition will also be found here. Since 1802 it has been a legal obligation in the United States of America to record here the date of copyright. Similar provisions were made for the United Kingdom by the Copyright Act of 1956. Currently, therefore, American and British practice conform to the usage recommended by the Universal Copyright Convention of the symbol © together with the name of the copyright owner and the date.

The statement of the number of copies printed

This statement can cover a number of factors. In its simplest form it may be solely a guarantee of the number of copies printed in a limited edition. This assurance is necessary because inevitably the purchase price of a limited edition will be higher than in the case of an unlimited edition. It is not always wise to take the statement "This issue is limited to 750 copies" at its face value. A regrettable practice is occasionally met with where "a few overs" are made available. This destroys the whole purpose of a limited edition and should always be regarded with extreme suspicion. The number of copies that are not available for sale should be clearly stated, e.g., "This edition is limited to 750 copies; of which Nos. 1-25 are not for sale." A statement of limitation does not always make reference to any unlimited issue of the

same work. For example, the signed edition of Sorenson's *Kennedy* (New York: Harper & Row, 1965) reads, "Of the first edition of KENNEDY, one thousand nine hundred and sixty three copies have been printed on special paper from the original type, specially bound, numbered and signed by the author,
THIS IS COPY NUMBER . . . ."
There was of course a very large unlimited edition issued simultaneously, of which no mention was made.

Another form of limitation, although not so common in modern times, is a statement of the number of copies in different format. For example, Dibdin's *The Bibliographical Decameron* (1817), of which the normal edition was in octavo, had fifty copies printed on large paper that had been reimposed in quarto.

A third, and very common, form of statement is found in plate books. Here the limitation is important on two counts. First, most plates from which the books will be printed have a limited life for the printing of first-rate illustrations. It is important to know that no more than a reasonable number have been printed so that the quality may be assured. Second, plates vary in their quality very much according to the kind of paper on which they are printed. It is therefore to be expected that any issue of plates will pay due attention to this kind of information. For example, the 1942 Fabiani edition of Buffon's *Book of Beasts*, for which Picasso produced thirty-one etchings, states that the printing consisted of 226 numbered copies: one on old laid paper with a suite on old bluish deckle-edged paper, 2–6 on Japanese deckle-edged paper with a suite of the etchings on Chinese paper, 7–36 on Imperial Japanese paper with a suite on Chinese paper, 37–91 on wove deckle-edged Montval, and 92–226 on wove Vidalon. This provides a full record of the main features of all copies.

Although, as is only natural, limited editions or issues are most frequently found in highly priced books in such fields as literature and fine arts, this is not exclusively so. Limitation of copy is found in many types of books for a variety of reasons.

The imprimatur

The imprimatur, or licence for publication, was granted by secular or ecclesiastical authority and usually carried not only the name of the licenser but also the date, which may not be that of the imprint. In England the "Regulation of Printing Act" of 1662 established the legal basis for one type of imprimatur. Categories of books had their official licensers: legal books were licensed by the Lord Chancellor, the Keeper of the Seal, the Lords Chief Justice, the Lord Chief Baron, or their assigns; books on divinity, philosophy, science, and arts, by the Archbishop of Canterbury and the Bishop of London or their assigns; books issued by the university presses, by the respective Chancellor or Vice Chancellor. The verso of the title leaf is a usual position in which to find the "imprimatur" statement within the book. This Act was in force from 1662 to 1679 and from 1685 until its final expiration in 1694.

The imprimatur is to be distinguished from the privilege of copyright ("cum privilegio ad imprendum solum") granted by the Crown to publishers in the first half of the sixteenth century in England. This was a privilege granted usually for a term of years and continued in a variety of forms in many countries for several generations.

The imprimatur is now rarely found except in circumstances as required by canon law of the Roman Catholic Church. It is granted by a bishop in respect to writings on Scripture, theology, and more general works related to religion and morality. In such cases the granting of the *imprimatur* itself (let it be printed), will be preceded by the recorded judgment of a censor in the form *nihil obstat* (nothing hinders it).

For example, Ronald Knox's *On Englishing the Bible* (1949) bore the following statement:

Nihil Obstat: Edvardvs Can. Mahoney, S.T.D.
Censor Depvtatvs
Imprimatvr: E. Morrogh Bernard
Vicarivs Generalis
Westmonasterii: Die XXVI Febrvarii MCMXLIX

The dedication

The habit of the dedication of books is of long standing. If the history of the tradition were written fully, it could reveal an extraordinary variety of motives, which in their turn could throw considerable light on literary, social, and cultural history.[3] It is important to recall that the act of dedication has much wider significance than a purely bibliographical one. It implies the setting apart of the object dedicated to a specific use and, originally, in a religious setting. The earliest records would therefore show examples of the dedication of temples, altars, and sacramental vessels. It is consequently not surprising to find many early dedications of books following this same theme. There are examples of dedications to Christ, to the Virgin, to the Trinity, and even to God the Father. A number of these, and especially in personal service books of the medieval period, such as Books of Hours, had a pictorial representation of a presentation: a frontispiece depicting the owner of the manuscript, for example, offering a book to the Virgin. As there had been purely secular dedications from Classical times, so also this pictorial dedication existed in nonreligious terms. One of the best-known examples of this is the "Lectionary of John, Lord Lovel" (MS. Harl. 7026, British Museum). The earliest picture in this book depicts John Siferwas, who was the painter of the miniatures in the Sherborne Missal, presenting his book to his patron, John, fifth Lord Lovel of Tichmarsh, who died in 1408. Into the period of the printed book the same theme is repeated in the engraved frontispiece in the one copy of Caxton's *The Recuyell of the Hystoryes of Troye,* c. 1475 (De Ricci 3.11) depicting an author, possibly Caxton, presenting his work to Margaret, Duchess of Burgundy.

Dedications have frequently fallen upon bad times. Bacon wrote, "Neither is the modern dedication of books and writings, as to patrons, to be commended: for that books (such as are worthy the name books) ought to have no patrons but truth and reason."[4] Certain categories of books were infrequently dedicated. Williams listed news pamphlets, corantos, chapbooks, broadside ballads, almanacs, proclamations, and service books as examples of this kind.[5]

The historical and bibliographical interest of dedications lies in their revelations of the friendships and indebtedness of authors. They frequently assist in reconstructing the milieu of writers and lead to the establishment of elusive biographical details. In books of some periods—English books of the sixteenth and seventeenth centuries, for example—it is often the only place where the author's name appears.

The preface

The main purpose of the preface is to permit the author an opportunity to publish afterthoughts or those comments that are not regarded as appropriate to the main body of the book. For the reader it frequently provides information as the purpose and scope of the book and consequently has occasionally been of particular use as first aid to reviewers. As a general rule all forms of prefatory material—prefaces, dedications, title leaves—are printed after the main body of text, at least in first editions. In such instances a clear indication will be given since these preliminaries must occupy a separate sheet and will therefore be separately signed. Because of this it provides a chance for the author to comment on any work bearing on the subject that has been published since the text was written or of which he or she has belatedly become aware.

Since the author steps out of the author's role in the preface and speaks more directly to the readers, it is not uncommon for references to be made to contemporary affairs, a feature that will sometimes help in solving problems of dating and general historical setting. The preface also frequently includes a list of acknowledgments to helpers. This is a courtesy that can be easily overdone, but very occasionally it provides linkages and suggestions regarding other people working in the same field.

Examples can readily be found of instances when the prefatory material comes to have an importance of its own. However specialized an instance they may seem to be, G. B. Shaw's *Prefaces* to his plays are a case in point in that they can be read without any reference to the plays of which they originally formed a part.

All of this kind of prefatory information can be found under a diversity of names. The old wording was simply "To the Reader." In more recent times a bewildering array of phrases have been employed to avoid the simplicity of early periods, from "Fore-talk" to "Front matter." A. P. Herbert's *The Thames* (1966) used "The Preamble" and was complimented by the *Times Literary Supplement* on "a nice change from introduction or preface."

In the 1955 Lippincott edition of Christopher Morley's *Parnassus on Wheels* John T. Winterich's prefatory offering was entitled "Certain Essential Preliminary Footnotage."

The introduction

This is the part of the preliminary material that is usually contributed by someone other than the author. It is often of particular interest when it is an introduction to a volume in a series when an explanation of the series or the project can be expected. As with the preface the main use may well be biographical and historical rather than strictly bibliographical since the introduction is frequently written as a commendation of the work by someone associated with the author or the subject.

Special circumstances obtain when the introduction is to a book that is being revived and probably reedited. In such circumstances, when the original author has no opportunity to comment, the "introduction" frequently takes the shape of an introductory essay and can be a major piece of writing in its own right. It is not difficult to find examples of books that reprint preliminary material from several earlier editions and thus demonstrate changing attitudes to the text. There are also examples of introductions of this kind to works that never appeared. Two of the best examples are in the bibliographical field: A. W. Pollard's *Shakespeare Folios and Quartos* was published in 1909 as a planned introduction to a series of facsimiles that were never published; McKerrow's *Prolegomena for the Oxford Shakespeare* in 1939 outlined the editorial method for an edition of Shakespeare that has not yet appeared.

The table of contents

This table is a part of the apparatus within the book to enable the reader to find required portions. The contents list, index, running headlines, glosses, and shoulder notes have this function in common and approach it in different ways.

The contents list has a value in that it can most conveniently deal with the subject matter of the book in the order in which it is treated. It is a function that contents lists fulfill in a variety of ways. The simplest method is a listing of chapter numbers with pagination: Chapter 1 ...... Page 1; Chapter 2 ...... Page 29; etc.[6] Only slightly more helpful in many instances is the contents list that repeats the chapter heading: Chapter 1 ...... Birth; Chapter 2 ...... Boyhood; Chapter 3 ...... Marriage.

There are many stages of contents lists at various periods of book history, from such simple enumeration to full analytical listing. At its least complex the analysis is purely systematic, giving the layout of the chapter in the order of the treatment of the subject and thereby the whole treatment of the book. In the most sophisticated examples analytical contents listing as presented in many books provides early examples of abstracting. Such instances are more generally found in works of a factual nature. The book of imaginative literature has tended to deal with the problem in a somewhat different manner.

A widespread habit among nineteenth-century novelists was the attempt to summarize the chapter in one telling sentence: "In which Pen is kept waiting at the door, while the reader is informed who little Laura was" (*Pendennis*, Chapter 8), or, "In which Mr. Warrington treats the company with tea and a ball" (*The Virginians*, Chapter 34).

The list of illustrations

This listing serves the same purpose for illustrative material as the Table of Contents did for the text. It should distinguish between figures in the text and plates, with each series having a separate sequence of numbers. At its simplest it may do no more than does the simplest form of contents listing, which is solely to accord a number to each plate. In many types of books, notably plate books, the bibliographical investigation of the plates is of paramount importance and not infrequently of great difficulty. It is consequently of great assistance when the table of illustrations leaves no doubt as to where each plate should be. The clearest indication, which gives maximum help to the bibliographer and indeed to the user of the book, is for the listing to bear the same caption as the item to which it refers. The list should also indicate the exact position of the plate in sufficient detail for there to be no doubt as to where it belongs.

Errata and addenda

The whole process of proofreading and proof correcting gives rise to a wide range of bibliographical features that affect books of all periods, both manuscript and printed. The full history of proof correcting is as yet imperfectly recorded, but such work as that done by Percy Simpson gives an indication of its importance.[7] Proof correcting that is completed during the process of printing should be undetected since a perfect text will result—although, as is now increasingly evident, correction was frequently done step by step during printing, which will result in variant readings in successive sheets and therefore in different copies. If errors were detected before the last sheet was run off, it was common practice to utilize a blank page or part of a page on which the corrections might be printed. If no such blank area presented itself, a slip could be printed and tipped into the book, becoming the necessary "errata" or "addenda," jointly known as the "corrigenda." Corrections of an important nature that became necessary after the completion of the book were dealt with in a more elaborate manner by means of *cancels,* of which more will be said later.

Copies will be found in which corrections are made by hand. The possibility always exists that such changes are individual to a copy and have been made by an owner. Nevertheless, it was a method of formal correction, especially in the sixteenth and seventeenth centuries. It is also important to be prepared at this period for other explanations of manuscript corrections due to some of the trade practices of the period. F. R. Johnson discusses one such interesting example in relation to the custom of "copy books" that prevailed in England until 1635.[8]

Corrigenda, in one form or another, are widespread, albeit regrettable. When they occur, there is often a natural inclination on the part of those involved to apportion blame. Seldom has this been done more delightfully than in the verse with which Robert Herrick prefixed his *Hesperides* in 1648.

> "For these Transgressions which thou here dost see,
> Condemne the Printer, Reader, and not me;
> Who gave him forth good grain, though he mistook
> The Seed; so sow'd these Tares throughout my Book."

Headlines

The first function of headlines was, and still is, to guide the reader turning over the leaves in search of a particular section.

It is therefore apparent that a variety of headings may be found within a single volume. A common form of heading is the "running title," which repeats the title of the book, or an abbreviated version of it, throughout. A full or shortened version of the chapter or sectional title is also commonly used and, less frequently, page headlines. It is normal practice to combine any two of these. The recto headline is invariably, judging from available evidence, of equal or less scope than that on the verso—never greater. A singular and entertaining example of analytical headlines is found in Thackeray's *The Rose and the Ring*, whose headlines form a complete running summary of the story in rhyming couplets, as for example:

> *Verso:* Much I fear, King Valoroso
> *Recto:* That your conduct is but so so.

The headline normally includes, at the outer ends, the pagination; but the pagination is also found in the middle of the foot of the page, an innovation in which there seems to be little advantage. Eccentricities of all sorts are found, such as pagination numbers in words instead of figures. At least one book exists in which the pagination occupies the centre of the head, and the headline is a footline.[9]

Headlines have been common in books of all kinds at all periods. There is an interesting letter from Daniel Macmillan to Charles Kingsley, dated December 12, 1854, regarding *Westward Ho!*

> Unless it runs counter to some deep-rooted theory of yours, pray let the novel have headlines. It is against all the usages to send out a respectable book otherwise. Why should not the title of each chapter be the heading? Don't let it go out like a Minerva Press novel. . . . Why behead your own book?[10]

These contradictions are primarily matters of book design. They are only of bibliographical significance insofar as they help to establish some kind of common practice in a country or among a particular category of book. In recent years a considerable body of work has been done on the bibliographical significance of headlines. Some of these applications are self-evident, such as helping to determine the individuality of separate pieces within, for example, a volume of tracts; but in this instance identity is unlikely to depend upon this piece of evidence alone. Disparity between running title and title-page title will sometimes help to reveal a reissue with a changed title on a reprinted title page. This is observed occasionally in twentieth-century books where, for purposes of transatlantic trade, the title of an English book may be changed for the American market, but only on the title page. For the body of the book the original sheets were used. In other instances evidence of headlines has helped to unknot more complex bibliographical problems, and it seems highly probable that it will be put to increasing use in the future.[11]

The plates

Plates are whole-leaf-sized illustrations that are printed separately from the text. The usual reason for this is that the process by means of which the illustration was reproduced is not one that can be printed at the same time as letterpress. In the years up to around 1800 this covered all the intaglio methods of illustrations. They were frequently printed on a pair of conjugate leaves so that they could be placed in position as a part of the gathering and secured firmly during the sewing operations in binding. On other occasions they were printed onto leaves slightly wider than the leaf size of the book, and a small part of that leaf folded around the sewing line, so that a small stub would appear where the conjugate leaf might be expected. Only in nineteenth- and twentieth-century books is there likely to be frequent use of "tipped-in" plates, where the illustration is secured into the book by adhesive only. It is regular to find a plate captioned with a descriptive phrase or note, the numbering of the illustration given consecutively and not as part of the pagination. It is somewhat less common, but not rare, to find a description of the plate's position within the book also included, e.g., "facing page 121."

Plates have frequently been supplied with "tissues," which serve to protect the facing page and the plate from any set-off while the ink is fresh. Such tissues are frequently loose, and a book would not be regarded as imperfect once they had been removed. Sometimes this interleaving is of more substantial a nature than tissue and in such cases frequently bears plate numbering and captions. When this occurs, the "tissues" must be regarded as a bibliographical part of the book.

Maps, plans, and other such types of "plate" that are designed for easy consultation while the work is being read are often printed on larger sheets that fold out clear to the text page. Folding plates of this nature have been frequent in books of many kinds since the issue of Breydenbach's *Sanctae Peregrinationes* in 1486.[12] This volume included seven large panoramic views of cities; that of Venice is approximately five feet in length. They have always been somewhat vulnerable, and many copies that should include folding plates are sadly damaged and imperfect. Material of this nature is frequently placed in pockets in the casing and in a few instances issued in a separate portfolio.

Illustrations that are printed as part of a text page, even when they have involved a second printing as with intaglio processes, are referred to as "cuts" or "figures."

Notes and references

Notes of various kinds have been commonplace in books throughout the whole of their history. They are most frequent in works that require extensive explanation and reference. For this reason they appear in scholarly works of all kinds and especially when very precise comment is necessary.

Marginal and interlinear glosses were favored in the manuscript period: they were natural positions given the total freedom of the scribe. Early printers tended, as in many other directions, to follow the manuscript tradition. A text page, set in two columns and framed all round with commentary and references in a smaller size of type, was a compositor's approximation to scribal habits. It is a method that makes undue demands on compositors and is usually regarded as lacking in aesthetic appeal. In modern times it is rare outside the field of Bible printing and some theological and legal printing. The general practice for the majority of books over the past two hundred or so years has been for notes and references to become "footnotes" at the foot of the page. More modern practice has been to congregate them at the end of a chapter or the end of the book.

Apart from their prime usefulness to the reader they can on occasion be of assistance to the bibliographer. They are of that same degree of priority as varieties of "internal evidence"; references may be made to events or publications that will provide assistance in questions of dating.

Index or indexes (indices)

There are several important kinds of index, apart from the user's natural division of good ones and inadequate ones. The simple alphabetical listing is the most widely known, but others will be regularly encountered.

Analytical indexes can avoid the unrevealing monotony of a list of numbers by breaking the subject down into its component parts and arranging them in some logical order. This is not necessarily an alphabetical order, and frequently an entry under a personal name will be arranged in the order of the sequence of the events within the book. The close similarity of function between the index and the contents list then becomes apparent.

Sectionalized indexes, which have a long and honorable history, are now frequently a bone of contention. Their advantages are obvious, their sole disadvantage being any indecision in the reader regarding the particular index to which reference should be made. They emphasize the fact, which cannot be stressed too much in dealing with indexes, that a good index can have a use apart from its main association with the book. The index to R. W. Chapman's collected edition of *Jane Austen's Letters* is a particularly apt example. It has the following eight parts to its index:[13]

  i. Jane Austen's family
  ii. Other persons
  iii. Places
  iv. General topics
  v. Authors, books, plays
  vi. Jane Austen's novels
  vii. Jane Austen's English
  viii. Names of ships

Each of these has a possible relevance of its own, and the editor has taken full advantage of the possibility. For example, the books listed in section v have a short quotation from the letters regarding each, so that the index provides a first résumé of Jane Austen's reading and her comments. It is an apt example because Dr. Chapman was a notable supporter of "pluralism" in indexes.

The imprint, or colophon, which may include the printer's device

The colophon (Greek: a summit or conclusion) is occasionally found in manuscripts, where it gives the scribe's name and the date. In printed books it first appeared on the Psalter printed by Fust and Schoeffer in 1457. It gradually became common but was driven out by the title-page imprint toward 1600.[14]

The colophon is an important repository of facts related to the printing and publication of a work, especially in the case of books that have no title leaves. Even when a title leaf is in existence, however, the colophon must still be scrutinized with care. Investigation of the detail given there may reveal information of general concern, not solely connected with the book in hand. Two examples will serve to demonstrate this: one that followed an investigation related to the precise date[15] and the other on the interpretation of one word in the colophon.[16]

In its full and original form it has been revived, particularly in the productions of the fine and private presses. It is very common among modern French books of this kind and is frequently the source of information regarding the bibliographical details of the book, such as the "justification du tirage."

When the development of the title page drew this information away to the beginning of the book, the imprint began to take its now traditional place at the foot of the title page, with the printer's device frequently centered on the page. In time the imprint and the device became those of the publisher rather than the printer as these two offices began to separate. Hence in modern books it is the devices of publishers, such as Longman's ship, Knopf's borzoi, and Heinemann's windmill, that became better known than those of printers.

As this transference took place, the older position of the imprint at the end of the book developed as one of the regular positions for the printer's imprint. The other common position is on the verso of the title page. In all books printed in the United Kingdom the printer's name must appear somewhere within the printing (2 and 3 Vict. c 12 s. 2.).

Even when the colophon is little more than a modest imprint for a printer, it is not without either problems or interest. A question that was raised some years ago in this connection indicates the bibliographer's need to explain every aspect of the book in as much detail as possible.[17]

Finis

It was an old habit of book makers to mark the end of the text with this word or, in later instances, the words THE END. It is not always quite so unnecessary a practice as might at first appear. In a multivolumed work this wording is usually kept for the last volume, the others ending END OF VOLUME I, etc.

Blank leaves

Blank leaves that are a part of the full sheet of the book must be included in any analysis and description of the book. Initially this may seem to be absurd, but the bibliographer is concerned with the completeness of the copy and is always haunted by the "might have been." A copy that should have blank leaves but in which they are lacking might have been a copy owned by Coleridge or Jefferson. On that blank leaf might have been the text of an unknown poem or the first draft of the Declaration of Independence. Only by seeing this blank leaf in a copy, *still* blank, can the bibliographer feel assured that this was not so.

It follows that the analysis of the book must be directed toward ascertaining whether such blank leaves are a part of the book proper—that is, part of one of the sheets that went onto the press—or whether they are a part of the process of binding or casing. The problem can be expressed in another way: it is important to distinguish clearly which are the endpapers in order that they may be ignored in establishing the book's collation.

Advertisements

Apart from the advertising element in title-page design and lettering, advertisements appeared in many books from the mid–seventeenth century onward. The early forms tended to follow two patterns, or at least two recognizably distinct versions of the same pattern. Printers took advantage of any blank area of a page at the conclusion of the text to advertise recent and forthcoming publications. The use extended to full pages and occasionally to any unrequired page areas on the whole sheet when less than the full sheet would meet the needs of the text.

In nineteenth-century trade issues publishers' advertisements commonly appear as a completely separate gathering within the book. Such groupings of advertisements are frequently dated, but the evidence of such dating has to be weighed with care. If supplies of the advertising section ran out during the casing of a book, it was not unknown for a publisher to insert an earlier advertising section of which stocks were still on hand. The study of advertisements may reveal detail about the book under review but additionally is a source of information regarding contemporary books.[18]

Much advertising was naturally conducted outside the book itself in trade listings that operated from time to time in different countries. One advertising medium, however, hovers between being external to the book and being a part of it. In the nineteenth century especially it was common practice to place an unattached insert in books containing publishers' or booksellers' notices. Many of these have unfortunately vanished with time and use. Where they still remain, care should be taken to preserve them.

Subscription lists

A common eighteenth-century practice, although of earlier origin, was the publication of works by subscription. A prospectus would be issued, frequently through newspapers, inviting subscriptions to a proposed work.[19] One of the terms of the arrangement was usually for a list of the subscribers to be published in the book. In certain types of lavish publication the listings themselves are somewhat elaborately produced. English listings of this style in the eighteenth century are often roll calls of the landed gentry. They are also some of the clearest evidence available regarding the reading taste of the period and the distribution of a particular work. Of similar interest, although with the individual subscribers less easily traced through normal biographical sources, are the subscription lists to some of the large part issues in the latter half of the eighteenth century. Names and addresses are more modest than the former category, but they are of extreme interest at a period when both reading tastes and book-distribution methods were beginning to exhibit significant change. Some new and very interesting work has begun in recent years on subscription book lists and should prove to be of considerable importance.[20]

Endpapers

These are not, bibliographically, a part of the book. The bibliographer may nevertheless have to spend a considerable amount of time on them determining exactly what are the endpapers in order that they may be ignored in the description. Or, to view the matter more positively, it must be determined how many of the leaves within the book are formed from foldings of the full sheet and how many are not. The basic function of the endpapers is to provide a pair of conjugate leaves one of which could be pasted down on the inside of the boards to cover the untidiness of the turn-over (or doublure) of the covering material and of the hinge of the binding. The leaf not pasted down would naturally create the fly endpaper. In modern books it is rare to find more than this pair of leaves serving as endpapers, but in older books two or three leaves may be found.

In instances where the binding is damaged, and even more in cases of rebinding, the endpapers are particularly vulnerable. They have unfortunately at times been a place for the printing of maps, plans, or genealogical data, which have often disappeared during the lifetime of a copy. Some nineteenth-century publishers, notably H. G. Bohn, used the endpapers for catalogs of their publications. The only common function of endpapers is decoration, and various forms of decorated and marbled papers have lent an air of distinction to their books.[21] Endpapers have frequently been the place for marks of ownership, a variety of manuscript notes, book plates, etc., and care should be taken to see that consideration of the preservation of these items is given at the time of any rebinding.

Dust jackets

These are known also as dust wrappers and as book jackets. These descriptions give a clear indication of their original purpose, which was quite simply to keep the covers of the book clean. Although "wrapper" has often been used in this connection, it is generally thought to be a confusing term. "Wrapper" is widely used to describe a cover that is attached to the publication and so has a close connection with the paperback. "Jacket" is a much less ambiguous term to describe the cover that can be removed. The earliest known use of a dust jacket was in 1832, but there are few extant examples until the late part of the century. From such partial amount of evidence as exists, the early dust jackets were of exceptional simplicity as compared with their modern counterparts, with nothing more than an announcement of the author's name and the book's title. In due course they also bore advertising material and became increasingly decorative. In current book production much time and money is spent upon these pieces of advertising material, and it is not surprising that they have been studied in their own right as pieces of artistic work.[22]

Bibliographically, however, they are not considered as a part of the book since they do not form any part of the sheets on which the book is printed, and they very easily become totally and permanently separated from the book. Bibliographers always hope that no information of importance will be committed to the dust jacket alone. Examples nevertheless exist in sufficient quantities for care to be taken in preservation of this "ephemeral" material.[23]

REFERENCES

1. CHAPMAN, R. W. "Thoughts on Half-titles." *The Colophon.* Part 7. 1931.

2. BLANCK, Jacob. *The Title-Page as Bibliographical Evidence.* 1966.
   DE VINNE, Theodore Low. *A Treatise on Title-pages.* 1904.
   NESBITT, Alexander, ed. *200 Decorative Title-pages.* 1964.
   POLLARD, A. W. *Last Words on the History of the Title-page.* 1891.
   SAMUEL, Ralph. "Four Centuries of Book-titles." *The Colophon.* Part 8. 1931.

3. WHEATLEY, H. B. *The Dedication of Books.* (The Book-lover's Library.) 1887.

4. BACON, Francis. *The Advancement of Learning.* i.iii.9.

5. WILLIAMS, Franklin B. *Index of Dedications and Commendatory Verses in English Books Before 1641.* 1962. p. xi.

6. A recent extreme example of this uninformative method of content listing is Elisaveta Fen's *A Russian's England* (1976). Two pages are solemnly devoted to a listing of "Chapter 1" to "Chapter 54," with simple page numberings and no more.

7. SIMPSON, Percy. *Proof-reading in the Sixteenth, Seventeenth and Eighteenth Centuries.* 1935.

8. JOHNSON, Francis R. "Printers' 'Copy Books' and the Black Market in the Elizabethan Book Trade." *The Library.* 5th Series. I: 1946–47. pp. 97–105.

9. MOLLOY, James L. *Our Autumn Holiday on French Rivers.* [n.d.]

10. HUGHES, Thomas. *Memoir of Daniel Macmillan.* 1882. p. 254.

11. BOWERS, Fredson. "The Headline in Early Books." *English Institute Annual, 1941.* 1942. p. 186.
    BOWERS, Fredson, "Notes on Running-titles and Bibliographical Evidence." *The Library.* 4th Series. XIX: 1938–39. pp. 315–338.
    BOWERS, Fredson, "Running-title Evidence for Determining

Half-sheet Imposition." *Papers of the Bibliographical Society University of Virginia.* I: 1948–49. pp. 199–202.
BUHLER, Curt. "The Headlines of William de Machlinia's *Year Book. 37 Henry VI."* *Papers of the Bibliographical Society University of Virginia.* I: 1948–49. pp. 125–132.
HINMAN, Charlton. "New Uses for Headlines as Bibliographical Evidence." *English Institute Annual, 1941.* 1942. pp. 207–222.
WILLIAMSON, William L. "An Early Use of Running Title and Signature Evidence in Analytical Bibliography." *Library Quarterly.* XI · 1970. pp. 215–249.

12. This is the title by which this work is usually known. The "correct" title is *Peregrinatio in Terram Sanctam* ....

13. CHAPMAN, R. W., ed. *The Letters of Jane Austen.* 2v. 1932.

14. POLLARD, Alfred William. *An Essay on Colophons, with Specimens and Translations.* 1905.

15. BUHLER, Curt F. "Dates in Incunabular Colophons." *Studies in Bibliography.* XXII: 1969. pp. 210–214.

16. RHODES, Dennis E. "On the Use of the Verb 'Facere' in Early Colophons." *Studies in Bibliography.* XXVI: 1973. pp. 230–232.

17. TODD, William B. "Arithmetic Colophons in Nineteenth-century Books." *Studies in Bibliography.* XIX: 1966. pp. 244–245.

18. TODD, William B. "On the Use of Advertisements in Bibliographical Studies." *The Library.* 5th Series. VIII: 1953. pp. 174–187.

19. Several interesting examples of this, together with other economic aspects of the book trade, are given in the chapter on "Financial Organization and Terms of Publication" in:

PLANT, Marjorie. *The English Book Trade: An Economic History of the Making and Sale of Books.* 2nd ed. 1965.

In addition, the John Johnson Collection in the Bodleian Library houses an important collection of prospectuses.

20. The Book Subscription Lists Project was established in the School of Education, The University of Newcastle upon Tyne. It is now called the Project for Historical Biobibliography. It is carrying out a number of research projects. One of the chief guides published so far is:

ROBINSON, F. J. G., and WALLIS, P. J. *Book Subscription Lists: A Revised Guide.* 1975.

which records some five thousand titles of books that were published by subscription.

21. LORING, Rosamund B. *Decorated Book Papers.* 2nd ed. 1952.

22. ROSNER, Charles. *The Growth of the Book Jacket.* 1954.

23. TANSELLE, G. Thomas. "Book-jackets, Blurbs and Bibliographers." *The Library.* 5th Series. XXVI: 1971. pp. 91–134.

3.
LANDMARKS IN THE DEVELOPMENT OF THE BOOK

Although human beings have been on this earth for more than a million years, it is only from within the last ten thousand that we have extant evidence of any attempts at permanent records of communication. Bibliography concerns itself very largely with the later period of manuscript work and the printed book, but it is important not to forget the area of what is sometimes called the "archaeology of the book." Cave paintings and drawings, such as those at Altamira, Lascaux, or on the rocks of Tassili, provide some indication that from a very early period the decorative urge and the desire to communicate have existed side by side. Papyrus rolls and baked clay tablets are of considerable importance in the evolution of our modern book. It is, for example, sometimes salutary to recall that the papyrus roll enjoyed a period of supremacy longer than that to date of the printed book. One of the lessons of historical bibliography is to expect change. To the bibliographer who is working with nineteenth-century novels or early Jacobean drama the problems of the decipherment of cuneiform inscriptions or the world of the papyrologist may seem to be very remote. They are both distinct fields calling for expertise of very different kinds. Nevertheless, the objectives of the researcher in all these and other similar fields are essentially the same: the documents have to be authenticated and the text thereon established bibliographically. Clay tablets and papyrus rolls are examined and described in a manner similar to that employed for printed books. They all come under what A. W. Pollard described as "the big umbrella" of bibliographical studies even though their practitioners may never meet and be largely ignorant of other areas of specialization.

One of the first important lessons to be learned from historical bibliography, therefore, is the broad sweep of events in the development of the "book" and an understanding of the turning points in its history. It will then be possible to delimit the periods within which there is a certain similarity of problem so that such expressions as "an Elizabethan pamphlet," "a late–eighteenth-century plate book," or "nineteenth-century three-decker" have some kind of meaning.

Many of the most important changes in the structure of the book were those contingent upon the introduction of new materials. One early change, however, was not. Although the papyrus roll continued as the main form of written material down to the end of the third century AD, some books were beginning to be produced in codex form from the beginning of the second century. This resulted in the "hinged" book as we know it today, in contrast to the rolled book. The main advantages were purely practical. The codex form was much more convenient to handle and especially so in referring to a specific passage. For this reason it is sometimes argued that lawyers were among the earliest supporters of this form. The other advantage of the codex was its economy in space; writing could be on both sides. The origins of the codex can be seen in the hinged tablets of Greek and Roman times, but it is chiefly in the membrane and paper manuscript and the paper printed book that it is remembered.

From the fourth century until the middle of the fifteenth it is the codex book written on parchment or vellum that is the mainstay of European book making. Toward the end of this period paper begins to appear, but the overall pattern is similar.

Public attention in the field of manuscripts has always been largely focused on the great specimens of illumination and decoration, and it is to these that most steps turn in our libraries and museums. They are so great a part of the glory of the manuscript age that it is difficult to resist this. It is important to realize that these are nevertheless only one part of the world of manuscripts. Many manuscripts have a preeminent textual importance, and it is all too easy for this aspect to be underestimated in a general survey of their history. The Dead Sea Scrolls are hardly beautiful to behold, but their importance cannot be gainsaid. It is inevitable that the majority of the world's manuscripts must fall into the "undecorated" category and correspondingly important that they should be surveyed as part of the contribution of the hand-produced book to the whole development.

It is difficult to put any articles into neat compartments appropriately labeled, and it is seldom more misleading than with works of art. Nevertheless, the student should learn to recognize a few broad categories of manuscript at the outset; further experience will soon begin to suggest the linkages among them. The following is an initial list of categories of manuscript that may help in the first steps toward recognition. Original manuscripts should ideally be seen in the great libraries and museums of the world, but in many areas these are few and far between. The next best, therefore, are good reproductions and especially those that are of the original size. The examples of the categories in the list are chosen not only because of the fundamental importance of the manuscripts but also because reproductions of them can be easily found:

(a)   *Classical Texts*, fourth–sixth centuries
      e.g.: Ambrosian Iliad
              Vatican Virgil

(b)   *Early Greek Uncial MSS of Bible*, fourth–fifth centuries
      e.g.: Codex Vaticanus
              Codex Sinaiticus

(c)   *Byzantine MSS* especially of sixth century
      e.g.: Vienna Genesis
              Rossano Gospel-book

(d)   *Celtic MSS*, sixth–eighth centuries
      e.g.: Book of Durrow
              Book of Kells

(e)   *English MSS*, sixth–eighth centuries
      e.g.: Codex Amiatinus
              Lindisfarne Gospels

(f)   *Carolingian MSS*, eighth–ninth centuries
      e.g.: Utrecht Psalter
              Charlemagne *or* Godescale Evangeliarium

(g)   *English MSS*, ninth–eleventh centuries
      e.g.: Benedictional of St. Aethelwold
              Arundel Psalter

(h)   Ottonian MSS, tenth–eleventh centuries
      e.g.: Otto Gospel Book
            Uta Codex

(i)   English MSS, twelfth century
      e.g.: Winchester Bible
            St. Alban's Psalter

(j)   English MSS, fourteenth–fifteenth centuries
      e.g.: Queen Mary's Psalter
            Luttrell Psalter

(k)   French MSS, fourteenth–fifteenth centuries
      e.g.: Rohan Book of Hours
            Très Riches Heures du Duc de Berry
            Bedford Book of Hours

(l)   Flemish MSS, fourteenth–fifteenth centuries
      e.g.: Li Romans d'Alixandre
            Grimani Breviary

(m)   Italian MSS, fourteenth–fifteenth centuries
      e.g.: Nicolò da Bologna's Missal
            Corvinus Breviary

   Frequent references will naturally be found to "the age of manuscript," and this will sometimes suggest a greater uniformity than in fact existed. It must be borne constantly in mind that the period so referred to lasted over a thousand years and was made remarkable more than any other feature by its diversity: a diversity that stemmed primarily from the differences of period, region, and nature of text.

The invention of printing

Printing from movable types was invented in China, preceding the European invention by four centuries. The employment of woodblocks for printing in the Far East was even more in advance of its European use. In the absence of definite evidence of dependence of Western inventors upon Eastern models or reports it is not possible to say more than that there had always been overland trade routes, however slow and indirect, and connection therefore is not impossible.[1]

Woodblock printing had been practiced in Western Europe for textiles, playing cards, figures of saints, and so forth, for perhaps a century before the invention of typography. Surviving cuts dated in the years around 1420 induced the belief that the "block-books," or books printed from woodcuts, were of the same date and that they were a stepping-stone to typography, but this is most probably not true. They exist in four forms: rudimentary block-books, in which the cuts are (a) merely pasted; or (b) directly stamped into spaces in MS books; (c) books in which the woodcut text and figures are printed on only one side of the leaf ("anopisthographic") and in writing ink that has turned brown with age; and (d) books printed on both sides of the leaf in printer's ink. The high period of the block-books was in the 1460s, and no date earlier than 1450 can be certainly assigned to any example of this class of printing.[2] Moreover, typography took its rise among workers in metal, and in spite of the assertions of several eminent scholars in the later decades of the last century, it now seems highly improbable that typography sprang directly from xylography. Woodworkers and metalworkers were organized, and closely organized, in quite separate guilds, and they had little contact. The advantage of the block-book was that a book of which frequent unaltered editions were wanted (especially if it were freely illustrated, like the scenes from the life of Christ called the *Biblia Pauperum*) could be reproduced without the labor of fresh setting of type. It is curious that block-printing was not perfected for this purpose, which is that fulfilled by the modern processes of stereotyping and electrotyping. In the fifteenth century the output of block-books appears to have been almost wholly German and Netherlandish, but in the early sixteenth France produced at least one and Venice a few. All are books of popular instruction, and the latest examples known are of about 1517.

A woodcut text can always be distinguished from one that is typeset by its variant, joined, or overhanging letters and other irregularities.

The frequent suggestion that sees in the Renaissance a source

of inspiration for the introduction of printing from movable type
into Europe is largely discounted. The motives of the inventors
were purely practical: to give the book-buying public what it
wanted in greater quantity and at a lower price than before.
There is not the slightest reason to suppose that they knew
anything of the Renaissance in Italy. There are indeed reasonable refutations of any such theory. In the first place, they were
inventors, but that did not make them prophets as well. The fall
of Constantinople, which if it did not create certainly gave body
to the Renaissance, occurred in May 1453: by this time the art of
printing was in its preparatory stage and possibly even being
practiced. Second, attention should be paid to the books they
first printed. Bibles, Church Service books, old standard theological treatises, indulgences, tell their own tale, and the impact of
the Renaissance on printing is not visible until the trade was well
established.

The actual invention is still surrounded by obscurity and has
given rise to an immense, very technical, and too often highly
controversial and prejudiced, body of writing. In the light of all
modern scholarly work there can be no serious reason to doubt
the claim for Johann Gutenberg as the one responsible for introducing printing from movable type into Europe. Equally there is
no reason to believe that he was in any way cognizant of the
developments in the Far East and thereby influenced by them.
He was an inventor in his own right even though the process had
been established elsewhere at an earlier date. Many of the basic
principles upon which book printing was established were known
to other trades and had been so for decades. The art of printing
had been applied to textiles as the art of engraving had been
applied in the gold- and silversmiths' trade. The new problem
was to produce a printing surface, capable of reproducing itself on
paper or membrane, that could be used again and again and that
could be built up without the labor of cutting out the letters
every time. It is therefore not surprising that, since what was
needed was a technology to apply some aspects of existing skills
to a new end, there should be rival claimants for the honor of the
European introduction. It would seem only logical to accept the
idea that others were working in the same field and that some
measures of success had attended their efforts also.[3]

Toward this end there had long existed the art of casting

"formae," or, as we say, "forms," slabs of metal with designs and lettering in relief. The next stage would be to stamp punches, a letter or line at a time, into clay or founders' sand at first, but later, more probably, using some soft metal like copper in which the depth of the punch was easier to control. Into the mold so formed molten metal could be poured, producing the printing surface. The process, somewhat akin to stereotyping, was, it is thought, called *jetté en moule*; we can call it metallography or cast-printing. Clear allusions to printing by *jetté en moule* are found in the *memoriaux* of Jean le Robert, Abbot of Saint-Aubert at Cambrai, who in 1445 and 1451 recorded the purchase at Bruges and Arras of copies of the Doctrinale "gette en molle." The Arras copies, he complained, were very inaccurately printed, but here is further evidence of the circulation of these cast-printed books and, what is more, two exact dates. Some writers have identified the Abbot's purchases with the "Costeriana" or typo graphically produced Dutch books, to be mentioned later, of which many fragments survive: but this seems less likely.

We know that as early as 1436 Gutenburg himself was at work at Strassburg on an invention that, however carefully he and his associates concealed its nature, involved a press and must have had to do with printing. Our knowledge is derived from the records of a lawsuit of 1439, which allege that Gutenberg had been in partnership with a certain Andres Dritzehen.[4] It may well have been from Strassburg that the knowledge of how to produce cast-printed books spread. If so, it spread not only to the Netherlands and to Mainz but also to the south of France. From contracts and receipts for the money involved we know that at Avignon between 1444 and 1446 a Bohemian goldsmith named Procopius Waldfoghel was engaged in an occupation (*ars scribendi artificialiter*) that sounds like printing. Waldfoghel, who in his previous career may well have met Gutenberg's Strassburg partner, worked in conjunction with one Girard Ferrose of Trèves. They possessed alphabets (including Hebrew letters) cut in steel and iron, as well as forms (*formas ad artem scribendi pertinentes*) of iron and tin. The letters, to judge by the hardness of the metals employed, must have been punches; the forms were probably cast blocks from which impressions could be taken, perhaps on to materials, or bindings, or, possibly, paper. No fragment identifiable as printed from one of them survives.

One much-debated group of typographically printed books has been held, but with their primitive appearance as the sole proof, to precede the first achievements in Mainz. In Holland, to judge by the type forms and the provenance of fragments, were produced a number of undated and very rudely printed editions, as already mentioned, of the famous Latin grammars of the Middle Ages, those of Donatus and Alexander Gallus (the Doctrinale). These appear to be earlier than the first datable Dutch incunabula, those printed at Utrecht in 1473 by Ketelaer and Leempt. These editions may possibly be the productions of a real person concealed behind the legend retailed by Hadrianus Junius in his *Batavia* (1588). Junius tells of a certain Laurens Janszoon Coster, an innkeeper of Haarlem (such a person existed there in the first half of the fifteenth century), who cut letters in wood and printed with them. These Donatuses and Doctrinalia are accordingly known as Costeriana.[5] An earlier and more important reference possibly to these books is a passage in the *Cologne Chronicle* (1499), quoting Ulrich Zel, the first Cologne printer, who had presumably gone there from Mainz (he was described as a *clericus Morguntinensis*) about 1464. Zel's testimony was to the effect that Mainz printing had come into being toward 1440 but had had a "Vurbyldung," or prefiguration, in some Donatuses printed in the Netherlands before that date. Junius's story that Coster's servant stole and fled with his types is hardly convincing to anyone who knows the weight of types and the rate of traveling in the fifteenth century. But Zel must have known Gutenberg, and the story in the *Cologne Chronicle* sounds likely enough, if we identify the Donatuses with the *gettes en molle,* and not with the Costeriana, which are probably later in date. This theory is enhanced if we allow the possibility (as in the "1468" Oxford imprint) of an error here of a decade and if we suppose that Zel gave 1450 and not 1440 as the date of the Mainz printing. This would be a date that more nearly suits the surviving books and documents and also covers the fact that Gutenberg was at Strassburg at least as late as 1442. Gutenberg's invention or improvement of the art must be pieced together from a combination of legal documents and surviving pieces of printing. The most individually important is the so-called Helmasperger Notorial document, which recorded in some detail one of Gutenberg's transactions. In 1455 Johann Fust, a goldsmith, sought by law to

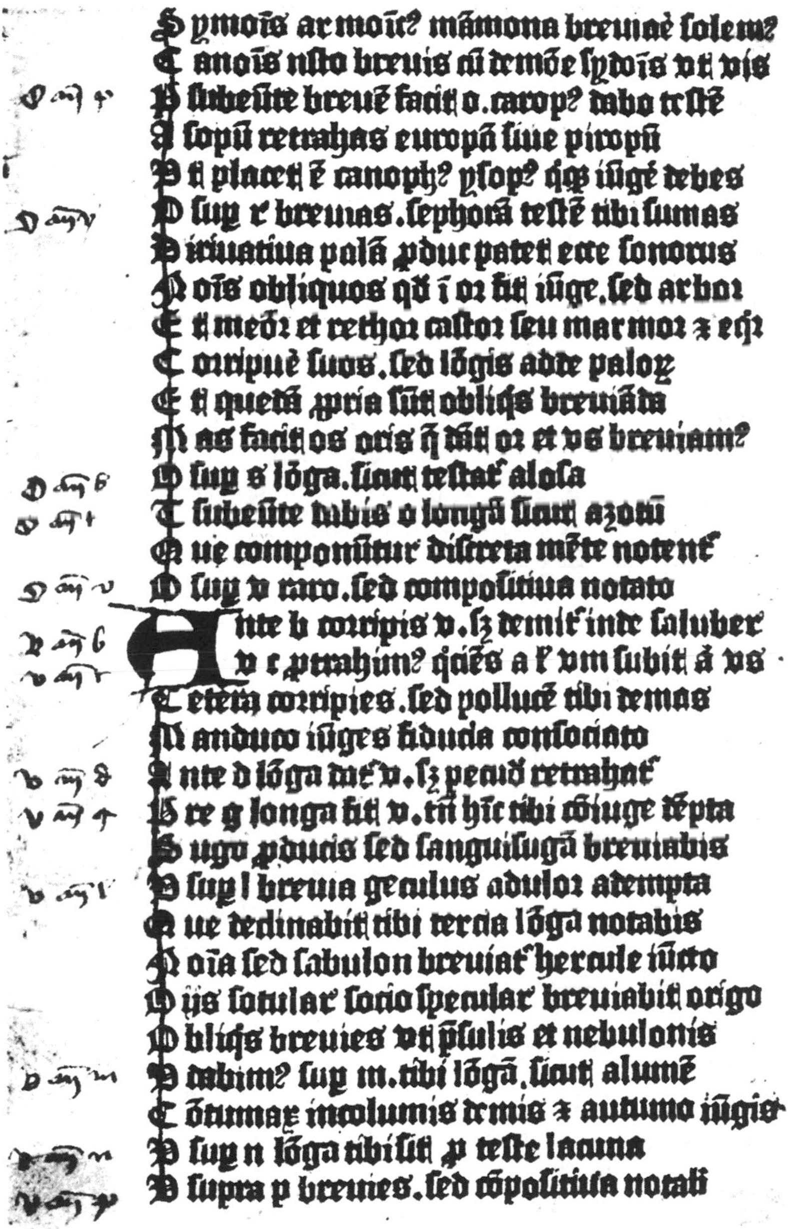
Symoīs ac moīc? mãmona breuiaē solem?
Canoīs nsto breuis cū demōe sydoīs vtꝭ vis
Subeūte breuē facitꝭ o. carop? dabo teste
Sopū cetrahas europã siue pircopū
Si placetꝭ ē canoph? ysop? quos iūgē debes
O sup r breuias. sephorā teste tibi sumas
Diuatiua palã pducpatetꝭ ecce sonorus
Noīs obliquos qd ī or fitꝭ iūge. sed arbor
Et meōr et rethor castor seu marmor ȝ ests
Corripuē suos. sed lōgis adde paloz
Et quetā ꝓpria sūtꝭ obliqs breuiāda
Mas facitꝭ os oris ꝗ dātꝭ or et vs breuiam?
O sup s lōga. sicutꝭ testat' alosa
Subeūte dabis o longā sicutꝭ azotū
Que componūtur discreta mēte notent'
O sup v raro. sed compositiua notato
Ante b corripis v. sȝ demit' inde saluber
Vc ꝓtrahūn? qdes a r' vm subitꝭ ã vs
Cetera corripies. sed pollucē tibi demas
Manduco iūges fiducia consociato
Ante d lōga dae v. sȝ pecuō cetrahat'
Sre g longa fitꝭ v. tñ hic tibi cōiuge tēpta
Iugo pducis sed sanguisugã breuiabis
O sup l breuia geculus adulor adempta
Que declinabitꝭ tibi tercia lōga notabis
Noīa sed sabulon breuiat' hercule iūcto
Ō ijs sotular sorio specular breuiabitꝭ origo
Obliqs breuies vtꝭ ꝑsulis et nebulonis
Dabim? sup m. tibi lōgã. sicutꝭ alumē
Cōtinmaz incolumis demis ȝ autumo iūgis
O sup n lōga tibi sitꝭ ꝓ teste lacuna
O supra p breuies. sed cōpositiua notabi

FIG. 1. *A Costerianum. Alexander Gallus,* Doctrinale

recover from Johann Gutenberg two loans of eight hundred guilders each, which he had made to him in 1450 and 1452. The purpose of the loans, on Gutenberg's statement, being for maintenance and all expenses while perfecting the art of printing. The security for the loans was the printing apparatus, which on Gutenberg's default would pass to Fust.

Before 24 August 1456 appeared the first substantial printed book, for on that date Henricus Cremer, Vicar of St. Stephen's at Mainz, finished rubricating a copy of a great folio Bible. This work is known as "The Gutenberg Bible"; "The Mazarin Bible," from the library where it was first noticed; or, more commonly now, as "the 42-line Bible," from the number of lines of text on a normal full page. The copy that Cremer rubricated is now in the Bibliothèque Nationale. There is no doubt now that this book was planned and begun by Gutenberg but carried to completion by Gutenberg's former servant, Peter Schoeffer, now in the service of Fust.[6] Fust and Schoeffer's names appear together in the following year in the first printed colophon, that to the fine Psalter of 1457, which is distinguished by its color-printed capitals.[7] Fust was no doubt only a financier (and a very trusting one, to have speculated in Gutenberg). Schoeffer must have been very young at the time, since he did not die till 1502.

Earlier than the 42-line Bible are several editions of an indulgence issued to those who should make gifts of money to help in the war against the Turks, which bear in manuscript the names of the recipients and dates in 1454 and 1455. There are also some undated Donatuses and other small pieces, such as might be put out by printers as specimens of their work. Among these smaller pieces are the fragments of early printing that were first noticed between 1834 and 1858 by Dr. Josef Muczkowski, librarian of the Jagellon Library in Cracow. The examination of these fragments has resulted in two notable conclusions: (a) that no positive evidence exists for any product of movable-type printing before 1454; and (b) that there is no extant piece of printing attributed to Gutenberg on either typographical or other grounds that satisfies the majority of critics. He may possibly have been responsible for the 1460 printing of the Balbus Catholicon. This bears no printer's name but glorifies God and Mainz for the invention of printing. A part of the colophon translates, "printed at Mainz in 1460 with the help of the Most

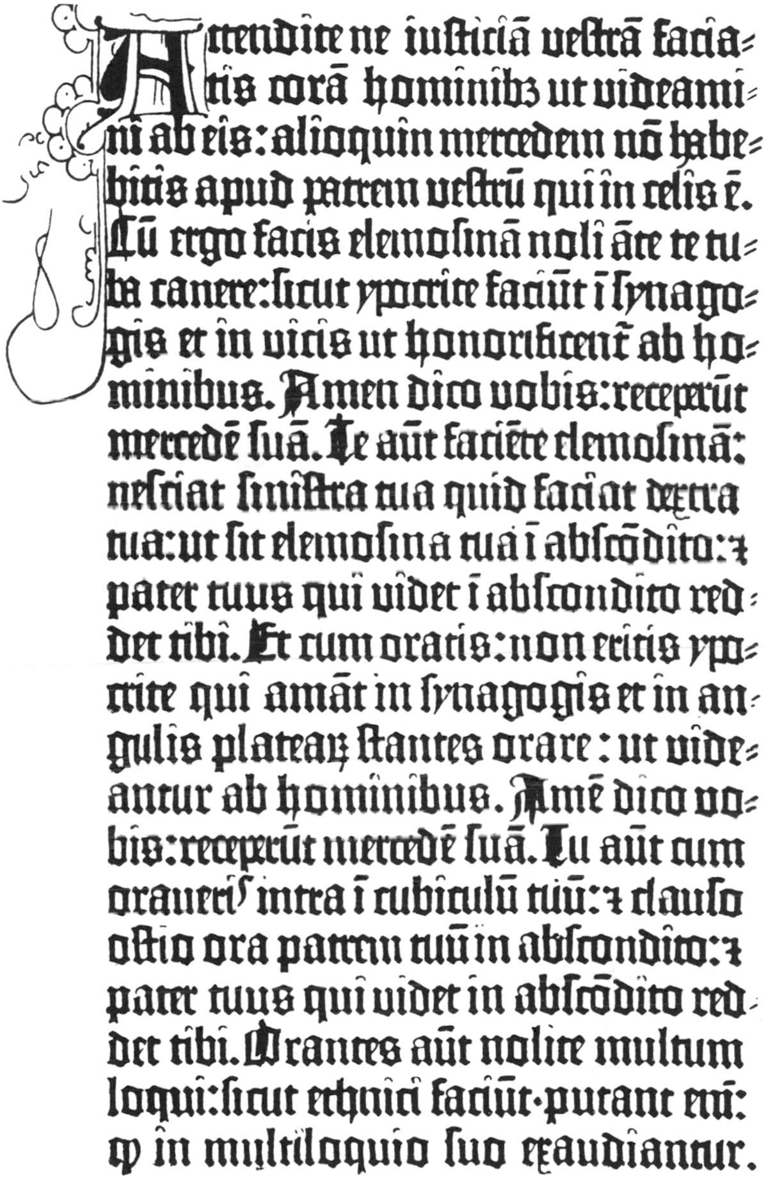

Attendite ne iuſticiā ueſtrā facia=
tis corā hominibꝫ ut uideami=
ni ab eis: alioquin mercedem nō habe=
bitis apud patrem ueſtrū qui in celis ē.
Cū ergo facis elemoſinā noli āte te tu=
ba canere: ſicut ypocrite faciūt i ſynago=
gis et in uicis ut honorificenſ ab ho=
minibus. Amen dico uobis: receperūt
mercedē ſuā. Te aūt faciēte elemoſinā:
neſciat ſiniſtra tua quid faciat dextra
tua: ut ſit elemoſina tua i abſcōdito: ⁊
pater tuus qui uidet i abſcondito red=
det tibi. Et cum oratis: non eritis ypo=
crite qui amāt in ſynagogis et in an=
gulis plateaꝝ ſtantes orare: ut uide=
antur ab hominibus. Amē dico uo=
bis: receperūt mercedē ſuā. Tu aūt cum
oraueriſ intra i cubiculū tuū: ⁊ clauſo
oſtio ora patrem tuū in abſcondito: ⁊
pater tuus qui uidet in abſcōdito red=
det tibi. Orantes aūt nolite multum
loqui: ſicut ethnici faciūt· putant eī:
ꝗ in multiloquio ſuo exaudiantur.

FIG. 2. *Part of a column of the 42-line Bible*

High . . . who oft-times reveals to the lowly that which he hides from the wise." It is often accepted that this refers to Gutenberg and the invention of printing and that it is language that suits the use by the inventor rather than by anyone else.[8]

The spread of printing

The event that contributed largely to the spread of printing from Mainz was the sack of the city in October 1462. From this date onward German printers, including many who had connections with Mainz, were taking the art of printing throughout Germany and subsequently throughout Europe. Two German cities, however, had begun printing before 1462. In about 1460 Johann Mentelin printed the third Bible at Strassburg, and that town became a center of considerable importance. Many of the early books are uninteresting until the Renaissance produced there, toward the end of the century, some delightfully illustrated classics, such as Terence. Mentelin was followed by his son-in-law and associate, Adolf Rusch, and between them they began to use types that showed some tendency toward roman. At Bamberg, Albrecht Pfister used the type of the 36-line Bible, the second of the two great early Bibles, to produce a group of small illustrated books to which it was not suited. These popular works, in which Pfister specialized, began to appear about 1461. Many of them had woodcut illustrations, an experiment that was not imitated for another decade. At Cologne, Ulrich Zel, already mentioned as the authority for the Netherlandish "Vurbyldung" of Mainz printing, established himself in 1464 and founded the local speciality of printing theological quartos, mostly mere pamphlets. In Augsburg (from 1468), Nuremberg (from 1470), and Ulm (from 1472) there was much use of woodcut illustrations and decorative capitals, both no doubt originally intended to be the groundwork for colors applied by hand but most pleasing when left in black-and-white. At Nuremberg, Anton Koberger (from 1472) developed an enormous business as both printer and publisher. Basel had in the person of Amerbach a scholar-printer and friend of scholars and in the next century became one of the great centers of learned printing.

In 1465 two Germans, both citizens of Mainz, Conrad

Sweynheym and Arnold Pannartz, carried printing into Italy. An imaginative description of the journey of the two printers may be read in Charles Reade's *The Cloister and the Hearth*. They produced, at the Benedictine Abbey of Subiaco, in the hills above Tivoli, on their way to Rome, four books, of which an edition of Lactantius bears the earliest exact date (*Fig.* 3). It is printed in a gothic type that is itself at least halfway on the road to Rome, and it is the first book containing Greek type.

Sweynheym and Pannartz established themselves at Rome in 1467 and started printing the *editiones principes* of classical authors from the manuscripts that scholars were then discovering. But like many of their followers they overestimated the demand and fell into financial difficulties. Printing was introduced into Venice in 1469 by another German, John of Speier. The chief figures in printing at Venice (which became the largest book factory in Europe) were a Frenchman, Nicolas Jenson (working there from 1470), formerly master of the mint at Tours, and famous for cutting a most beautiful roman type, which has had much influence on later fonts (*Fig.* 4), and a native Italian, Aldo Manuzio, commonly called Aldus. He was the founder of the family and the press bearing his name and also the inventor of the dolphin-and-anchor device that marks an "Aldine." After printing, from 1495 onward, a number of Greek and Latin books, including a splendid Aristotle and the *Hypnerotomachia Poliphili* of Francesco Colonna (1499), with its wonderful woodcut pictures, Aldus began in 1501 (with a Virgil) to print the long series of pocket classics by which his name is best known. It was for this last series that he caused to be cut the first italic type.

The first generation in Italy saw many wandering printers, who printed a book here and a book there. In Florence from 1476 printing in Greek types was carried on, and between 1490 and 1510 Florentine presses produced a large number of small quartos illustrated with charming woodcuts of a well-marked local style.

The first press in France was academic, and the first type accordingly was roman. In 1470, at the invitation of two professors of the Sorbonne, Heynlyn and Fichet, a press was set up in the Sorbonne itself by three German printers, Gering, Crantz, and Friburger. Three years later Guillaume le Roy started printing romances and other popular books at Lyons. Later the printing of vernacular books spread to Paris, where the most prolific

menatur. Nam hoc corpufculum. quo induti fumus. homis receptaculū eft.
N m ipe homo neq; tangi : neq; afpici. neq; comphendi poteft.qa later intra
hoc qd uidetur. Qui fi delicatus ac tener in hac uita fuerit. q ratio eius ex-
pofcit : fi uirtute contempta. defideriis fe carnis addixerit : cadet et premet
in terram. Si aūt ut debet ftatū fuum q rectū recte fortitus eft : et prompte
conftanterq; defenderit : fi terrę quā calcare ac uincere debet non feruierit :
uita merebit fempiternam.   Ipeus conclufio   . Cxx·

HEc ad te Demetriane interim paucis & obfcurius fortaffe q decuit :
pro rerū ac teporis neceffitate perorani. qbus cōtentus eē debeas.
Plura et meliora laturus. fi nobis indulgeria cęlitis uenerit : tunc & ego te
ad uere philofophie doctrina. et planius & uerius cohortabor. Statui eni
q multa potero literis tradere : que ad uite beate ftatū fpectēt.et qdem cōtra
philofophos. quonia funt ad pturbandam ueritatem perniciofi & graues.
Incredibilis eni uis elopuēte. et argumetandi differendiq; fubtilitas :q uis
facile deceperat. quos partim noftris armis : partim uero ex iporū inter fe
concertatione fumptis reuincemus.ut appareat eos induxiffe potius erro-
rem q fuftuliffe. Fortaffe mireris q tantū facinus audeam. Patiemur ne igr
extinguit. Aut oppmi ueritatē. Ego uero libēdius fub hoc onere defecerim.
Nam fi Marcus Tullius eloquentę ipius unicum exemplar. ab indoctis &
melioqbus : quia tame pro uero mitebatur : fepe fupatus eft. Cur defpere-
mus ueritatem ipam. contra fallacem captiofam q facundiam fua,ppria ni
et claritate ualitura. Illi qdem fe pronos ueritatis,pfiteri folent. Sed quis
pot eam rem defendere : qua non didicit.aut illuftrare apud alios : ipe non
nouit.Magnū uideor polliceri. fed cęlefti opus eft munere : ut nobis facul-
tas ac tepus ad,ppofita perfeqda tribuat. Quod fi uita ē optāda fapienti :
profecto nullā aliam obcaufam uiuere optauerim : q ut aliqd effici. quod
uita dignū fit. et qd utilitatem legētibus. et fi nō ad eloqtiam : qa tenuis in
nobis fac idie riuus eft : ad uiuendum tame afferat. quod eft maxie necef-
farium. Quo perfpecto : fatis me uixiffe arbitror. et officiū hois impleffe : fi
labor meus aliquos hoies ab erroribus liberatos : ad iter cęlefte direxerit.

Lactantii Firmiani de diuinis inftitutionibus aduerfus gentes libri feptem.
necnō ciufdej ad Donatū de ira dei liber unus.unacū libro de opificio hois
ad Demetrianū finiunt. Sub ano dni.M.CCCC.LXV. Pontificatus Pauli
pape.ii.anno eius fecūdo.Indictiōe.xiii.die uero ānpenultia menfis Octo-
bris. In uenerabili monafterio Sublacenfi.   Deo gratias.

FIG. 3. *The first book printed in Italy. Sweynheym and Pannartz,
Subiaco.* Lactantii Firmiani de Divinis Instit. Adversus Gentes.
1465.

୬ q̃maxīe ad præcepta accōmodatos curare poteris.
In imaginibus collocādis exerceri quotidie cōuenit.
non enim ficut a cæteris ftudiis adducimur nonnūq̃
occupatione:ita ab hac re nos poteft caufa deducere
aliqua.Nunq̃ eft enī quin aliquid memoriæ tradere
uelimus:et tum maxime cum aliquo maiore officio
detinemur.Quare cum fit̄utile facile meminiffe nō
te fallit:quod tantopere utile fit:q̃to labore fit appe⸗
tendum: quod poteris exiftimare utilitate cognita.
Pluribus uerbis ad eā te adhortari non eft fententia:
ne aut ftudio difficili:aut nimis q̃ res poftulat dixiffe
uideamus. De quarta parte rethoricæ deinceps dice⸗
mus.tu primas quafque partes frequenta: et quod
maxime neceffe eft:exercitatione confirma.

VONIAM In hoc libro Herēni de
elocutione confcripfimus:et quibus
i rebus opus fuit exemplis uti:noftris
exēplis ufi fumus:et id fecimus præ⸗
ter cōfuetudinem græcoᵖ qui de hac
re fcripferūt: neceffario faciendū eft:ut paucis rōné
confilii noftri demus. Atque hoc nos neceffitudine
facere non ftudio fatis erit figni:q̃ in fuperioribus
libris nihil neq̃ ante rē neq̃ præter rē locuti fumus.
Nūc fi pauca quæ res poftulat dixeriūs tibi id quod
reliquū eft artis:ita uti iftituimus perfoluemus.Sed
facilius noftrā rōnem itelliges:fi prius quid illi dicāt
cognoueris. Compluribus de caufis putāt oportere:
cum ipfi præceperint: quo pacto oporteat ornare

FIG. 4.   *Nicholas Jenson, Venice. Cicero. Rhetorica. 1470.*

printer for this market, Antoine Vérard, produced a series of romances of chivalry of which copies on vellum, decorated like manuscripts, but rather coarsely, were bought by the thrifty Henry VII and are now in the British Library. The most distinctive feature of Parisian books in the last two decades of the fifteenth century is the large device, with short title above and publisher's imprint below, that is constantly found on title pages. The printer, who here began to be differentiated from the publisher, printed his imprint, as hitherto, in the colophon. Paris became (with Venice) the great center for printing service books; it held almost a monopoly of Hours of the Virgin and (notably for English bibliographers) of those of the use of Sarum. The most finely decorated Hours were those from the press of Philippe Pigouchet. The English market was also being served at the same time by the presses of Rouen.

Books for the English market were equally a work of the Antwerp press, especially that of Gerard Leeu. The date for the introduction of printing into the Low Countries depends upon the interpretation of Costeriana, but the date usually accepted is 1473, when printing begins in Utrecht and Alost.

Doubt also surrounds the date of the earliest printing in Spain, but it is possibly as early as 1473. Throughout the fifteenth century, however, the output of the Spanish press remained small. The only certainty is that Spain, like so many other European countries, received printing at the hands of German craftsmen.

Those who have inherited the English language are naturally most interested in Caxton of all the prototypographers, and he was in fact a more striking figure than the men who introduced printing into Italy, France, or Spain in that he was a public man, a man of letters, and an amateur.[9] Caxton's first printings were produced at Bruges, where he printed one of the earliest books in French and the earliest in English. They were the *Quatre Dernieres Choses* (1475) and Caxton's translation (1474) of the *Recueil des Histoires de Troye*. (*Fig. 5*).

Caxton had established himself in the Sanctuary of Westminster Abbey by the end of 1476, and began, as most printers did, by printing some small pieces while larger works were preparing. A copy of one of these, an indulgence printed for John Sant, Abbot of Abingdon, was identified in 1928 in the Public Record Office.

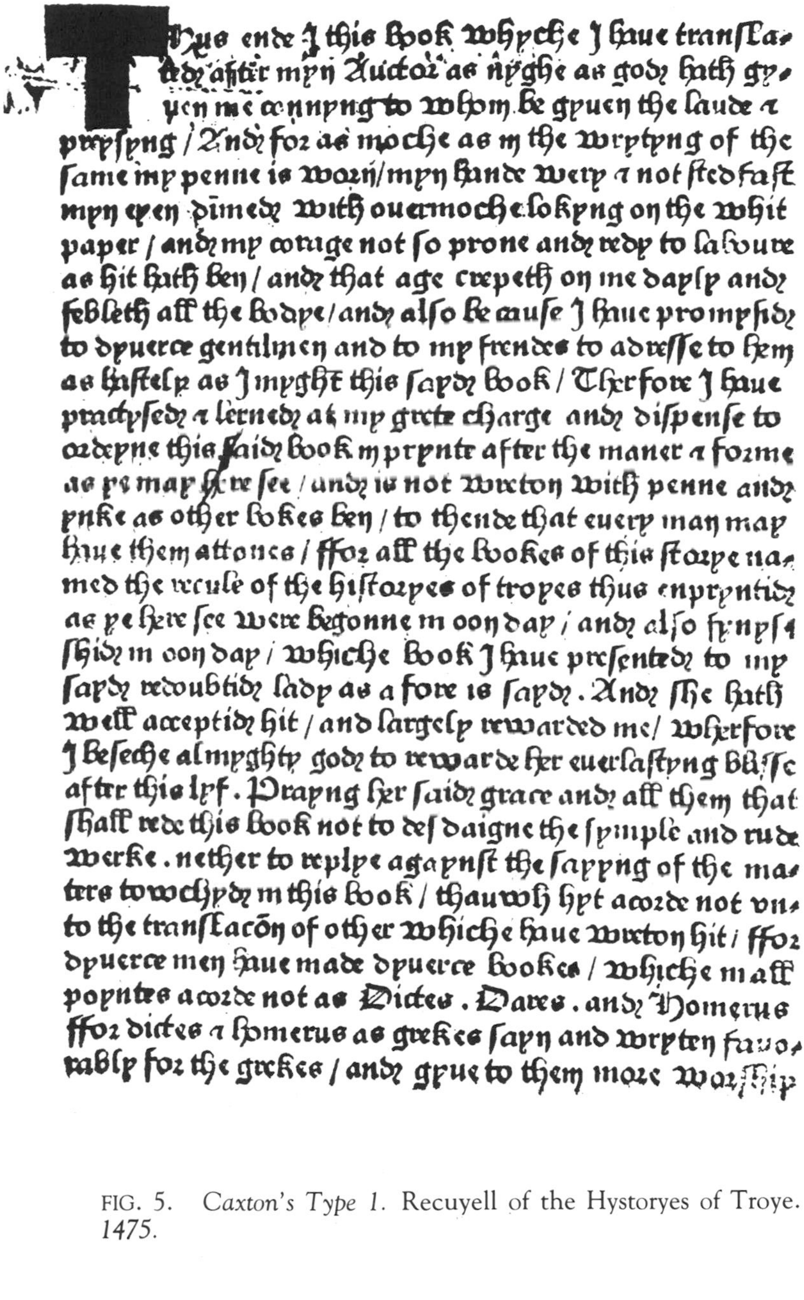

Tus ende I this book whyche I haue translated aftir myn Auctor as nyghe as god bath gyuen me connyng to whom be gyuen the laude and
pryssyng / And for as moche as in the wrytyng of the
same my penne is worn / myn hande wery and not stedfast
myn eyen dimed with ouermoche lokyng on the whit
paper / and my corage not so prone and redy to labour
as hit hath ben / and that age crepeth on me daylp and
febleth all the bodye / and also be cause I haue promphid
to dyuerce gentilmen and to my frendes to adresse to hem
as hastely as I myght this sayd book / Therfore I haue
practysed and lerned at my grete charge and dispense to
ordeyne this said book in pryntr after the maner and forme
as ye may here see / and is not wrixton with penne and
ynke as other bokes ben / to thende that euery man may
haue them attones / ffor all the bookes of this storye named the reculé of the historyes of tropes thus enpryntid
as ye here see were begonne in oon day / and also fynysf-
shid in oon day / whiche book I haue presentid to my
sayd redoubtid lady as afore is sayd. And she hath
well acceptid hit / and largely rewarded me / wherfore
I beseche almyghty god to rewarde her euerlastyng blysse
aftir this lyf. Prayng her said grace and all them that
shall rede this book not to desdaigne the symple and rude
werke. nether to replye agaynst the sayyng of the ma-
tere towchyd in this book / thauwh hyt acorde not vn-
to the translacon of other whiche haue wrixton hit / ffor
dyuerce men haue made dyuerce bookes / whiche in all
poyntes acorde not as Dictes. Dares. and Homerus
ffor dictes and homerus as grekes sayn and wrytyn fauo-
rably for the grekes / and gyue to them more worship

FIG. 5.   *Caxton's Type 1.* Recuyell of the Hystoryes of Troye.
1475.

It is filled up in pen and ink to Henry Langley and his wife, Katherine, and is dated partly in print and partly in manuscript, December 13, 1476. Caxton's first substantial book printed in England and dated was the *Dictes or Sayengis of the Philosophres,* 18 November 1477: like the Troy book a translation from the French, though not by Caxton himself. Although it is possible that the *Dictes* were preceded by the undated translation of the romance of Jason, the lapse of time from Michaelmas 1476, when Caxton took his lease from the Abbey, shows how slow were the preliminaries in setting up a press in a country where none existed.

Caxton's output till 1491, the year of his death, consisted largely of romances, varied by devotional books, which were assured of a sale. As George Parker Winship pointed out, "His venture, even though it was intended primarily for his own purposes, did not cost him more than need be." The most famous works printed by him were Chaucer's *Canterbury Tales* (two editions, 1478 and 1484(?), from different MSS); Malory's *Morte d'Arthur,* 1485; Gower's *Confessio Amantis,* 1483; poems by John Lydgate; *Reynard the Fox,* 1481; *Aesop's Fables,* 1484; *The Golden Legend, or Lives of the Saints* (1483); and more than one English chronicle. The debt of English literature to Caxton is thus very great. What more he may have printed, of which no copy has come down to us, can only be guessed. A high proportion of his books exist in single copies and fragments since they were popular and copies worn out. Other works, such as Mandeville's travels, are books that he planned to print but never brought to fruition.

Caxton's press was carried on from his death till 1534 by his foreman, Wynkyn de Worde. Caxton's work is primitive and suggestive of the manuscript; much of de Worde's was poor and suggestive of little but cheapness. The eight hundred or so pieces that he produced in his forty years of independent activity do not really imply great productivity, since with rare exceptions they are hardly more than pamphlets, and a large number, such as the stock Latin grammars of the day, were printed over and over again. But those that survive are so rare that many more must have been lost, and with them possibly much attractive early Tudor verse.

Meanwhile, in 1478–1487, Theodoric Rood printed, at first in a Cologne type, a few academic books at Oxford. The first, S. Jerome (or rather Tyrannius Rufinus) on the Apostles' Creed, had the date misprinted MCCCCLXVIII for MCCCCLXXVIII and thereby appears to give Oxford priority over Westminster in English printing. Classical and scholarly books, however, could be produced much more cheaply and accurately by the well-equipped presses of such towns as Lyons and Venice, and for a century and more classical printing was only sporadic in England. Oxford had two other short-lived presses (Scolar and Kyrforth) in 1517–1519, and Cambridge one (Siberch) in 1521–1522; but printing was only permanently established in the universities in 1584 (Cambridge, T. Thomas) and 1585 (Oxford, J. Barnes). The Cambridge press was set up under the university's printing charter of 1534.

A law-press had been set up in London in Caxton's time; the printers were John Lettou (the Lithuanian) and his partner, William Machlinia (of Mechlin or Malines), 1480–1491. They were succeeded by Richard Pynson, a Norman, who printed from 1490 till 1529 and was a much better printer than de Worde, varying his style and achieving some dignity. He was appointed Royal Printer in 1508 and introduced roman type in 1509, a result of his closer connection with Continental printers.

In 1480–1486 the schoolmaster of the Abbey School of St. Albans printed a few books and deserves mention here on account of the celebrity of one of them, the *Bokys of Haukyng and Huntyng, and Also of Cootarmuris* (i.e., heraldry), 1486, generally called *The Book of St. Albans* and attributed to a certain unknown Dame Juliana Barnes or Berners. The printer got his type from Caxton.

Printing appeared sporadically in various English provincial towns in the first half of the sixteenth century but nowhere for long or to very much effect. John Oswen, who printed at Ipswich in 1548 and at Worcester in 1549–1552, and was skillful enough to print the first Prayer Book of Edward VI, was the chief provincial printer. In London, Thomas Berthelet (1528–1554), who was also Royal binder, printed large quantities of the law Year Books. The most distinguished work was done by Richard Grafton, who made free use of a very pretty italic, and Reynald Wolfe, who was Royal printer in Latin, Greek, and Hebrew and who introduced Greek printing into England in 1543, whereas in

1520 Siberch at Cambridge had had to have Richard Croke's *Introductiones in Rudimenta Graeca* printed abroad. The first printing in Scotland was in 1508 from the press of William Chepman and Androw Myllar. A volume discovered in 1785 and now in the National Library of Scotland contains unique copies of eleven pamphlets from the press. Three of these are dated: *The Maying and Disport of Chaucer*, 4 April 1508, which is Lydgate's *The Complaint of the Black Knight; Golagrus and Gawain*, 8 April 1508; and *The Porteus of Nobleness*, 20 April 1508. In 1505 and 1506 Myllar had two works printed for him by Pierre Violette in Rouen, editions of Garlandia, *Multorum Verborum Interpretatio* and the *Expositio Sequentiarum Sarum*. The Sarum book bore the most decorative "rebus" device (*Fig.* 6) used in Britain, except Grafton's tree, or "graft," springing from a "tun." Myllar's device was no doubt cut by a Rouenese or Parisian artist. Scottish printing did not reach any great competence till the latter half of the sixteenth century. It is worth noticing that (as a glance through the earlier pages of H. G. Aldis's list of Scottish books printed before 1700 will show) few reprints of English books came from Scottish presses.

The books of the period of the establishment of printing form a group that possesses sufficient unity for them to be studied as a body. By the end of the fifteenth century the press had spread widely over Europe and had achieved a technical proficiency that allowed it to produce millions of copies and an artistry that could reach the standards of the 1457 Psalter and the *Hypnerotomachia* of 1499. The next era made a major concentration on the texts and established its reputation largely on its scholarly printing.

The scholar-printers

The sixteenth century on the Continent was the age of the scholar-printer-publisher. Josse Bade, of Aasche, better known as Iodocus Badius Ascensius (and his press as the "prelum Ascensianum," figured in woodcut devices) printed a number of scholarly works, although perhaps without high technical distinction. But he was the father-in-law of two famous learned printers, Michel Vascosan and Robert Estienne, and through the latter was connected with a third, Simon de Colines (Col-

FIG. 6.   *Printer's device of Androw Myllar, first printer in Scotland (fl. 1503–1508)*

inaeus). This group of men completely converted French book buyers from the medieval to the Renaissance taste in printing. The movement was from the rich and heavy effects of gothic to the light effects of roman, with woodcuts designed to match. Nor were they mere imitators of Italian models, though they were influenced by them both directly and through the designer Geof-roy Tory, whose *Champ Fleury*, 1529, studied the theory of proportion and beauty in lettering in the new manner and who took from Aldus the idea of publishing cheap editions of Greek and Latin classics for students. François I was the active patron of good printing as of the other arts and saved Robert Estienne, who leaned to the Reformed Church, from persecution till the King's death in 1547, after which (in 1550) the Estiennes had to re-move to Geneva. François also promoted Greek and Latin print-ing by his foundation of the Collège de France and its professor-ships in 1530. The Estiennes (Stephani, or, *anglice*, Stephens) were themselves scholars and edited or wrote some of the most important works they printed. Robert wrote the *Thesaurus Lin-guae Latinae*, 1532, and Henri the *Thesaurus Graecae Linguae*, 1572, but the latter's best-known work today is the anecdotic *Apologie pour Herodote*. The family device, introduced by Robert, is an olive-tree.

The only French city to vie with Paris was Lyons. Early print-ing there had been vernacular, but trade routes connected Lyons, at the head of the navigable Rhone, more closely with Basel and with the Mediterranean than with Paris. Basel had early had in Johann von Amerbach (printed 1478–1512) a printer who was a friend of the men of the new learning, notably of Sebastian Brant, author of *The Ship of Fools*. Erasmus's friend and pub-lisher, Johann Froben, or Frobenius, (printed 1491–1527), who had been in Amerbach's service, carried on the tradition. Ac-cordingly we find Renaissance scholarship in such printers as Sebastian Gryphius (d. 1556), who printed small texts in the Aldine style with his griffin in place of the dolphin and anchor; Etienne Dolet, who was hanged for heresy in 1546; and Jean de Tournes. De Tournes was distinguished as a publisher by issuing the works of the Lyonnese literary set, notably the poet Louise Labé, and as a printer by his use of magnificent arabesque title-borders and tailpieces strongly suggestive of metal lantern-supports (*culs-de-lampes*).

In Italy the house of the Aldi, as the Manuzio family of Venice were called, carried on the business till the end of the sixteenth century, though with less originality than the founder had shown. The Guinti, who had begun at Venice in the fifteenth century, printed mainly at Florence in the earlier and middle sixteenth century, and the Florentine lily, their device, is the mark of sound work (as the Sessas' cat is of bad). They hardly rivaled in excellence of workmanship the Florentine ducal printer, Lorenzo Torrentino, but they were important for the quantity of solid work, as well as imitations of Aldines, that they turned out. With them should be studied Gabriel Giolito of Ferrara, who printed at Venice from 1539 to 1578; had book-shops at Naples, Bologna, and Ferrara; and specialized in decorated books.

Spanish printing, though it does not boast a figure like these, unless it be Coci of Saragossa, has a remarkably constant national quality that makes it interesting. Even when the types are roman, the feeling is medieval. A page of a Spanish book of the fifteenth or sixteenth century, especially if decorated, has a rich, somber, and stately appearance that is unknown in the productions of other countries but that is consonant with the other arts in Spain in that period. The greatest single achievement of a Spanish press is the polyglot Complutensian Bible printed at Alcalá de Henares (Complutum) in 1514–1517 by Arnald Guillen de Brocar under the patronage of Cardinal Ximenez.

Almost the first really good printing done in the Low Countries was that of Christopher Plantin, a French bookbinder by origin, who settled at Antwerp and in 1555 commenced work as a printer and publisher. He obtained patents for printing from the Spanish authorities and produced many service books, but also many large and handsome illustrated works in the sciences. His most ambitious production was the polyglot Bible in 1572. Plantin's house was the resort of learned men and continued to be a successful publishing office till the nineteenth century in the family of his son-in-law, Moretus. It is now a museum, full of the archives and material of the sixteenth-century printer, and a place of pilgrimage to the bibliographer.

A little later than Plantin there arose in Holland a family of printers and publishers who, with less learning but more business instinct, repeated the success of Aldus. These were the Elzevirs of Leyden (Lugdunum Batavorum), and later of Utrecht and Amsterdam also. Louis, the founder, began at Leyden in 1580, but the next two generations were the more famous, especially Bonaventure. They were excellent men of business and produced handy books, both texts of the classics and books of reference, such as those on the different countries, entitled "Respublica so-and-so." They employed scholars to edit the books, but with-

out contributing much, if anything, to scholarship. Nor are Elzevirs pretty or easy to read. Their vogue in their own time may
possibly be accounted for by the amount of time that courtiers
had to spend waiting in anterooms, which could be beguiled by
reading pocket volumes in the window embrasures. They are
frequently referred to in general books on book collecting, but
they are not now so highly prized as formerly.

The importance of the scholar-printers lay not only in the high
standard of much of their work but also in the motivation that
led them into printing. For the majority of printers throughout
history it is obvious, and not at all to their discredit, that they
were engaged in a trade. Their main objective had been to make
money. A few have had other reasons for their printing. The
scholar-printers were those to whom the scholarly importance of
the texts was of prime importance. They had to master the arts of
printing in order to make their texts available to the world. The
printing office to them became a scholarly academy, with the
press as the machine at the end to assist in the process of dis-
semination. They presage the activities of the great modern university presses in the disinterested manner in which they ensure
the publication of works of enduring scholarship.

The STC period

All stopping points in human development are obviously artificial, but some have the advantage of convenience. The period of
early printing is frequently thought of as ending at 1520, which
has advantages in that it stops short of the flood of Lutheran
pamphleteering. Another date of equal convenience and one
that has become of greater bibliographical importance is 1640. In
England it provides a date that nearly coincides with the closing
of the theaters in 1642, an act that brought to a conclusion the
great period of Elizabethan and Jacobean drama. It became the
natural end point for Greg's great bibliographical survey of this
material.[10] Again in England it avoids the spate of pamphleteering of the Civil War and Commonwealth period, the quantity of
which can be judged by reference to the British Museum catalog
of the Thomason Tracts.[11] In the context of printing in English
it also coincides with the beginning of printing in North

America. For Europe as a whole the seventeenth century was sufficiently a period of rapid change to make a midway point acceptable. It also acknowledges the impact that the Thirty Years War had on the social and economic life of Europe. It is a date that has now become entrenched bibliographically in that it has provided a limitation for a number of bibliographies and catalogs and, from them, has taken the title of the STC period.[12]

One of the distinguishing marks of the period is the way in which the book trade, as distinct from the actual business of book making, was established. At the end of the reign of Philip and Mary, in 1557, the Company of Stationers of London, a body that had existed since the beginning of the fifteenth century, was incorporated by Royal Charter.[13] Attached to the rights of that state were duties by which the Company practically became the Crown's instrument in controlling the press. A monopoly of printing was given to the members of the Company and extended rather later to the universities of Oxford and Cambridge. By the *Injunctions* of 1559 nothing was to be published without licence by the Crown, Privy Council, and Archbishops or Bishops of London, and the licences were to be entered in a register for the keeping of which the Company was responsible. By this ingenious plan the Crown secured a real, if never quite complete, control over printing. Provincial printing, of which there had in fact been but little before 1556, disappeared, with the exception of the universities and of the Royalist presses of the Civil War period, until after the desuetude of the Licensing Acts in 1695. The period at which the Company was incorporated was so stormy both in dynastic and in ecclesiastical politics, and the right of every government to control opinion so universally practiced and allowed, that the action of the Marian government was merely natural and was, moreover, in its method one of the very few signs shown by Mary of the statecraft of her father and sister.

These provisions brought into existence the foundation stone of English bibliography: the Register of the Stationers' Company.[14] This Register was at first kept fully, but in the seventeenth century the entries decline, in spite of the obvious convenience of having a record of copyrights. By 1911, when the Copyright Act tacitly abolished it, the Register was very little used. Up to the date of the first Copyright Act (1709) it is accessible in print; the rest may be consulted at the Stationers'

Hall. As a documentary source of knowledge in the history of books it is only rivaled by the records of the French book trade—but they have not been so extensively published.[15] They reveal a similar pattern in the organizational growth of the trade in the seventeenth century. Beginning as early as the thirteenth century the developing parts of the trade continued primarily under the aegis of the university until 16 June 1618. From that date the Syndical and Royal Chamber of Booksellers, Printers and Binders of Paris occupied a position in France not markedly unlike that of the Stationers' Company in England. The early basis of the organization in Germany was essentially that of the trade. The Frankfurt catalogs from their origin in 1564 were issued by publishers and booksellers but became the responsibility of the Town Council from 1598. Neither in Frankfurt nor in Leipzig was the trade organization as highly developed as in London or Paris, but the foundations were laid for a long and virtually uninterrupted book-trade bibliography to the present day.

In its long-term effect one of the main events of the early seventeenth century must be the establishment of a permanent press in North America. The earliest press to be set up anywhere on the American continent had been that of Juan Pablos in Mexico City in 1539. Juan Cromberger, a leading printer of Seville, had been commissioned by the Spanish Archbishop in Mexico to print a catechism in the Nahuatl dialect. Work began in Seville, but in order to complete it satisfactorily Cromberger decided to establish a press among the people for whom the book was designed. Accordingly he despatched Pablos to accomplish this, and from 1539 to 1560 a number of works issued from this press.[16] Although printing spread widely throughout Spanish America, it was a century later, in North America, that the art developed most greatly.

Stephen Day, a locksmith of Cambridge, England, arrived at Boston, Massachusetts, in September 1638. In that same month an earlier pilgrim, John Harvard, had died, leaving his three hundred books to the College of Newtown. The College took Harvard's name and Newtown was renamed Cambridge. It was there that in 1639 Stephen Day set up his press and issued his first works, the *Freeman's Oath* and an *Almanack*.[17] No copies of these are extant, and a 1640 printing of *The Whole Booke of*

Psalmes Faithfully Translated into English Metre, known as "The Bay Psalm Book," is the first book of which any copies are known.[18] Some years later two printers who followed Day at Cambridge, Samuel Green and Marmaduke Johnson, printed the first Bible in the New World, a translation into the Algonquian language by John Eliot the missionary. The New Testament was issued in 1661 and the whole work, when the Old Testament had been completed, in 1663.[19]

1660–1800

The unity of this period lies in its demonstration of the hand-produced book at its peak period.[20] This was especially so in the decorative aspects of the book, binding and illustration, but these are specialist concerns and somewhat outside the general development of the trade.

This was preeminently the period of the earliest publishers who were not also printers. One of the first, if not the first, was Humphrey Moseley, who throughout the Commonwealth and earlier Restoration period issued poetry and play-books in quantity. His success as a publisher of contemporary writers and one who bought up available copyrights of many Elizabethan and Jacobean playwrights made him the most enterprising and successful publisher of his day. More celebrated publishers succeeded him in the persons of Henry Herringman (c. 1630–1703/4), who had a share in the Third Shakespeare Folio; of Jacob Tonson (1656?–1736), publisher to Dryden and many other men of letters; of Bernard Lintot (1675–1736), who published for Pope, Gay, and Steele; and of the notorious Edmund Curll (publ. 1706–1747), who, while deserving most of the ill-repute he has, was also a very intelligent publisher. The publisher begins now for the first time to be an important figure in literature, and we have fortunately in the letters and remains of Swift, Pope, and other writers a mine of knowledge of the trade—but nowhere more so, nor more curious, than in the *Life* of John Dunton, himself a bookseller. Although Dunton was a verbose and rambling writer and one on whom it is dangerous to place too much reliance, his detailed picture of the trade of his day cannot be ignored.[21] It was a period also that witnessed a revival of interest in scholarly printing. Distinguished new publishing houses, such as that of the brothers Robert and Andrew Foulis of Glasgow (1741–1776), which was noted for its scholarly and textually accurate editions of the classics, and the revival of the Oxford University Press, later called the Clarendon from its acquisition of the copyright of Clarendon's history of the Civil War, the profits of which contributed toward the building of the printing house.[22]

From the middle of the eighteenth century onward can be seen the establishment of the profession of authorship. Authors become figures in their own right, and the business relationships that were established between successful authors and their publishers provide a graphic description of the new economic situation in the trade.[23]

From the early sixteenth century publishers increasingly had shared the cost and the copies of publications, normally having their name and address printed on the title pages of their copies. De Worde and Pynson occasionally did this, and another notable early example is the 1542 Chaucer.[24] At the end of the seventeenth century publishers exchanged parts of editions after publication, and in these cases only the first publisher's name will appear on any copy. About 1730 there grew up a regular system of taking shares in a new book; and now all the shareholding publishers' names would appear on all copies. By the end of the century, possibly because publishers were more highly capitalized, the practice began to disappear.

In the seventeenth century the Stationers' Company was harassed by continual edicts limiting the number of printers and type founders. By a Star Chamber decree of 1637 the number was restricted to twenty. After the Commonwealth period the Act of 1662 reimposed this limit; but in the following year L'Estrange estimated the number of master printers at work in London at sixty. Nor, in spite of Milton's *Areopagitica*, was the press any more free during the power of the Parliament than during that of Laud before or of Sir Roger L'Estrange after. The restriction of printing to London, with all other censorship, apart from that of the common law, lapsed in 1695, from this period date the earliest permanent provincial presses other than those in the universities.

The general situation of the book trade in England, which is well documented in contemporary records, is similar to that which obtained in other European countries. France again provides the clearest picture due to the quantity and quality of the records. It showed the same growth in the book trade in spite of the taxes on bookselling and publishing. Control of the numbers of printers, entailing a curtailment of their strength, brought about a situation, largely for political reasons, similar to that in England largely built around the guild structure.

The physical nature of the book and the methods of its distribution depend at all times on manifold aspects of the social life of the period. This can be seen clearly in the late seventeenth and the eighteenth centuries. It is arguable, for example, that the coffeehouse and the newspaper/periodical trade created each other, as it were. That the rise of overseas trade and mercantilism increased the need for pure news element in the newspaper. That the demand for easily and cheaply accessible fiction brought the rise of serialization in journals.[25] That the same demand brought about the development of the subscription list from a roll call of the gentry to a list of modest subscribers to part issues of the great accounts of late–eighteenth-century voyages of exploration.[26] That the rise of the book club and the circulating library both created a new reading demand and a change in the book.[27] This was a connection as close as the relationship between the circulating library and the three-decker in the late nineteenth century. There was, also of necessity, a very direct relationship between the book and certain internal factors within the trade itself. For example, the size of book papers increased after the Restoration, and all the formats therefore naturally differ in general appearance from their earlier counterparts. An Elizabethan octavo is a very small book; one of 1750–1800 is about twice its size. Late in the eighteenth century there arose (especially among women readers) a taste for very small books, which were made up in twelves or twenty-fours and issued in two or more volumes.

The preeminently "trade" aspects were also to the fore in the development of the North American book trade during this period. For a long time after its establishment the American trade was dominated by European, and especially British, printers and booksellers. Most basic supplies, from the presses themselves to smaller pieces of equipment, had to be imported. The importation of European books was an essential requirement for a population that was still close to its intellectual roots and that wished to maintain that contact, especially at a time of intellectual ferment, as was evident in eighteenth-century Europe. Gradually, and especially after the War of Independence, there was a natural urge to free the new society from ideologies and influences that appeared repugnant. The work of such noted printers and individualists as Benjamin Franklin and Isaiah Thomas did much to establish a purely American tradition in printing and publishing.[28] Allied to this the establishment of such trades as paper making and type founding helped to create a publishing trade that would increasingly stand on its own feet.[29]

Nineteenth century

The nineteenth century witnessed, in many respects, the height of prosperity of the book trade. The emergence of a strong trade in the eighteenth century was reinforced by the application of industrial processes to the business of book making in the nineteenth. If, as can readily be established, this situation brought about undesirable influences on the general standards of book design, this was accepted in the mingling of wishes for greater profits and a genuine desire to spread the benefits of wider and cheaper reading material. Aethestic standards, which appeared to be lost completely throughout much of the century, were given renewed consideration before the century closed.

The early nineteenth century was in many ways the golden age of English publishing and printing, though not of type design. The orderly sequence of centuries is once again broken because there is something of a natural unity in the period of 1785–1825 approximately. Within this short span the press became mechanized and was soon capable of high-speed work. Paper was machine made and, again, by the end of this time span, widely available in increasing quantity. The long-established art of binding gave way to cased books. Fine illustration processes, especially the most recently developed, aquatint and lithography, created some of the most splendid plate books of all time. France required time to recover from the disastrous effects of the Revolution; in much of Europe the early nineteenth century had undertones of political strife; in the United States publishing sought to use its power to establish a national identity.[30] In Britain the commercial instinct was most unmistakably to the fore. The country's wealth was greatly increased, and the Romantic Revival had brought with it a love of the picturesque and an interest in antiquities. These produced together not only such futilities as artificial ruins but also many splendid and useful publications, and notably county histories.

British publishers exhibited a wide range of capabilities and interests throughout the century. Some were responsible for establishing practices that had lasting effects on the trade. One such was the alliance of William Pickering, the publisher, with Charles Whittingham the younger, which commenced in 1828. Pickering started early in life as a bookseller and in 1820 began with *Horace* his well-known series of "diamond" classics, which it must be confessed are more curious than beautiful, but which served to attract attention to their publisher. Pickering was the first publisher to issue books in cloth casings, with the paper labels that preceded gold-stamped title blocks. The calico that he used was not entirely successful until improved by Archibald Leighton, but it was an important step forward with vast repercussions upon the whole book industry.

In 1828 he commissioned work from a young printer, Charles Whittingham the younger, of the Chiswick Press in Tooks Court. This press had been started in 1789 and in 1810 transferred to Chiswick. Whittingham started alone and adopted the well-known device, based on that of Aldus, of the dolphin and anchor with the legend *Aldi discipulus Anglus.* The Press will always be noteworthy for the important influence that it exercised on English printing by Pickering and Whittingham's revival of Caslon's old-face roman font. Between them Pickering and Whittingham enormously raised the level of English printing, especially in printing liturgical and semiantiquarian books, in which fields they owed much to the patronage of Oxford Movement scholars. But the Chiswick Press showed a very wide range of interests and did all sorts of work well. After the death of Pickering in 1854 and Whittingham's retirement in 1860 the main activity of the Press was over. It had an important period of revival under C. T. Jacobi beginning in 1885, but the Press finally came to an end in 1962.

Other publishers are rightly remembered not solely for the variety of trade practices that they demonstrated but for the importance or interest of the texts for which they were responsible. It is difficult to imagine any study of literary movements in the early nineteenth century that does not take note of the work of John Murray, or of the rise of cheap literature without consideration of Charles Knight, or of the popular novel without Bentley. As it is impossible to pursue any bibliographical work up to the mid–seventeenth century without a clear understanding of the operations of the printing house, so any aspect of nineteenth-century bibliography demands an understanding of the problems of publishing and distribution.

This highly competitive nature of the trade brings economic considerations to the forefront of attention more than in many other periods. The economic development of the trade is of concern at all times, and insufficient attention has hitherto been paid to it. In the nineteenth century, however, because of the increased emphasis, it is of paramount importance.[31]

Of equal importance, and going along hand in hand with developments in publishing, was the improvement in the status of the author. Many of them, especially the writers of popular works, were household figures in their day to a degree that was common neither before nor since. Scott, Dickens, Balzac, Hugo, Melville, Poe—all were writers of wide contemporary interest whose methods of working and standards of financial remuneration are of importance in considering the bibliographical problems connected with an author's work.[32] Following directly on the changes in the status of the author from the mid–eighteenth century the author has now achieved economic as well as literary stature. Grub Street had not disappeared, but it was much less an automatic limitation for the whole profession.

American publishing history moved on similarly developed commercial instincts, with such publishers as Harper, Carey, and Lea well in the forefront. Because they shared a common language with the United Kingdom overlapping interests were inevitable. This brought about deeply felt views on copyright and decades of acrimonious dispute.[33] It has also led to a very confused situation regarding transatlantic editions of most British and American authors of the period.[34]

Another feature of the century, of particular importance in the

United Kingdom, was the rise of publishing societies. The Royal Society had issued its *Philosophical Transactions* since 1665 and the Society of Antiquaries the *Archaeologia* since 1770. The early years of the nineteenth century witnessed the creation of a crop of antiquarian literary societies, notably the Roxburghe Club (1812), founded by T. F. Dibdin to celebrate the sensational sale of the Duke of Roxburghe's library, and the Bannatyne Club (1823), founded by David Laing and others for printing early Scottish poetry. These were followed by the foundations of that remarkably dynamic scholar Frederick James Furnivall, of which the Early English Text (1864), Chaucer (1867), and New Shakspere (1874) Societies are the chief. These were not quite like the academies of the Continent, which were mostly crea-tions of the seventeenth and eighteenth centuries. They were, and are, an entirely reputable device to secure subscriptions for antiquarian reprints or specialist studies that might not seem a good speculation to the ordinary publisher. They are really only a variety of the publication by open subscription, which, largely owing to Johnson's onslaught on Lord Chesterfield (1755), had taken the place of the earlier system of private patronage.

At the other end, as it were, of the book's life history, it is unwise to ignore the bibliographical importance of the great book sales. Most of the great private collections have been chiefly composed of books printed before the end of the eighteenth century, but many of these have come under the hammer in the nineteenth and twentieth centuries. Major book sales, frequently resulting in important bibliographical tools, have been an integral part of the book trade throughout the past two hundred years. Among many may be mentioned those of Richard Heber (sold 1834–1837), Henry Huth (cataloged 1880, sold 1911–1920), and the Christie Miller or Britwell (sold 1910, 1916–c. 1925). This last was largely founded from the Heber, and much of it has passed into the Henry E. Huntington, now en-dowed and public, at San Marino, California. Of the many other great American collectors the chief are perhaps Robert Hoe (cataloged 1903–1905, sold 1912) and Pierpont Morgan (father and son), whose collection is now endowed and public in New York. Even the most random thoughts on English book collect-ing would not be complete without some mention of the stormy career of Sir Thomas Phillipps (1792–1872), which resulted in

the splendors of his collection—mainly notable for its manuscripts. The sale of this great library, begun in 1886, resulted in
the publication of some memorable catalogs, especially from W.
H. Robinson. In addition, there have been the revealing studies
of the development and dispersal of the collection.[35]

Finally, throughout the whole of the nineteenth and twentieth centuries one social factor has dominated the activities of
the book trade. The spread of education and the overall advance
in literacy as a necessity brought about the production of cheap
reading matter. The proliferation of popular periodicals and
newspapers, the part-issue publication of nineteenth-century
novels, have been obvious signs of this need. Surpassing all these
in importance to the book trade of the present day, however, has
been the success of the paperback book.

The modern paperback has had a reasonably long history,
since it is recognizable in cheap reprints issued by Tauchnitz in
Leipzig from 1841 onward. British publishers from time to time
attempted to launch such series, but for many years their efforts
culminated in failure. The natural conservatism of the British
public led them to reject what they regarded as an "unpleasant
Continental" habit. The great change came on 30 July 1935, a
date of special importance to the British book trade. On this day
the first ten "Penguin" titles were issued. In defiance of much
reputable opinion Allen Lane not only succeeded in this venture, he succeeded grandly. The earliest titles were reprints, but
original titles joined the lists within a year or two. New series
proliferated, and Penguin Books has now made great writings
available in enormous quantity. The careful attention that has
been devoted to typography, illustration, and layout has ensured
a remarkably high standard of production throughout. The Penguin has joined the ranks of the great printers' and publishers'
devices.

Since the end of World War II the paperback explosion has
continued and branched out in one other important direction.
Penguin Books created a particular market for the serious,
scholarly nonfiction work in paperback form. This has now
grown into the immense provision, by a variety of publishers, of
the "egghead" paperbacks. Advanced works of scholarship,
textbooks, and standard treatises are all available, many from the
great university presses, in this cheap form. The probable effect

of such a plenitude of widely disseminated scholarship can hardly be overestimated.

REFERENCES

1. CARTER, Thomas F. *The Invention of Printing in China and Its Spread Westward.* 2nd ed. 1955.
   TSIEN, T. H. *Written on Bamboo and Silk, The Beginnings of Chinese Books and Inscriptions.* 1962.

2. One of the most interesting modern investigations of this dating of block books can be read in:

   STEVENSON, Allan. "The Quincentennial of Netherlandish Block Books." *British Museum Quarterly.* XXXI: 1966–67. pp. 83–87.

3. The literature on the origins of printing in Europe is great in quantity and variable in quality. At the outset the following should be read:

   BLUM, André. *The Origins of Printing and Engraving.* Trans. H. M. Lydenberg. 1940. This is a translation of two of the three parts of the author's original *Les Origines du papier de l'imprimerie et de la gravure.* 1935.

   BUHLER, Curt F. *The Fifteenth Century Book.* 1960.
   BUTLER, Pierce. *The Origin of Printing in Europe.* 1940.
   FEBVRE, Lucien, and MARTIN, Henri-Jean. *L'Apparition du livre.* 1958. English translation: *The Coming of the Book: The Impact of Printing.* 1976.
   HAEBLER, Konrad. *The Study of Incunabula.* 1933.
   HELLINGA, Wytze and Lotte. *The Fifteenth-century Printing Types of the Low Countries.* 2v. 1966.

   The student should also read the appropriate sections in the collected papers of one of the greatest modern incunabulists.

   SCHOLDERER, Victor. *50 Essays in 15th and 16th Century Bibliography.* 1966.

4. Documents relating to Gutenberg's career are contained in:

   FUHRMANN, Otto W. *Gutenberg and the Strasbourg Documents of 1439: An Interpretation.* 1940.
   McMURTRIE, Douglas C. *The Gutenberg Documents.* 1941.
   STILLWELL, Margaret B. *The Beginning of the World of Books . . . with a Synopsis of the Gutenberg Documents.* 1972.

5. LINDE, A. van der. *The Haarlem Legend.* 1871. Reprinted 1968.

6. It is reasonable to assume that Fust secured control of Gutenberg's press through the operation of the penalty clause in the loan document when Gutenberg defaulted on his payments. Schoeffer, as Gutenberg's assistant, would also have passed to Fust but later secured his position by marrying Fust's daughter.

   LEHMANN-HAUPT, H. *Peter Schoeffer.* 1950.

7. This is not an easy work to see in the original, but a good impression of it can be achieved through:

   MASSON, Sir Irvine. *The Mainz Psalters and Canon Missae 1457–1459.* 1954.

8. GOFF, Frederick, R. *The Permanence of Johann Gutenberg.* 1970.
   LEHMANN-HAUPT, Hellmut. *Gutenberg and the Master of the Playing Cards.* 1966.
   RUPEL, Aloys. *Johannes Gutenberg sein Leben und sein Werk.* 2nd ed. 1947.
   SCHOLDERER, Victor. *Johann Gutenberg.* 1963.

9. Caxton's work was first studied by a typographical expert in:

   BLADES, William. *The Life and Typography of William Caxton.* 2v. 1861–1863.

   which Blades revised in:

   BLADES, William. *Biography and Typography of William Caxton.* 1877.

   One of the leading British incunabulists provided a good short life:

DUFF, E. Gordon. *William Caxton.* 1905.

and for many years the best biographical survey was the introduction to:

CROTCH, W. J. B. *Caxton's Prologues and Epilogues.* 1928.

An account of the copies of Caxton's books that was complete as to known copies at the time of its publication and that is still invaluable, although it now needs augmenting, is:

DE RICCI, Seymour. *A Census of Caxtons.* 1909.

The quincentennial celebrations of Caxton's first printing produced a spate of new writing, for example:

BLAKE, Norman F. *Caxton: England's First Publisher.* 1976. *Journal of the Printing Historical Society.* XI: 1975–76.
PAINTER, George D. *William Caxton: A Quincentenary Biography.* 1976.

10. GREG, Sir Walter Wilson. *A Bibliography of the English Printed Drama to the Restoration.* 4v. 1939–1959.

11. BRITISH MUSEUM. *Catalogue of Pamphlets, Books, Newspapers, Manuscripts Relating to Civil War, Commonwealth, and Restoration (1640 1661).* Collected by G. Thomason and edited by G. K. Fortescue. 2v. 1908.

In 1641, at the outbreak of the Civil War, George Thomason, a Scottish bookseller in London, perceiving the value that the fugitive literature of a disturbed time would have if methodically collected and carefully preserved, procured so far as he could everything published, other than folio volumes, and on most of the pieces he noted the day of receipt. His collection, which he ceased to make in 1661, after the Restoration of Charles II, failed for a century to find a purchaser. But on his accession George III bought it for £300 and presented it to the newly founded British Museum, where in consequence Thomason's twenty-two thousand books, pamphlets, and sheets long bore the title of "the King's Tracts." They have been cataloged chronologically, as Thomason's written dates allow, an arrangement that has obvious advantages in dealing with historical sources and that might well

be adopted for similar catalogs for other periods. Their importance as original historical sources for their period must not be
forgotten; it is to be wished that we had similar collections, similarly cataloged by date of publication, for other periods. Carlyle
said of them that they are "greatly to be preferred to all the
sheepskins in the Tower and other places, for informing the English what the English were in former times."

12. The major contribution of the Bibliographical Society to this
field, and possibly the most influential single work yet published
by them, is the well-known "STC":

POLLARD, A. W., and REDGRAVE, G. R. A Short-title
Catalogue of Books Printed in England, Scotland and Ireland, and
of English Books Printed Abroad, 1475–1640. 1926.

This is an author list and has been under revision for a number of
years. One half of the new edition, covering the letters I–Z, was
published in 1976, and the other half is expected soon. It is one
of the best examples in bibliographical work of the spur that a
good tool can give to the study of the subject.

A useful index to this work has been published by the Bibliographical Society of the University of Virginia.

MORRISON, Paul G. Index of Printers, Publishers and Booksellers
in A. W. Pollard and G. R. Redgrave: Short-title Catalogue. . . .
1950.

Many catalogs of English books printed before 1641 (in some
cases before 1600) had appeared before the STC, and some are
still of importance as giving fuller information than a short-title
catalog can. Two stand out:

BRITISH MUSEUM. Catalogue of Books in the Library of the
British Museum Printed in England, Scotland and Ireland, and of
Books in English Printed Abroad, to 1640. 3v. 1884.

which is arranged by authors and has indexes of titles (including
some class headings, such as "Plays") and of printers, the latter
hard to use.

CAMBRIDGE UNIVERSITY LIBRARY. Early English Printed

Books in the University Library, 1475–1640, Edited by C. E. Sayle. 4v. 1900–1907.

Commonly known as Sayle, though largely the work of the University Librarian, Francis Jenkinson, it is arranged by presses, with author and other indexes.

13. A considerable literature has grown up around the Stationers' Company, of which the best general and informed account is:

BLAGDEN, Cyprian. *The Stationers' Company.* 1960.

A brief account of the Company in modern times:

UNWIN, Philip. *The Stationers' Company 1918–1977.* 1978.

14. STATIONERS' COMPANY. *Transcript of the Registers of the Company. . . . 1554–1640.* Edited by Edward Arber. 5v. 1875–1894. Continued for 1641–1708, edited by G. E. B. Eyre, transcribed by H. R. Plomer. 3v. 1913–1914.

The registers should be used in conjunction with the two volumes so far published of the transcripts of the court records of the Company. They contain a wealth of detail that illuminates much in the imprints of the period.

GREG, W. W., and BOSWELL, E. *Records of the Court of the Stationers' Company, 1576–1602.* 1930.
JACKSON, W. A. *Records of the Court of the Stationers' Company, 1602–1640.* 1957.

Two other publications provide guidance through this incomparable source material.

GREG, W. W. *Licensers for the Press, etc. to 1640; A Biographical Index Based on Arber's Transcript. . . .* 1962.
GREG, W. W. *A Companion to Arber.* 1967.

15. The best general account, drawing on these records is:

POTTINGER, David T. *The French Book Trade in the Ancien Régime, 1500–1791.* 1958.

16. THOMPSON, Lawrence S. *Printing in Colonial Spanish America.* 1962.

17. WINSHIP, George Parker. *The Cambridge Press, 1638–1692.* 1945.

18. HARASZTI, Zoltan. *The Bay Psalm Book: A Facsimile Reprint of the First Edition and the Enigma of the Bay Psalm Book.* 2v. 1957.

19. There are several accounts of early printing in North America:

HAMILTON, M. W. *The Country Printer.* 2nd ed. 1964.
LEHMANN-HAUPT, H., ed. *The Book in America.* 2nd ed. 1951.
THOMAS, Isaiah. *History of Printing in America.* 2v. 1810. 2nd ed. 1874.
WINTERICH, John T. *Early American Books and Printing.* 1935.

20. The bibliographical coverage of the period is limited:

WING, Donald G. *Short-title Catalogue of Books Printed in England, Scotland, Ireland, Wales and British America and of English Books Printed in Other Countries, 1641–1700.* 3v. 1945–1951. 2nd ed. 1972–

Morrison has provided an index similar to that for the basic STC.

MORRISON, Paul G. *Index of Printers, Publishers and Booksellers in Donald Wing's Short-title Catalogue, 1641–1700.* 1955.

In 1668 began to be published a current classfied list of new books, pamphlets unfortunately being excluded, which appeared once in each law term (Hilary, Easter, Trinity, and Michaelmas); it originally bore the title of *Mercurius Librarius* and was the venture of the booksellers Starkey and Clavell; it has been republished, although with an inadequate index, as:

ARBER, Edward. *The Term Catalogues, 1668–1709, with a Number for Easter Term, 1711.* 3v. 1903–1906.

In every country the bibliographically darkest period is that intermediate between the early period, the slightest productions of which are collected for their rarity and historical interest, and the contemporary period, in which the trade makes current lists of new publications for its own use and in which the national libraries gather by privilege the output of the press. In England the eighteenth century is ill served, except by the special bibliographies of the greater writers, which are numerous. The London Catalogue, which began in 1773 nominally providing a trade list of books published since 1700, is for its earlier issues entirely worthless, and the best source we have is certainly:

WATT, R. *Bibliotheca Britannica, or, A general index to British and Foreign Literature.* 4v. 1824.

Watt was a Glasgow doctor, who originally intended a medical and scientific catalog but whose appetite grew with what it fed on till he aimed at universality. The British part, however, is much larger and more valuable than the foreign. The work is in two parts, Authors and Subjects, with Anonyma entered in the latter.

21.   PARKS, Stephen. *John Dunton and the English Book Trade.* 1976.

22.   The work of the Foulis brothers is seen in:

GASKELL, Philip. *A Bibliography of the Foulis Press.* 1964.

and of the Oxford University Press in:

BARKER, Nicolas. *The Oxford University Press and the Spread of Learning, 1478–1978.* 1978.

23.   COLLINS, Arthur S. *Authorship in the Days of Johnson.* 1927.
COLLINS, Arthur S. *The Profession of Letters, 1780–1832.* 1928.
KENT, Elizabeth E. *Goldsmith and His Booksellers.* 1933.
McLAVERTY, J. *Pope's Printer.* 1976.

24.   STC 5069 to 5074 inclusive.

25.   WILES, R. M. *Serial Publications in England Before 1750.* 1957.

26.   Special attention should be paid to the work of the Project for Historical Biobibliography (formerly the Book Subscription Lists project) at the University of Newcastle upon Tyne and its publications, such as:

ROBINSON, F. J. G., and WALLIS, P. J. *Book Subscription Lists: A Revised Guide*. 1975.

27. WILLIAMS, Harold. *Book Clubs and Printing Societies of Great Britain and Ireland*. 1929.

28. WROTH, Lawrence C. "Book Production and Distribution from the Beginning to the American Revolution," in LEHMANN-HAUPT, H., ed. *The Book in America*. 2nd ed. 1951.
WROTH, Lawrence C. *The Colonial Printer*. 2nd ed. 1938.

29. SILVER, Rollo. *The American Printer, 1787–1825*. 1967.
SILVER, Rollo. *Type-founding in America, 1787–1825*. 1965.

30. There was much to support Emerson's comment in his famous address to the Phi Beta Kappa Society in 1837 that: "Our day of dependence, our long apprenticeship to the learning of other lands, draws to a close."

31. BARNES, J. J. *Free Trade in Books: A Study of the London Book Trade Since 1800*. 1964.
PLANT, Marjorie. *The English Book Trade*. 3rd ed. 1977.

32. The best and most interesting example of this that is readily available is:

BUTT, John, and TILLOTSON, Kathleen. *Dickens at Work*. 1957.

This should be read in conjunction with the Pilgrim edition of his letters and the prefaces to the Clarendon Dickens. More generally, see:

HEPBURN, James. *The Author's Empty Purse and the Rise of the Literary Agent*. 1968.
SUTHERLAND, J. A. *Victorian Novelists and Publishers*. 1976.
TILLOTSON, Kathleen. *Novels of the Eighteen-forties*. 1956.

33. NOWELL-SMITH, Simon. *International Copyright Law and the Publisher in the Reign of Queen Victoria*. 1968.
BARNES, J. J. *Authors, Publishers and Politicians*. 1974.

34. The bibliographical guides to nineteenth-century literature are

numerous but very uneven in quality and usefulness. Efficient trade lists, which lapsed with the Term Catalogues, began again with the gradual improvement, in the first half of the nineteenth century, of the London Catalogue and the foundation in 1853 of a rival, the British Catalogue. These were amalgamated by Sampson Low in 1864 into:

The English Catalogue of Books, 1835–1863.

A retrospective volume, covering 1801–1836, edited by R. A. Peddie and Q. Waddington, was published in 1914. The period after 1863 is covered by a series of cumulative volumes up to those of our own time.

This source is naturally a very general one and provides only the bare bones of bibliographical information. Another general source but with groupings under an author's work is in the third volume (1800–1900) of the:

New Cambridge Bibliography of English Literature.

An example that is good in the coverage of its own field and serves as an example of the type of tool that is of greatest use is:

SADLEIR, Michael. *XIX Century Fiction: A Bibliographical Record, Based on the Author's Own Collection.* 2v. 1951.

The first work to give serious treatment to one of the major bibliographical problems of the nineteenth century, the vast spread of periodical literature:

HOUGHTON, Walter E., ed. *The Wellesley Index to Victorian Periodicals, 1824–1900.* Vol. 1. 1966–. In progress.

The coverage for the United States is similar. The beginnings of American printing are dealt with in:

EVANS, Charles. *American Bibliography: A Chronological Dictionary of All Books, Pamphlets and Periodical Articles Printed in the United States of America from the Genesis of Printing in 1639 down to and Including the Year 1800; with Bibliographical and Biographical Notes.* 14v. 1903–1959.

Covering largely the same period but including much additional material is a work usually referred to as *Bibliotheca Americana* or *Sabin* and probably the most frequently consulted of bibliographies in this field:

SABIN, Joseph. *Dictionary of Books Relating to America from Its Discovery to the Present Time.* 29v. 1868–1936.

Whereas Evans is arranged chronologically, Sabin is arranged alphabetically by authors.

These are followed chronologically by a series of contemporary trade records:

ROORBACH, Orville Augustus. *Bibliotheca Americana, 1820–1860.* 4v. 1852–1861.

Roorbach is arranged alphabetically by author and title; much the same kind of information (publisher, date, size, price) is given in its continuation:

KELLY, James. *American Catalogue of Books Published in the United States from Jan. 1861 to Jan. 1871.* 2v. 1866–1871.

The next in sequence is:

American Catalogue of Books, 1876–1910, 9v. in 13. 1876–1910.

These bibliographies are now receiving support from:

BLANCK, Jacob. *Bibliography of American Literature.* 1955–. In progress.

This work is arranged alphabetically by author and devotes considerable attention to bibliographical details.

American Bibliography (covering 1801 to 1819) followed by *American Imprints* (covering 1820–. In progress)

A more detailed study, in relation to a few authors, of the complexities of transatlantic publishing can be found in:

BRUSSEL, I. R. *Anglo-American First Editions 1826–1900. East to West.* 1935.

BRUSSEL, I. R. *Anglo-American First Editions. Part Two: West to East, 1786–1930*. 1936.

35. MUNBY, A. N. L. *Phillipps Studies*. 5v. 1951–1960.
MUNBY, A. N. L. *Portrait of an Obsession*. 1967.

In addition to the specific references above, there is a wide range of more general texts that will give the student more detail in areas of particular interest and widen the general background. The following are suggestions for these purposes:

ALTICK, R. D. *The English Common Reader*. 1957.
BENNETT, H. S. *English Books and Readers, 1475 to 1557*. 1952.
BENNETT, H. S. *English Books and Readers, 1558 to 1603*. 1965.
BENNETT, H. S. *English Books and Readers, 1603–1640*. 1970.
BRITISH MUSEUM. *Guide to the Exhibition in the King's Library*. 1939.
CARTER, Harry. *A History of the Oxford University Press*. Vol. 1. (to the year 1780). 1975.
CLAIR, Colin, *History of European Printing*. 1976.
CLAIR, Colin. *A History of Printing in Britain*. 1965.
DAHL, Svend. *History of the Book*. 1958.
DE RICCI, Seymour. *English Collectors of Books and Manuscripts, 1530–1930, and Their Marks of Ownership*. 1930. Reprinted, 1960.
GOLDSCHMIDT, E. P. *The Printed Book of the Renaissance*. 1950.
GREG, W. W. *Some Aspects and Problems of London Publishing Between 1550 and 1650*. 1956.
HANDOVER, P. M. *Printing in London from 1476 to Modern Times*. 1960.
HELLINGER, W. G. *Copy and Print in the Netherlands, An Atlas of Historical Bibliography*. 1962.
KENYON, Sir Frederick. *Books and Readers in Ancient Greece and Rome*. 2nd ed. 1951.
McKENZIE, D. F. *The Cambridge University Press, 1696–1712. A Bibliographical Study*. 2v. 1966.
McLEAN, Ruari. *Victorian Book Design*. 1963.
MILLER, E. H. *The Professional Writer in Elizabethan England*. 1959.
MORISON, Stanley, and DAY, Kenneth. *The Typographic Book, 1450–1935*. 1963.
MUIR, Percy. *English Children's Books, 1600–1900*. 1954.

REED, Talbot Baines. *A History of the Old English Letter Foundries.* New ed. rev. and enl. A. F. Johnson. 1952.
SHEAVYN, Phoebe. *The Literary Profession in the Elizabethan Age.* 2nd ed. 1967.
SIEBERT, Frederick S. *Freedom of the Press in England, 1476–1776.* 1952.
STEINBERG, S. H. *Five Hundred Years of Printing.* New ed. 1962.
SUTCLIFFE, Peter. *The Oxford University Press: An Informal History.* 1978.
THOMPSON, J. W. *The Medieval Library.* 1939.
WROTH, L. C., ed. *A History of the Printed Book; Being the Third Number of "The Dolphin."* 1938.

It is also important to become familiar with the:

Annual Bibliography of the History of the Printed Book and Libraries (ABHB). Vol. 1 covered 1970 publications and was published in 1973. It has been annual since that date. Prior to this there was an annual "Selective Check List of Bibliographical Scholarship" (including historical bibliography) published in *Studies in Bibliography* up to and including Vol. 27 (1974).

4.

PAPYRUS, PARCHMENT, VELLUM, PAPER

A variety of substances has been used for several distinct purposes in the manufacturing of the material means for the transmission of texts. Many of these—the materials used in binding, for example—can be regarded as ancillary to the main purpose. The substance on which the text is recorded has an importance above all others. Since bibliography must cover the production of "books" of all periods, it must concern itself with all the materials of the record itself. Varied as these have been in successive civilizations, a few have been of especial importance.

The first writing material was stone, and the first implements were designed for scratching, engraving, and painting on that surface. The earliest known marks of this kind are still visible in the numerous surviving examples of palaeolithic cave art in Western Europe. This evidence suggests a history of writing surfaces of some fifteen thousand years. The cave paintings and engravings of these early years may have been designed more for decorative purposes than for those of communication, but these two elements have been inextricably entangled throughout the whole long history of book making. In any event, it was here that human beings made a first attempt to break out of the isolation of their own person other than by speech. They chose a surface that was ideal in many respects. It had that degree of permanence for which many generations of book makers have sought and that has been the subject of so much research in our own day. Its disadvantages were few, but one of them was vital. It was static.

When it became necessary to record minor transactions and to set down ceremonies, rituals, dedications, and such like, in something more portable than cave walls and stone blocks, the Sumerians incised clay tablets and hardened them by baking. These tablets, being well-nigh indestructible, are extant in large quantities, and examples can easily be seen in libraries and museums. The jabbing action of a stylus into the damp clay produced a wedge-shaped impression, with the result that the name "cuneiform" came to be applied to this particular form of writing. Although the shapes and sizes of the tablets vary considerably, the majority indicate that they were shaped between the hands. Cushion shapes and cones are among the more common forms, but a considerable range can be found.

Early materials such as these rarely come into the regular consideration of bibliographical problems; they are more often associated with historical and archaeological investigations. Nevertheless, they are an essential part of the whole range of bibliographical materials, and they enjoyed a longer life than the modern paper that we now take for granted. It is impossible to overlook them completely in any survey of bibliographical evidence, but other materials have supplanted them in general importance. Over the most fully documented period of the history of the book three basic materials reigned supreme: papyrus; animal skins, especially parchment and vellum; and paper.

Papyrus

Papyrus, from which came our words "paper" and "Bible," was manufactured from the pith within the stem of a river plant that once grew freely in the Nile valley and still grows sparsely in a few areas of the world. Our knowledge of its manufacture is based on the account given by Pliny in his *Natural History* reinforced by illustrations in Egyptian tombs and manuscripts.[1] There have been several recorded instances of the modern making of pieces of papyrus, the first probably in the seventeenth century.[2] I can attest to one additional experiment. During the summer of 1962 a group of students in the University of California (Los Angeles) made a sheet of papyrus, possibly the first ever made in California, working entirely and successfully by Pliny's instructions. Strips of the pith were cut thinly and laid side by side; a second layer of strips was laid transversely over the first and the sheet beaten, pressed, and polished. Doubt is sometimes expressed as to whether these layers were pasted or not. Most modern opinion suggests that they were not, and this was certainly not necessary with the Californian sheet. Papyrus is the material of practically all the books of antiquity. As we see it today, it is a frail-looking brown substance, which can only be handled between sheets of glass. When new, there is no doubt that it was strong, white, and pleasant to the eye.

The size of a sheet of papyrus depended upon the length of the strip used in its manufacture. The maximum height of any known sheet is 47–48 cm. but this is a Book of the Dead (Papyrus Greenfield B.M. 10554) and was therefore designed for burial rather than for reading. The more usual height of a sheet was much smaller, and 20–24 cm. was nearer to the average. If a larger piece were needed, one sheet would be pasted to another to form a continuous roll. Some rolls were of considerable length. Egyptian rolls sometimes exceeded one hundred feet in length and often exceed fifty; the longest known, the Great Harris Papyrus (B.M. 999), is one hundred and thirty-three feet long. Greek papyri, on the other hand, were shorter, and thirty-five feet appears to be the longest normal Greek literary roll.[3] References suggest that wooden or bone rollers were sometimes attached to the ends of the rolls and ornamented with projecting knobs (*cornua*, or *umbilici*). This is true of Roman rolls, but it is not a device found in those of ancient Egypt. In such cases tickets bearing the titles of the works could be attached to the umbilici as a means of identification. The whole could be kept rolled up on the handles and stored in pigeonholes. From the Latin word for a roll, *volumen*, comes our word "volume." The roll was written on in ink with a reed instrument, which, originally shaped to form a fine brush, later developed to a more penlike instrument pointed and split in two like a quill pen. The writing was in columns, usually on one side only, the side on which the strips ran horizontally. If text was written on both sides, then the roll is known as an *opisthograph*. The columns of text crossed the roll, whereas in the skin rolls, used during the later Middle Ages for accounts and chronicles, the writing was in a single immense column down the whole length of the roll.

Papyrus was used in Egypt from the third millennium at the latest, and there is a considerable body of papyrus rolls extant that date from about 2000 BC onward. It continued in use in many other areas as late as the eleventh century AD but in diminishing quantity, perhaps because of some failure in the supply of the plant. In any case, it was eventually driven out by parchment and vellum. The other vegetable materials that served similar purposes, such as the Oriental palm-leaf and the birch-bark of the American Indians, do not affect the history of the book as known in Europe, but it is worth remarking that the Latin *liber* originally meant the inner bark of trees.[4]

Superficially the papyrus book seems very dissimilar to its modern counterpart, but the basic elements have much in common. Written on a manufactured surface, capable of taking decoration and illustration, with a rudimentary form of binding, it exemplified the real function of the "book" as an instrument for the communication of ideas. In one important respect, however, there was to be a major evolution.

The roll form prevented easy and rapid reference to any particular passage in the text. As the need increasingly arose for more specific reference, particularly in law digests and Bibles, so the physical form evolved also. The roll was gradually superseded by the hinged form of the book, the codex, which is now the most familiar of all forms. The word "codex" means block of wood, probably from the wooden covers.[5]

The codex form of manuscript is associated chiefly with vellum, and the changes in form and material proceeded side by side. There are, however, examples of papyrus codices, instances in which the form changed but the material remained constant. The most notable of them are the eleven Chester Beatty Biblical papyri, whose dates are estimated to range from the second to the fourth or fifth centuries AD. It is still an open question as to the probability that the roll form is associated with pagan literature and the codex with Christian. The proposition has been debated in many writings concerned with papyrus and the evolution of the codex.[6]

Parchment and vellum

Animal skins came into use as writing surfaces at a very early period, and in many communities they had obvious advantages. In the case of other materials the writing surface was the prime, sometimes the only, result of the process of manufacture. When skins were used, they were by-products of other processes, and the capability of a community to make skins into writing surfaces depended also on the economy of the community and the ability to eat or otherwise utilize the flesh of the animal. Also, skins were less likely to be transported distances than many other materials, and consequently their treatment assumes a more completely localized practice. It has long been known that animal skins were used in a less sophisticated manner of preparation than parchment and vellum. The discovery of the Dead Sea Scrolls and the investigation of the materials on which they were written has awakened a new interest in these substances. The Dead Sea Scrolls, which were written on skins, date from the very beginning of the Christian era, and the probability is that the animals used were goat and sheep. The skins were tanned and treated in much the same manner as modern leathers. The resultant surface was markedly unlike that of parchment and vellum.

Confusion is occasionally caused because the names parchment and vellum are frequently so loosely used as to be almost interchangeable. Strictly speaking, parchment is made from the skins of sheep or goats and vellum is made from calfskin. They were known, and probably used, as early as 1500 BC but were not used extensively until the beginning of the Christian era. There is a tradition that Eumenes II, King of Pergamum in Asia Minor (197–159 BC) incurred the displeasure of the King of Egypt, who thereupon forbade the export of papyrus. The people of Pergamum then reverted to the use of skins as writing material and, perfecting the methods of treatment, produced a more durable substance than papyrus, although heavier and more expensive. Pergamum, from which parchment took its name, was probably the center of the trade, and by the end of the third or the beginning of the fourth century it had become the leading material in Europe. Vellum, taking its name from the animal whose skin was employed, had a much finer and whiter surface than parchment and was used for some of the choicest examples of manuscript decorative art. The finest of all vellums, known as "uterine" vellum, is believed to have been the skin of the unborn or stillborn calf.

Because vellum was the finer surface of the two, a curious and misleading habit grew of using "vellum" as an adjective and referring to a finer surfaced parchment as a "vellum parchment." The confusion becomes possible because parchment made from the skin of a young sheep or goat, carefully prepared, can achieve a surface that is not dissimilar to a less-fine vellum. There must naturally be an overlapping area in which only technological analysis can determine which of the two materials any one example is. Because of this difficulty, and because in many instances it makes little or no difference to the librarian, curator, or bibliographer, there is an increasing modern habit of calling them all "membrane books."

Parchment and vellum were prepared in a manner similar to each other. The skins were placed in a pit or vat of lime and then scraped to remove the flesh and hair. The skins were stretched on a frame and dressed with a substance like alum and finally dusted over with a fine powder to create the necessary writing surface.

Parchment and vellum were made up into books in the codex form by cutting the prepared skins into rectangular pieces that, when folded, made two leaves of the size required. (Paper, on the other hand, is brought by successive foldings to the smaller book sizes.) The parchment or vellum sheets were so arranged that the pages of each opening were of the same texture, both being either the fine "flesh" side or the "hair" side, which was spotted with the roots of the hair. This fact is often of use in determining obscure questions as to the makeup of particular manuscript volumes.

Parchment and vellum books require very special treatment in libraries, especially with regard to temperature and humidity. Although the danger may be greater when the materials are used in binding because of the greater exposure to the air, it is important in all cases. If membranes are stored in too dry an atmosphere, they will become extremely brittle. If the surroundings are damp, there is a tendency for the membranes to cockle and in extreme cases, over relatively long periods, to powder away to complete disintegration. It is not possible to provide the same kind of preventative or restorative treatment to membranes as writing surfaces as is possible with the same materials in binding. The only "cure" is prevention. Membrane books require the storage conditions that are satisfactory for rare books in general; that is, a temperature of about 62° and relative humidity of between 45 and 50. These conditions should be capable of very rigorous control.[7]

Paper

Paper is of great antiquity, and there is no reason to doubt the well-established tradition that it was invented in China. It is generally accepted that the inventor was Ts'ai Lun and the year of his discovery was AD 103. The translation of a near-contemporary account stated that the materials that he used were "rags, fish nets, bark of trees, and hemp well prepared." During the course of his explorations in Chinese Turkestan in 1907 Sir Aurel Stein discovered nine letters written on paper. They were not dated, but documents in the vicinity were not later than AD 137. The first movement of paper manufacture outside China was in the eighth century. Chinese prisoners, captured by the Arabs in what is now Russian Turkestan, taught the art to their captors at Samarkand in AD 751. The introduction of flax in manufacture at this time is believed to be due to the Arabs. Oriental papers were always of a thicker, creamier, and more vellumlike quality than European ones.

With the Moslem power and civilization, then much greater than the Christian, the manufacture and use of paper moved westward: to Bagdad in the late eighth century, to Damascus, and to Egypt by AD 900, then crossing the Mediterranean into Europe.

Paper entered Europe by two main routes. That from Damascus, which for several centuries was Europe's main source of paper, entered through Constantinople and paper from Africa through Sicily. The earliest extant example of the use of paper in Europe is a document in the Escorial, a deed of Count Robert of Sicily written in Greek and Arabic, dated 1109. At Palermo is a second example, of exactly a century later.

By 1151 Xativa in Spain had a well-established paper mill; in 1189 there is one recorded at Herault on the French side of the Pyrenees; the first mill in Italy was at Fabriano by 1276, the first in Germany at Nuremburg in 1391, the first in England in 1496.

The spread of paper was very slow. It appears with increasing frequency in archives but was not really made in quantity till the manufacture was stimulated by the invention of printing. It is significant that of the very earliest books many copies survive printed on vellum, but of books of half a century later very few indeed, while in England its use in printing was rare from the first.

In practically every country into which paper making was introduced there was a period during which only imported paper was used. This means that the bibliographer can usually rely on a fairly distinct period of imported paper in books under examination. At the latter end of such a period there is obviously an overlap of time during which both imported and domestically produced papers were employed. The total length of time during which wholly or primarily imported papers were in use varies with the passing of time. In England, for example, paper had been in use since the early part of the fourteenth century. It was not until 1495 that John Tate the younger established the first paper mill in England in Hertfordshire—a fact that is attested by its use in that year by Wynkyn de Worde, who calls attention to it in the often-quoted *prohemium* to his English edition of Bartholomaeus (Glanville) Anglicus *On the Properties of Things*. Tate's enterprise seems to have been short-lived, and English printers still relied heavily on imported paper for a considerable time. Similarly in North America, when printing began in 1639, paper was readily available but it was imported. The local manufacture of paper, however, when it began at Germantown in Pennsylvania in 1690, could satisfy but a small proportion of the needs of an expanding press, and the importation of paper continued. Although the history of paper making is still a comparatively new study, much work has been done in recent years and a considerable amount of fundamentally important material has been published.[8]

By 1500 paper making in general in Europe had established itself in a fairly settled pattern. Over the following centuries two main areas of change affected paper making as it spread worldwide: changes in the basic materials that were used in the pulp and in the methods of manufacture.

Materials of paper

To the downward succession of the Ages of Gold, Silver, and

Iron must now be added the Age of Paper, in which we live. Paper has become one of the most ubiquitous and obtrusive of all the stuffs of daily life. The huge use of it and the diminishing resources of material create difficulties that are far from resolution. All modern reports and surveys have drawn attention to the steeply rising curve of use at the same time as natural resources are declining rapidly. Similar situations have arisen in the past, notably in the middle of the nineteenth century, but the pressure of demand has never been as great as at the present time. Acute shortages are definite possibilities unless and until new materials are discovered or the demand can be abated.[9]

At the same time it has become more and more apparent that many of the papers that are being used are not capable of fulfilling their long-term function. Not all books are designed to last, but many of those for which this good fortune may be hoped are printed on paper that precludes the possibility. In any event, librarians and archivists are a race apart in that they seek to preserve for posterity, in some form or another, material that was designed by its producers to be ephemeral. Bibliographers in their turn are concerned with all the physical aspects of the book, of which paper must inevitably form a major part. Some knowledge of the chief ingredients of paper is therefore highly desirable.

Paper is vegetable fiber disintegrated and reintegrated in water; this distinguishes it from vellum and parchment, which are animal skins, and from papyrus, which is vegetable leaf not disintegrated but simply dressed by drying, rolling, and polishing.

The final quality of the paper will depend upon a number of combined characteristics of the basic materials, but no feature is more important than the fibers themselves. These must be long, tough, flexible, and easy to separate from the raw bulk, of which they should form a high percentage. The durability of the paper is in inverse ratio to the amount of chemical action needed to separate the fibers from the intercellular matter of the plant. In addition to this, it has to be remembered that the strength and longevity of the fibers will vary considerably according to the plant of their origin and the care with which they are treated during manufacture.

From the time of its invention until the middle of the nineteenth century cotton and linen rags formed the staple basic material of the trade. Since cotton is an extremely pure form of cellulose and since flax is one of the strongest and hardest of fibers, it follows that rag paper, which is usually a mixture of these two, stands as the most durable of papers. Such papers are found today in perfect condition, white and strong, and it is only of them that we can state from experience that they reach what may be called absolute permanence. Certain newspapers, notably *The Times* of London, have from time to time printed a special issue on an all-rag or part-rag paper so that it might be preserved without difficulty. *The Times* ceased to publish their "Royal Edition" on 31 December 1969.

As early as 1719 René Réaumur, a French industrialist and physicist, suggested the use of wood pulp as a substitute for rags in paper manufacture. He communicated his remarks in a treatise to the French Royal Academy. His observations were that American wasps formed very fine paper through extracting fibres from common wood. His opinion was that, given similar wood, it should be possible to make a satisfactory paper of the whitest quality. "While the consumption of paper increases daily, the production of linen remains the same. The wasp seems to teach us a means of overcoming these difficulties."

Réaumur's proposals were carried no farther until a German, Jacob Christian Schaeffer, actually made paper from wasps' nests. In 1765 he published the first volume of his work on paper making, containing specimens of papers from a variety of materials: wasps' nest, moss, vines, bark, cabbage stalks, thistles, Indian corn husks, potatoes, reeds, horse-chestnuts, walnuts, tulips, and linden leaves, among others.

The eighteenth century was primarily one of experimentation so far as materials other than rags were concerned. It was not until the nineteenth century that there was a real breakthrough. In 1800 Matthias Koops, an Englishman, developed a paper made from straw, and by 1829 an American, George Shryock, made a straw-based paper as a commerical proposition.

Wood pulp appears in two forms in paper making, and it is important to distinguish between the pair because of their completely differing qualities. Chemical wood paper, in which the cellulose fibers are released by chemical action, is the best of the nonrag papers. If carefully made, it stands the tests remarkably well. Mechanical wood, which is ground up instead of being chemically disintegrated, has no length of fiber and makes a paper that soon turns brown and brittle under light since it retains all the intercellular matter that is removed in the other processes. The latter became a possibility after 1840, when Friedrich Keller perfected his machine for grinding wood. Mechanical wood pulp became a major ingredient for newsprint but was not adaptable for book papers. The former stemmed from 1851, with the initial processes in England of Hugh Burgess and Charles Watt in producing the soda pulp by chemical processes. The processes were later refined by Benjamin Tilghman in America in 1866 and further still by George Fry and C. B. Eckman working in England and Sweden and patenting their improved sulphite process in 1884.

These two varieties of paper are found in increased quantity in books from the middle of the nineteenth century onward and rapidly displaced rag papers from their long-established monopoly. This change was hastened by the American Civil War, which virtually cut off the supplies to Europe from a major distributing area.

This same event, together with the steady growth of the book trade, was also responsible for the spread of the third important nonrag material. *The Times* newspaper sponsored the development of esparto grass as a raw ingredient in 1854, and it came into general commercial use in 1861. Papers manufactured from esparto grass, which is imported from North Africa and Southern Spain, have, when well made, only little less lasting power than chemical wood. Esparto grass is a fine and tough fiber but, when specially beaten, can bulk out considerably and was largely used in the manufacture of "featherweight" papers. It is also preferred for the body of art paper.

For over a century now these have been the chief fibers in use. Unless the rate of growth of the consumption of paper can be slowed down in some way, new materials may be needed in the near future as in the last half of the nineteenth century. The most promising opening to date would seem to be in the utilization of synthetic fibers as opposed to the natural fibers that have served hitherto.

Other materials are used in the production of paper in addition to the basic fibers. All of these are important, and some, notably those that leave distinct traces in the finished product, are of crucial importance. Dyes of various kinds are employed because few book papers are dead white, and much experimentation still needs to be done on the possible effects of papers with definite colorations. Rosin and alum are used primarily for surfacing purposes and especially for creating a surface that will not permit too much penetration by the ink. China clay and titanium oxide serve as loading agents to increase the opacity of the paper and to fill in the interstices between the individual fibers.

The material that is used in greater quantity than any other in making paper, however, is water. Although, if as completely pure as it should be, it may leave no residual traces in the finished product, its role in manufacture is so crucial that it cannot be ignored. One estimate is that about two thousand gallons of water are needed in order to make one ton of paper; or to phrase it in another way, each paper-making machine will consume approximately twelve thousand gallons each hour. So vast a required quantity has naturally dictated the places of paper manufacture very precisely over its history.

A few special materials and papers are worthy of note:

(a) *Japanese vellum:* This is a fine strong paper, made of Japanese shrubs, notably the Broussonetia; it has a creamy tint and smooth surface like vellum and is much used for engravings. The surface is delicate and will not, for instance, survive the use of india-rubber.

An imitation is made by treating thick ordinary paper with sulphuric acid so as to melt and coagulate the surface into a resemblance of that of Japanese vellum. It has no merits.

(b) *China paper:* Very thin and silky, used for proofs of woodcuts.

(c) *Ramie:* One of the finest materials, normally used only for textiles and bank-notes. A certain amount of textile waste is used for paper.

(d) *India paper:* Very thin and strong, thoroughly made of rags and rendered opaque by judicious loading. A small consignment was brought from the East (in old parlance, all farther Asia was "the Indies") in 1842 and used by the Clarendon Press; in 1875 this was successfully imitated by the Wolvercote Mills and later manufactured for Oxford University Press by Thomas Brittain and Sons, of Hanley, and is now familiar. Very popular for private use, and especially for pocket editions, being only one-third as thick as ordinary paper.[10]

Manufacture of paper

Whatever may be the basic raw materials of a paper, the first step is always the treatment, either by chemical or mechanical means, to change the material into its constituent fibers. The methods have changed over the centuries, but the basic principles have not. There is a strong unity among papers up to 1800, which is as genuine a watershed date as can be found in the history of paper. Until then no truly revolutionary changes had occurred that affected the actual nature of the paper itself. The initial steps are common to all processes and to all types of paper. A pulp has to be made of the fibers in suspension in water. This pulp is the vital element in the finished sheet; strength and durability both depend upon it. To it were added at any given period such other materials as were appropriate to the manufacture of one particular kind of paper.

The first processes to which rag material is subjected are the cutting, sorting, and dusting. The strips are then thrown into a large vessel, in which they are boiled in water containing some kind of alkaline solution. Originally the amount of boiling seems to have been minimal and in certain countries even restricted to the heat generated by the fermentation of bundles of rags kept constantly dampened. The procedure was refined considerably in course of time, but the main changes were introduced gradually as new raw materials began to replace rags.

The purpose of this boiling is to loosen or dissolve any noncellular matter, leaving behind the fibrous material. It will also partially remove dyes, depending upon their color and fixity. Esparto grass and straw, after dusting and cleaning, are boiled under pressure in "digesters" with caustic soda. In the case of mechanical wood the logs are brought into contact with a revolving grindstone and the pulp so created is washed away by a stream of water. For the chemical wood pulps the wood, after having been sliced into chips, is boiled in a digester with chemicals. The bisulphite process of chemical wood pulp manufacture will use sulphur dioxide with bisulphite and magnesium bisulphite. The alkaline process, which originally used caustic soda, now frequently uses sodium sulphate.

The pulps that result from these processes next pass into yet other receptacles, called "breakers." The object of this part of the operation is to separate the fibers from each other in the pulp, and the extent of the treatment will vary greatly from one material to another. Much of this was originally accomplished by a process of flailing or stamping, but during the eighteenth century the invention and spread of the "Hollander" completely revolutionized this part of the procedure. Even after this introduction some mills retained their old stamping machines for the initial task of breaking the rags and then used the Hollander to continue the process of beating. This first or breaking stage resulted in the creation of half-stuff, as the pulp is called at this stage, and now is passed on for "beating." Here mixtures will be made of various pulps, size will be added in the case of engine-sized papers, and filling materials will be added for loaded papers. This stage is also used for bleaching. Bleach is mixed with the stock, which is subsequently passed into further receptacles in which it is washed to rid it of the residuary bleach, a fertile source of deterioration if allowed to remain. Most important of all, however, is the fact that the paper will vary greatly depending on its treatment in the beater. The pulp will be passed between a beater roll, which is a drum fitted with protruding metal bars and the bottom, or "bed plate," of the beater. If the bars are blunt, the fibers will be torn apart, but, if sharp "tackle" is substituted for blunt, the fibers will be chopped short and a paper of featherweight or blotting-paper quality will result.

At this point machine- and hand-making diverge; hitherto they have only differed in the greater care and patience lavished on paper to be made by hand. The pulp, with the addition of any necessary coloring matter, is further mixed with water for machine-made paper since it has to be poured into the mold. For hand-making a thicker consistency is kept.

Hand-manufacture

In hand-making the mold was a wire sieve set on a large oblong wood framework. The mold is of two types: The first is the "laid" mold, making "laid" paper, consisting of a close mesh of fine wires, running lengthwise and crossed at intervals of about three-quarters of an inch by stouter wires. Till the beginning of the nineteenth century nearly all paper was "laid." The second is the "wove" mold, a very fine mesh, closely woven. The first wove paper was made in the beginning of the latter half of the eighteenth century, but its general spread was never very wide.

Over the top of this frame fits another, called the deckle, rather like an empty picture frame, the object of which is to restrict the area of the mold over which the pulp can flow. The edge of handmade paper, known as the "deckle-edge," is the rough and wavy edge that uncut books have and is due to some of the liquid pulp's seeping under the deckle frame. It may be considered that too much stress is laid by some kinds of book collectors upon having the complete deckle edge of a book untouched, and its artificial production in a machine-made paper is an absurd falsification, yet the presence of the deckle is evidence that the binder has not cut down the book's original margins. In parenthesis it must be pointed out that a careful distinction must be kept between a book that is "uncut" and one that is "unopened." As discussed above, the former term is used when the margins of a book have not been trimmed since its original issue. The latter means that the bolts, the folds at the top and fore-edges due to the folding of the original sheet into the gathering, have not been cut or opened. There is a point in preserving it in the former state but none in preserving it in the latter, in which it cannot be read.

The vat-worker takes the mold, dips it into the vat, and lifts it up covered with a layer of semiliquid pulp. The mold is then shaken as the water begins to drain through the mesh and so causes the fibers to cross and interlace. It is a very delicate and subtle craft, which nothing but the human hand can accomplish, and it is upon this that the strength of the paper chiefly depends.

The mold is then passed to the coucher, who turns the sheet onto a bed of felt. As the sheets are turned out one by one, they are interleaved with layers of felt. This "post" of sheets is then pressed to commence the drying process. The felting process also provides the first gentle pressing of the sheet in order to compress the fibers. The sheets are then hung in a loft to dry. When dried, it is still what is called "water-leaf," that is, it readily absorbs water. The next process is to give it a nonabsorbent surface, on which printer's or writing ink will not run. For this it has to be "sized." Any unsized paper will act as blotting paper.

Size is animal gelatin, into which the leaf is now dipped, being said to be "tub-sized." If tub-sized papers lose their size by the action of damp or of bacilli, they can be dipped again and resized. Inferior paper is "engine-sized" in the beater with rosin and various acids, which have an injurious effect. The paper is then air-dried, smoothed, and pressed and is given a glazing, which if moderate may actually add to its strength by compressing the fibers, but if excessive, bruises and breaks them.

Machine manufacture

Paper making by machinery is a lower level of the craft, but one that is nevertheless capable of producing a durable material. The machine process was invented just before 1800 by Nicolas-Louis Robert, an employee in the French publishing house of Didot, but it was first practiced in England. The basic idea of the machine was taken to England by Didot, Robert's employer, and John Gamble, a brother-in-law of Didot. Economic conditions in France in the last decade of the eighteenth century were not conducive to such development there. An agreement to finance the manufacture and sale of the machine was made by two British wholesale stationers, Henry and Sealey Fourdrinier. A young engineer, Bryan Donkin, developed and improved the machine, with the result that one was operational by 1803; the machine, known as the Fourdrinier, was patented in 1807. The principle is that of an endless wire mesh onto which the pulp flows. As this mold passes along the water falls through the mesh, the belt is shaken from side to side in an attempt to simulate the shake of the hand paper maker. This is successful only up to a point since it can shake from side to side but not backward and forward, while the vat-worker can shake in both directions. The strength of handmade paper is thus in two directions, that of machine-made paper is one only. To test whether paper is handmade, tear off a piece and drop it into water. A handmade paper will turn up—i.e., contract—in all directions. Machine-made paper will turn up two edges only, because its matting runs chiefly one way. A machine-mold–made paper, on the other hand, can be produced with little difference between the strength of the two dimensions.

More water will be removed from the pulp by suction boxes over which the mesh will pass and will also be squeezed out under rollers. In what always seems to be a surprisingly short time the paper will be strong enough, although still very damp, to be transferred from the wire mesh to pass between felting and surfacing rollers. A variety of surfaces can be achieved in papers according to the number and type of cylinders between which the paper passes. At length it will be wound onto reels, and the manufacturing process can be regarded as virtually completed.

The new process, which was considerably refined and improved as the nineteenth century progressed, produced papers in sufficient quantity and of sufficient quality to meet the rising demand of the nineteenth-century popular press. Above all, machine manufacture allied with the new raw materials produced a wider selection of papers than had hitherto been possible. It was upon this feature that the varied economic ranges of nineteenth-century book production depended.

Mold-made paper

One interesting variation in method produced a paper that for quality came midway between handmade and machine-made papers. Mold-made paper was first made in England by John Dickinson in 1809. It involved a method in which a hollow drum with a mesh similar to a paper maker's mold was fixed around the circumference. This drum rotated in a vat upon the mesh. The water drained through the mesh causing a layer of fiber to be deposited on the outside of the mesh area as the drum revolved. This was picked off by a roller and so passed through a series of felting rollers. A later development produced individual sheets rather than a web by introducing wooden slats onto the couching roller and so dividing the length into separate portions.

Laid marks and watermarks

Paper made on a laid mold shows the lines of the wires lighter and more transparent than the rest when held up to the light. These markings in the paper are known as "laid marks"; the thicker ones, caused by the cross wires, are "chain lines"; the thinner ones, caused by the lengthwise wires, are "wire lines." The wove papers show similarly a faint network that gives a rather mottled appearance to the paper. This is because the soft wet pulp is thinner where it has rested on the wire or metal; the marks are not the structure of the fiber, which is to be seen in cloudy masses when a piece of paper is held up to the light.

There may also be seen a pattern or device in transparent lines. This is the watermark, which was made by interweaving wire into the mesh or by soldering the wire onto the surface of the mesh. Although it has now assumed considerable importance as bibliographical evidence, the original and lasting purpose of the watermark was solely that of a trademark. It was first introduced in Western papers, the earliest date known being 1282 in a paper from the Italian mill at Fabriano. Many papers, especially from the sixteenth century onward, bore a mark in addition to the watermark. This was the countermark, consisting frequently of initials or a date associated with the watermark itself. Its usual position was in the center of the other half of the mold from the watermark and therefore found in the center of one half of the full sheet of paper. Oriental papers did not bear marks until two or three centuries later.

The watermark in machine-made paper is not made by the mold but by a special roller called the "dandy," which revolves over the mold and impresses at every revolution upon the moving pulp the device that is in relief upon it. The watermark is of small value in collating books printed on machine-made paper.

Sheet sizes

The important size in the consideration of paper is that of the whole sheet. Sizes have varied considerably from country to country and from period to period. Although hundreds of sheet sizes have been in use over the centuries, only a few were common in the manufacture of one country at a particular time. The knowledge of the standard sizes of the period is a prerequisite to the detailed investigation of a group of books. A good example of a chart of paper sizes in relation to analysis and description can be found in Allan Stevenson's "Hunt Botanical Catalogue."[11]

The nomenclature for the description of paper sizes has been reasonably stable for a long period of time even though actual sizes have varied within each definition. In English the terms Foolscap, Crown, Large Post, Demy, Medium, Royal, Large Royal, and Imperial Elephant are of long standing, as are the French terms of Tellière, Grand-cornet, Carré, Royal, Grand-Jésus, Impérial, and Grand-Colombier, or the Dutch terms of Pro patria, Bijkorf, Groot post, Kl. mediaan, Gr. mediaan, Royaal, Super royaal, Imperiaal, and Oliphants.[12]

The deterioration and preservation of paper

Librarians and bibliographers alike have to be concerned over the dangers that threaten the life of paper. Some of the most obvious problems are those that concern its basic strengths. It has always been recognized that papers made from different basic materials and manufactured by different methods can vary considerably in such vital regards as weight, tearing strength, resistance to folding, and so on. It is equally obvious that certain broad categories of paper will be preferred to others in these respects. For example, it does not matter which way a handmade sheet is folded in book making—the folds will have equal strength. But machine-made paper should not be folded along the flow (i.e., the direction in which the pulp moves on the mold), or the fold will not cross the fibers and will lack strength and in time will probably split. The direction in which the paper is cut, however, is perfectly arbitrary, since the sheet is endless and is not originally a limited oblong, as in handmaking but is subsequently cut to the required size and shape. Methods have varied considerably from one manufacturer to another in this regard, and it is difficult to see anything that can be regarded as general practice. Nevertheless, research into paper technology of recent years has opened up a number of areas of investigation, of which one has shown the most hopeful results.

In the early years of the nineteenth century the problem of the durability of paper began to be of some concern. Papers made before 1800 were found to be still in good condition, while many of those made in the nineteenth century were showing signs of decay. In 1823 John Murray contributed some notes to the *Gentleman's Magazine*, [13] which in 1829 he expanded into a pamphlet entitled *Practical Remarks on Modern Paper*. [14] He saw the problem as one that above all affected modern books. "I have in my possession a large copy of the Bible printed at Oxford, 1816 (never used), and issued by the British and Foreign Bible Society, *crumbling literally into dust.*" He believed the main causes of decay were:

(a)   damage to the fibers on the machine;

(b)   mineral loading;

(c)   alum, used in the sizing, which reacted with any excess chloride of lime, used in the bleaching, to form muriatic acid; and

(d)   excessive bleaching, which damaged the fibers.

Although the situation was demonstrably bad in the early part of the century, it worsened and became further complicated during the period 1840–1860 by the introduction of new raw materials, such as mechanical wood, chemical wood, and esparto grass.

In the latter half of the nineteenth century there were numerous investigations throughout Europe regarding the problems of paper deterioration. The causes were clearly established, and apart from considerations of the manufacturing process itself attention was directed to the part played by the integral qualities of the fibers themselves. It became clear that it was virtually impossible for a finished paper to be better than the nature of the raw products permitted. Consequently there was wide acceptance of the report issued in 1898 by a Special Committee of the Royal Society of Arts, *The Deterioration of Paper*. [15] In it paper fibers were arranged in four main classes. In descending order of permanence they were:

Class A: cotton, flax, hemp;
Class B: wood celluloses;
Class C: esparto grass and straw celluloses; and
Class D: mechanical wood pulp.

The first half of the twentieth century occupied itself largely, but not exclusively, with matters of the manufacturing process. Committees set their eyes on the ideal that, if paper mills made only those papers that exhibited none of the intrinsic demerits to which decay was now attributable, then all would be well. The whole tenor of *The Durability of Paper Report* issued in 1930 by the Library Association of the United Kingdom is typical of this outlook.[16] It approved the classification of fibers in the Royal Society of Arts Report, but it saved much of its main analysis for the problems created by poor-quality papers, such as featherweight papers and art papers. The main recommendations of the report were specifications for two main grades of durable paper.

About fifty years have now passed since the investigations of *The Durability of Paper Report*, and during that time an unprecedented amount of research into the problems of paper has been conducted. Indeed the Report is by now so much a document of the past that it could with some reason be forgotten were it not for two considerations. First, it was the last large-scale report prior to the spate of investigation and reports since the end of World War II and consequently helps to underline the considerable advances that have been made within a comparatively short time. Second, it was the last of the reports to place the main emphasis on the avoidance of the problems entirely through manufacturing processes. Since then responsibility has been divided between manufacture and the problems of storage and proper conservation methods, with increasing attention being paid to the latter.

During the postwar years one man above all has been associated with the investigation of these interrelated problems. The first major report issued by W. J. Barrow of the State Library of Virginia came in 1956. Since that date a series of reports has been issued based primarily on his researches that in total now present the fullest picture available of the problems and some suggested solutions.[17] A summary of Barrow's conclusions will give some indication of their scope. First: although the inherent strength of the fibers did contribute in some measure to the increasing rate of deterioration, this was not the only, nor possibly the most potent, cause. Of even greater significance was the use of acid sizing in machine-made papers. Handmade papers as well as some of the early machine papers had been tub-sized with animal gelatin. This was abandoned largely as an economic measure to avoid the second separate operation. Animal glue was unsuited to engine-sizing because it would not stay in suspension in the pulp and rosin in an acid medium was substituted. This left a residue of acidity in the paper, which was a major cause of decay and was augmented by the absorption by the paper of further acidity from the atmosphere during the years of the book's storage and use. Barrow evolved several methods for the deacidification of papers and was eventually successful in producing one that was simple in its application. He also evolved a lamination method that sealed the paper in a thin covering that would prevent further absorption of acid. This method was particularly suited to papers in which decay was already advanced and where there was an equally urgent need to preserve the paper from physical disintegration following upon chemical decay. This created a logical alternative to the old-established method of silking paper documents as a method of repair and preservation.

Barrow also investigated the effect of temperature control on paper deterioration and produced evidence that may in the long run have the most important result of all on storage conditions.

In 1964 the Association of Research Libraries issued a report that studied the implications of these researches to the role of the librarian.[18] Naturally one of the most alarming of Barrow's discoveries is the size of the problem. The Report summarized his conclusions as follows:

> Of a sample of books printed in the U.S. during the forty-year period 1900–1939, about 40% were found to be so weak that if given only moderate use they will be unusable by the general reader within another twenty years, and another 50% (or a total of 90%) will be too weak for general use within about forty-five years.

There can consequently be no doubt as to the magnitude of the problem for librarians or bibliographers. The Report also summarized the findings as to the effect of temperature on the problem.

> Paper deteriorates not only because of acid, but also because of other complex chemical reactions. It is a well-established fact that most chemical reactions vary directly with the temperature, being speeded up at higher temperatures and slowed down at lower ones. Research has demonstrated that this general law also operates in the case of paper deterioration, and that if paper is stored at a low temperature its life expectancy is significantly lengthened. The evidence indicates that the longevity of any particular paper (except newsprint) will be increased about seven and a half times for each decrease of 36°F drop in temperature. For example, a particular book with a life expectancy of twenty-five years if untreated and housed under usual library conditions, would have a life expectancy of six hundred years if de-acidified and stored at 34°F, and of over four thousand years if de-acidified and stored at −2°F.

The Committee also viewed with concern any easy acceptance of the microfilming of such vulnerable materials in order to secure their permanent preservation. Proposals on these lines had been made frequently during the postwar years, with commonly a suggestion that, if this were done, there need not be too much regard for the safety or accessibility of the originals. The Committee drew attention to two points: (a) that for many bibliographical purposes a photographic version of any kind can never provide an adequate substitute, and (b) that microfilm negatives themselves appear, according to current research, to be subject to deterioration.

Bibliographers can therefore take heart from the fact that the materials that they need are capable of long-term preservation if librarians and archivists can introduce modern methods of storage and preservation. To this end the Committee proposed a program of a nationally centralized storage scheme for materials deemed suitable for preservation "by de-acidification and storage at the lowest practical temperature (or by improved techniques if such should be discovered by future research)." Although such a scheme is not perfect, it would certainly result in the preservation of significant materials in accordance with the best information currently available as to the reasons for decay.

Bibliographical evidence of paper

The study of paper and the application of such evidence to the understanding of bibliographical problems is of comparatively recent origin. In 1908 it was not unusual for so eminent a bibliographer as A. W. Pollard to write that "in the present section of this catalogue very little use has been made of the evidence which may be lying hidden in the various kinds of papers used by the early printers, and the devices with which these papers are watermarked," and with particular reference to watermarks Pollard wrote, "But this method is laborious and not free from uncertainty, so that other kinds of evidence are almost always preferable."[19]

In the time since then the study of paper has scored notable successes in the unraveling of bibliographical problems, with the result that it now ranks high in bibliographical esteem. Much of the advance has been due to the work of Allan Stevenson. The major successes before his contribution had been individually important but limited in number. The initial success of real importance was the role of the watermarks in the understanding of the Pavier quartos, to which reference has already been made. It is evidence that also played a significant part in the unmasking of the T. J. Wise forgeries and in the revelation of the true date of the Constance Missal. Even so it would be naïve to suggest that the battle has now been won and that every bibliographical investigation now pays due attention to paper evidence. Stevenson himself wrote, "Among some bibliographers and scholars there is a belief that paper can be of little use in solving problems concerning manuscripts and printed books. In their opinion, paper and watermarks have been tried and found wanting."[20] On the other hand, some of the recent bibliographical successes of paper evidence have encouraged others to expect that almost any problem can be solved in this fashion. Stevenson again has warned against overoptimism as clearly as he warned against neglect.

The only answer I know is that paper evidence has contributed to the resolution of many minor questions of date and a few major questions of date, and that when we learn better how to use it, it should contribute more. I say "contribute" because I see no virtue in trying to solve problems through one sort of evidence alone. My thought is that an understanding of paper and an understanding of type can be of mutual assistance. To be sure, paper evidence is often beclouded with ambiguities. But so is typographical evidence. That is why they need each other.[21]

The area of paper evidence that has registered the most important success recently is undoubtedly watermark evidence and especially its application to the problem of dating. As has already been said, the function of the watermark is that of a trademark. Thus it shares a similarity of purpose, and not infrequently of design, with printers' devices, masons' marks, merchants' bale marks, and sword markings. Since watermarks are the result of the thinning of the paper caused by the raised wire design on the paper maker's frame, it follows that they are susceptible to wear. The wire design wore, broke, or merely deteriorated. If it was repaired, as distinct from being replaced, solder marks or wire ties might be visible in the watermark. These variations in the appearance of the watermark provide assistance in the process of dating. The theory behind such work is disarmingly simple. Assume that a paper mill adopts a cornucopia as the watermark design. The mill would certainly have more than one frame on which paper was made. The wire design for the mark would need to be woven into the mesh of each frame and would need complete replacement after a number of years. Since the mark was intended solely as a trademark, there would be no reason to attempt an exact remodeling of the design. Variations between the designs of individual marks have been the subject of a number of special studies, which have recorded such variations and ascribed a date to them. This has been made possible by the appearance of watermarks in a large number of dated books and the fact that at certain periods some watermarks have themselves included a date. Works like those by Briquet, Churchill, and Heawood provide examples of such studies.[22] The accepted procedure, therefore, is to discover the watermark in the paper of the book under discussion, compare its design and state with one in one of the reference sources, and so move logically to a date.

Practice does, however, add a few complications to this simple route. The basic injunction to find the watermark in the paper itself raises difficulties. A student handling a first example for bibliographical analysis may not immediately appreciate a fact that later becomes obvious—that the first sheet in a copy was not followed through the press by the second sheet in that same copy but by the first sheet in another copy of the work. Assuming a printing of five hundred copies and imagining, simplistically, a pile of sheets by the press, the sheet for the first gathering within a copy would be followed in the next gathering by the 501st sheet in the pile, then by the 1001st, the 1501st, and so on. This kind of realization reduces any initial surprise that there should be several different watermarks in a single copy, especially if it is a large work.

Experience will also be needed in the location and above all in the transcription of the watermark. The relationship between format and position of a watermark is dealt with in more detail in a following chapter, but it will be readily apparent that, given a sheet with a regularly placed watermark, only in a folio format will a whole watermark be found (*Fig.* 10). In other formats it will be divided into halves by the sewing (quarto), into quarters in top inner corners (octavo), and so on. In such instances the watermark design needs to be assembled from the parts, and in some designs this is far from straightforward. Before a comparison can be made with any other watermark, however recorded, the mark must be drawn or traced. A watermark in a folio, obscured in the center of a leaf by heavy printing, or in sections in other formats, is frequently neither seen nor recorded without difficulty. Suitable facilities are available in all too few libraries or research centers. There is nevertheless an insistence that such recordings should be minutely accurate in order that detailed comparisons may be made. A realization of these problems also raises questions as to the accuracy of the drawings in such tools as Briquet, with which the comparisons will be made. Differences between one watermark and the most clearly similar one to it in any of the reference works is frequently minute. A beginning student will discover that adequate light sources for viewing watermarks are not found in many libraries, that it is difficult to trace the watermark accurately with normal facilities, and that vital adjuncts to the design itself, such as sewing dots, are at first difficult to spot.

In the postwar years technology has made a major contribution to the study of watermarks, creating a revolution that will have a radical effect on paper and watermark evidence. In the new method a glass or plastic plate, impregnated with a Beta-radiographic isotype, is placed against the leaf from which it is necessary to reproduce the watermark. A piece of photographic film or sensitized paper is placed on the other side of the leaf and the book closed for a short time. The result will be a clear record on the film in which the watermark will be shown as a light design against a dark background and without any interference from the reproduction of type, or of writing, stains, and such like. It is the most perfect method for the reproduction of watermarks so far devised.[23]

The description of paper

Descriptive bibliography sets out to record the basic bibliographical features of a book or document. It has therefore changed as bibliographical investigation has advanced and produced more information that it was essential to record. Much of the most important study of paper has been in the last twenty-five or so years; consequently it is not surprising that many bibliographers have in the past made no reference whatsoever to paper in their descriptions. It is much more difficult to understand why, with the importance of paper evidence clearly established, bibliographers of the present day can still disregard it in their published statements. One bibliography and one catalog of recent years have provided virtually the only substantial attempts to include such information. The first was Philip Gaskell's bibliography of John Baskerville[24] and, second, Allan Stevenson's portion of the catalog of the Hunt Botanical Library.[25] The lack of practical applications in bibliographical work is matched by the paucity of any serious discussion as to the information that such a part of an entry should contain. The clearest guidance is given by Stevenson in his introduction in the first part of the second volume of the Hunt Catalogue and by Tanselle in one paper that was published after both Gaskell and Stevenson and so able to refer to both.[26]

The basic information relating to paper that it is now reasonable to expect to find recorded in a description would include:

(a) The size of the sheet. This refers to the whole sheet as it went on to the printing press. This will involve a calculation on the part of the bibliographer. A start must be made with the measurement of the single leaf multiplied as appropriate according to the format of the book. Thus a folio in which a leaf measured, untrimmed, 15 inches in height by 10 inches in width would be a sheet 20″ × 15″; a quarto from that same sheet would measure 10″ × 7½″ and an octavo, 7½″ × 5″. This is an area where more investigation needs to be done in order to clarify the nomenclature and actual sizes that have been utilized. Enough has been done, however, to enable a useful attempt to be made even though it may lack the ultimate precision that is desirable.

(b) Water marks and laid marks. Watermarks, including countermarks when present, should be described in sufficient detail to allow certain identification. This should include the measurement of the mark given, as is common with all bibliographical measurements, in the form of height by width. Whenever possible they should be identified with reference to any bibliographical record of them. There should be a statement as to whether the paper is laid or wove and, if the former, the measurement between chain lines should be given.

(c) The measurement of a normal leaf within the book. This should be the actual measurement, that is, not allowing for any reduction in this particular copy for trimming or for shrinkage. The variations which would thereby be on record relative to several copies of a single work could be of prime importance to the bibliographer in a study of the work as a whole.

Examples will show how Gaskell and Stevenson applied their general principles in two particular instances:

Gaskell 20. *The Book of Common Prayer*, 1762.

Paper: Thin, medium quality laid, marks Fleur-de-lys in a shield crowned over LVG/IV; no uncut copy seen but size of sheet at least 20½ x 16¼ in., so probably *Writing Medium.*

Stevenson 473. Langley, Batty. *A Sure Method of Improving Estates.* London. 1728.

Paper: Demy, Italian, fine, marked GF with "spectacles" in corner, except sheet E, marked I with "spectacles" in corner. Plate: ordinary paper, probably English, countermarked IV. Leaf 7.6 × 4.9″.

In addition to these essential elements in a description, Tanselle suggests three additional ones: thickness, color, and finish. Given these six items, there is no doubt that the evidence of paper would be recorded in bibliographical descriptions at a level far in advance of general modern practice. It might be argued that to provide as much detail as this in every case would produce a superabundance of detail. Something similar to this could be urged in respect of any other category within a description. They do, however, represent the headings within which the bibliographer should feel obligated to provide information if it is appropriate to the work under scrutiny.

REFERENCES

1. PLINY. *Natural History*. XIII, Ch. 11–12.

2. CERNY, Jaroslav. *Paper and Books in Ancient Egypt*. 1952. p. 6.

3. KENYON, Frederic G. *Books and Readers in Ancient Greece and Rome*. 2nd ed. 1951. pp. 52–55.

4. LEWIS, Naphtali. *Papyrus in Classical Antiquity*. 1974.

5. Kenyon, pp. 87–120.

6. ROBERTS, C. H. "The Codex." *Proceedings of the British Academy.* XL: 1954. pp. 169–204.

7. REED, Ronald. *The Nature and Making of Parchment.* 1975.

8. CLAPPERTON, R. H. *Modern Paper-making.* 3rd ed. 1952.
COLEMAN, D.C. *The British Paper Industry, 1495–1860.* 1958.
HUNTER, Dard. *Paper Making; The History and Technique of an Ancient Craft.* 2nd ed. 1947.
HUNTER, Dard. *Paper Making Through Eighteen Centuries.* 1930.
LABARRE, E. J. *Dictionary and Encyclopedia of Paper and Paper Making, with Equivalents of the Technical Terms in French, German, Dutch, Italian, Spanish and Swedish.* 2nd ed. 1952.
LEIF, Irving P. *An International Source Book of Paper History.* 1978.
PAPER PUBLICATIONS SOCIETY. *Monumenta Chartae Papyraceae Historiam Illustrantia, or, Collection of Works and Documents Illustrating the History of Paper.* 1950–. General editor: E. J. Labarre. Contents:

v.1. Heawood, Edward. *Watermarks, Mainly of Seventeenth and Eighteenth Centuries.* 1950.
v.2. *The Briquet Album.* 1952.
v.3. *Zonghi's Watermarks.* 1953.
v.4. *Briquet's Opuscula.* 1955.
v.5. *The Nostitz Papers.* 1956.
v.6. Shorter, A. H. *Paper Mills and Paper Makers in England, 1495–1800.* 1957.
v.7. Tscheidin, W. F. *The Ancient Paper Mills of Basle and Their Marks.* 1958.
v.8. Eineder, G. *The Ancient Paper Mills of the Former Austro-Hungarian Empire and Their Watermarks.* 1960.
v.9. Uchastkina, Z. V. *A History of Russian Hand Paper Mills and Their Water-marks.* 1962.
v.10. Lindt, J. *The Paper Mills of Berne and Their Watermarks.* 1964.
v.11. *Tromonin's Watermark Album.* 1965.
v.12. Subirà, Oriol Valls I. *Paper and Watermarks in Catalonia.* 2v. 1970.
v.13. Mošin, Vladimir. *Anchor Watermarks.* 1973.

9. UNESCO. *Paper for Printing: Today and Tomorrow. By the Intelligence Unit of The Economist.* 1952.

10. SUTCLIFFE, Peter. *The Oxford University Press: An Informal History.* 1978. pp. 39–40.

11. *Catalogue of Botanical Books in the Collection of Rachel McMasters Miller Hunt.* Vol. II. 1961. p. ccxxvii.

12. GASKELL, Philip. "Notes on Eighteenth-Century British Paper." *The Library.* 5th Series. XII: 1957. pp. 34–42.
    POLLARD, Graham. "Notes on the Size of the Sheet." *The Library.* 4th Series. XXII: 1941–42. pp. 105–137.

13. *The Gentleman's Magazine.* XCIII: July 1823. pp. 21–22.

14. MURRAY, John. *Practical Remarks on Modern Paper with an . . . Account of Its Former Substitutes.* 1829.

15. ROYAL SOCIETY OF ARTS. Report of Committee on *The Deterioration of Paper.* 1898.

16. LIBRARY ASSOCIATION. *The Durability of Paper.* Report of the special committee set up by the Library Association. 1930.

17. BARROW, W. J. *Manuscripts and Documents; Their Deterioration and Restoration.* 1955.
    CHURCH, Randolph W., ed. *Deterioration of Book Stock, Causes and Remedies.* Two studies . . . conducted by W. J. Barrow. 1959.
    CHURCH, Randolph W., ed. *The Manufacture and Testing of Durable Book Papers.* Based on the investigations of W. J. Barrow. 1960.
    Permanent/Durable Book Paper. Summary of a Conference . . . Sponsored by the American Library Association and the Virginia State Library. 1960.

    The W. J. Barrow Research Laboratory has also issued a series of reports from 1963 onward entitled *Permanence/Durability of the Book.* These are concerned with the problems of the book as a whole but include material on later researches into paper.

18. *The Preservation of Deteriorating Books: An Examination of the Problem with Recommendations for a Solution.* Report of the ARL Committee on the Preservation of Research Library Materials. 1964.

19. BRITISH MUSEUM. Catalogue of Books Printed in the XVth Century. . . . Part 1. 1908. p. xv.

20. STEVENSON, Allan. Observations on Paper as Evidence. 1961. p. 11.

21. STEVENSON, p. 19.

22. The main basic work on watermarks is:

BRIQUET, C. M. Les Filigranes, dictionnaire historique des marques du papier. 2nd ed. 4v. 1923. Reprinted 1966.

Briquet followed watermarks up to 1600. Other works have gone beyond this point chronologically, while others have surveyed related areas. Examples of these that are important are:

CHURCHILL, W. A. Watermarks in Paper in Holland, England, France, etc. in the XVII and XVIII Centuries and Their Intercommunications. 1935.
HEAWOOD, Edward. Watermarks, Mainly of the Seventeenth and Eighteenth Centuries. 1950.

23. The method was first described in a Russian journal by D. P. Erastov in 1960. It was first communicated in English by J. S. G. Simmons in an article, "The Leningrad Method of Watermark Reproduction," in Book Collector, X: 1961, pp. 329–330. The clearest example of the use of this new technique and certainly the best statement of its advantages over older methods is in Allan Stevenson's The Problem of the "Missale Special," 1967. Chapter V, "Time Lag and Identity," is especially relevant, but the whole book should be read as one of the outstanding bibliographic detective stories of this century. Another, much briefer, article by Stevenson that also makes the advantages of the method clear is "Quincentennial of Netherlandish Block Books," in British Museum Quarterly, XXXI: 1966–67, pp. 83–87. Further research has been conducted with such results as those communicated by J. S. G. Simmons, "The Delft Method of Watermark Reproduction," in Book Collector, XVIII: 1969, pp. 514–515. There has also been investigation of other methods, such as T. L. Gravell's "A New Method of Reproducing Watermarks for Study," in Restaurator II: 1975. pp. 95–104.

24. GASKELL, Philip. *John Baskerville: A Bibliography.* 1959.

25. *Catalogue of Botanical Books in the Collection of Rachel McMasters Miller Hunt.*
    Volume II Part 1. Introduction to Printed Books 1701–1800. Compiled by Allan Stevenson. 1961.
    Volume II Part 2. Printed Books 1701–1800. Compiled by Allan Stevenson. 1961.

26. TANSELLE, G. Thomas. "The Bibliographical Description of Paper." *Studies in Bibliography.* XXIV: 1971. pp. 27–67.

5.

TYPOGRAPHY

The process of book production, or, as A. W. Pollard called it, "book-building," has been many times described and in its elements is quite easy of comprehension. It must now be outlined because the bibliographer, in examining books, will constantly be faced with problems that can only be solved by reconstructing in the mind exactly what happened in the printer's office. As McKerrow said:

> The numerous processes through which all books pass are perfectly simple, and very little trouble will suffice for the understanding of them. What is needed is that they shall be grasped so clearly as to be constantly present to the mind of the student as he handles a book, so that he sees this not only from the point of view of the reader interested in it as literature, but also from the points of view of those who composed, corrected, printed, folded and bound it; in short, so that he sees it not only as a unit but as an assemblage of parts, each of which is the result of a clearly apprehended series of processes. [1]

The first three of these processes are included in the generic term "printing."

When we speak of printing, we generally mean book printing, but if so we are using the term loosely. "Printing" covers the very ancient art of taking impressions from blocks of wood or metal on paper or on textiles. In all its forms, from early textile printing to printing from woodblocks onto paper and then to unsophisticated methods of printing from movable pieces of type, the Far Eastern contribution preceded any known experimentation in Europe. Gutenberg's achievement in Mainz was the introduction of movable-type printing into Europe, and without almost any shadow of doubt his was a discovery quite independent of what had passed in the Far East. It is this that is usually referred to simply as printing: the taking of multiple impressions from an inked surface composed of individual movable letter units, or "types." The art and science of creating, designing, and adapting letter forms to this particular use is the business of typography as distinct from printing, which is the use of material so created. The complete collection of "sorts" (*a*, *b*, etc., being each a "sort") of any one design makes up one particular "font" (*anglice,* "fount"). The artist's original design for each is transferred to a tool, or "punch," of hard metal, on which it is cut in relief. The punches are practically eternal, and a font of which the punches survive can always be revived—as occurred when Whittingham and Pickering had recourse, about 1840, to the old firm of Caslon for their round fonts of the early eighteenth century.

The punch is stamped with force into a block of soft metal, frequently copper, which thus becomes the "matrix," in which the face of the type is cast. Hand-cast type was manufactured in a small mold that could be held in the type founder's left hand. It consisted of two parts, brought together for the operation itself, and the appropriate matrix was inserted into the mold. With a long-handled ladle the founder poured molten type metal into the mouth of the mold, shook the mold vigorously to prevent air bubbles (which would weaken the type), and so created a single sort. The excess metal at the foot of the sort was broken off and the shank was smoothed. According to Moxon's estimate a good worker could cast four thousand pieces a day. There are a number of representations of type founders at work[2] and some early descriptions of their methods;[3] in some museums pieces of the actual equipment can be seen.[4] The type metal is an alloy of lead, tin, and antimony; their proportions have varied over the centuries, and at any one time according to its use, but the alloy is and always has been largely lead.

The craft of the type founder began to be separated from that of the printer in the fifteenth century, and specialist type foundries were set up throughout Europe. At first all printers were their own type founders and very probably their own type cutters also. But as early as 1493 Nicolas Wolf of Brunswick was established as a "fondeur de lettres" in Lyons. Others followed, and there were eighteen type founders in Lyons alone in the first half of the -sixteenth century. Claude Garamond (*c.* 1480–1561) was one of the forerunners in concentrating on founding types, a trade that was expanded to international proportions by Robert Granjon

(c. 1510–c. 1590). Great type foundries were established at numerous places in Europe, some, like the Enschédé factory in Holland, surviving to the present day. Important houses, such as Plantin's at Antwerp in the sixteenth century or Clarendon Press today, maintain their own type foundries, but the normal practice is for printers to purchase type from the foundries by font and weight, a pound of type containing letters of each sort in a recognized proportion for any language. These proportions were worked out by the founders and presented to the purchasers as "bills of type" or "bills of letters." This ensured the correct quantities of individual letters, punctuation signs, spaces, etc., within any given weight.[5]

The diagram below shows the shape and the names of the parts of a piece of type. Type is of a standard height, from foot to face, of .918 of an English inch, so that the faces, which stand up in relief and take the ink that is rolled over them, make an even surface and give a consistent impression on the paper.

Measurement of type

A font of type is normally made in a variety of sizes. These sizes used to be known by a number of picturesque traditional names, differing from country to country and in any case not easy for any but a printer to keep in the memory. In England there were many names used over the centuries, some of them long lasting from one printing generation to another. Such names as Canon, Great Primer, English, Pica, Long Primer, Brevier, Nonpareil, and Pearl were in constant use. The problems arose from lack of any standardization within those names. C. J. Jacobi, a printer of great experience, wrote that the old system "resulted in chaos, for as a rule no two fonts of the same body made by different founders could be used together." The problem was compounded by the fact that French, German, Dutch, Italian, and Spanish foundries used names that were only rarely recognizable as bearing any relationship to each other for the approximate, not the actual, similar sizes.

Early in the eighteenth century French typographers made the first substantial efforts to regularize the system of type measurement. The first truly successful scheme was formulated by Pierre

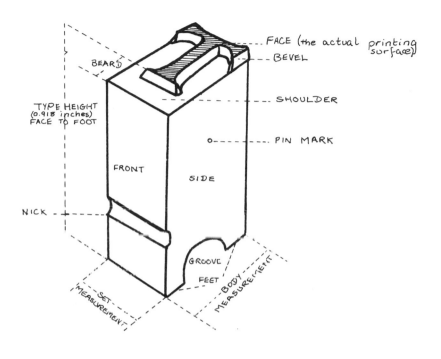

FIG. 7.   A *piece of type*

Fournier in 1737, followed by another improved system by Didot in 1780. The unit of measurement in both cases was the *point*, one unit of which in Fournier's scheme measured .0137 of an English inch and in Didot's .0148. England, Germany, and Italy were slow to adopt the revised method of measurement. In America, where much of the type was still imported from Europe during the first half or so of the nineteenth century, the evolving American type-founding industry maintained the old name system. The point system was introduced into American type founding around 1870, and it was the American system that was finally accepted in Britain in the early years of the twentieth century, mainly under the influence of the Monotype machine setting.[6] In this version the point measured .013837 or approximately 1/72 of an English inch. It is still too early to say whether the widespread move toward metric measurement and new economic regional groupings will have any effect on systems of type measurement or whether they will become redundant with the advent of new printing methods.[7] There are no exact equations between the point sizes as they are expressed in 8, 10, 12 point, and so on, with the old names that they have replaced.

The measurement of type is made by the distance between the front and back of a piece of type, the measurement being known as the "body." It is important to remember that the measurement is *not* of the typeface itself. Thus, when faces are cast on larger bodies in order to save leading (that is, the space between lines), as is now common, such expressions as "an 11-point type on a 12-point body" are used.

The "set" of a type—its width—is also measured in points. Certain fonts are spoken of as having a "wide set" or a "narrow set," meaning that the letters are inclined to be wide or narrow in relation to their size. This is a matter of some importance when a type design is being chosen for any work, affecting as it does the amount of paper that will be necessary. Type is measured laterally and the extent of a piece of composition is reckoned in "ens." An en is half the measurement of an "em," which is the square of the body height of the type and therefore variable. Thus in a 10-point type an em equals 10-point, or in an 18-point type an em equals 18-point. In modern printing parlance an em is frequently regarded as 12-point, since this is the type size in the most general use. Opinions vary as to whether the word "em" had any connection with the letter *m*. The early types, however, were cast solid (that is, the face height equaled the body height), as can be tested by laying a rule along the tops of the ascenders of a line of print and noting if the descenders of the line above touch it. Otherwise the type may be either leaded or cast on a large body, and either is comparatively rare in the early period of printing. When the letter *m* is cast solid, the piece of type would be practically square, and the letter *n* would be about half the width of the letter *m*. It is thus difficult to believe that the words "em" and "en" originally meant anything but the letters. From the late eighteenth century, and increasingly through the trade agreements of the nineteenth, the en became the basis of calculation for compositors' wages.

All questions of good type design and problems of legibility must be viewed against the background of the function of type. It is sometimes easy to overlook the fact that type is not there to be admired for its own sake. The old cliché says that type should be invisible; like most clichés it has an element of truth. If the eye and the mind pause to admire a type design, it has to some extent failed in its purpose, which is to transmit the author's message. Because of this it is often said that any eccentricity or marked peculiarity of design must be bad. This is true, and on this statement much could be built if only human beings, whether printers or readers, could agree as to the limits of eccentricity. Ligatures, which many modern readers regard with abhorrence, were regarded by Aldus as one of the commendable features of his italic font. To many readers the mixture of upper-case forms with lower-case forms in the lower case of the King's Font of the Avon Press was eccentric, but it does not affect all readers equally. When matters of pure design are discussed, purely aesthetic considerations rule the judgment. On these we can never expect, nor should we hope, to achieve an unanimity of opinion. Never has this dilemma been more clearly expressed than in Stanley Morison's celebrated essay "First Principles of Typography":

> Typography may be defined as the art of rightly disposing printing material in accordance with specific purpose; of so arranging the letters, distributing the space and controlling the type as to aid to the maximum the reader's comprehension of the text. Typography is the efficient means to an essentially utilitarian and only accidentally aesthetic end, for enjoyment of patterns is rarely the reader's chief aim. Therefore, any disposition of printing material which, whatever the intention, has the effect of coming between author and reader is wrong.[8]

Type can, however, be analyzed and discussed from a purely factual standpoint. One font has a wider set than another; one is large on the body, another small; one has a wide range of sizes and series, another is limited; one is available for machine setting, another is not. These are important matters for consideration and have clear and direct results; they are precisely the aspects of the type that need to be recorded in a description. They do not become entangled with questions as to whether it is a good design or not, or whether it is suited to the printing of any particular work or kind of works.

Matters of legibility will also loom large, and some of the discussion here may turn again on matters of design. On the whole, however, design is legible in proportion to its familiarity to the eye. Other considerations can affect matters more fundamentally. Experiments have always indicated that there are at least two different considerations of type in this respect. There can easily be shown to be a difference between immediate legibility and long-term readability. For the former, as with display work—the title pages of books, for example—the chief requirement is instant recognition. An unusual design in general or shape of particular letters can help achieve this. Sans serif types, although sufficiently familiar by now not to appear as eccentric, come within this category because they lack the required qualities for long-term readability. Another factor is the relationship between types and paper both for color and texture. Strong contrasts can be accepted when the criterion is for immediate legibility only, such as black ink on yellow paper. Long-term readability, on the other hand, can be achieved by serifed types with more subtly toned relationships between type and paper. The contrast here must not be as startling as can be used for display purposes, and indeed too black an ink on too white a paper is not desirable. This was the contemporary objection raised to the standards of Baskerville's printing and, exaggerated though it might have been, it has some sound basis in fact. Baskerville did, however, demonstrate one relationship that is still held to be valid. He used a wove paper in order that no irregularity of paper surface should detract from the beauty of his classical type designs. In this he was right. For the full demonstration of its quality, including some measure of legibility, modern-face type needs a smooth-surfaced paper. This should not be taken to imply a shiny surface. No text requires a shiny surface if it is to retain any measure at all of readability. Old-face or old-style types, on the other hand, need a matte surface if they are to achieve their full effect. The overall principle is clear, that type design must be attuned to the quality and surface of the paper if it is to achieve its full effect. Legibility of type is therefore a combination of related factors. To these must be added considerations of spacing, length of line, and so on, when the problems of composition are faced.

All discussions on typography lead to one inevitable conclusion. *What is really at issue is not type design but letter design.* The reader is looking at letter forms in the book, with only scant regard for the manner in which they arrived on the paper. The manuscript scribe was not limited by what the "soldiers of lead" could accomplish. Some book makers, such as the printer of the *Theuerdanck* (1517) and William Blake, strove to overcome such restrictions. The advent of photocomposition, of which more will be said later, has permitted the book designer to exercise greater freedom in typography. This emphasis on letter forms is one of the many major contributions of Stanley Morison to this study. His interests covered not only typography, with which his name is most readily associated, but also carved inscriptions, calligraphy, writing books, manuscript book hands—anything that symbolically conveyed a message. His friend and colleague Beatrice Warde, who shared this catholicity, was excited by the illuminated signs used for "textual" purposes along New York's Broadway and Times Square. Many of the greatest type designers, notably Eric Gill, conveyed this in the breadth of their work. It is an outlook that must be borne in mind when looking at the main families of typefaces.

Typefaces

1. GOTHIC

In the age of the manuscript every large district had its own peculiar style of handwriting, and these fell into the broad classes of cursive, rapid book hand, and formal book hand. In certain instances, when the quantity of manuscript work was considerable, manuscript styles could exhibit recognizable peculiarities within a very limited area. Although these national, regional, and highly localized variations occurred, equally recognizable similarities existed also. Until the middle of the fifteenth century manuscript hands in Europe still demonstrated their common origins from the script of the Roman Empire. The hands used up to this moment of the introduction of movable-type printing are known now as *gothic* hands. Contrary to some general impressions, this is not a particularly "German" hand. Its use was widespread in Europe.

When early printers came to produce their earliest type designs, it was only natural that they should lean heavily upon the manuscript traditions. They set out initially to provide something closely resembling the manuscript book in all important essentials, and accordingly their fonts of type reproduced the book hands of the locality. To these early local styles the name *gothic* was again applied or in the descriptive English phrase, "black letter," as opposed to roman or "white letter." As manuscript hands had introduced variations, based not solely on locality but also on the kind of text being written, so were similar styles developed for early book types. Some of the most significant divisions in the classification of early type designs were in fact based on this kind of analysis.

It is now usual to divide the early gothic fonts into four main classes. First is one representing the formal, pointed, upright scripts reserved for Bibles and service books for choir desks. This category includes the most formal of all the Gothic fonts and is called *textura* by the Germans and *lettre de forme* by the French. Second is a smaller and more cursive type used for other Latin books. It retained very marked Gothic qualities but was considerably less formal than textura. This second class was known as *fere-humanistica* or *gotico-antiqua* by the Germans and *lettre de somme* by the French. Still less formal was the third class of *rotunda* types, which is largely an Italian style of gothic and shows a much more open quality. Lastly, most cursive of all, used chiefly for books printed in the vernacular, was the *lettre bâtarde* or, in the German, *bastarda*. In Germany there was developed out of bastarda, which is cursive, the *fraktur*, a pointed cursive of an unexampled ugliness, which in the sixteenth century ousted the other styles and reigned supreme till the nineteenth century. An extreme case of the length to which the flourish could go in German *fraktur* is seen in the books lavishly printed by Schönsperger at Nuremberg in and about 1517 under the patronage of the Emperor Maximilian II, notably Melchior Pfintzing's *Theuerdank*. It is said that technically such printing was very difficult. One might go farther, and, like Dr. Johnson, wish that it had been impossible.

In France and the southern Netherlands a local variety of bastard (*lettre bâtarde*) was used in the fifteenth century, especially for French vernacular and secular literature. The forerunners of these types can also be identified in earlier and contemporary manuscripts. French manuscripts of some of the great tales of chivalry and romance were written in a hand strikingly similar to the "lettre bâtarde" fonts, which can be seen, for example, in the popular books in the vernacular printed by Antoine Vérard in Paris. This is the general style of Caxton's first fonts, both those that he used with Colard Mansion at Bruges and his earliest Westminster fonts, though the latter were of a more fantastic and pointed kind. Unhappily for early English printing Caxton's models were more the Burgundian bastarda that enjoyed a vogue in the Netherlands rather than the French style, and they were undoubtedly the worst of all. It remained for Pynson, who benefited English printing in so many ways, to introduce the French pattern. Luckily this was the dominant element in the later use of this type in England until it finally passed out of general use around 1535. The characteristic of true bastard (to use a paradoxical phrase) is that the letters are narrow and slope somewhat as in italic; that there are more descenders, such as the *f*, ending in a point; and that the ascenders are usually looped. The whole effect is strikingly cursive.

Except in Germany, where it has persisted into this present century, gothic was driven out by roman in the course of the first century of printing. Yet even in Germany, where Gothic has in modern times appeared to be so securely established, the possibility of change has long been apparent. German type designers have attempted to break into new fields, if only into the functionalism of the "Bauhaus" roman. Modern German designers, such as Hermann Zapf, have done their best work in roman designs. In Italy gothic was from the beginning excluded from the service of the new learning, though it was used for legal and medical books. Its native form was a rather narrow rotunda, except in Naples, where Spanish influence was strong and the typical book of the finer kind showed a rich and stately combination of heavy gothic text and solid black border decorations or woodcut illustrations. E. P. Goldschmidt has shown how closely in this instance the subject matter and general tenor of the book significantly affected the type in which the text could be printed.[9] In France gothic was driven out in the third and fourth decades of the sixteenth century by the roman types and correspondingly light decorations of Tory and his pupils and followers. In Spain, the Netherlands, and England it lasted longer.

Early English black letter had heaviness and illegibility without being redeemed by beauty. Early models were unfortunate in their choice, and for some reason native ingenuity and qualities of design were unable for a long time to improve upon them. Updike's conclusion was that

> if the earliest types cast in England were somewhat unattractive in design and rough in execution, it was not because the types were early types, for at that same time in other countries types were better; nor because of any lack of good models, for English black-letter manuscripts were often very beautiful. But in England few early native types had what we should call "feeling." Type cutting and type-designing did not, apparently, at first come easily or instinctively to the English. Their best early types were imported.[10]

It was chiefly for the printing of law books that the use of gothic was retained in England and for the English text when it had to be differentiated from Latin. For these purposes it can frequently be found well into the seventeenth century. After that time it has been largely out of favor, and even William Morris failed to restore it to fashion. Although his Troy type was a very simplified font, and there is no doubt that two pages of gothic type, owing to its thick lines, and especially when combined with solid woodcut decorations, are a very handsome spectacle, unfortunately to the modern unaccustomed eye it is not highly legible. Nevertheless, it must be pointed out that much of the modern popular antipathy to the Kelmscott Press gothic books is due to their having been seen mainly through reduced facsimiles rather than in the original.

It is indeed altogether too easy for the modern eye to reject gothic as a typographic aberration and to lose sight of its place in the development of letter forms. In countries where the tradition of roman lettering is strong and where few examples of Gothic type in books of recent centuries exist—throughout the English-speaking world, for instance—the modern use of Gothic type does not help the situation. Although it rarely appears in book form, its use is common as a differentiation type in much jobbing printing. Such faces might generically be granted the title of gothic or black letter, but they are usually versions with no historic pedigree and with minimal resemblance to the genuine article.

2. ROMAN

Italian humanists in the half-century that preceded the introduction of printing into Italy had been using for Classical texts a small book hand based on the beautiful "caroline minuscule," the hand taught under Alcuin's influence in the schools of Charlemagne. This hand was afterward called, in Italy and France, *lettera rotunda, lettre ronde,* or round letter, and elsewhere *antiqua.* This became the basis for some of the best known and most widely appreciated of all type designs that are generally known as "roman" and used, by printers in English, almost to the exclusion of all others. To the minuscules so designed were added majuscules based on the inscriptions of ancient Rome, and from first to last the finest roman upper case has always been that which smacked most of its origin.

A humanistic type first appeared in Italy when Sweynheym and Pannartz printed the *Lactantius* at Subiaco in a type that was rather more roman than fere-humanistica (*Fig.* 3). Stanley Morison has shown how closely this type did in fact follow its calligraphic origins, and he has suggested that it can be called the first roman type without any reservation.[11] Following soon after this Adolf Rusch used at Strassburg a purer roman, and before his recent identification he was known as "The R-Printer" from the distinctive upper-case R that he used in that font. Germany also produced, among its comparatively few roman types, one that was used by Lienhart Holle at Ulm in 1482 to print his edition of Ptolemy's *Geographia.* As A. F. Johnson pointed out, however, this was a type that, while still roman in its general characteristics, retained "a gothic g and a rather angular e."[12] For the first decades type designs thus indicated a variety of influences, and it was to be the role of Italian printing to produce the first fully-fledged Roman types of remarkable legibility and outstanding beauty.

Sweynheym and Pannartz went on in 1467 from Subiaco to Rome, where they used a purely roman form; but a better design was produced at Venice in 1470 by Nicolas Jenson, a Frenchman, who had been master of the Mint at Tours. This type has often been called the most beautiful ever cut and has been the inspiration of many later roman fonts of importance, including William Morris's Golden, Bruce Rogers's Centaur, and the American Type Founders' Cloister type. Even so, it has probably been less influential than that of Aldus.

The earliest roman types that were produced for Aldus by his type designer and cutter, Francesco Griffo, were influential in their own time and have remained so to the present day. The later state of them, however, as used in his 1499 printing of Colonna's Hypnerotomachia Poliphili, had an even greater effect, due possibly in some measure to the regard in which the book has always been held. It deserves its considerable reputation as much for its type as for its woodcuts, and not less for the harmony of the two.[13]

Aldus's roman, and also his italic, was the model used in France about 1530 by Claude Garamond, a pupil of Geofroy Tory, who had studied in Italy. Tory was one of the greatest of all printing craftsmen in the sixteenth century, and in his attractively written book Champ Fleury (1529) had made a study of the design of roman letters. The types of Garamond, used by the royal printers of France, together with those of Robert Granjon, both of which were used by the great Antwerp printer Christopher Plantin, dominated type design in Europe for a couple of centuries.

The most attractive achievements of French printing in the later sixteenth century, the small books printed by Jean de Tournes at Lyons, owe perhaps less to type design than to his lovely arabesque ornaments. The Wars of Religion threw a blight over French printing, though not so badly as did the Thirty Years War in the next century over Germany. Louis XIV founded in 1640 the Imprimerie Royale, with at least the active cooperation of Cardinal Richelieu, and made Sebastien Cramoisy the first director. In 1692 Philippe Grandjean cut for it an immensely influential type, the *romain du roi*, in which the movement of the succeeding century toward lightness and the effect of engraving, which culminated in Bulmer, Bodoni, and Didot, is already to be seen. But it was Simon Pierre Fournier, called le jeune, best known by his *Manuel Typographique* of 1764–[1768] and by being the first author of the Continental point-system of measuring types, who designed types with shading and decoration, adapting them to the engraved vignettes by Eisen, Moreau le jeune, and others, which characterized the dainty little French *livres à gravures* of the eighteenth century.

Roman type had appeared in England in the hands of Pynson in 1509. It was used for Latin at first, but by the end of the century it had pretty well ousted black letter. Except for John Day, few English type founders deserve praise. In 1672 Dr. John Fell, anxious to present the University of Oxford with a printing outfit, had to send emissaries to Holland, and they, with infinite difficulty, purchased matrices from Dutch founders. The Fell types are still in use at the Clarendon Press and are well known.[14]

In 1722 William Caslon the First cut for William Bowyer his very pleasant round roman, resembling the old Dutch and not the new French royal model. This soon came into general use, only falling out at the end of the century, to be revived forty years later as what is called "old-face."

Caslon is remembered and revered for the unobtrusive sturdiness of his design, a quality that was so much to the fore in the Dutch styles that influenced him. Recent advances and fashions appear not to have affected him at all, and few type designs have been more subservient to their textual matter. If, as has been suggested, the function of type design is to be invisible, then Caslon was successful to a remarkable degree.[15]

At the time when Caslon was working, however, a greater and more fundamental change was beginning to take place. From the time of Aldus onward the roman letter was based on the manuscript hand and showed, in spite of all expressions of typographic individuality, clear traces of that origin. The types based on that model form the group that we now know as old-face types. The general characteristics are: (a) a tendency toward an evenness of shading over the whole of the letter, and (b) rather solid and chunky, or, at least, triangular serifs to the letters. When any

variation in the thickness of the stroke—that is, the shading—
was apparent, then it was a diagonal emphasis, as would follow in
writing when the pen was held at an angle. In the early part of
the eighteenth century calligraphers began to prepare their designs for production by copper-engraved plates. In doing so the
pen was held at right-angles to the paper, which produced a
vertical rather than an oblique stress, and a marked variation
became apparent between the somewhat exaggerated thickness
of the main stroke and the fine thinness of the hairline. In due
course these changes in calligraphic styles began to influence
type designs, and what we know as modern-face type was on the
way to its birth. It is important to realize that two completely
distinct and opposing traditions of design do not exist. All type
designs are made up of a mixture of influences and trends and can
consequently exhibit these in a variety of ways. There are type
designs that can be labeled as distinctly old-face as there are
designs that can be classified as markedly modern-face. In between the indisputable cases are those in which the influences
are mixed. Before types were produced that exhibited to the full
all the characteristics of modern-face, there were those in which
the influences can be' seen to emerge and that accordingly are
frequently called transitional types.

The first printer in whose work the new influences can be seen
was John Baskerville of Birmingham.[16] He was formerly an engraver and writing master and so fully aware of the developments
in calligraphic styles. Beatrice Warde has pointed out that he was
in fact translating into type a style that was already the vogue
among calligraphers.[17] In 1757 he produced the quarto *Virgil*
with types, cut by himself, of greater lightness and regularity
than had before been seen in any English font. In the following
year he was appointed printer to the University of Cambridge, an
office that he held for ten years, printing notably a very fine
Bible in 1763. His printing was appreciated in France, where it
was in the movement set on foot by Grandjean with his *romain
du roi* toward a light and engraved appearance of the printed
page. After his death Baskerville's types were bought by
Beaumarchais, together with his stocks of paper and the secret of
hot-pressing, and used for printing two editions of Voltaire.

After a long sojourn in France, Baskerville's original punches and matrices have now returned to their own country, the gift of M. Charles Peignot to the University of Cambridge.[18]

Types of the latter half of the eighteenth century became narrower and lighter, notably in the hair strokes; serifs lost the air of the pen's first touch on the paper, and were square; the shading and stress of letters was vertical rather than oblique; and types were either cast on bodies much larger than their faces or were extravagantly leaded. This culminated in the true and full-blooded examples of modern-face type. The first was cut by Didot in 1784, John Bell's (1788) was the first English and the first in England not to include the long s. The extremes were reached in England by William Bulmer (1757–1830) and Thomas Bensley (d. 1833) and abroad by the Didots and Bodoni. Although several of the most important designers of modern-face began work in the eighteenth century, their most violent examples, accentuated by a fattening of the thick strokes, were not cut until well into the nineteenth century. Bulmer in fact used old-faced types in the earlier part of his career. The modern-faced style is thought by some to have been influenced by Pine's *Horace*, 1733, of which the whole, text and all, is engraved. The condensed or narrow style was by now accepted on the Continent, not only in France but in Holland, and notably in the Enschédé foundry at Haarlem.

The outstanding examples, however, can be found in the productions of two great printers. The Didot family in Paris owned and operated a printing and publishing establishment in which, in the late years of the eighteenth century, seven members of the family were engaged. They made remarkable contributions to printing developments as well as to typography. The modern-face types that the Didots introduced in 1784 were developed until they reached their finest expression in the *Virgil* of 1798. They were enormously popular not only in France but almost universally. As a result Firmin Didot was invited, in 1812, to survey and reform the typography of the Imprimerie Impériale. The other full flowering can be seen in the works of Giambattista Bodoni of Parma.

Bodoni was the son of a printer and began his career as an apprentice in the press of the Propaganda Fidei in Rome. His truly independent career as a printer began in 1768, when at the request of the Duke of Parma he assumed control of the Stamperia Reale at Parma. His earliest types were importations from the Fournier type foundry in Paris, but within a few years he began to design his own fonts and to write on typographic design. His press became famous among collectors and connoisseurs and, for many of them, one of their scheduled stops on the "grand tour." With this encouragement he widened the range of his books, printing volumes in Italian, Latin, Greek, French, Russian, German, and English. He printed on fine paper and occasionally on vellum, and many of his productions are large, handsome folios. Although, as Updike said, they "lacked intimacy and charm" and although he paid much less regard to the accuracy of the text than the Didots, his books are a triumph of their kind. The great collection of Bodoni's books is at Parma, where his matrices are also preserved.[19] Five years after his death his widow published the second edition of his *Manuale Tipografico* (1818), which included his preface. The preface is not as detailed an account of his printing beliefs as we might wish to have, but the *Manuale* provides the perfect survey of his type designs. An excellent modern facsimile edition has once again made this easily available.[20]

Modern-face reigned supreme till about 1850, when, almost simultaneously in England and in France, there began a revolt against it and a return to the round letter. Charles Whittingham had been in the habit of getting gothic type from the Caslon foundry for printing for Pickering. From at least 1840 he obtained from the same source small quantities of "old-face," the round early–eighteenth-century roman cut by William Caslon the First. The first whole book observed as printed in old-face by Whittingham is Herbert's *Temple*, 1844.

In France it fell out rather differently. Louis Perrin of Lyons, commissioned to print de Boissieu's *Inscriptions antiques de Lyon* (1846–1854), declared that the available Didot types were only fit for printing railway timetables. By studying the inscriptions that were the matter of the book he designed the beautiful round roman well known to most readers of French literature from its use in the series of classics printed in it for MM. Lemerre. Old-face has not had the success in France that it had in England, and narrow fonts are still common.

Modern-face type designs enjoyed a considerable fashion in the United States, where printing was really beginning to establish itself with a national tradition at the time of their chief vogue. Benjamin Franklin, the most ubiquitous of all Americans, corresponded with both Baskerville and Bodoni and left no doubt of his admiration for their work.

In spite of this interest it would be nothing more than a crude generalization to suggest that any one style has been dominant in any major book-producing country during the last century and a half. What has in fact happened can only be indicated in the broadest possible terms. The partial return to old-style fonts in the nineteenth century was accompanied by a very considerable increase in the total amount of printing. The increasing mechanization of the trade added greatly to the number of printers and of the kinds of work with which they were engaged. The number of type designers and founders increased, and, although it can be argued that this spread was not primarily responsible, there can be little doubt of the general decline in standards. A considerable number of type designs from about 1860 onward are of quite amazing ugliness, a situation relieved only in part by the excessive ingenuity of some of the display types.

Much of the change that has brought events around to the present extremely good and interesting typographical situation can be attributed to two factors, both of them initially events of the last decade of the nineteenth century. First was the introduction of the earliest successful type-composing machines and the subsequent creation of two corporations. Nothing has done more during this present century to spread the production and use of first-class typography than the Monotype and Linotype organizations. They have been able to commission designs from the world's leading typographers and to make them readily available. The second factor, which goes along hand in hand with the first, was the completely fresh outlook on typographical matters that can be dated from the rise of the private- and fine-press movement. What was, in the long run, of particular significance was the realization once again that good typography is only one part of book design and that all elements are very closely related. Nowhere was this more fully appreciated than at the beginning of the movement. Although its earliest important successes were in

books that were designed to give particular meaning to the revived use of gothic type its lessons were just as applicable to work
with roman type.

This revival in England at the end of the century was immediately inspired by the first Arts and Crafts Exhibition in 1888
and by the lecture given at it by Mr. (later Sir) Emery Walker. It
probably owed something also, even if less directly, to the Caxton celebrations of 1877. In 1891 William Morris, with Emery
Walker's assistance, set up the Kelmscott Press at Hammersmith.
In the next seven years—in fact, till Morris's death—they
printed a noble series of books, in which Morris's genius for
design found play. His Chaucer is possibly the most splendid
book ever printed in England. Morris hated the Renaissance, and
after his first type (the "Golden"), which was based on Jenson's
roman, he went back to German gothic, which gave a richer
effect, especially when enclosed in his elaborately designed
woodcut borders. The Kelmscott Gothic was a simplified fere-
humanistica, the simplest form of gothic to start with, in two
sizes, called respectively after the books for which they were cut,
the "Troy" and "Chaucer" types.

Morris was the first to enunciate clearly the vital truth, acted
on instinctively by good printers, that the aesthetic unit in a
book is not the page but the opened facing pair of pages. His
books are mostly too rich and heavy in appearance for comfort-
able reading, and his influence was more really valuable than his
own achievement. All subsequent fine printing sprang largely
from his inspiration, and the high standards of modern commercial press work owe a very great deal to the private- and fine-press
movement, which he did so much to initiate.

The Kelmscott woodblocks were deposited in the British
Museum, not to be used for a hundred years. The types are in the
custody of the Cambridge University Press.

When the Kelmscott Press came to an end, Emery Walker
started again with T. J. Cobden-Sanderson, better known
perhaps as a binder, at the Doves Press, Hammersmith. There,
from 1898 to 1916, they printed a long series of famous books,
mostly small but culminating in a magnificent Bible, in a style
that was the antithesis of Morris's. The Doves type was a roman,
based on Jenson's, but lighter and purer than Morris's Golden;
the very perfect inking heightened the effect. A straight-tailed y,

a too-conspicuous feature of it, may be useful for recognition. At the close of the Press's activity Cobden-Sanderson threw the types into the River Thames, so that they might not become "staled with unthinking use."

Already it will be apparent to what an extent the early private presses drew on their knowledge of early type designs. The study of the history of type began to have a fresh relevance for typographers, and a new era opened in that field as well. The Ashendene Press, after an early use of Caslon and Fell types, used a somewhat more gothic version of the semigothic roman with which at Subiaco in 1465 Sweynheym and Pannartz brought printing into Italy. Later, use was made of a fine roman based on the Ulm *Ptolemy* of 1482.

The private and fine presses proved to be among the comparatively few institutions or organizations that actively encouraged type design and the new and as yet unestablished type designer. No better example of the need for this kind of experimental environment can be found than the career of Eric Gill. Gill was one of the truly great designers of the present century, and the breadth of his interests—sculpture, woodcarving, illustration, and typography—served to strengthen the impact that he made. Gill produced designs for the two presses that he helped to establish and also during the years of his association with the Golden Cockerel Press. Versed as he was in the whole history and development of typography, it is perhaps surprising that his designs should have been so individual and so apparently little rooted in designs of the past. This is perhaps tantamount to saying that Gill had a genius that defies exact classification. One of his best-remembered designs is the Gill Sans, probably the most popular sans serif type of modern times. Its origin was in the capital letters that he designed for a fascia board for the bookshop of his friend Douglas Cleverdon, in Bristol. At the suggestion of Stanley Morison, Gill turned these letters into type design, in capitals only, in 1927. The rest of the font followed within a few years. The relationship between letter design and typography is apparent here just as it had been in the formative years of the fifteenth century. Much of the credit for modern typography must therefore be shared by those who have been responsible for the modern resurgence of interest in calligraphy. Here few greater figures can be found than Edward Johnston, whose delight in medieval book hands seems at first sight not to be the obvious background for the sans serif letters that he designed for the London Underground. From such examples, from fascia boards to railway-station lettering, it may be correctly inferred that the main use of such type is outside book printing. Its importance is largely in display, since a sans serif type is not ideally suited to long-term reading. But Gill was far from restricted to this one design. He was also responsible for superb book faces, of which Perpetua is not only the best known, but is deservedly so.

Gill's achievement, great as we now know it to have been, was not the limit of his accomplishment. His designs, coupled with his somewhat controversial writings on typography, inspired others with the result that much lettering design, as much sculpture and carving, has been unmistakably in the Gill manner.

Other great designers also received their impetus from fine printing. F. W. Goudy, a remarkable man who surmounted setbacks with the fortitude of a Plantin, contributed greatly to good letter design in the United States. Over one hundred of his designs spread his wide range of styles and left an indelible mark on modern American printing. D. B. Updike, less prolific in the quantity of his design, achieved a similar influence due additionally to his writing. His one great historical survey of printing types has done much to give to budding typographical students a critical awareness of their heritage.[21]

The commerical world of printing and publishing has played a large part also. One of the great modern types had its origin in 1932, when *The Times* newspaper commissioned Stanley Morison to design its new typeface. Created originally for newspaper work, it has achieved widespread use as a book face. For character and for clarity it is a peer among type designs, and to this achievement must be added Morison's work as the historian of newspapers; vigorous writer on typographical principles; and guide, mentor, and friend to the Monotype Corporation. Few have had more influence on printing and typographic practice.

The university presses have made their contribution, which can be measured not only in the general excellence of most of their work but also pinpointed by their highlights. In 1929 Oxford University Press commissioned an American designer to design the Oxford lectern Bible, eventually issued in 1935. For this outstanding piece of modern printing Bruce Rogers designed a type that was a larger-size recutting of his Centaur type, first issued in 1915. Centaur is one of the most delicate of modern types, taking Jenson's roman once again as a model. Both in this form and the recutting for the Bible it is a supreme achievement of a great modern designer.

Typography is one of the most living of all the book arts of the present day. Work of such people as Jan van Krimpen has carried on the tradition of design, and such designers as Hermann Zapf have stressed the fundamental relationship between calligraphy and type design. To repeat, in the final analysis it is letter design, rather than type design, that is of fundamental importance.

3. ITALIC

Italic type, unlike gothic or roman, is definitely the creation of a single printer, Aldus of Venice. He had it designed for a pocket series of octavo classics, beginning with a Virgil in 1501, though a few words of italic had appeared in his edition of the *Letters of St. Catherine of Siena* in 1500.

The type was cut for him by Francesco Griffo of Bologna from one of the countless specimens of the scholarly cursive of the fifteenth century in Italy, and it was first called "Chancery" (*cancelleresca*) or "Aldine." The statement, often repeated, that it was based on Petrarch's handwriting is due to an egregiously careless misreading of Aldus's statement that his text of Petrarch's *Cose Volgari*, 1501, is "tolto con sommissima diligenza dallo scritto di mano medesima dal Poeta"—in other words, that it was based on a holograph manuscript of the author.

At first Aldus's italic had a sloping lower case but no upper case of its own, therein imitating the manuscripts on which it was based. To most modern eyes, though there were professed exceptions, the addition of its own upper case, which came soon, was a great improvement on the small roman capitals used at first.

It has been stated that Aldus introduced italic because he could not print such small books in roman. This is ridiculous, but Aldus began his series with Virgil, and what is true is that italic is a narrow (or condensed) type, and that an equally narrow roman (in which a hexameter would not overrun a line) would be intolerable and a smaller font would be needed. The result can be seen in the small Elzevir classics, which, though neat, are far less legible than the Aldines. Aldus's small classics and his type were immediately copied, expecially at Lyons, though he did his best to protect his rights.

The early part of the sixteenth century was a great period for calligraphy and nowhere more so than in Italy. With the advance of movable-type printing it lost its prime place as a book hand, but it enjoyed increasing use in official and diplomatic documents as well as in personal correspondence. From 1514 onward series of writing books were issued, and among them were those of three of the greatest of the masters: Ludovico degli Arrighi (called Vicentino) published his *La Operina* in 1522, Giovanantonio Tagliente his *Lo Presente Libro Insegna . . .* in 1524, and Giovanni Battista Palatino his *Libro Nuovo D'imparare a Scrivere* in 1540. The connection between manuscript hands and contemporary type design, a subject of perennial interest, is underscored by the fact that Arrighi also cut a notably original italic type. It was a simpler, more formal style than the Aldine italic and avoided the large number of ligatures of which Aldus had been so proud. Arrighi's italic first appeared in 1523, with modifications of the original design following a few years later. The Aldine and Arrighi italics are the antecedents of all italic designs, although they were modified further and adapted to new uses by later designers. The most noted of these was Robert Granjon of Lyons, who took elements of both designs and, through his great influence as a type designer, gave to Europe its italic tradition. Garamond and Granjon, the chief type cutters of the day, sold types to many European printers, and not least to Plantin. They appear to have divided the field among them, with Garamond achieving preeminence in roman designs and Granjon in italic. Italic type was first introduced into England by Wynkyn de Worde in 1528, and in the earliest days of its use there it was Arrighi's earlier type that proved popular. From the seventeenth century on italics have always been designed in relation to the romans with which they were to be associated; before that they had been independent. In the sixteenth century whole books of verse, and especially Latin verse, were set in italic. By degrees the use of italic diminished except for its modern function, which is chiefly as a differentiation type.

4. GREEK

The earliest books to contain Greek type are both dated 1465. One is the Cicero, *De Officiis*, printed by Fust and Schoeffer at Mainz; the other is the Subiaco *Lactantius* of Sweynheym and Pannartz. In the former it is indecipherable, what was intended to be οτι μονου το χαλου αμαθου appearing as an unintelligible phrase, since type cutter and compositor alike knew no Greek; and for some time after this most printers preferred to leave blanks for Greek words to be filled in by hand. The Subiaco type and its successors (all Italian) were book hands, broad and upright, intended to go with roman, and are called graeco-roman. The most successful of the very early ones is that of Joannes Philippus de Lignamine, Rome, 1470, which shares the lapidary quality of its owner's roman and which would not have been neglected by modern type cutters had more of it been in existence; the letters are bold and square, and ascenders and descenders occur very sparsely.

At Venice, Nicolas Jenson cut in 1471 a Greek font of the same family character as the Subiaco, but much better. In fact it is worthy of his famous roman and was in its way almost as influential in the modern revival of type cutting.

The earliest continuous Greek texts printed were edited by teachers of Greek, and the types in which they were printed were no doubt designed by them, for they are more cursive and more genuinely Greek of the style of the day, having in particular narrow and ugly Byzantine upper case. The first book entirely printed in Greek is the πιτομη, or Greek grammar, of Constantine Lascaris, Milan, 1476, and this was followed by some of the great classics. *Theocritus* (Milan, c. 1480), *Homer* (Florence, 1488), *Aristotle* (Venice, 1495), and *Aristophanes* (Venice, 1498) appeared before the end of the fifteenth century, side by side with the *editiones principes* of the Latin classics. The last two of these were printed in Venice by Aldus, in a style of type that was to its predecessors very much what his italic of a few years later was to roman. He gave the regular slope to the strokes that survives into our own time, and the style may well be called "graeco-italic."

But while Aldus's italic was a boon, his Greek proved to be a curse and the more so in that it dominated Greek types for four centuries. While printers had, for practical reasons of simplifying composition, in fifty years gone far to clear ligatures and contractions out of the roman case, Aldus enormously multiplied them in the Greek case, thus adding simultaneously to the cost of printing and the difficulty of reading. Even the fine layout of such books as his Aristophanes cannot conceal the ugliness of the types themselves, closely modeled on script though they be, with all the pen's running flourishes. Proctor went so far as to call Aldus "a man of phenomenal bad taste for his time."

One famous exception to the vogue of the Aldine Greek was the stately round graeco-roman of the New Testament (1514) of the Complutensian polyglot Bible printed for Archbishop Ximenes by Arnald de Brocar at Alcalá de Henares (Complutum), which was based on Jenson's Greek of 1471.[22] It had no successors for nearly four hundred years, and the rest of the world preferred Aldus's graeco-italic to the graeco-roman. The finest graeco-italics of the heavily contracted kind were the *grecs du roi* cut in 1543–1544 by Garamond with the aid of a Cretan scribe named Angelos Vergetios. The fonts were cut to the order of François I, as part of his scheme for printing the Greek classics in the Royal Library. The year 1543 also saw the first book printed in Greek type in England, a Chrysostom edited by Sir John Cheke and printed by Reynald Wolfe.

In his *Greek Printing Types* Dr. Victor Scholderer wrote, "Such beauty as the contemporary Greek penmanship which he [Aldus] was imitating possessed consisted wholly in the abundance and freedom of its ligatures and contractions, and to reproduce these in the exceptionally unsuitable medium of type was not really a business proposition."[23] But it was not until the mid–eighteenth century that this was thoroughly realized, and there are several great landmarks that mark this period of change: the simple Greek printing of the brothers Foulis at Glasgow, notably their famous Homer of 1756–1758, in which Robert Foulis persuaded the designer, Alexander Wilson, to omit contracted sorts; the large-text Greek of Bodoni, as shown in the Longus of 1786, into which he introduced the peculiar qualities of extreme modern-face roman; and the Porsons of the Cambridge University Press, which are the plain but very clear graeco-italics on which so many scholars in England were brought up.

In 1895 the stirring of the waters by Morris produced an experiment in a graeco-roman cut for Macmillans by Selwyn Image. This was fat-faced and painful to the eye, probably in deference to Morris's admiration of gothic. It deserves the credit of being a first experiment on the right lines, though it had been preceded both in France and England by some upright types that were in essence Porson pushed up out of the slant. Soon after this Robert Proctor designed the "Otter," a modification of the Complutensian font, and an *Oresteia* and *Odyssey* were printed in it. They are splended books, but Proctor's Otter type was not well adapted for reduction to a size suitable for normal texts. This adaptability has been found in the New Hellenic, designed in 1927 for the Hellenic Society by Dr. Scholderer of the British Museum, and based on a Venetian graeco-roman of the 1490s. This Greek type is available in varying sizes on monotype.

5. HEBREW

Italy also saw the beginnings of Hebrew typography from as early as 1475. Abraham ben Garton of Reggio di Calabria and Meshullam of Pieve de Sacco were first in the field, with a commentary on the Pentateuch and a Jewish law book respectively. Hebrew books soon followed from a number of other centers, such as Ferrara and Bologna. Perhaps the most famous location, however, was a small village near Cremona from which a German born family from Speier took their name of Soncino. Two sons of the original founder of the business established presses, the elder Joshua in Naples, where he died in 1492. The younger son, Gerson, "the greatest Jewish printer the world has ever known," wandered through about six Italian towns, thence to France, and finally to Constantinople and Salonika, where he died in 1534.

Trade was sufficiently good for printing in Hebrew to become a valuable monopoly. Daniel Bomberg, also of German descent, obtained the privilege for such printing from the Venetian Senate from 1515 to 1549. In Paris, Robert Estienne was appointed, by letters patent, as Printer and Bookseller in Hebrew and Latin on 24 June 1539, as distinct from Conrad Néobar's appointment as royal printer for Greek. Guillaume Le Bé, "the most famous cutter of Hebrew type in his generation" and, according to the younger Fournier, "the disciple of Robert Estienne," learned his trade in the Estienne foundry, then departed for Venice.[24] He was later the source of Hebrew fonts for Garamond and Plantin. There was a considerable use of Hebrew types in the Low Countries and Spain, although it has always been relatively small compared with the other families of type.[25]

Description of type

In the description of books no single item is more difficult than the problem of describing the type in which the work is printed. Attention has long been paid to the transcription of the title page, and this has occasionally included a very simple statement of its main typographical features. Very rarely indeed, however, has an attempt been made to record the type or types in which the body of the work was printed. Incunabulists have been accustomed to classifying type according to Haebler's classification scheme for the gothic upper-case M and accompanying that with a measurement of twenty lines of the type. Outside of these two areas, title pages and incunabula, little has been attempted. Even the most advanced "scientifically bibliographical" works have paid scant attention to this difficult task. In his Lyell Lectures, Harry Carter expressed his view on this issue:

> As compared with bibliography of the modern analytical kind the study of type historically considered has been amateurish. People have written about post-incunabular types because they like them and thought them beautiful. They concentrated attention on typefaces that were the best of their kind. This is like bibliography in the time of Dibdin: we must try, without taking the delight out of the subject, to modernize it. That we can do by applying, broadly, the methods of the incunabulists to the later phenomena.[26]

Justified as this comment is, it does not in itself help to resolve the problem of the classification and description of type. It does, however, draw attention to one aspect of typographical his-toriography that may on occasion serve to help the bibliog-rapher. Because attention has been largely directed to the designs that were admired and considered to be "the best of their kind," it follows that the most influential designs have been adequately studied. Assuming a large family tree covering the main families of type, the historical developments of fonts within each family, the linkages and dependencies that typographical study and documentary evidence permit, then the broad beginnings are established, as is done, for example, for languages and alphabets. The overall pattern of development of type styles is an essential preliminary to an understanding of the problems of type descrip-tion. The kind of description that appears in the colophons of an increasing number of modern books is not a model that can be projected into past centuries. The printer of earlier periods would not, even had the wish been there, have been able to attain a precision similar to that of the printer of the present day, who can draw upon very detailed classifications of type measurement and design. It is therefore of some importance to understand what the desirable information regarding type is thought to be. To this end it must be remembered that the purpose of a biblio-graphical description is to set apart, step by step, the work or copy being described from all other works and all other printings and copies of the same work. Harry Carter's stated objective was:

> I think a typeface is sufficiently identified if the name of the man who cut the punches for it is known, if it can be named by the conventional body on which it was meant to fit, and if the style of the face can be described by one of the adjectives commonly used by palaeographers, palaeotypographers, and neotypographers.[27]

G. T. Tanselle has tackled the problem and, in his own words, made "two suggestions."[28] They were suggestions toward the ambitious solution mentioned, in a passing manner, by Stanley Morison that there was need for a "Descriptive principles of typography" as an equivalent to Professor Bowers's "Descriptive principles of bibliography." Tanselle's suggestions covered two basic areas, "the two essential ingredients in any identification of type," the first of which is "the indication of size." Certain measurements have traditionally been standard: the measurement of the type page, number of lines to the page, and the measurement of twenty (or as is sometimes proposed for modern books ten) lines of text. If the lines were set solid—that is, without leading—the measurement of the lines of text would provide the necessary measurement of the type, but the simplicity of this is ruined whenever the type is leaded or the typeface is set on a larger body. These occurrences are sufficiently frequent to cause a major problem. Since there is no sure way of deducing from the printed page in such circumstances the actual measurement of the type, Tanselle suggested an alternative. Although the type itself may long ago have vanished and in any event is practically never available to the bibliographer, what is left is the impression of the typeface on the paper. The alternative proposed was for the recording of the measurement of the typeface in place of the type size. In his discussion Tanselle raised one issue that deserves attention because it goes to the heart of descriptive bibliography:

> The system outlined here would inevitably require modification in practice, but my concern is not so much with details of notation as with the concept lying behind these details. The descriptive bibliographer who records only type-sizes, however valuable and accurate his information, may appear to be working backward, for description must precede analysis, and the naming of type size from the examination of a printed page is an act of inference rather than observation.

Good descriptive bibliographers have always provided an impetus to further research and do not sit imperiously on the throne of ultimate certainty. If the measurement of typefaces were accurately recorded in bibliographical descriptions, there would certainly be much more information than is currently available to aid in typographical research.

Stevenson's notes on type in the Hunt Botanical Catalogue make very much the same point as Carter. "The study of eighteenth-century types has not progressed beyond the half-way point. There is even an opinion, encouraged by some devotees of early printed books, that they may not be worth the trouble."[29]

His requirement was for identification by font, size according to the country of use, by font-family, measurement of ten lines of type, and a statement of the number of lines on a typical page. Typical entries in Stevenson therefore read as:

Pica roman leaded 47.5: A2 = 32 lines.

English roman 46: B2 = 32 lines.

Small pica roman 37: A2 = 37 lines.

Beyond this it is unusual, and extremely difficult, for any bibliographer to go at present.

It is only to be expected that a special interest in type might be found in a bibliography of a printer. There are two, both by Philip Gaskell, that are worth special study.[30]

Dealing with Baskerville's type, Gaskell discussed its background in the introduction to his *John Baskerville: A Bibliography* and in the prefatory "Conclusions Drawn from the Bibliography." Factors that are important, therefore, to an understanding of his use of type are found here in such statements as: "Baskerville cut and cast his type about a size larger than normal; his *Pica*, for example, was in both face and body about the same size as Caslon's or Wilson's *English*." The fonts of type and the ornaments were for the most part those that appeared in Baskerville's Specimen Sheet, a facsimile of which appeared on an inserted sheet within the book. This achieves a basic identification of the type, as expressed in the two entries for type in the first and second editions of Baskerville's *Virgil* (Entries Nos. 1 and 2):

1. Text, *Great Primer* leaded; Subscribers, *Small Pica*; and see the note on the type of the second edition.
2. As first edition, but in a later state; the set (width of body) of both the *Great Primer* and the *Small Pica* is wider by 6 or 7 per cent; and some of the letters (e.g. the *Double Pica* italic "Y" on p.1, 1.3) are from different punches.

Gaskell's treatment of the Foulises' types was different, as befitted a different situation. Each text type used in the Press's books was illustrated by about nine lines of text and its detailed characteristics noted. In this description, in addition to general notes on the design, dates were given of first and last uses in the Foulises' books. Each font was given a reference number, and these constituted the descriptions of type throughout the bibliography. Entries would then appear in such forms as:

RSP1, RLP1, RP2.

GGP, RSP1.

RLP1, RB2.

In both these bibliographies great reliance is placed on reference to facsimiles of the designs within the works themselves rather than on descriptions that stand by themselves.

There have been, as mentioned earlier, more attempts to distinguish among sizes and varieties of fonts employed on title pages than in the text. The examples just given from Stevenson and Gaskell are comparatively rare examples of the latter sort. It is obvious that title pages are a special problem in this respect in that they can display such a bewildering variety: hence the proposals for photographic transcription that is discussed in Chapter 10. Some of the proposals, such as the scheme proposed by the Oxford Bibliographical Society, have sometimes been regarded as yielding results hardly worth the labor.[31] It must, however, be said that this method has been well put into use in a number of cases.[32]

Tanselle's second suggestion concerned the problem of describing the style or design of a typeface. The describing eye is here plagued by subjective attitudes, as were not apparent in dealing with factual matters of measurement. This has always been apparent in much of what has been written about type. Type design is an easy target for writing on a purely aesthetic level that does not translate easily into terminology that has wide general acceptance. The tradition of naming typefaces, which can simplify matters greatly in this present century, is very recent and can provide no assistance in the vast majority of cases. Tanselle's suggestion is important not necessarily for the specific tools that he proposed as aids but rather as a principle that opens up areas of investigation. The British Standard *Typeface Nomenclature* (BS 2961: 1967) covered basic issues and produced acceptable terms to cover weight and width of type. The German Standard (DIN 16 518) provided a numerical classification of styles that permits considerable flexibility in a multilevel approach to type classification.[33] The two systems in conjunction present greater opportunity for accurate record than the somewhat haphazard methods that have served in general so far.

Tanselle regarded both suggestions as having value for "their general pragmatic drift." They also make it obvious that much more research into typographic history and many more efforts to achieve satisfactory classification schemes for type are necessary before descriptions can be truly satisfactory.[34]

REFERENCES

1. McKERROW, R. B. *An Introduction to Bibliography for Literary Students.* p. 4.

2. One of the clearest is the woodcut in Jost Amman's *Beschreibung aller Stände und . . . Handwerker* (Book of Trades), Frankfurt, 1568. Another of the same period was used by Jost Lamprecht, a printer in Ghent in 1545. They are both reproduced in Harry Carter's *A View of Early Typography,* 1969, as Figures 10 and 7 respectively. Carter's book also includes photographs of the molding equipment.

3. The earliest is probably in Leonardo Fioravanti's *Dello specchio di scientia,* Venice, 1564. Another is contained in the section on printing in Jacques Grevin's *Dialogues françois pour les jeunes enfans,* printed by Plantin in 1567. The earliest English description is contained in a translation of a French work, Louis Le Roy's *Of the Interchangeable Course, or Variety of Things in the Whole World,* 1594. The most accessible to students is in Joseph Moxon's *Mechanick Exercises,* 1683, in the modern edition edited by Herbert Davis and Harry Carter, 2nd ed., 1962.

4. Many museums have pieces of equipment, but none can rival the Plantin-Moretus Museum in Antwerp. The foundry of this great press is still in excellent condition. See descriptions in: *Penrose Annual* (1921), *Printing and Graphic Arts* (1953 and 1955), *British Printer* (1960), as well as in the publications of the Museum itself.

5. Some examples of these figures are given in:

   SMITH, John. *The Printer's Grammar.* 1755. Reprinted 1965. pp. 38–48.

6. HOPKINS, Richard L. *Origin of the American Point System for Printers' Type Measurement.* 1976.

   For British adoption of point system see Chapter 8, pp. 79–87.

7. ETTENBERG, Eugene M. "Is Type Measurement Overdue for Change to the Metric System?" *Inland Printer/American Lithographer.* CLXII: 1969. p. 48.

8. The essay appeared originally in the seventh (and final) volume of *The Fleuron.* It has since had wide separate publication in a number of languages.

9. GOLDSCHMIDT, E. P. *The Printed Book of the Renaissance.* 1950.

10. UPDIKE, Daniel Berkeley. *Printing Types, Their History, Forms and Use.* 2v. 3rd ed. 1962. Vol. 2. p. 88.

11. MORISON, Stanley. "Early Humanistic Script and the First Roman Type." *The Library.* 4th Series. XXIV: 1943–44. pp. 1–29.

12. JOHNSON, A. F. *Type Designs, Their History and Development.* 2nd ed. 1959.

13. If the original can not be consulted easily, recourse may be had to the excellent facsimile published by the Eugrammia Press in 1963.

14. BARKER, Nicolas. *The Oxford University Press and the Spread of Learning, 1478–1978.* 1978.
    CARTER, Harry. *A History of the Oxford University Press.* Vol. 1. *To the Year 1780.* 1975.
    MORISON, Stanley. *John Fell.* 1968.

15. BALL, Johnson. *William Caslon, 1693–1766.* 1973.

16. The most important modern survey of Baskerville's work is to be found in:

GASKELL, Philip. *John Baskerville: A Bibliography.* 1959.

In conjunction with this students should read a review of the book by L. A. HANSON in *The Library.* 5th Series. XV: 1960. pp. 135–143, with additional notes, pp. 201–206. This is an outstanding example of the way in which an authoritative review can add to the importance of a book. Also:

PARDOE, F. E. *John Baskerville of Birmingham: Letter Founder and Printer.* 1975.

17. *Monotype Recorder*, September–October 1927.

18. DREYFUS, John. "The Baskerville Punches 1750–1950." *The Library.* 5th Series. V: 1950–51. pp. 26–48.

19. The great collection of Bodoni material is now housed in the Bodoni Museum at Parma. Accounts of this collection may be found in: *Printing and Graphic Arts* (1957), *British Printer* (1964), *Times Literary Supplement* (1964).

20. BODONI, Giambattista. *Manuale tipografico.* 2v. Reprinted 1960.

21. A good survey of modern typographers is:

GRANNIS, Chandler B. *Heritage of the Graphic Arts.* 1972.

22. WOODY, K. M. "A Note on the Greek Fonts of the Complutensian Polyglot." *PBSA* LXV: 1971. pp. 143–149.

23. SCHOLDERER, Victor. *Greek Printing Types, 1465–1927.* 1927.

24. ARMSTRONG, Elizabeth. *Robert Estienne.* 1954.

25. HOWE, Ellic. "An Introduction to Hebrew Typography." *Signature.* V: 1937.
HOWE, Ellic. "The Le Bé Family." *Signature.* VIII: 1938.
MORISON, Stanley. *L'Inventaire de la fonderie Le Bé.* 1957.

POSNER, Raphael, and TA-SHEMA, Israel. *The Hebrew Book: An Historical Survey.* 1975.

26. CARTER, Harry. *A View of Early Typography.* 1969. p. 1.

27. Carter, p. 3.

28. TANSELLE, G. Thomas. "The Identification of Type Faces in Bibliographical Description." *PBSA* LX: 1966. pp. 185–202.

29. *Catalogue of Botanical Books in the Collection of Rachel McMasters Miller Hunt.* Vol. II. 1961. pp. clxxx–clxxxiii.

30. Gaskell, *John Baskerville.*
    GASKELL, Philip. *A Bibliography of the Foulis Press.* 1964.

31. MADAN, Falconer; DUFF, E. G.; and GIBSON, S. "Standard Descriptions of Printed Books." *Oxford Bibliographical Society: Proceedings and Papers.* Vol. I. Part I. 1923. pp. 56–64.

32. For example:
    MURPHY, Gwendolen. *Bibliography of English Character Books, 1608–1700.* 1925.

33. DEUTSCHE INDUSTRIE NORMEN-AUSSCHUSS. *Klassification der Druckschriften.* (DIN 16 518). 1959 (draft) and 1964.

34. Some of the interesting examples, other than those to which reference has already been made, are:

    BASTIEN, Alfred. *Encyclopaedia Typographica.* Vol. 1. 1953.
    BURT, Sir Cyril. *A Psychological Study of Typography.* 1959.
    DOWDING, Geoffrey. "Type-faces: A Plea for Rational Terminology." *Typographica.* IV: 1951. pp. 9–13.
    GASKELL, Philip. "A Nomenclature for the Letter-forms of Roman Type." *The Library.* 5th Series. XXIX: 1974. pp. 42–51.
    GASKELL, Philip. "Type Sizes in the Eighteenth Century." *Studies in Bibliography.* V: 1952–53. pp. 147–151.
    MORISON, Stanley. "On the Classification of Typographical Variations," in *Type Specimen Facsimiles,* edited by John Dreyfus. 1963. Reprinted in MORISON, Stanley. *Letter Forms.* 1968. pp. 1–132.

MOSLEY, James. "New Approaches to the Classification of Typefaces." *British Printer.* LXXIII: 1960. pp. 90–96.

TANSELLE, G. T. "Langage visible. Recherches typographiques. L'identification des caractères dans la bibliographie descriptive." *Arts et techniques graphiques.* LXXXVI: 1972. pp. 41–55.

THORP, Joseph. "Towards a Nomenclature for Letter Forms," *and* "Experimental Applications of a Nomenclature for Letter Forms." *Monotype Recorder.* Nos. 240: 1931, and 246: 1932 respectively.

VOX, Maximilien. *Pour une Nouvelle Classification des caractères.* 1954.

There are also many general books on letter design and typography. The following will provide introductions:

BALTIMORE: Walters Art Gallery. *2,000 Years of Calligraphy.* 1965.

BIGGS, John R. *An Approach to Type.* 1949.

DAY, K. *Book Typography, 1815–1965, in Europe and the United States of America.* 1966.

DENMAN, Frank. *The Shaping of Our Alphabet.* 1955.

DOWDING, Geoffrey. *An Introduction to the History of Printing Types.* 1961.

GILL, Eric. *Typography.* 1931.

GRAY, Nicolete. *Nineteenth Century Ornamented Typefaces.* 1976.

JASPERT, W. P.; BERRY, W. T., and JOHNSON, A. F. *The Encyclopaedia of Type Faces.* 4th ed. 1970.

LEGROS, L. A., and GRANT, J. C. *Typographical Printing Surfaces.* 1916.

LEWIS, John. *Typography: Basic Principles.* 2nd ed. 1967.

MORES, Edward Rowe. *A Dissertation upon English Typographical Founders* (1778), with a catalog and specimen of the typefoundry of John James (1782). Edited by Harry Carter and Christopher Ricks. 1961.

MORISON, Stanley. *A Tally of Types.* 1973.

MORISON, Stanley. *On Type Designs; A Brief Introduction.* New ed. 1962.

MORISON, Stanley. *The Typographic Arts.* 1949.

REED, Talbot Baines. *A History of the Old English Letter Foundries.* Edited by A. F. Johnson. 1952.

SIMON, Oliver. *Introduction to Typography.* 2nd ed. 1963.

VERVLIET, H. D. L. *Sixteenth-century Printing Types of the Low Countries.* 1968.
WARDE, Beatrice. *The Crystal Goblet: Sixteen Essays on Typography.* 1955.

Journals that should be scanned regularly, covering some aspects of printing as well as typography:

Journal of the Printing Historical Society. 1965–
Penrose Annual. 1896– [under various titles until 1935–]
Typographica. 1949–
Visible language 1967– [from 1967 to 1970 appeared as *Journal of Typographical Research.*]

6.

COMPOSITION AND PRESS WORK

Hand composition

The whole process of composition and printing remained comparatively unchanged in any real essential from the middle of the fifteenth century until 1800. Even though the nineteenth century witnessed vital and important changes, the origins are still apparent in all of today's advanced techniques. The methods have been improved, accelerated, and refined, yet the basic principles remain constant. It is also a sobering thought that, in spite of all that nineteenth- and twentieth-century technology has accomplished, the standards of workmanship of some of the great masterpieces of the fifteenth century have not been excelled.[1]

At all periods of printing the initial decision has been the settlement of the "layout" of a new book—that is, the type or types to be used, the number of lines to a page, whether leaded or solid, the length of the lines, the format of the book, and so forth. This process, known as "casting-off," enables the printer to determine into how much text-type the work will set and therefore what quantity of materials are necessary.[2] The actual method of operation would naturally vary somewhat from printer to printer and from period to period. It is to be expected that the methods of a scholar-printer like Robert Estienne would differ from those of an Elizabethan printer of polemical pamphlets. Nevertheless, it is a necessary step in the process at whatever level of work. In larger printing houses, or with longer texts, decisions would have to be taken as to any division of work among compositors or printers. Many books, on analysis, will demonstrate evidence that such allocation of work was a normal occurrence. Following this, the copy was handed to the compositor to "set up" or "compose."

In the days of hand composition the compositor stood before a "case" with the copy in view. The case was a sloping cabinet of shallow pigeonholes, each of which contained all the pieces of type of a single sort. The "lay of the case," or the manner in which these compartments were arranged, has not been unchanged over the centuries. There have been period and regional variations, and these would need to be taken into account before any individual book was studied in detail in order to give reasonable assurance that it was being viewed in the right context.[3] The two main patterns were the single lay and the divided lay, the latter being the more common in English use. In the divided lay the two cases would be set at different angles so that both would be placed conveniently to the printer's hand. The upper case was devoted to the majuscules, hence called the "uppercase" letters, and the lower to the minuscules, called "lowercase."[4] In the upper case the equal-sized compartments are arranged in a clear order, which is broadly alphabetical and numerical. The lower case, however, is organized in a convenient order according to the frequency of use, as on a typewriter. The quantity of each sort, and hence the size of the compartment, vary for the same reason combined with the size of the letter. Because of this, although *e* and *i* are both letters of high frequency, *e* has the larger compartment because it is the larger of the two.

In the compositor's left hand was the curiously named "stick," a small shallow tray capable of holding as many lines of type as were not uncomfortably heavy. The later version of the stick was provided with an adjustable end, which was screwed before work began to the required length of line. Picking them out of the case, the compositor placed the types in this stick, using (as the typist and pianist do) not the eye but the habit of hand to find the pigeonhole holding the right sort. In order to produce the proper impression the type had to be set upside down and backward, and printers acquire a peculiar facility in reading type in this position. In this setting the hand-compositor has always been helped by the nicks on the front of the piece of type, which will be uppermost when the type is correctly set in the stick.

After each word a space (or sort consisting of body and no face, which will therefore not reach the paper or make an impression) was inserted; when the end of the line was reached, these spaces (which were made in different breadths) were graduated so as, if possible, to end the line with the end of a word. This process is called "justification." In the earliest days of printing the line endings were often left uneven; this is one of the tests by which the frequent undated books of the early printers can be, at least approximately, dated, since having acquired the trick of justification printers may naturally be assumed not to have relapsed. Irregularity of line endings is very occasionally found in some modern presses, where it has no bibliographical significance and is a pure affectation.

The spacing is one of the tests of good printing. The conscientious printer always tried not to allow the gaps between words to be wide, nor to position them one above another so as to give an effect of a crack (a "river") down the page. Too closely compressed, the page of type looks handsome but is less legible. These considerations are not mentioned for purely aesthetic purposes, although that is a perfectly legitimate way in which to regard a book. The bibliographer is always alert to any indication, of whatever nature, that might help to suggest that a work is carefully or carelessly put together. It is in the composition and the press work that such clues manifest themselves almost over any other area of production. Ends of paragraphs were filled up by long spaces, called "quads." Often in proof—and occasionally in the finished book—these have jumped up and printed a solid black square. If it had been decided that the type was to be "leaded," the compositor placed along the foot of the line (actually above it in the stick) a strip of base metal. This, like spaces and quads, was of body-height, having no face, and was not intended to touch the paper. This served to separate the lines of type. It is always important in a book with a wide page that there should be a fairway for the eye to run back from the end of one line to the beginning of the next. The leading provided that fairway. Types were frequently specially cast on a larger body so that the effect of leading was obtained without the labor.

A type page that has very little spacing presents a more solid, uniform, and, to many eyes, more decorative appearance than one that is widely spaced. Because of this some printers and book designers have sought to achieve their desired effect by abolishing paragraph-breaks, indentations, and sentence-ending spaces. This kind of experimentation has occasionally displeased the traditionalists and at other times, as notably with the Doves Press Bible, has been greeted with enthusiasm. Other book designers have felt impelled to break away from the "tyranny" of the neat rectangle of the type-page area. While not all such attempts have been successful, it seems only reasonable that a designer should wish to try. The "Mouse's tail" page in Chapter 3 of Alice in Wonderland has long been accepted, and indeed any attempt to restrain this text within rectangular form would surely meet with opposition.[5]

When the first line had been set and leaded as necessary, others were added until the stick was full. In the earliest days of printing these lines of type were gathered on the press-stone until sufficient had been set to produce the number of lines already decided upon for the page. At a later stage the galley was introduced.[6] This was a larger tray into which the composed lines of type could be slid. They were made in different sizes, but for book work they normally held about three octavo pages. Stickful followed stickful of type in the galley tray till the column of type filled it. The "matter," as standing type was called, was then made fast and a proof taken, or "pulled."

Because the whole description of hand-composition is written in the past tense it must not be generally assumed that it is completely a thing of the past. Much hand work is still done, but it is largely for specialized purposes, and it now has very little to do with normal commercial book printing and publishing.

Mechanical composition

In recent times the labor of composition has been minimized by the invention of machines for the purpose.[7] These have not simply accelerated the basic operation but, during this present century, have brought a completely new dimension to the business of composition. Throughout the first half of the twentieth century the chief machines have been the Linotype and the Monotype. During the second half of the century an even more basically revolutionary change has been the introduction of the photocomposition machine.

Linotype, and its almost exact equivalent Intertype, is based on a principle that was first brought into effective use about 1890. It consists of a single machine on which the operator, by striking the keyboard, resembling that of a typewriter, brings into position in a line the appropriate matrices. When the line is completed, the matrices are moved up to the mold in front of the orifice of a cauldron of molten type metal. The whole line is then cast in a solid "slug," a peculiarity of the process to which it owes its name. The slugs are passed direct on to the galley, while the matrices are automatically redistributed into the magazine. Spacing is achieved by means of thin metal wedges, called "spacebands," which are automatically inserted between words as the compositor taps the space key. As the line of matrices move upward toward the casting box, the line is justified by being wedged out to its predetermined length. The lines of type that are assembled in the galley are proofed and dealt with in the same manner as hand-set type.

The Monotype method, which was introduced a year or two later than Linotype, involves two machines. On the first the operator strikes the keyboard and in so doing punches a series of holes in a spool of paper, resembling that used in the pianola. The spool finished, the operator marks it in pencil with the title of the book, the font to be used, etc., and passes it to the casting room. Here it is affixed to the monotype casting machine, which, like the linotype, has a cauldron attached. The operator selects, according to the instruction penciled on the spool, the die-case of the appropriate font. This die-case is a small square of steel in which are sunk matrices (usually brass) of all required sorts. The spool is fixed over an air-pressure bar, the blast from which, passing through the holes punched in the spool, and passing there only, sets the die-case in motion, bringing the appropriate matrix over the flow of molten type metal. Single letters are thus cast, whence the more scholarly name of this process. They are extruded one by one on to the galley, and when the line is complete it is automatically moved up, and a fresh line begins to form beneath it.

It will be seen that both the linotype and monotype processes have certain marked advantages over hand setting. First, and most obvious, is the saving in time, even in monotype, where two operators and two machines are involved. Against this must be set the initial cost of the apparatus. Second is the complete elimination of the whole process of redistribution, since the type, when "broken up," is simply thrown into the melting pot and cast afresh on the next occasion. As a result there can never occur (unless by damage to the die-case itself) battered or broken letters; the type is cast afresh for each printing operation. Nor can "foul-case" occur, that is, the placing of a letter after use in the case belonging to another sort. It is possible, though not a frequent occurrence, in linotype for a wrong matrix to get into the magazine and so produce recurrent wrong font.

In monotype too the spool can easily be stored and stereotyping saved; but, as the spool will not carry the corrections, this advantage is limited to matter that is practically "clean." The original corrected proofs can of course be kept and used for the amendment of the text type. The advantages of being able to store a paper spool instead of heavy type-metal plates are obvious, but the disadvantage of not having the forms ready for printing has to be borne in mind. Linotype, on the other hand, has the advantage, as in the case of some cumulated bibliographical tools, of lending itself to this kind of operation. Three or four slugs can more easily be inserted into a sequence than lines of individual sorts.

The chief difference between monotype and linotype is that implied by their names. Monotype-set matter, consisting of single types, is naturally corrected by hand letter by letter. But in linotype the unit is the line, and the correction of a single letter means throwing out and resetting the line in which it occurs.

Probably the most important change of all that the Monotype and Linotype Corporations have effected has been due to their great and scholarly interest in typefaces. For each of these machines there is now a fine range of first-class fonts, the range of which is being steadily increased.

This same range of designs is now being made available through the newest of the major developments, the photocomposing machines. Increasingly during the last fifty or so years reprints of books have been produced by photographing the original and using the photographic image to create a photomechanical plate. Photolithography has been widely used for this purpose. The basic idea behind the photocomposition machines was that they should produce the photographic image from the outset and not simply bring it into being at a secondary stage. In other words, as these machines were developing, books were being produced in greater and greater numbers without the use of any hot-metal type at any stage of the production. Although each

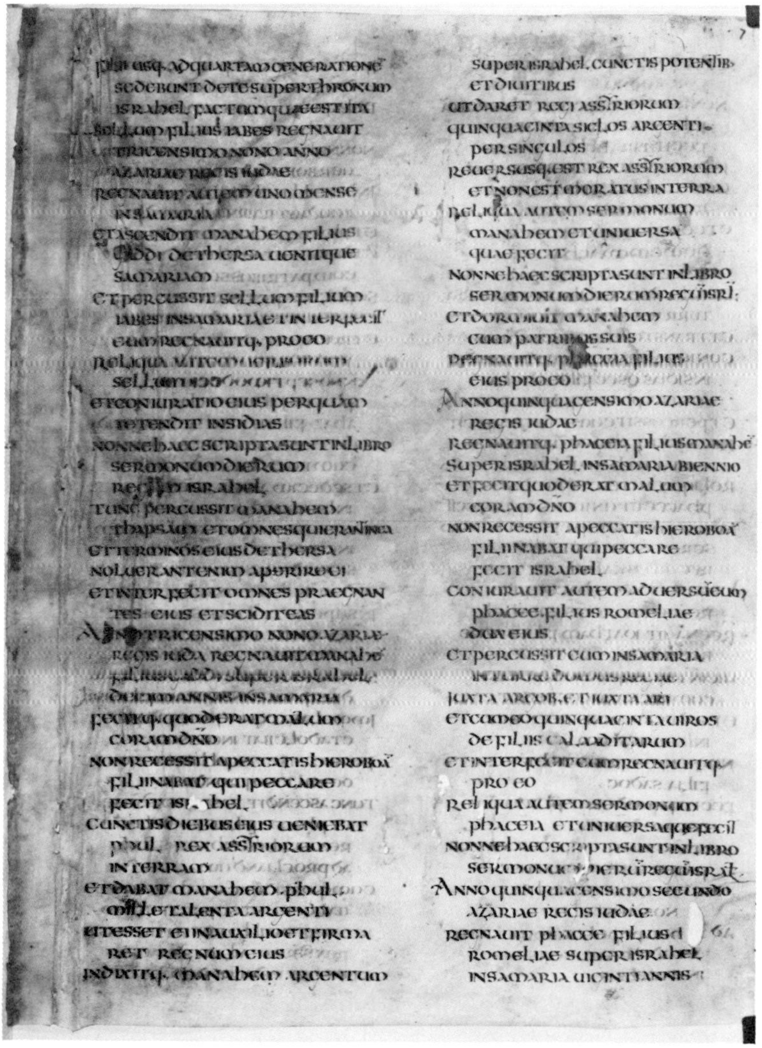

1. Early-eighth-century Northumbrian Bible

2. Sixteenth-century European paper mill

3. English wooden press, early eighteenth century

4. Seventeenth-century printing office

5. Nineteenth-century composing room

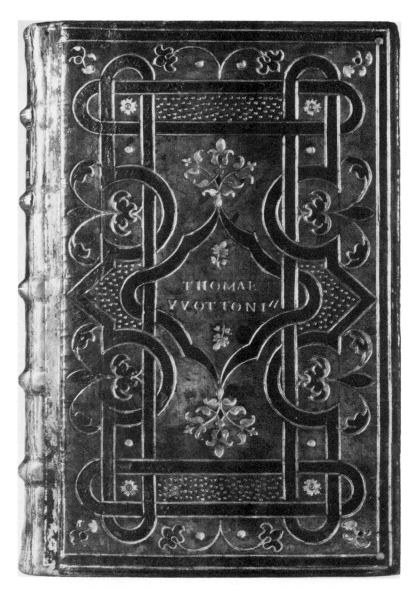

6. Wotton binding

7. St. Cuthbert Gospel: front cover

8. St. Cuthbert Gospel: back cover

machine works in a different way, the general principle of photo-composition is clear. It consists of a method whereby transparencies of all the characters of a font are embedded within a matrix and this matrix is brought into position with source of light, lens, and film. A positive or negative transparency can be produced for use according to whichever photomechanical means is to be used for printing. Because the process is photographic the same set of matrices can set text over a wide range of type sizes. Correction and paging of the text have both caused difficulties during the development stages and are two parts of the whole process that tend to make it still an expensive operation. Advances in techniques are, however, occurring at such speed that only current journals can reveal the latest advantages, problems, and solutions. Assuredly the designer has a new freedom over letter design in such matters as kerned letters and in generally being able to feel released from the restrictions of metal type. The Monotype, Linotype, and Harris-Intertype Corporations have continued to make their regular typefaces available in the new medium. Many other machines are available that demonstrate constantly new advances, such as, for example, those that utilize various forms of computerized composition.

It has not been easy to secure authoritative agreement as to which were the *incunabula* of photocomposition, but the probability is that the "42-line Bible" was Peter Gray's *Handbook of Basic Microtechnique*, published commercially in New York in 1952, while the first British books so produced were Luis Henderson's *A Child's Book of Dogs* and E. Joseph Dreany's *A Child's Book of Horses* in 1952.

Although the actual method of printing following upon photocomposition could be by any of the photomechanical methods, much of it has in fact been by offset-photolithography. This has at the same time been not only a popular but also an increasingly satisfactory method for printing illustrative material. Once again, therefore, text and illustrations are being produced by the same process, giving to the book a unity in design that it has achieved only rarely, and then usually expensively, since the great age of the woodcut illustration.

During these same recent years, however, much as it may be resented and deplored by traditionalists, fresh dimensions have been added to the normal printed book. For a considerable

number of books that can only hope to enjoy modest circula-
tions, the usual process of printing and publication is too uneco-
nomical. At least a partial answer to this dilemma seems to lie
with typewriter composition allied, once again, to the possibilities of photolithographic printing. Early attempts were
crude and amateurish, in the worst sense of the word, but a
steady improvement has been maintained. The limitation of
typefaces was at least as real a drawback to their use as the lack of
precision in the machines. This has now changed, and new
typefaces are being marketed regularly. The situation is rapidly
arising when there need be nothing second-rate about a typewriter, or cold-metal, composed book, especially for those of
rather short runs.

The second aspect, or perhaps a variation on this first innovation, is an increasing quantity of publication stemming from
computer printouts. These bear considerable resemblance to the
typewritten mass-produced text except insofar as the printing
face is concerned. While typewriter faces have improved, the
printing styles of the majority of computer printouts are hideous
to the point of unreadability. Improvement is possible but not
inevitable since utilitarianism is the order of the day. In any
event the bibliographer is compelled to be concerned with whatever form in which textual material is presented, without regard
to artistic standards.

The third new form of publication is the appearance of original
material published in microform. In the early days of micro-
techniques it was used almost exclusively for republication.
Although this is still a major part of micro publication, the
growing percentage that represents first publication gives the
bibliographer a new area of concern.

Another modern development has already had considerable
influence upon composition but of a different order. The computer is being used increasingly to secure justification of lines
more easily than can be done by hand. Under this method the
compositor composes the text in the normal way, except that
there is no concern with justification. The composing machine
produces a punched coded tape that is fed into the computer, and
the justification is done. Already, however, this is clearly only a
small part of what the computer may soon accomplish in the field
of the preparation of the text. Computerized concordances and

book catalogs are already with us, and new developments are evolving regularly. In December 1959 it seemed a far cry from some of the original teachings on bibliography when James Moran read a paper to the Bibliographical Society on "Filmsetting—Bibliographical Implications,"[8] but it is already clear that his paper was only the forerunner of other investigations that will be necessary to keep abreast of the changing situation.

Although the most advanced methods of composition and printing seem remote from the usual problems of bibliography, they are as much a part, at this end of the time scale, as are baked clay tablets at the other. The most modern developments, as well as the most embryonic, are within the purview of bibliographical studies.

Proofing

Not very much real and tangible evidence exists regarding the history of proofreading.[9] This is only to be expected since proof sheets are usually discarded and consequently are not extant to add their testimony. Such evidence as does exist suggests that it began in a somewhat rudimentary fashion, although it had existed in some form or other for a long time. McKerrow was strongly of the opinion that the galley proof, as it is now understood, was a very late addition to the scene and was probably unknown until the early nineteenth century. Once the galley proof had been introduced the possibility of good clean texts increased many-fold, and in due course the use of page proofs followed as the final stage of correction prior to publication. In this method, when the composed type has been gathered together in a galley tray in sufficient quantity to make, say, two or three pages of an octavo book, a first proof is taken, or "pulled," on a handpress kept for the purpose. Machine presses can only be used economically for the rapid printing of large runs. This first rough proof does not usually reach the author but is read by the printer's reader; a second and cleaner proof goes to the author. Corrections need to be made at this stage of galley, or "slip," proof: once the matter is locked in the chase in pages (see below) corrections involve much more work. Any corrections that must be made should be made with a clear conception of the work that will be caused and an active conscience or at least consciousness of the bill for author's corrections.

In the earlier years of printing such proofreading as was done was usually done on the printed sheets as they came off the press and any amendments made by stop-press corrections. This meant that, contrary to modern practice, the copy would be read after the type pages had been prepared and imposed ready for printing. A usual procedure would be for the first sheet printed to be checked by the "corrector" and returned to the compositor for the necessary corrections to be made. The number and methods of the correctors would vary from press to press. In some cases there would be several; in a small press it is probable that the pressman would serve in a dual capacity. [10] The compositor would make changes as required—not adding any new errors in the process, it is to be hoped—and the form is ready for its final printing. Such a procedure, when carried out efficiently, should give a good clean final text. The neat pattern is frequently disturbed by there being several successive corrections to each form during the printing of a sheet, which result in a complex relationship of variant readings when all the sheets were finally brought together in book form.

Imposition

At this stage the matter that will make the first sheet (e.g., if the book to be printed be an octavo, pages 1–16) is transferred to a large metal-topped table called (from its older form) the "stone." The title page and other preliminaries will of course be printed last and will make a separate section, unless the book is a plain reprint. The type will be made up into pages and duly provided with pagination, headlines, and signatures where necessary. In the earliest printed books none of these is found; like the capitals at the head of chapters, they were left to be filled in by the hand of the rubrisher or owner, as they had been in the manuscript book. Fairly early, however, there began to be printed at the head of each recto page not a page number (pagination) but a leaf number (foliation); pagination was very rare till 1500 and not really common for another half-century. The printer took little interest in either, as it was a device intended only for the reader's convenience in reference, and early foliation and pagination alike abound in gaps, repetitions, and errors of all sorts.

The type pages will now be divided into outer and inner "forms", in other words into the set that will be printed on the recto of the open sheet of paper, the same side as page 1, and those that will be printed on the verso, the same side as page 2. In the press the form, and not the sheet, is the unit.

The type pages required to print one of the forms are then enclosed in an iron frame called a "chase." The spaces between, which will constitute the margins on the printed sheet, are filled in with furniture consisting of iron bars, wooden blocks, and wooden or metal wedges ("quoins"). Wood was used as being more elastic than metal, but nowadays is frequently replaced by metal furniture, which can be expanded by means of a ratchet. The proportion of the margins to the type pages is an important part of imposition. It will be noticed that the type page never lies in the center of the page of paper. William Morris stated the reason for this rule, which is that what the eye sees when a book is opened is not the single page but the pair of pages, with due allowance made for a little trimming by the binder, and for the optical illusion caused by the reader's thumb covering a part of the margin.

Once the type is properly positioned it is "locked up" by hammering in the wedges or securing the furniture. The finished result is the "form," which is the actual unit of printing laid on the bed of the press. Flat pieces of wood are then laid over it and gently hammered, so that any pieces of type that have been raised by the pressure are knocked down level with the rest without the face being damaged. The whole can then be lifted bodily and either stood on its end in store or sent direct to the press.

The arrangement of the type pages within the form for different formats is, at first encounter, one of the most complex of the problems of imposition. The "format" of a book is the term used to describe it in accordance with the number of times and manner in which the original sheet was folded. Thus a sheet folded once, creating two leaves or four pages is described as a folio. The pages on the outer side of the sheet would be 1 and 4 and on the inner side 2 and 3. Consequently the imposition of the type pages within the chase for the outer form would be 1 and 4, and for the inner form 3 and 2, so that page 2 would back on to 1. However, in order to save sewing and prevent a somewhat ill-shapen book, a folio was frequently made up with four sheets to a single gathering. The outer sheet would then be printed from an outer form, which held pages 1 and 16, the inner form pages 15 and 2. The second sheet would require an outer form with pages 3 and 14, the inner form 13 and 4, and so on. In other words, the imposition is determined not only by the format of the book but also by the way in which that format will be "made up" within the book. Folios, for example, were seldom sewn in single sheets before the eighteenth century but more usually with three sheets ("folio in sixes") or four sheets ("folio in eights").

Quartos were frequently sewn in single sheets, producing four leaves or eight pages, with an outer form of pages 1,8,4,5 and an inner of 7,2,6,3. If, however, it were sewn two sheets together, eight leaves or sixteen pages, then the outer form of the outer sheet would contain 1,16,4,13, the inner form of the same sheet, 15,2,14,3. Impositions therefore exist in far greater numbers than simply the quantity of the different formats, as a glance at any of the printer's manuals will confirm.

In recent years attention has been paid to a compositorial and printing habit that seems to have been more widespread than was previously believed, namely, setting by forms. For example, in a folio in sixes the pages included in the first gathering would be numbers 1 to 12 inclusive. It seems logical that the compositor would start setting at page 1 and follow logically through with the next until page 12 had been set. The problem with this method was that the form containing page 1, the first to be set, could not be printed until page 12 was finished. Indeed no form would be ready for printing until the completion of page 8, when the outer form of the inner sheet, containing pages 5 and 8 would be ready for the press. If, however, the process of casting-off could be carried out accurately and a good estimate made of the text that would be carried on each page, then an alternative method was possible. Two compositors started with pages 6 and 7; one worked backward to page 1 while the other set forward to page 12. Each compositor worked at an individual case of type, set the type, and then distributed the type back again into the case. The result is that broken or recognizable sorts recur with some regularity. If the casting-off was accurate, then the "join" should scarcely show. Problems arose when there had been faulty calculations, which affected the compositor working backward. Since the previous six pages were already in print the compositor had no recourse but to make some amendment to the setting, such as varying the number of lines to the pages or, in some circumstances, make more drastic amendments to the text. This method would enable the inner form of the inner sheet, containing pages 6 and 7, to be printed as soon as composed, followed by 5 and 8, 4 and 9, and so on. Charlton Hinman's study of the First Folio is the best-known example of this, but others make it clear that this was not an isolated example.[11]

One other practice was general enough to make it convenient for consideration at this point, that of "half-sheet imposition." By this method all the type pages for the printing of a sheet, which would usually be imposed in two forms, were instead imposed within the single form. Following first printing the sheets were then perfected from the same form, with the paper turned end to end, cut into halves, each half bearing precisely the same layout of pages. These half-sheets were then folded ready for the binder.[12]

The press and press work

Our knowledge of the wooden handpress that was used with little alteration, and none in principle, from the time of the invention of printing until 1800 is built up from a variety of pieces of evidence.

First, there are several sixteenth-century woodcuts, a number of which were used as the design in printer's devices. That used by Froschover at Zurich in the middle of the century shows as clearly as any the essentials of the press as well as of the composing cases. Apart from these a few illustrations exist that show the press in operation, such as Dürer's drawing of 1511 or the fuller and much more detailed delineation of the whole of the printer's office as shown in Abraham von Werdt's woodcut.[13]

Second, the detailed measurements of the handpress with sufficient detail to understand the basis of its operation are given in Joseph Moxon's *Mechanick Exercises*, first published in 1683 and within recent years superbly edited and reissued. Much later information can be gleaned from the several printers' manuals that were issued both with regard to the operation of the press itself and the whole organization of the printing office.[14]

Third, as McKerrow stressed, there is the evidence of the books that were printed on the press. In many instances of detail the books bore traces—pinholes, for example—of their origin, and the evidence needs interpretation. This is an area of bibliographical investigation in which much work has been conducted in recent years.

Fourth, and most important of all, is the existence of a number of old wooden handpresses today, many of which are in operational order. European museums have several, as have those of the United States.[15] Of them all the most impressive for quantity and condition are those in the Plantin-Moretus Museum in Antwerp. Here are not only the presses but also all the equipment and paraphernalia of the printing shop exactly as it existed when it was functioning. A number of modern replicas can be found, constructed chiefly for educational purposes.[16] There is also a quantity of nineteenth-century iron presses, which bestraddle these two worlds; some of them are in museums while many of them are in use for bibliographical instruction.[17]

The wooden press resembled an old-fashioned linen-press, and the framework reached from floor to ceiling, as befitted a structure that had to work with so heavy a weight of metal. The screw was turned, and the impression made, by pulling a long handle. Under the screw was a flat, heavy board, the "platen," which the action of the screw brought down upon the paper and type.

The form was laid upon the bed of the press and inked. In modern press work the inking is done by a mechanically regulated flow of ink from a supply tank, the ink being carried over the form by rollers. But in the handpress of the fifteenth to the eighteenth centuries the ink was dabbed on by heavy "ink-balls," as may be seen in Figure 8. In spite of this apparently primitive method, uneven inking was much rarer in those years than might be at first supposed.

The problem was to position the paper so that the platen could press it upon the inked form and take the impression. A frame was necessary, and this is called the "tympan" (Greek: a

FIG. 8. *Earliest known illustration of a printing press.* Danse Macabre, *Lyons. 1499.*

drum). The frame of the tympan was covered by a piece of stout parchment and hinged at one end to the bed of the press. It was on this bed that the sheet of paper was placed. At the other end of the tympan is hinged another light frame. This is the "frisket," and its purpose was to double in over the tympan and so to come between the paper and the inked surface when the tympan and frisket are together turned down upon the form. In this way the margins were protected from the ink. The frame of the frisket was fitted with a sheet of stout paper or parchment, which was first of all brought down on the type and inked, and out of which the inked type-page areas were cut, like windows, to admit the paper to the type just where it was wanted and nowhere else.

The paper for the printing of the book was brought into the printing shop from the warehouse and prepared for printing. The main step in this preparation was the dampening of the sheets in order to secure a good impression. This was a careful process since any lack of judgment would result in a distorted sheet. When the paper was ready for use, it was placed on a low bench conveniently situated by the press, as may be seen in the foreground of the von Werdt illustration.

When the sheets had been printed on one side, they were piled up ready to be "perfected," i.e., printed on the other side from the second form. This part of the operation had to be completed soon after the printing of the first side if distortion of the sheet was to be avoided as the paper dried. The major problem at this stage was that of register, that is, of ensuring that the paper was in the same position on the tympan during the perfecting process as it had been for the printing of the first side. The early printer solved this in an ingenious fashion. Two adjustable pins, fastened to the frame of the tympan, pierced the paper along the central fold of the sheet. When the sheet was perfected, the sheet was returned to the tympan so that the pins again went through the holes already made and ensured the overall register of the sheet. The pinholes so created are an important part of bibliographical evidence and a significant body of writing has grown up on the subject.[18] Printing with more than one color, or printing from two different surfaces, such as relief and intaglio, onto the same sheet nearly always necessitated a separate impression. One of the most common secondary colors to be used in printing was red, and the fact that red printing was from the earliest times done by an independent impression is clear from the fact that red and black often overlap, which would be impossible at a single impression.

Before the form could be printed off, or "put to bed," it was necessary to make sure that the face of the whole type surface was absolutely even, as otherwise those parts that were standing the least bit above the level would make too strong an impression on (and perhaps even into) the paper, while those below it would not be impressed strongly enough, and the result would be the familiar one of alternating patches of heavy black and of grey.

This process is called "making ready," and it completed the work begun by the hammering flat of the typeface. It should first be explained that the tympan was padded with layers of paper and textiles, in order to prevent the type from cutting through the paper. A first trial pull showed which parts of the form were printing too heavily or too lightly. The worker took sheets of paper to add to the padding of the tympan, and from this cut out patches corresponding to the heavy patches in the impression and pasted on extra pieces of paper corresponding to the light patches. This corrected the inequalities by pressing the paper farther down into the light patches and allowing it to be pressed not quite so far down into the heavy patches. It will readily be imagined that making ready was the work of a highly skilled hand and eye, and that there was nothing mechanical about it.

The quality of the ink was also of importance, but really poor printer's ink was not so common as is thought. Printer's ink differs entirely from writing ink. The latter is liquid made (at its best) from oak-gall and water; the former is a very viscous substance made from linseed oil and lampblack. The best printers of all periods have been distinguished by the care with which they selected, or frequently made for themselves, the inks that they were to use. Baskerville and Morris are two well-known examples of this kind of perfection. Many others, with equal thought for the standard of their work, bought their supplies from specialist manufacturers. It is not a subject to which a great deal of attention has been paid in bibliographical work, but it is one of fundamental importance.[19] Some of the block-books that are contemporary with the first generation of typography are printed with liquid writing ink that has turned brown with age; but it seems to have been perceived at once by the pioneers of printing with movable types that black (and red) oil-based ink was the only suitable medium.[20]

The design of the press made one other practice necessary to which reference is often made. The measurement that Moxon gave for the platen was 9″ × 14″, but the measurement of the tympan was 22″ × 15″. As we have already seen, paper sizes were also appreciably larger than the platen. It is therefore clear that the platen was not large enough to cover the whole of the sheet being printed, and no question can possibly arise of there being any impression made on paper not covered by the platen.

Johnson, in his *Typographia*, makes the process quite clear when comparing the old "Wooden Press" with the new metal press: ". . . it was necessary to pull twice with every full forme."[21] This method of printing was known as "two pulls to the forme."

Stereotyping and electrotyping

Stereotyping and electrotyping are both methods of converting the form of movable letters into a solid block. The object is to avoid resetting of the type for later editions in which alterations are not required. Stereotyping may be said to have been anticipated, in principle, by the block-book, which achieved the same result without the use of type, and by the experiments with *jette en molle*. The more modern experiments, however, that led eventually to a successful method are primarily in the eighteenth century.

The early history of stereotyping is extremely confused, no single account can be said to set the record straight. A general pattern of inventive activity is nevertheless fairly clear, and the several independent inventors can be placed in some kind of perspective.[22]

A minister of the German Lutheran Church in Holland, Johann Müller, is credited with the first successful attempt to print from plates made in this manner. This is believed to have resulted in a small prayer book in 1701, followed by the following surviving books printed by his process: a Syriac Lexicon (1709), a Dutch Bible (quarto, 1711; folio, 1718), and a Greek New Testament (1716).

The better-known attempts, long thought generally to be the first that were successful, were those of William Ged, an Edinburgh goldsmith, around 1727. He spent a number of frustrating years in partnership with men whose views were not as disinterested as his own. Eventually, however, a small duodecimo volume of Sallust appeared in Edinburgh in 1739, stating on the title page that it had been printed "not with movable type, as is usual, but with cast plates." It seems to have been recognized for the breakthrough that it in fact was; John Carter recorded having seen some contemporary bindings labeled SALLUST/FROM/ PLATES.

Ged's process was probably forgotten soon after his death and was again independently invented by Alexander Tilloch in Scotland and by F. I. J. Hoffman in Paris. These early stereotyping methods, which all depended upon molds of plaster of paris, lasted until about 1830. The one other name of particular interest in this period is that of one of the greatest of innovators of the time, Earl Stanhope (1753–1816). He made some important advances in technique around 1800 in conjunction with a London printer, Andrew Wilson. Stanhope was a well-rounded figure in the technological life of the time, but Andrew Wilson has only recently begun to assume any substance related to his part in these developments.[23] The nineteenth century witnessed great changes in plating methods. The new printing machinery, and especially the rotary printing press, made such advances necessary, and the whole course of long printing runs and cheap book production justified such developments as had never been necessary prior to 1800. Genoux of Lyons introduced paper in place of plaster of paris in 1839. This paved the way for the long reign of papier-mâché, alternate layers of blotting paper and tissue paper with a noninflammable paste. This was known as "flong."

This was the basis of the method used throughout the nineteenth and much of the twentieth century. Flong was mechanically pressed (formerly brushed) over the original printing surface, and the molds so made, which are light and yet lasting, can be stored until required. Type-metal casts are made from these molds and mounted "type high" for printing. A great advantage of the process was that the printing face could be not only perpetuated but also multiplied, so that where a "long run" was in question the same form could be printed at several presses simultaneously. These factors made possible much of the popular-book publication of the last two-thirds of the nineteenth century and the first half of the twentieth. The demands of the press and the need for finer work were met by the introduction of electroplating in about 1840. Copper was deposited on a wax or lead mold taken from the face of the type and was then backed up to bring it to type-height. For more lasting surfaces in longer runs nickel-faced electros were also employed.

In all these cases the plates could easily be rounded, or cast curved, in order to suit the rotary presses of the nineteenth and twentieth centuries. The main drawback to printing from plates was that once the molds had been made, correction was difficult. Words or phrases that can be cut out and replaced by words or phrases occupying the same amount of space are comparatively simple, but such occasions are naturally rare. Otherwise, fresh typesetting and complicated printing methods are involved. As can be readily appreciated, such an event will frequently result in irregularities in pagination and signatures, which must be watched. Methods of plating developed in America at about the same time as in Europe.[24] Because there was such a flow of titles between British and American publishers it is not uncommon to find complex examples among such transatlantic transplants. The bibliography of American books is further complicated by the fact that most American books after 1860 were printed from plates, electro or stereo, and not from type. It was not uncommon, in those American books that still carried signatures, for the printing to have been done from plates that were signed in such a way as to allow the printer to choose one of several formats. W. A. Jackson reported a copy of

> Conan Doyle's A *Study in Scarlet*, Philadelphia, J. B. Lippincott Co., 1890. This is a 12 mo. bound in sixes, with three sets of signatures: (a) roman capitals by twelves, (b) italic lower-case by eights, and (c) arabic numerals by sixes, with asterisked repeated numbers for the inserted two-leaf conjugates.[25]

It is always necessary to approach with extreme caution any book that is known, or suspected, to be printed from plates.

The power-driven press

The whole of the nineteenth century was one of considerable technological change, and the central object of the entire operation, the printing press itself, was no exception. The first step in this direction was the change from the old wooden press that was brought about by the advent of the Stanhope press. This was the first to have an iron frame, with a compound lever action and a platen that was large enough to cover the whole form. It was designed by Lord Stanhope, who deliberately refrained from taking out a patent on his invention so that the trade could benefit from it to the maximum. Other models, with successive improvements, followed in rapid succession; the unsuccessful Ruthven Press in Edinburgh in 1813, the successful Columbian

Press of George Clymer of Philadelphia in 1813, and the Albion Press of R. W. Cope around 1822. These, however, were all handpresses—the mechanization had yet to come. William Nicholson had made tentative proposals for a powered press as early as 1790, but they were never developed. The true inventor was Frederick Koenig, born in Thuringia in 1774, who became a printer. After early experiments he went to London in 1806, continued his experiments, took out a patent in 1811, and constructed his first successful machine in 1812. Commercial success was virtually ensured when *The Times* newspaper ordered early models of the press, and the first issue printed on the new machine was that for 29 November 1814. The subsequent history of the power-driven press, its increasing speed and sophistication, is of less importance than the speed with which the printing industry was revolutionized after this date. The role of *The Times* in this is difficult to overestimate. The newspaper was gaining rapidly in prestige, sales, and size at this time, and it needed every technological advance to maintain its position. The original Koenig machine, which could produce eleven hundred impressions an hour, was improved and modified by both Edward Cowper and his brother-in-law, Augustus Applegath. John Walter II, the proprietor of *The Times*, then commissioned them to build a new machine, which went fully into action in 1828. It was capable of printing four sheets at a time on one side of the paper and was capable of printing forty-two hundred sheets an hour. By 1830 the basic revolution had been accomplished. The handpress, which was capable of perhaps two hundred and fifty sheets an hour, had been overtaken, in a matter of fourteen years or so, by one that could operate at least sixteen times that speed.[26]

REFERENCES

1. The beginning student needs a sound, but nontechnical, introduction to the printing processes and the elements of book design. The following are suggestions for an initial survey:

   EDE, Charles, ed. *The Art of the Book.* 1951.

JENNETT, Sean. The Making of Books. 4th ed. 1967.
LEE, Marshall. Bookmaking: The Illustrated Guide to Design and Production. 1965.
McLEAN, Ruari. Modern Book Design. 1958.
Practical Printing and Binding: Odham's Complete Guide to the Printer's Craft. 3rd ed. 1965.
UNWIN, Sir Stanley. The Truth About Publishing. 8th ed. 1976.
WILLIAMSON, Hugh. Methods of Book Design. 2nd ed. 1966.

2. BOND, W. H. "Casting Off Copy by Elizabethan Printers." PBSA. XLII: 1948. pp. 281–291.

3. A good introduction to this complicated matter is:

GASKELL, Philip. "The Lay of the Case." Studies in Bibliography. XXII: 1969. pp. 125–142.

These variations can also be put into perspective by reading the accounts of them and the operations connected with them in the printers' manuals, for example:

HANSARD, Thomas C. Typographia. 1825. pp. 406–409.
JOHNSON, John. Typographia or the Printer's Instructor. 1824. Vol. II. pp. 96–118.
MOXON, Joseph. Mechanick Exercises on the Whole Art of Printing. 1683–84. (Davis-Carter. 1962 ed.) pp. 27–30.
SAVAGE, William. Dictionary of the Art of Printing. 1841. pp. 95–102.

For a slightly different viewpoint, emphasizing the variety of models, see:

PRYOR, Lewis A. "The History of the California Job Type Case." Journal of the Printing Historical Society. VII: 1972. pp. 37–50.

4. The term "capitals" is strictly kept for the large decorative letters at the beginning of chapters ("Capita"); but printers speak of "caps" and "small caps."

5. One interesting modern example of a break with the traditional type-page area is:

THOMPSON, Elbert A., and THOMPSON, Lawrence S. Fine Binding in America. 1956.

6. A clear date for the introduction of the galley proof is still uncertain. For various aspects see:

HARGREAVES, G. D. "'Correcting in the Slip': The Development of Galley Proofs." *The Library.* 5th Series. XXVI: 1971. pp. 295–311.
JONES, John Bush. "British Printers on Galley Proofs." *The Library.* 5th Series XXXI: 1976. pp. 105–117.
JONES, John Bush. "Galley Proofs in America." *Proof.* IV: 1975. pp. 153–164.
McKERROW, R. B. "The Use of the Galley in Elizabethan Printing." *The Library.* 4th Series. II: 1921–22. pp. 97–108.

7. Although success was not achieved until late in the nineteenth century, there had been earlier experiments, notably by an American inventor, Dr. William Church (1779–1863), on whose efforts Johnson poured such scorn in his *Typographia,* 1824. Vol. II. pp. 545–546. For more detail see:

HUSS, Richard E. *Dr. Church's "Hoax."* 1976.

See also:

MORAN, James. *The Composition of Reading Matter.* 1965.

8. MORAN, James. "Filmsetting—Bibliographical Implications." *The Library.* 5th Series. XV: 1960. pp. 231–245.

9. The most important work in this field is:

SIMPSON, Percy. *Proof-reading in the Sixteenth, Seventeenth and Eighteenth Centuries.* 1935.

The student should also see the most detailed examination of a single work yet produced that bears on this subject:

HINMAN, Charlton. *The Printing and Proof-reading of the First Folio of Shakespeare.* 2v. 1963.

In addition, there are a number of studies of proof-correcting procedures of individual printers:

BROWN, John Russell. "A Proof-sheet from Nicolas Oke's Printing-shop." *Studies in Bibliography.* XI: 1958. pp. 228–231.

CRAVEN, Alan E. "Proofreading in the Shop of Valentine Simmes." *PBSA*. LXVIII: 1974. pp. 361–372.
McKENZIE, D. F. "Eight Quarto Proof Sheets of 1594 Set by Formes." *The Library*. 5th Series. XXVIII: 1973. pp. 1–13.

10. A good short survey of the work of the corrector is:

HELLINGA, Wytze Gs. *Copy and Print in the Netherlands*. 1962. pp. 142–152.

11. Hinman's study, listed above under reference 9, is the best known. Others that record similar procedures are:

CRUICKSHANK, D. W. "The Printing of Calderon's *Tercera Parte*." *Studies in Bibliography*. XXIII: 1970. pp. 230–251.
FLORES, R. M. *The Compositors of the First and Second Madrid Editions of "Don Quixote": Part 1*. 1975.

This last title shows an interesting example of change in compositorial method during the course of printing.

12. POVEY, K. "On the Diagnosis of Half-sheet Imposition." *The Library*. 5th Series. XI: 1956. pp. 268–272.

13. A good reproduction of the Dürer drawing with commentary may be found in the edition published by the Department of Printing and Graphic Arts at Harvard:

NASH, Ray. *Dürer's 1511 Drawing of a Press and Printer*. 1947.

Abraham von Werdt's woodcut appeared in:

DIEDERICHS, Eugen. *Deutsches Leben der Vergangenheit in Bildern*. (Jena.) 1908.

and is reproduced in this volume as Plate 4.

14. The most important of the printers' manuals are, listed chronologically:

MOXON, Joseph. *Mechanick Exercises on the Whole Art of Printing*. 1683.
WATSON, James. *The History of the Art of Printing*. 1713.

SMITH, John. *The Printer's Grammar.* 1755.
LUCKOMBE, Philip. *The History and Art of Printing.* 1771.
STOWER, Caleb. *The Printer's Grammar.* 1808.
JOHNSON, John. *Typographia or the Printer's Instructor.* 1824.
HANSARD, Thomas C. *Typographia.* 1825.
TIMPERLEY, Charles H. *The Printer's Manual.* 1838.
SAVAGE, William. *A Dictionary of the Art of Printing.* 1841.

The student is fortunate that a modern edition of Moxon is available from Oxford University Press (2nd ed. 1962), and modern editions of all the others in the series of *English Bibliographical Sources* (Series 3· Printers' Manuals), edited by D. F. Foxon and published jointly by the Gregg Press and the Archive Press.

See also the paper:

GASKELL, Philip; BARBER, Giles; and WARRILOW, Georgina. "An Annotated List of Printers' Manuals to 1850." *Journal of the Printing Historical Society.* IV: 1968. pp. 11–32; and VII: 1971. pp. 65–66.

For the development of the press itself there is:

MORAN, James. *Printing Presses, History and Development from the Fifteenth Century to Modern Times.* 1973.

15. GASKELL, Philip. "A Census of Wooden Presses." *Journal of the Printing Historical Society.* VI: 1970. pp. 1 32.
   HARRIS, Elizabeth M. "The American Common Press· The Restoration of a Wooden Press in the Smithsonian Institution." *Journal of the Printing Historical Society.* VIII: 1972. pp. 42–52.
   HARRIS, Elizabeth, and SISSON, Clinton. *The Common Press, Being a Record, Description and Delineation of the Early Eighteenth-Century Handpress in the Smithsonian Institution.* 2v. (text and plans). 1978.

16. GASKELL, Philip. "The Bibliographical Press Movement." *Journal of the Printing Historical Society.* I: 1965. pp. 1–13.

17. KAINEN, Jacob. *George Clymer and the Columbian Press.* 1950.
   MORAN, James. "The Columbian Press." *Journal of the Printing Historical Society* V: 1969. pp. 1–23.
   SILVER, Rollo G. "An Early Time-sharing Project: The Intro-

duction of the Napier Press in America." *Journal of the Printing Historical Society.* VII: 1971. pp. 29–36.
STONE, Reynolds. "The Albion Press." *Journal of the Printing Historical Society.* II: 1966. pp. 58–73; and III: 1967. pp. 97–99.

18. MASLEN, K. I. D. "Point-holes as Bibliographical Evidence." *The Library.* 5th Series. XXIII: 1969. pp. 240–241.
MASSON, Sir Irvine. "Digression on Pinholes and Their Interpretation," in *The Mainz Psalters and Canon Missae, 1457–1459.* 1954. pp. 16–22.
POVEY, K. "Pinholes in the 1457 Psalter." *The Library.* 5th Series. XI: 1956. pp. 18–22.

19. One of the few recent occasions when ink was used as bibliographical evidence was in the investigation of the "Vinland Map." The map, which had been believed to date around AD 1440, was found to have traces in the ink of a form of titanium oxide that was invented in the 1920s.

20. BLOY, C. H. *A History of Printing Ink, Balls and Rollers, 1440–1850.* 1967.
CARVALHO, David N. *Forty Centuries of Ink.* 1904.

21. Johnson, *Typographia,* ii, p. 504.

22. CARTER, John. "William Ged and the Invention of Stereotype." *The Library.* 5th Series. XV: 1960. pp. 161–192, with a postscript, *The Library.* 5th Series. XVI; 1961. pp. 143–145; and *The Library* 5th Series. XVIII: 1963. pp. 308–309.
Printing and the Mind of Man. Catalogue of the Exhibitions. . . . 1963. pp. 60–62.

23. TURNER, Michael L. "Andrew Wilson: Lord Stanhope's Stereotype Printer, a Preliminary Report." *Journal of the Printing Historical Society.* IX: 1973–74. pp. 22–65.

24. SILVER, Rollo G. "Trans-Atlantic Crossing: The Beginning of Electro-typing in America." *Journal of the Printing Historical Society.* X: 1974–75. pp. 84–103.

25. NOWELL-SMITH, Simon. "Signatures in Some Nineteenth-

century Massachusetts Duodecimos: A Query. *The Library.* 5th Series. III: 1948–49. pp. 58–62.

JACKSON, W. A. "Signatures in Nineteenth-century American Printing." *Ibid.* p. 224.

HAZEN, A. T. "Signatures in Nineteenth-century American Printing." *Ibid.* pp. 224–229.

HAZEN, A. T. "Signatures in Nineteenth-century American Printing." *The Library.* 5th Series. VII: 1952. p. 134.

26. BERRY, W. T. "Augustus Applegath, Some Notes and References." *Journal of the Printing Historical Society.* II: 1966. pp. 49–57.

GREEN, Ralph. "Early American Power Printing Presses." *Studies in Bibliography.* IV: 1951–52. pp. 143–153.

Printing and the Mind of Man, pp. 74–81.

TIMES NEWSPAPER. *Printing The Times Since 1785.* 1953.

7.

ILLUSTRATION

From the very earliest times books have been decorated or elucidated—as we say, "illustrated"—by drawings and paintings or other reproductions. It is necessary for the bibliographer to know something of the history and technique of the various processes in order to recognize and adequately describe them. For this purpose no theoretical training is worth anything by comparison with the study of examples of the processes themselves in books and in print galleries. In each area of the work students should locate several examples and study them with great care. A few examples of the processes will be presented in this chapter, but for each one given another hundred could serve equally well. It may also prove useful to consult some of the texts on the recognition of prints.[1]

Decoration in books is almost as old as the idea of the book itself. The earliest known extant example of illustrative work of this nature is the *Ramesseum Papyrus*, a roll dating back to the twentieth century BC. In this instance the text is of a ceremonial play, but many of the best-known examples, such as the *Hunefer Papyrus*, are superbly illustrated copies of the Book of the Dead. The world of Graeco-Roman illustration included examples of pure illustration for such works as herbals as well as the more decorative elements in early books, such as the *Ambrosian Iliad* or the *Vatican Virgil*, both dating from around the fourth or fifth centuries AD.

In the period that followed, the great development of illumination, which was the regular form of book decoration through to the close of the Middle Ages and one of the chief channels of art for nearly a thousand years, was fostered by two influences in the Eastern Empire: first, the sumptuous taste of Byzantine society, and second, the spread of Pergamene vellum, which provided a more solid and opaque ground than papyrus for gold and colors. Three types of decoration ensue:

(a) *Rubrication,* or in old English, "rubrishing." Originally this term covered whatever was written in red. Marginal glosses were frequent examples of this practice; hence the name "rubrics" came to be applied to them. The development of decoration brought coloring, other than gold and silver, to individual letters, especially capitals. Capitals, in the manuscript tradition, were not what the printer was later to term "upper case" but the large initials of chapters for which the scribe had left space. The early printer frequently followed this scribal practice and left spaces for the letters to be added by hand. Although, etymologically, all this type of decoration should be in red, the term "rubrication" came to be applied to similar work in other colors also, chiefly blue and less frequently green.

(b) *Illumination,* the decoration of the manuscript in gold or silver. In the earlier period these were applied, whether to the letters or as general decoration, in liquid form. After the thirteenth century application was in the form of gold or silver leaf burnished on to a prepared surface. The silver has nearly always oxidized black, but the gold has kept its color.

(c) *Miniature painting,* the painting of scenes, sometimes purely decorative but frequently appropriate to the matter of the book. Initial letters, and especially those that had bowls to them, such as *B, D, O, P,* and the wide margin at the foot of the page were popular locations. The paintings were called "miniatures" not because they were small but because the artist originally worked largely in *minium,* a scarlet paint. Hence the artist became a *miniator* and the work itself a *miniature.*

These three processes were frequently combined within a single book and were generally the work of different hands. At this stage of development it also becomes increasingly apparent that two distinct yet interrelated functions are emerging. At its purest possible level illustration exists to elucidate certain parts of a text. It can almost be said in these instances that the text is deficient unless illustrated: herbals and anatomical and architectural writings were among the earliest of this kind. The other instinct, and this must be present to some degree in pure illustration, is the decorative element. Here the artwork can scarcely be called essential unless it is in setting a tone for the book as a whole.

The Byzantine art passed west through Italy and met the Celtic at the court of Charlemagne, producing the Carolingian style. Apart from the remarkable Anglo-Saxon school of outline drawing of the tenth and eleventh centuries this was the basis of the style of Western Europe till the thirteenth century, when national styles began to be generally divergent. Books became smaller in the next two centuries, and certain features became stereotyped. The border decorations, which were designed to flow out from a capital, were at first delightfully fresh and restrained, showing plenty of margin; they often ended in grotesque monsters, hares hunting men, and so forth. Gradually the fashion settled on smaller books, passing in the fifteenth century from the Psalter to the Hours of the Virgin, as it had earlier passed from Bibles and Apocalypses to the Psalter. The margin illumination became more mechanical, until the margins were filled with a solid framework, and little vellum was visible. At the same time in the French and Flemish schools the enclosed miniature reached the highest point of beauty and delicacy, but also became common. Books of Hours of the later fifteenth and earlier sixteenth centuries, the product of the stationers' shops, abound, and these are generally of small merit.

Illuminations and miniatures are not only worthy of study for their own sake as monuments of medieval art; they frequently enable us to fix the date and country of origin of manuscripts, which very rarely contain that information in their colophons.[2]

The advent of printing killed illumination, though not at once. There are copies of books from the earliest Mainz presses that are elaborately illuminated; and in Italy the art, strongly colored by the Renaissance, survived in printed books and manuscripts into the sixteenth century. The best combination of the printer's and illuminator's arts is to be found in North Italian books of about 1470–1475, which often have the opening page of text exquisitely decorated with an illuminated capital set in a border of white vine-tendrils on a background of colors.

But it is not in human nature to go on applying costly decoration to a cheap article, and the normal decoration found in early printed books consisted of rubricated capitals in red and blue, with more or less decoration. Printed decorative capitals, but in metal, were tried by Fust and Schoeffer at Mainz as early as 1457 but were not successful; and it was only some twenty years later that the woodcut capital was introduced in the presses of South Germany and in the next twenty years gradually took the place of rubrication.

It is now time to turn to the production of printed illustrations.

Technically these may be divided into three classes

(a) *Relief.* In this group the printing is done from a raised surface, as with normal letterpress printing. In most cases it is the design that is left standing while the background is cut away. The reverse of this is true in the case of wood-engraving, which, in spite of its name, is a relief process. The great advantage of relief illustration processes is that they can be set up and printed at the same time as normal type and plates can be taken from them.

The most important relief processes are woodcuts, wood-engravings, halftones, and line-blocks.

(b) *Intaglio.* Here the design is incised in the block or plate, which is then cleaned, inked, and wiped. Thus the engraved lines of the design alone retain the ink and the impression is made by strong pressure so that the paper is forced into the incisions.

All intaglio engravings will normally show a "plate-line"; the paper, which is pressed by the plate, is smooth and sunk, while beyond the edge of the plate it keeps its natural surface; the resulting line dividing these two areas is the plate-line. When the plate-line is absent, it will be for one of three reasons: (i) The leaf has been cut down by the binder. When this is so, the engraving is reckoned imperfect, as there may be lettering, or even part of the design, cut away. (ii) The plate was as large or larger than the sheet. This is common in small steel-engravings of the early nineteenth century, which seem to have been regularly engraved together on a single plate as large as the open sheet, so that when cut for issue the leaves show no plate-line at all. (iii) The illustration was printed by the offset method.

The strong pressure needed for printing all intaglio plates makes it impossible to print at the same time with typeset text. They are sometimes printed on a page bearing letterpress, but by a second impression; and normally they appear alone on inserted plate leaves.

The action of the press flattens the edges of the incisions in the soft copper, and the finer lines gradually grow faint, so that a late impression is much less crisply defined than an early one and is usually much less valuable.

The designer's name, when it appears, is generally given at the foot on the left, followed by the word "del" (*delineavit:* drew) or "pinx" (*pinxit:* painted), and the engraver's on the right, followed by "sculp" (*sculpsit:* engraved, literally carved, the Latin for an engraving being *sculptura*). These abbreviations are said to have been mistaken by the beginner for surnames of singular frequency. The right way to express it in description is: Plates by So-and-So (the Engraver) after So-and-So (the Artist)— e.g., by Blake after Lawrence.

The chief intaglio methods of illustration are line-engraving, drypoint, etching, stipple, mezzotint, aquatint, and photogravure.

(c) *Planograph.* The design is neither raised nor incised but is on a flat surface. Printing is accomplished because certain areas will accept ink while others will reject it.

The chief planographic processes are lithography, including photolithography, and collotype.

Woodcut and wood-engraving

In a woodcut the drawing is made on or transferred to a smooth block of wood, planed along the grain. The cutter with a knife cuts away everything that is to be left white. Since both the woodcut and the page of type are in relief the two can easily be printed together. Moreover, if the strength of line of each is chosen so as to harmonize with the other, a pair of pages of text and woodcut makes an entirely harmonious whole, and accordingly this style of illustration has always proved attractive to book designers. Woodcut and line-engraving on copper were both in existence in Germany at the time of the invention of printing. The technical advantage of woodcut over engraving, in not needing a separate printing, no doubt caused it to be the more popular of the two, as well as the difficulties met by early printers in taking impressions from an intaglio surface.

Woodcut printing (xylography) was employed as early as the twelfth century for the decoration of stuffs; but it was only with the spread of paper in the later fourteenth century that it was used for separate pictures. Examples of these, which are believed to have been sold or given to pilgrims at shrines, are found bearing lettering cut, like the picture, in the wood. One of the Virgin at Brussels bears the date 1418; one of St. Christopher in the John Rylands Library, 1423; while one at Paris has been assigned to 1408.

Late in the fifteenth century, and particularly at Paris, soft metal was used instead of wood, often punched with holes (*criblé*) to relieve the black mass. Metalcuts do not have so sharp-edged an effect as woodcuts, and of course they never show wormholes or cracks, which often help the bibliographer to arrange in their true order undated editions of books illustrated with woodcuts.[3]

The first use of woodcuts in printed books was made by Albrecht Pfister of Bamberg in 1460–1462; but they were not used again until a decade later, when they flourished in South German towns. Early German woodcuts used a bold strong line and were very vigorous, if often crude. In Italy, where the art was late to be introduced, they were more graceful: the famous *Hypnerotomachia Poliphili* of 1499 at Venice is perhaps the highest point reached. But the school of Florentine cutters of 1490–1510 produced much charming work, using, as well as line, black silhouette lightened by white-line engraving.

In the sixteenth century woodcut gradually sank before the rise of line-engraving, which superseded it in the seventeenth and eighteenth centuries, leaving it to the jobbing printers for ballads and the like. Toward the end of the eighteenth century, however, woodcut met with a revival in the form of wood-engraving, first in France and then notably in England, at the hands of Thomas Bewick (1753–1828), whose *Select Fables*, 1784; *General History of Quadrupeds*, 1790; and *History of British Birds*, 1797–1804, brought wood out of disrepute into favor again.

Wood-engraving differs from woodcut in that a harder wood is used, generally box, and the design is cut into the surface with a graver, not a knife, working against the grain on the end of the plank. As a result, although the block is still a relief block, it is the background and not the line that takes the ink. In the words of the British Museum's *Guide to the Processes and Schools of Engraving*, the design "prints white."[4] There is nothing to prevent the use of black-line and white-line together on one block.

Wood-engraving flourished during the nineteenth century in England following its great use by Bewick, and some beautiful work was done after many of the best artists. Later in the century wood was used in an attempt to produce something like a photograph but of lesser quality. When photographic blocks became cheaper, they killed the art. At the very end of the century William Morris in his Kelmscott Press books went back for decoration as well as typographical inspiration to the fifteenth century in Germany. He used woodcuts for illustrations, borders, and capital letters with bold black line that harmonized with his types. During this present century the concentration has been mainly on wood-engraving, and in no other field of book illustration and decoration has so high a level been reached and maintained. Thanks mainly to the inspiration and encouragement of the private- and fine-press movement, there is now a body of first-class wood-engravers whose work can be found in the ordinary commercial-press book.

The actual woodcut is not often used in printing in modern times; in order both to save it from accident and to enable simultaneous printing to be done at more than one press electrotypes are made, which give a facsimile.

Another development on the same lines is the linocut, in which the block is surfaced with linoleum. It does not differ in principle from woodcut, but it is coarser and not widely used in book illustration. In similar fashion, any surface that is capable of being cut can be pressed into service for the wood-cutting princi-

Illustration ๙ 207

ple, even to the, at first, unlikely medium, capable of only a few impressions, of the potato cut.[5]

Line-engraving

Line-engraving is executed on a plate of polished metal, generally copper. The engraver pushes the graver or burin, which cuts the line, into the soft copper, throwing up a burr, or furrowridge, of copper. This is scraped away, and the plate is inked and then wiped, the ink remaining only in the lines, whence it is transferred to paper by very strong pressure, as the paper must be forced into the incisions to take up the ink.

Few illustrations engraved on copper are found in the fifteenth century. At Bruges and Florence, where engravers were at work, they appeared as early as 1476 or 1477; and in 1481 the Florentine press of Nicolaus Laurentii produced the Dante with cuts once thought to be (and possibly are) after designs by Botticelli. At Cologne an isolated Kalendar of L. Beham (1476?) has coppercut astronomical tables; and a series of service books of Würzburg and Eichstätt of 1479 and the next decade, printed by the Reysers, seems to owe its engraved illustrations to episcopal patronage. For map making the process was eminently suited, as giving a finer line; and it was used for the purpose in the Rome Ptolemy in 1478 (planned by Sweynheym in 1474) and the Bologna edition of 1482, in which year the splendid edition of Ulm was produced with woodcuts.

Practically wherever the process appeared in book illustration it preceded woodcut and was superseded by it, no doubt on account of the technical difficulty of combining the printings of incised and relief surfaces. Laurentii's Dante of 1481 is evidence that it was a pioneer process. Only nineteen of the many illustrations planned are known; of these only three are pulled on the leaf itself, the rest being pulled on slips and pasted in.

A very remarkable line-engraving in an early book is that of an author, possibly Caxton, presenting his book to Margaret, Duchess of Burgundy, Caxton's patroness, which is found in one copy only (the Chatsworth-Huntington) of the *Recuyell of the Hystoryes of Troye*, 1475;[6] but it is doubtful whether this can be considered as an integral part of the book. If it were, it would be the earliest engraved book illustration. It may, however, have been added to this one copy.

Line-engraving became common in books toward the middle of the sixteenth century, particularly to reproduce fine topographical drawings, maps, etc., of which many were being produced. Woodcut, even in such choice books as the Ulm Ptolemy of 1482, was by comparison coarse. In England copper drove wood out of all but popular use in the seventeenth century, and it was very much used for frontispiece title borders and portraits, of which Droeschout's portrait of Shakespeare in the First Folio of 1623 is one of the most famous and one of the worst. Engravers developed the use of shading and "cross-hatching" to give tone, which was not only laborious but was also never really beautiful. It was mainly the deficiencies of this process for tonal reproduction that prepared the way for the triumph of mezzotint as a tone process. Line-engraving (or "copper-plate") was also used for the copybooks of the writing-masters, such as Cocker, for which, by its delicacy and the slow and careful movement of the hand imposed by the process on the engraver, it was admirably suited. Otherwise, in spite of Faithorne, it fell on evil days, till it was revived on steel in the early nineteenth century. There is some use of copper-engraving today, but it is almost entirely limited to occasional fine book productions.[7]

Steel-engraving

The softness of copper, which prevented very many successful impressions being taken, was against the use of coppercut for large editions. A more resisting material came into use in the nineteenth century. In America in 1810 Jacob Perkins used steel in place of copper for the engraving of bank notes. Its use spread to book illustration in such volumes as A. B. Durand's engravings in W. C. Bryant's *The American Landscape* in 1830. By about 1823 artists in Europe were employing the medium, and in England there were countless steel-engravings illustrating the works of Campbell, Rogers, Byron, Scott, and others. The Keepsakes and almanacs of the period were in many instances illustrated with engravings of very high quality. The most famous of them, *The Keepsake* (flourished 1828–1857), included some contributions by Turner and much that showed his influence. Turner was one of the outstanding steel-engravers in England of the time, and his work in Rogers's *Italy* (1830), *Poems* (1834), and *Rivers of France* (1833–1835) shows the medium at one of its highest points.

The extreme hardness of steel enabled the engravers to outdo the delicacy of the line in copper, and the work is often microscopic; in fact it is a line process attempting tone. At its best it has great beauty, and it will always be associated with the Romantic movement. By the middle of the nineteenth century it was fading rapidly from a position of real importance in Europe, although it persisted for another twenty or so years in America.

Drypoint

The engraver draws freehand on the copper with a pencil of steel, which throws up a great deal of burr to the side of the line. This burr is not removed but is carefully preserved. When the plate is inked and wiped (with very great care), the ink is retained by the burr as well as in the engraved line itself. The result is an incomparably soft and deep line. But it takes very few impressions to flatten it down and destroy the beauty, and in consequence only a very few books, produced in small editions, are illustrated with drypoints. As in other intaglio processes, the life of the plate can be extended by steel-facing the printing surface, but this is not a common occurrence.

Because there is always uncertainty as to the use of drypointing in a print it is not possible to be precise as to its first appearance. It probably was used in the fifteenth century; Dürer's *St. Jerome in the Wilderness* and *Man of Sorrows*, both dated 1512, provide early examples.

Etching

In the process of this class the lines are incised not by a tool but by acid. The copper plate is protected by a "ground" of a transparent waxy composition, and at the back and sides by varnish.

The etcher smokes the grounded face over a taper to make it opaque and then draws the design on it with a blunt "needle," removing the ground but not cutting the copper. The plate is then placed in a bath of etching acid, which bites the copper where the needle has exposed it. If only one uniform length of biting were given, the etching would show only one thickness of line and would bear some resemblance to a line-engraving. It has been used in this manner by a number of very fine etchers. When the etcher requires greater variety of line, the plate is removed from the bath when the lightest lines have been deeply bitten, and "stopped out" by varnishing them over. The plate is then replaced to give the rest of the lines a rebiting, and so on by stages till the lines are in every required strength from feathery touches to black patches where the lines have fused. The process is thus one of immense range and power.

Etching can often be distinguished from line-engraving by the irregular (or, in the etcher's phrase, "juicy") edges of the line, since the acid does not bite evenly, and also (though not so certainly) by the yellowish impression of the film of ink that is often deliberately left on the plate. Also, being freehand, it gives more the effect of sketching. In this and in the irregular line it is still more like drypoint; and the two processes are often used together. Blake used etching to produce a relief printing surface, biting away the background, a process that he described as "relief etching." He also referred to it in his memoranda as "woodcut on copper," which describes the principle exactly and underlines its basic similarity to photographic line-block making.

The new popularity of sketching in the latter half of the eighteenth century produced varieties of etching to reproduce the crayon and pencil line. The next three processes to be mentioned were the leading methods, and they were frequently used in combination with each other and with normal line-etching.

Soft-ground etching

Here the etcher covers the plate with a soft granulated ground and draws on thin paper stretched evenly over it. The design is drawn on the paper with a lead pencil, causing the waxy ground on the lines to adhere to the paper, which lifts it when raised, but does not leave the lines clean, a certain amount of ground remaining. The etching process is applied normally with the result that the acid bites irregularly round these grains. The line that results is composed of flecks, like that left by crayon or lead pencil on rough drawing paper.

Crayon-etching

Much the same effect is produced by drawing with a toothed roulette instead of a needle. The ground is pierced in points and the printed line is accordingly made of dots, which can be distin-guished from those of soft-ground etching by their regularity. Crayon-engravings were sometimes printed in a reddish-colored ink the further to enhance the similarity of the print to a red chalk drawing. The process was invented in France around 1750 and much used in England in the late eighteenth century.

Stipple

Stippling is a method of giving some semblance of tone to a line illustration. It can be used with both engraved and etched pro-cesses. The general principle is to create a slightly pitted surface in the plate that will hold the ink in a manner similar to the main lines of the design. It has practically the same effect on the finished print as cross-hatching but produces a dotted, in place of a line, semblance of tone. The ground, or the copper itself, is pierced with roulettes and multiple-pointed tools, such as a mace-head, and the resulting print, etched or engraved, shows a close mass of dots, which imitate soft pencil shading or light wash very well.

The early cutters had sometimes got a halftone effect by punching the wood or metal block; and in the desire for tone the seventeenth-century engravers "flicked" the surface of the plate with the graver. Stipple, discreetly used in conjunction with other processes, is more delicate than these. Late in the eighteenth and during the first decade or so of the nineteenth century it was often used alone, particularly in small frontispiece portraits. These are not often successful because the process lacks the strength to stand alone, as will be seen in the plates of Francesco Bartolozzi (1727–1815). Bartolozzi, a Florentine by birth, was invited to England to engrave the Guercino drawings at Windsor Castle and in 1764 was appointed engraver to George III. His best-known work, and hence the best-known stipple engravings, were from the works of Angelica Kauffmann, Francis Wheatley, and the single plate of *Death of Chatham* from J. S. Copley's oil painting.

Mezzotint

Late in the seventeenth century engravers were given a more powerful medium for reproduction of continuous tones than stipple (which was not used till much later), and that was mezzotint. Some uncertainty still surrounds the invention of mezzotint, and a variety of claims can be documented. There seems little reasonable doubt, however, that it was invented by Ludwig von Siegen (1609–af.1676), a Dutchman of German and Spanish parentage. Seven plates by Siegen are known, of which the earliest is a portrait of *Amelia Elizabeth*, the Landgravine of Cassel. In a letter dated August 1642, addressed to the Landgrave, he made a definite claim for his invention. Prince Rupert of the Rhine (1619–1682), for whom claims as the inventor were once made, was surely responsible for its introduction into England and for raising the standard of work. His print of the *Great Executioner*, after a painting by Ribera, which was dated 1658, is one of the finest of early mezzotints and guarantees Prince Rupert a firm place in the history of the art. Much of the early work was of poor quality, and the process appears to have had some initial difficulty in establishing itself. Once the method had been perfected, almost certainly at the hands of Abraham Blooteling (1640–1690), its future was assured. Blooteling began mezzotinting around 1671 after an apprenticeship in line-engraving. He was in England from 1672 to 1676, when he did some of his best work, notably in his plates after Lely.

The process in its fully developed form differs from all others in that the mezzotinter normally works from black to white. The surface of a polished copper plate is first roughened over the whole of its surface. In the early days of the process the roughening was probably done by a roulette wheel with the artist working from light to dark areas—that is, the reverse of the later accepted method. The change came with Blooteling, who introduced the "rocker," a curved serrated tool named from its similarity to that of a cradle. This throws up a burr in all directions, so that if inked, wiped, and printed from it will give a more or less uniform black mass. At this stage the mezzotinter *may* make use of a lightly etched outline, and of course any line may be engraved or etched in afterward; but the essential part of the process is entirely lineless. In the parts to be all but as deep as the absolute black, the burr is very slightly scraped down; in the next lighter parts a little more, so as to hold less ink, and so on to the high lights, which are not only scraped but burnished, so that, when wiped, they can hold no ink at all and are left white in printing. In other parts of the plate the work of the rocker can often be seen.

Mezzotint for fine illustration, especially for portrait frontispieces, drove out line-engraving in England, where it became so naturalized as to be called by the French *la manière anglaise.* For cheaper work line-engraving, for all its laboriousness, continued to be used.

The great contribution of mezzotint lay in its effectiveness as a purely tonal process. No other process could give in the same way the gleam of sky and water in topographical illustrations or the gloss on armor, hair, velvet, and satin in portraiture. It is therefore logical to expect that in England, where for reasons that cannot be wholly explained mezzotint made its natural home, the best work should be found in the period of great oil painters. Some of the finest of English work is consequently in the eighteenth and the very early nineteenth century. John Faber the younger (*c.* 1695–1756), who engraved after Kneller; John Simon (1675–1751), also after Kneller; Valentine Green (1739–1813), one of Reynolds's greatest engravers; John Jones (*c.* 1745–1797), who worked after Romney and Reynolds; and John Raphael Smith (1752–1812), himself a painter, print publisher, and, as an engraver, an interpreter of Reynolds, Romney, and Gainsborough: these are among the men who raised the English mezzotint of the period to an art form.

The later landscape period also had its interpreters. A pupil of J. R. Smith, William Ward (*c.* 1762–1826) achieved his fame with his prints of the landscapes and animals of his brother-in-law, George Morland. The greatest landscape artist of them all, John Constable, was perhaps the most fortunate, in the numerous prints done of his paintings by David Lucas (1802–1881). It is important that time should be spent in finding original prints of some of these engravers in order to appreciate fully the strength of the mezzotint process and the stature of some of the practitioners.

The eighteenth century also contributed to print history by the emigration to America of Peter Pelham (c. 1684–1751), who went to Boston in 1726 and in the following year with his portrait of *Rev. Cotton Mather*, launched the art of mezzotinting in that country.

The great age of the mezzotint was over after the first quarter of the nineteenth century, although it was far from defunct as a process. Innumerable cheap reproductions were produced by this method, and evidence hangs framed on cottage walls. For this writer, at least, the firelight that in Blunden's *Almswomen* falls on "pictured kings and queens grotesquely bright," must surely have fallen on mezzotints. The twentieth century has not abandoned the medium, but it would be difficult to suggest that it has contributed significantly to it.[8]

Aquatint

While Mezzotint had established itself for the reproduction of oils, it gave rather too rich and somber an effect for wash and wash-color drawings, which were very popular in the second half of the eighteenth century. Some uncertainty exists as to the precise allocation of credit for the invention of the aquatint process. A number of plates exist that were produced by processes described by Hind as "on the borderland of aquatint."[9] This will serve to demonstrate once again that few discoveries of any kind spring ready-formed at a particular date. The credit is, however, by consensus usually given to Jean Baptiste Le Prince (1734–1781). His earliest dated aquatints are of 1768, and he exhibited twenty-nine of them in the Paris Salon of 1769 with a note on the new process. In this process the work of the mezzotint rocker is accomplished less laboriously by acid, and at the same time the plate is nowhere roughened so as to print so continuously black as in mezzotint. The plate, first grounded with finely powdered resin, is then warmed so as to fix it—that is, to soften the grains so that they will adhere to the plate as tiny hard globules of acid-resistant resin. With back and sides given a protective coating against the acid, the plate is then transferred to an etching bath. In the bath the acid bites, as in soft-ground etching, around the grains of the ground. The plate is removed from the bath at intervals, stopped out, and rebitten until all the required gradations of tone, from light to dark have been obtained. As in mezzotint, a guiding outline can be etched in at first, and any lines required afterward.

As the etching acid bites into the plate to varying depths, the small areas covered by the resin dots are protected from the acid and therefore remain as areas of undisturbed, polished, copper plate. Their purpose is that when the plate is wiped after inking they will provide a bearing surface on which the wiper will ride. In this way the ink is not wiped out of the pits, which retain the correct amount of ink to print the required tones. One result of this, useful in the identification of aquatints, is that the printed surface shows a network of white dots, where the ground has been protecting the plate, against the background of ink.

The process has varied in some aspects over the years. One such change is associated with the early use of the process in England. Several conflicting stories exist regarding purchases of the details of the process from Le Prince, and it is difficult at present to determine where credence should be placed. The first important practitioner, however, was Paul Sandby (1725-1809), the watercolorist. His first series of aquatints, *Views in Aquatinta from Drawings in South Wales,* was published in 1775. In the British Museum there is a manuscript of Sandby describing the process that he "discovered." In this he describes the preparation of the plate with a fluid ground consisting of resin dissolved in spirits of wine. This may indeed have been the discovery that Sandby claimed, and it was certainly an increasingly popular alternative method among aquatinters.

This inaugurated the great age of the English aquatint, when it was enormously popular for books of picturesque travel, and indeed for every other sort of illustrated book, until about 1830, when it gave way to lithography. The great name of this period is that of Rudolf Ackermann (1764–1834), who published some of the major series of aquatints from his "Repository" in the Strand, where he kept colorists busy tinting the plates. Topographical books are particularly well represented, quantitatively and qualitatively, among aquatint plate books. One of the finest, William Daniell's A Voyage Round Great Britian (1814–1825), with three hundred and eight colored plates, is a magnificent example of this type of work. The best survey of plate books of the late eighteenth and early nineteenth century is the catalog of Major J. R. Abbey's collection, and students should use this to locate the originals that they need to see.[10]

Until modern times aquatint was not a process that attracted the attention of many great artists; one of the few was Goya (1746–1828), notably in his collection Los Caprichos (1799). A notable variation of the normal aquatint process was the "sugar aquatint," a process introduced in the eighteenth century, used by Gainsborough but then neglected until modern times. Several modern French artists, especially Rouault in his illustrations to Suarez's Passion (1939) and Picasso in Buffon's Histoire Naturelle (1942), have used the medium to advantage.[11]

Lithography

This process differs from all others in that the plate is neither carved out in relief nor incised. The design is drawn out and printed from the flat surface of the stone or metal. This apparent impossibility is achieved by means of the basic lithographic principle of two mutually antipathetic surfaces. The process always leads to certain areas of a plate that will accept ink and others that will reject it. Based on this principle, later processes, such as aquatone or, more notably, collotype, can be seen to operate in the same manner. On a polished stone surface the lithographer draws the design with a specially prepared greasy chalk pencil or with a pen using a greasy ink, or makes a greasy solution and lays it on with a brush. Chemical solutions applied to the stone fix the design. The stone is then dampened and the water is absorbed everywhere, except where the grease in the line rejects it. Printing ink is then rolled on, and is rejected by the wet spaces, but accepted by the greasy areas of the design, since they also contain oil. As a result only the design is reproduced upon the paper, which is placed over the stone and pressed down upon the surface.

The surface on which the drawing or painting is done is obviously of great importance. Apart from such qualities as it will need during the printing process, it will also need to be porous during the actual period of work by the artist.[12] Stone is the most porous material that has ever been used for this process but is not the only one. Zinc can be used, and especially so when it has a slightly grained surface. It has come to be a relatively common medium, especially when cheapness is a factor to be considered. In more recent times plastic plates have been used for some very high-grade commercial work. Instead of drawing or painting directly onto the stone, use is also frequently made of lithographic transfer paper. By this method the artist draws, with the usual greasy medium, onto specially prepared paper. The grease in the design is then transferred onto the stone by simple pressure and the stone worked up in the normal manner.

Lithography is the only major process of which the name of the inventor and the date of its invention are known with any certainty. Alois Senefelder discovered the process in 1798, and it had an immediate and widespread effect. Senefelder took out patents in many countries; in England the process was first seen generally in a portfolio of prints published by Senefelder's partner, Philip Andrée. This was the *Specimens of Poly-autography* (1803), which included designs by Benjamin West and Henry Fuseli and the only lithograph known to have been drawn by William Blake. As a means of book illustration it had its first use in J. T. Smith's *Antiquities of Westminster* in 1807. Throughout the nineteenth century lithographic work abounds. At its best it can be seen to be extremely good in such volumes as Gould's famous bird books. The reverse side of the coin was that the technical facility of the process encouraged less-skilled practitioners to try their prentice hands. There is much that is inferior especially in England, where few fine artists tried the medium. The general poor quality was emphasized when color was added to the print. Color printing crept into all the illustrative processes in the nineteenth century, as opposed to the older method of tinting or coloring a monochrome print. Nowhere else than in the chromolithograph did it arrive quite so flamboyantly.

Digby Wyett's *Industrial Arts of the Nineteenth Century*, published
in 1851 to commemorate some of the specimens housed in the
Great Exhibition, gives a clear idea of what it can accomplish
applied to subject matter typical of its period. The use of the
chromolithograph in pure book work is best illustrated by the
works of Noel Humphreys and Owen Jones. Humphreys published
his *Illuminated Books of the Middle Ages* in 1844 and gave one of
the first clear indications that lithography could produce illustrations that appeared to be an integral part of the book. His later
The Parables of Our Lord (1847) and *The Book of Ruth* (1850)
show the same qualities. Jones also deserves honorable mention
for his work in his *Grammar of Ornament* (1856) and *Victoria
Psalter* (1861). The modern eye is fully accustomed to the use of
lithography as a means of reproducing text just as much as illustrations. The harbinger of this vast field was a well-known, now
very scarce, book, Edward Lear's *The Book of Nonsense* in 1846.
The advantage of lithography lay in its ability to reproduce the
work of an artist without the necessity of any intermediary. Because of this it brought out the very best of many artists, such
as Daumier, whose output of approximately four thousand lithographs is the major part of his life's work. The series of lithographs
drawn by Manet for Edgar Allan Poe's *The Raven* in 1874 and
the works of Degas and Toulouse-Lautrec underline the artist's
freedom in the use of this medium.

The twentieth century has continued to use autolithography
in addition to its vast use of photolithography, and many of the
leading book artists of modern times have worked in it. Picasso,
Edward Bawden, Barnett Freedman, Rojankovsky, Roger
Duvoisin, and dozens more have contributed in Europe and in
America to liveliness of this process in modern books.[13]

Photographic illustration

With the exception of lithography, none of the hand processes
described above was, however beautiful, entirely satisfactory
either to the artist or to the scientist responsible for an illustration. For each of these people wants, above all, an absolutely
exact facsimile, faithful to the last touch of the artist's design and

the least detail of the plan or object reproduced. But the design had to be rendered by hand of the engraver, and while some engravers were meticulously careful, others were not. Even the careful ones were human and frequently were artists in their own right, incapable of divesting themselves of their personality. When, therefore, photography was added to the illustrator's resources, it was not an unmixed evil. All facsimile work was thenceforward on a firmer basis, although in nearly all photographic processes the merely mechanical work produces unsatisfactory results. The block or plate is generally fine-etched or otherwise worked over by a skilled engraver's hand.

It will be found that, just as each hand process specially represents one variety of hand design (e.g., line-engraving representing pen-and-ink drawing and aquatint watercolor), so each photographic process represents one or more of these pairs and is specially adapted for reproducing them.

Most of the photographic processes that have been evolved depend upon the fact that certain chemicals are hardened by light. A transparency of the subject (negative in all cases except that of photogravure) is exposed to light over a sensitized plate. The light, passing through the white lines or areas of the transparency, hardens the sensitive emulsion. Where no light passes through the black areas, the emulsion remains unhardened and soluble and will be washed away. The design of the original in hardened emulsion will thus be left on the surface of the plate. This, in brief, is the general principle behind the photographic processes. The actual adaptation of this principle to each process and the treatment of the plate will be seen as each process is regarded in more detail. Before the full impact of the photographic processes was felt in the latter half of the nineteenth century considerable experimentation had already taken place. The great increase in the quantity of books and prints produced, made possible by the revolutions in printing methods previously discussed, were making apparent the need for change. The new reading public needed, in the strictest sense of the word, illustrations in order to benefit fully from the variety of publications they used. Nineteenth-century bibliography is vastly complicated and in no respect more so than in the bewildering number of illustration processes that came and went so rapidly. In turn this brought about significant increases in the number of individuals and firms engaged in the manufacturing process as well as the artists, of every level of competency, who had a newly enlarged field of opportunity. No adequate bibliographical tools yet exist to provide guidance through the maze of processes and practitioners, but it is an area that is now beginning to receive serious attention.[14]

Most of the modern photographic processes can in one way or another be adapted for use on high-speed rotary presses. Curved plates are placed on the press and printed either directly onto the web of paper or indirectly by offset process. This latter method is now widespread and has the great advantage of increasing the variety of papers onto which the text or illustrations will print. In offset printing, a rubber- or composition-surfaced roller is interposed between the plate and the paper. The plate will print onto the offset roller and then the roller onto the paper. In normal printing practice the final print impression is the reverse of what is on the plate; in offset printing, the printed version will be identical with the plate. Since the rubber or composition surface possesses greater resiliency than the original block or plate, coarser-surfaced papers can thus take an accurate impression of the original.

Zincography

Zincography, commonly called "Zinco" or "line-block," is a relief etching on metal. It will be remembered that Blake was a forerunner in this field when he produced etchings in relief instead of intaglio. Other examples of this use can be found between the time of Blake and the advent of photography.

A photographic negative is exposed to light over the sensitized surface of a sheet of zinc. The image is thus transferred to the zinc in hardened emulsion. The unhardened emulsion is then washed away in water. The remaining design is dusted over with powdered rosin, which forms an acid resist, and the plate is then etched. The background is eaten away, leaving the design in relief. The plate is then mounted type high and is ready for printing.

Zincography is admirable for reproducing pure line and solid silhouette and is greatly used in printing facsimiles of woodcuts, title pages, other type pages, and pen-and-ink drawings. Of itself it cannot reproduce tone, but attempts are made to give an appearance of tone by the use of Ben Day media or Bourges tints. These methods can produce fine line patterns over parts of the plate and so create an illusion of tone.

Halftone

Halftone, the common photographic stipple print, is most easily recognized in its crudest form in any newspaper.

The original photograph or drawing is photographed through a halftone screen. This screen consists of two glass plates that are etched with fine diagonal lines. The lines are then filled in with black pigment and the plates are cemented together, the diagonal lines crossing each other and so producing a multitude of tiny diamonds of clear glass. Halftone screens are measured by the number of black lines that reach the edge of the plate to the inch. The coarsest screens have about forty-five lines to the inch, the finest have two hundred or even more on certain occasions.

Photographing the original through this screen breaks the image up into a multitude of dots of varying size. The dots that correspond to the dark areas of the original will be large, and those corresponding to the light areas will be small. This negative is then printed onto the surface of a sensitized copper plate. The dots are thus transferred to the copper as hardened emulsion, and when the plate is etched, as in zincography, these hard spots will be left in relief. When inked and printed, they will reproduce the tonal qualities of the original.

The spots are so minute that the etching can only be of the lightest and the resulting relief of the shallowest, so shallow indeed that the copper plate has to be held slanting to the light before the design appears to the naked eye. Consequently only the coarsest screens are suitable to paper of ordinary surface, and for fine work a smooth surface is necessary. To meet the need clay-coated "art paper" was introduced, and the use of this is the fatal defect of halftone. It is, however, possible to use a substantial paper in which the mineral is a loading and not a coating, and the surface is produced by calendering. Also, with the development of offset printing, owing to the surface of the offset roller being able to reach all the surface, a rougher paper could be used for coarser-screened plates.

For special qualities of work varieties of screens can be used in which the lines were engraved in other than diagonal directions. These include such things as "one-way" screens, "curved one-way" screens, "linen" screens, and "Erwin" screens.

Photogravure

This process is too expensive for any but the best work, or for "runs" amounting to tens of thousands of copies. Technically it is a photographic aquatint, but the general effect is darker than that of aquatint and closely resembles mezzotint, which it reproduces perfectly. Like mezzotint, it is admirably adapted to the reproduction of oil paintings or anything that relies for its effect on good, rich tonal qualities. Its range, however, is very wide and, especially in magazine work, frequently reproduces text as well as illustrations.

As this is the only photographic intaglio method, a transparent *positive* will be used and not a negative as in the other photomechanical methods. This positive is then printed onto a sensitized sheet of paper known as the "carbon" sheet. This sheet is then laid over a prepared copper sheet or cylinder and the design is etched through the gelatin, which is the main substance of the carbon sheet. Originally the copper plate was "prepared" by grounding it with powdered bitumen, around which the acid would bite, as in an aquatint. Now a ruled screen of very fine lines is applied photographically in order to achieve the same effect. Etched pits of varying depth on the plate will hold varying amounts of ink and thus achieve varying tones when printed.

Photolithography

For modern commercial work lithography exists today mainly as photo-litho-offset. It is widely used for the production of unaltered reprints of books.

Instead of the design being drawn onto a stone, it is transferred photographically onto a sheet of zinc or aluminum. The design is then worked up, inked, and printed. The use of offset in connection with modern lithographic work is very general.

Collotype

For facsimiles in which tone as well as line is to be shown, such as facsimiles in elaborate catalogs of pages of printed books or manuscripts in which the tone of the original paper is to appear, illuminations, or bindings, the most suitable process is collotype. The plate is of thick plate-glass and is covered, as in other processes, with sensitized gelatin. This dries into a network of fine wrinkles that constitute the grain, the delicacy of which regulates the amount of ink held when the plate is dampened and inked. Collotypes normally show a pale lithographic background, darker than the paper, to the plate edge, but this can be cleaned out. The setting of the gelatin depends on a warm, dry atmosphere in the shop, and there are many fewer firms able to produce good collotypes than other types of illustration. It is without doubt the finest of all reproduction methods, but it is also an expensive one. It has the great advantage for scientific facsimile that no retouching is required as in the other methods.

Colored illustration

Printing in more than one color was the object of early experiment, since the finer manuscript book had been richly decorated in colors, and even the commoner book normally had rubrisher's capitals in red and blue. There is, however, the technical difficulty that, unless the form is very meticulously inked, the sheet has to go through the press twice or more, once for each color. That this is so can often be seen in practice, as with the combination of type and engraving, in the overlapping of one color upon another, which could not occur at a single impression.

At first rubrics were left blank, but they soon began to be printed. Decorative color, however, was not used early with much success or often. There is no doubt that the outline woodcuts in early books were meant to be hand-colored, as they in fact often were.

Fust and Schoeffer, Gutenberg's successors at Mainz, used, in the Psalter of 1457 and in later books, metalcut initials, imitating the decorative work of the rubrisher, and printed them in two colors (making three with the black text). In such cases the red or blue letter nearly always had the background ornamentation printed in the converse color. But their use was only occasional, and no other firm imitated them. In 1487 Erhard Ratdolt returned from Venice to Augsburg, at the Bishop's invitation, to print service books for the Diocese, and in these and others he used woodcut devices of a bishop and the arms of the diocese, printed in three or four colors.

The beginnings of what was to become the revolutionary method of printing colored illustrations lay in the development of chiaroscuro woodcut. It began almost simultaneously in Germany and Italy early in the sixteenth century, the earliest dated print of this nature being *The Emperor Maximilian on Horseback* (1508), by Hans Burgkmair. The method consisted in making several blocks of different tones of the same color or, occasionally, of closely related colors. These would be printed with a key block that gave the outline of the illustration.

It is obviously only a step forward from this technique to the process more widely known as the "multiple-block" method. It releases itself from the etymological restraint of the chiaroscuro method (Italian: bright-dark) with the emphasis on gradations between lights and shades, to assume the full range of colors.

The black part of the picture when using multiple blocks, whether a mere outline or including mass, is cut alone, ignoring all else, on one block and printed first as the "key"; then one (say) for the red; and so on. Each is inked with its appropriate pigment, which can be rolled or (in early days) dabbed on without the special care needed to keep it clear from the other colors at the meeting-lines of the masses. It is in securing exact "register," or superimposition on the key at each printing, that this process requires care. If a block is printed out of register, the whole mass will be out of place and the fact can easily be seen. In modern times colored lithographs and wood-engravings have been largely produced by means of multiple stones or blocks. Examples familiar in England are the children's books illustrated by Randolph Caldecott, Kate Greenaway, and Walter Crane; those of Roger Boutet de Monvel afford a later parallel in France.[15]

With the principle established, numerous variations became possible, even to a mixture of processes. The well-known Baxter prints, for instance, were the creation of George Baxter (1804–1867), who in 1835 patented a method by which an aquatint or mezzotint background was colored by the application of ten to twenty suitably colored woodblocks. Much of his work was applied to prints rather than book work, but the method was used by some cheap book producers in the mid–nineteenth century, such as J. M. Kronheim, who printed many illustrations for books of Warne and Co., the Religious Tract Society, and other publishers.

By the multiple-block method each color must lie in a separate mass or masses of even tone; the appearance of greater depth can be secured by black shading on the key block, but in no other way, and designs to be reproduced by this method must be specially colored for the purpose in flat masses. An advance on this, at least in its ability to represent gradations of color, was the manner in which a simple mixture of colors could be obtained by superimposition in printing. This was obtained in chromolithography, but the results were not invariably fortunate. Greater subtlety in the blending of color, as in nature or in ordinary painting, was achieved by color printing *à la poupée*. The single plate was painted or dabbed before each printing with dollies or rag stumps carrying inks of various colors. But this requires the presence at the press of an artist, preferably the original artist, to refresh the plate regularly, and it is obvious that any process that can be applied by a roller with reasonable care and skill must be much cheaper. It is consequently found that though true color prints were produced in some quantity in the great period of experiment in engraving, that is, in the latter part of the eighteenth century, and when good they are much prized by connoisseurs, books were rather infrequently illustrated in so expensive a manner.

A more usual method of putting books with colored illustrations on the market was for the publisher to employ professional colorists to color the engravings by hand in a limited number of copies. Some of the most notable examples of this are to be found in the aquatint books of Rudolf Ackermann. Hand-coloring was largely applied to separately published engravings also, and these are to be distinguished from true color prints. The most careful colorist cannot prevent the brush from wandering in color printing by either of the methods described above. A small amount of hand-color work has continued to be produced in this century, but only in rather special circumstances.

The difficulty of reproducing the natural gradations of colors in nature and consequently in printing has been overcome up to a point by the "three-color process," by which the colors of the original are split up into the three primary colors and then recombined in printing into their original combinations.

There is nothing to prevent this color separation from being done by hand, relying solely on an artist's skill in differentiating the appropriate areas for each primary color. Photography has nevertheless brought a new ease to this task, and its chief benefits have therefore been experienced in the modern photomechanical methods.

The primaries are yellow, red, and blue. A negative is made by photographing the original through a light filter that allows only the yellow rays to pass onto the plate, then one for the red, and finally a negative for the blue. From each of these negatives (or positives in the case of photogravure) a block or plate is made for each color according to the illustration process being employed. Each plate is then inked with its appropriate color ink and printed in succession, one being most carefully superimposed on the previous printing. It will be apparent that much of the success of this depends upon the care taken to ensure the most faultless register of the printings. If there is any error, an untidy edge of one color will be seen and the whole impression will be blurred. If, however, the colors used are good, if there is absolute register and very careful press work, then the results can be excellent. But these are not easily or cheaply obtained. A carelessly printed color plate is a most miserable spectacle.

In what is termed a three-color printing there is usually a fourth plate printed. This is a black plate, used to give density to some of the color areas and frequently to add line. Extra plates are often added in order to reproduce any especially important colors or to secure greater delicacy. It is not unusual to meet up to seven-color processes, but it has to be remembered that with each extra printing the dangers of bad register increase.

In printing, the colors should not lie one over another in too solid a mass, or there will be obliteration instead of mixture. In color halftones it is usual to shift the position of the screen between each of the exposures so that the dots that combine to produce a color (e.g., yellow and blue for green) are not exactly superimposed. If the eye picks up a yellow dot not completely covered by a blue dot, it will gain a truer impression of green than if the blue dot entirely covers the yellow. In photogravure this problem is met by the more fluid inks employed, which are inclined to mix under the speed and pressure of printing.

Description of illustrations and plates

It is of paramount importance that students should study examples of each of these methods for themselves. There is no substitute for such firsthand experience. At the same time the purpose of such study must not be forgotten. The interest is not that of the artist, the art historian, or the art critic but solely that of the bibliographer, and the need is to be able to recognize certain features in the published print. In the final description of a work the part that is concerned with the diagrams, illustrations, ornamental capitals, borders, plates, etc., must include a statement of the process or processes involved, and this is dealt with in context in Chapter 10. The names of the artists involved, including engravers, etchers, colorists, and so on, must be established in as much detail as possible. The type of wear to which a block or plate is subject must be understood in order that the progressive states may be established. This is frequently of the same degree of priority as attempts to establish variants in textual matters. There is no period of the book trade in which this kind of concern with the "illustrative" features of the book is not relevant. The practices of fifteenth- and sixteenth-century woodcutters; the styles and methods of engraving in the seventeenth and eighteenth centuries; the problems of the late–eighteenth- and early–nineteenth-century plate books, not excluding those plates included in the illustrated part-issues of this period; and the complexities of reengraved plates in long nineteenth-century runs of popular books—all these emphasize the importance of the study of the illustrative content of the book.

REFERENCES

1. Good examples are:

   IVINS, William M. *How Prints Look.* 1943.
   WILDER, F. L. *How to Identify Old Prints.* 1969.

2. There are many books that cover different aspects of illustration in the book world prior to the introduction of the printed book. There are also many that give the student who is distant from any of the great libraries an opportunity to view them through reproductions. The following is an initial selection only:

   BRITISH MUSEUM. *Illuminated Manuscripts in the British Museum, with Descriptive Text by F. F. Warner.* 4 parts. 1899–1903.
   BRITISH MUSEUM. *Schools of Illumination.* 6 parts. 1914–1930.
   DIRINGER, David. *The Illuminated Book.* 1958.
   HERBERT, J. A. *Illuminated Manuscripts.* 1911.
   MILLER, E. G. *English Illuminated Manuscripts.* 1926–1928.
   OAKESHOTT, W. *The Sequence of English Medieval Art.* 1950.
   PACHT, Otto, and ALEXANDER, J. J. G. *Illuminated Manuscripts in the Bodleian Library.* 1966–.
   ROBB, David M. *The Art of the Illuminated Manuscript.* 1973.
   WEITZMANN, K. *Illustrations in Roll and Codex.* 1947.
   WEITZMANN, K. *Late Antique and Early Christian Book Illumination.* 1977.
   WEITZMANN, K. *Studies in Classical and Byzantine Manuscript Illumination.* 1971.

3. Examples of these, not very common, illustrations may be found in the British Museum Catalogues, *Woodcuts and Metal Cuts of the Fifteenth Century Chiefly of the German School.* 1914. and:

Prints in the Dotted Manner and Other Metalcuts of the XV Century. 1937.

also:

WASHINGTON, D.C. NATIONAL GALLERY OF ART. *Fifteenth Century Woodcuts and Metalcuts.* 1965.

4. BRITISH MUSEUM. *A Guide to the Processes and Schools of Engraving.* 4th ed. 1952.

5. HIND, A. M. *An Introduction to a History of Woodcut, with a Detailed Survey of Work Done in the Fifteenth Century.* 1935.
    HODNETT, E. *English Woodcuts, 1480–1535.* 1973.
    LINTON, W. J. *A History of Wood-engraving in America.* 1882.
    WOODWARD, David. "The Decline of Commercial Wood-engraving in Nineteenth-century America, *Journal of the Printing Historical Society.* X: 1974–75. pp. 57–83.

6. Reproduced as the frontispiece to:

    DE RICCI, Seymour. *Census of Caxtons.* 1909.

7. HIND, Arthur M. *A History of Engraving and Etching from the 15th Century to the Year 1914.* 3rd ed. 1923.

8. DAVENPORT, Cyril J. H. *Mezzotints.* 1904.
    WHITMAN, Alfred. *The Masters of Mezzotint.* 1898.

9. Hind, *A History of Engraving,* p. 300

10. *Scenery of Great Britain and Ireland in Aquatint and Lithography, 1770–1860, from the Library of J. R. Abbey. A Bibliographical Catalogue.* 1952.
    Life in England in Aquatint and Lithography, 1770–1860, from the the Library of J. R. Abbey. A Bibliographical Catalogue. 1953.
    Travel in Aquatint and Lithography, 1770–1860, from the Library of J. R. Abbey. A Bibliographical Catalogue. 2v. 1956.

11. PRIDEAUX, Sarah T. *Aquatint Engraving: A Chapter in the History of Book Illustration.* 1909.

12. TWYMAN, Michael. "Lithographic Stone and the Printing Trade in the Nineteenth Century." *Journal of the Printing Historical Society.* VIII: 1972. pp. 1–41.

13. TWYMAN, Michael. "The Tinted Lithograph." *Journal of the Printing Historical Society.* I: 1965. pp. 39–56.
TWYMAN, Michael. "The Lithographic Hand Press, 1796–1850." *Journal of the Printing Historical Society.* III: 1967. pp. 3–50.
TWYMAN, Michael. "A Directory of London Lithographic Printers, 1800–1850." *Journal of the Printing Historical Society.* X: 1974–75. pp. 1–56.
TWYMAN, Michael. "Thomas Barker's Lithographic Stones." *Journal of the Printing Historical Society.* XII: 1977–78. pp. 1–32.
WAKEMAN, Geoffrey. *Aspects of Victorian Lithography.* 1970.
WEBER, Wilhelm. *A History of Lithography.* 1966.

14. BAIN, Iain. "Thomas Ross & Son, Copper and Steel Plate Printers Since 1833." *Journal of the Printing Historical Society.* II: 1966. pp. 3–22.
DYSON, Tony. "The Ross Records: 1833 to 1900. Notes on the Forthcoming Catalogue of a Plate-printer's Nineteenth-century Archive." *Journal of the Printing Historical Society.* XII: 1977–78. pp. 52–67.
FILDES, Paul. "Phototransfer of Drawings in Wood-block Engraving." *Journal of the Printing Historical Society.* V: 1969. pp. 87–97.
GERNSHEIM, Helmut and Alison. *The History of Photography from the Earliest Use of the Camera Obscura in the Eleventh Century up to 1914.* (Part 6: "Photography and the Printed Page.") 1955.
HARRIS, Elizabeth M. "Experimental Graphic Processes in England, 1800–1859." *Journal of the Printing Historical Society.* IV: 1968. pp. 38–86; V: 1969. pp. 41–80; VI: 1970 pp. 53–89.
WAKEMAN, Geoffrey. "Anastatic Printing for Sir Thomas Phillipps." *Journal of the Printing Historical Society.* V: 1969. pp. 24–40.
WAKEMAN, Geoffrey. *"Victorian Book Illustration, the Technical Revolution."* 1973.

15. EVANS, Edmund. *The Reminiscences of Edmund Evans.* Edited and introduced by Ruari McLean. 1967.
LEWIS, C. T. Courtney. *George Baxter the Picture Printer.* 1924.

LEWIS, C. T. Courtney. *The Story of Picture Printing in England During the XIXth Century.* 1928.
McLEAN, Ruari. *Victorian Book Design and Colour Printing.* 2nd ed. 1972.
MITZMAN, Max E. *George Baxter and the Baxter Prints.* 1979.
MUIR, P. H. *Victorian Illustrated Books.* 1971.
WAKEMAN, Geoffrey, and BRIDSON, G. D. R. *A guide to Nineteenth Century Colour Printers.* 1975.

The following books will also be necessary for reading or reference:

BLAND, David. *A History of Book Illustration.* 2nd ed. 1969.
BLAND, David. *The Illustration of Books.* 3rd ed. 1962.
CURWEN, Harold. *Processes of Graphic Reproduction in Printing.* 3rd ed. 1963.
GOLDSCHMIDT, E. P. *The Printed Book of the Renaissance.* 1950.
HOFER, P. *Baroque Book Illustration.* 1951.
IVINS, W. M. *The Artist and the Fifteenth Century Printer.* 1940.
IVINS, W. M. *Prints and Books.* 1926.
IVINS, W. M. *Notes on Prints.* 1930. Reprinted 1967.
IVINS, W. M. *Prints and Visual Communication.* 1953.
JAMES, Philip. *English Book Illustration, 1800-1900.* 1947.
LEJARD, A., ed. *The Art of the French Book.* (English translation.) 1949.
MUIR, P. *English Children's Books.* 1954.
PITZ, H. C. *A Treasury of American Book Illustration.* 1947.
POLLARD, A. W. *Early Illustrated Books.* 3rd ed. 1926.
POLLARD, A. W. *Fine Books.* 1912.
STRACHAN, J. *Early Bible Illustration.* 1957.
THORPE, J. *English Illustration: The Nineties.* 1935.
WEITENKAMPF, Frank. *The Illustrated Book.* 1938.

8.

BINDING

Historical styles of decorated binding

It is a general human instinct, comparable with Nature's *horror vacui*, that impels us to decorate any accessible blank surface; and few blank surfaces demand decoration more loudly than do the flat covers of books. There has always been a purely utilitarian aspect to binding. Clay tablets were frequently protected by the earthenware jars in which they were stored and by small fabric envelopes into which they were placed. This much was needed for straightforward protective purposes. When some of the clay tablets were discovered in the late nineteenth century, there were also discovered near to the tablets small triangular inscribed labels, which had previously been attached by fibrous cords. Similarly papyrus rolls were often protected by a wrapper of parchment that in some instances was decorated. The title of the work was written on a projecting label of papyrus or vellum. The rolls were then sometimes stored on shelves or in buckets.[1] With the advent of the codex form a different style of binding became both possible and necessary, and the result was that decoration became that much easier.[2]

The outer sides of the ivory diptychs, or folding tablets, used by the Romans, from which the codex was evolved, were some-times carved. The idea was carried further by the use of metals, enamels, and inset jewels on the covers of the finest manuscripts of the Gospels and other sacred texts that were treasured in the richer monastic churches. This type of binding persisted throughout the Middle Ages, but the earlier examples, dating from the seventh to the ninth centuries, are more impressive than the later. Examples can be found in such bindings as the eighth-century Gospel book from Lindau, formerly in the Ashburnham collection and now in the Pierpont Morgan Library at New York, or the simpler one that bears an inscription stating that it was given by Theodelinda, Queen of the Lombards (d.

625), to her newly founded Cathedral of Monza, where the covers (without the book) are preserved. In later centuries the tendency to overelaboration, high relief, and the insetting of large jewels degraded the art. It must be remembered in their favor, however, that such projecting covers, however inconvenient now when books stand upon shelves, were not so when the books, and especially gorgeous examples like those mentioned, were kept lying on altars or in treasure-chests and ambries.[3]

Leather covers, laid over wooden boards, were also decorated in early times, in the West as well as in Near Eastern countries, such as Egypt. There were two chief methods: incision with sharp tools and stamping with blunt tools. The first method, though common in the Middle Ages, has only rarely survived into later times, except where inlay work in colored leathers is in question. One famous and beautiful specimen is the Gospel Book of St. Cuthbert, known as the Stonyhurst Gospels which was found in the coffin of St. Cuthbert, who died in 687. The body was reburied in a more elaborate coffin eleven years later, and it is probable that it was at this time that this Gospel of St. John was placed in the coffin. The manuscript that it contains was written in Wearmouth-Jarrow toward the end of the seventh century. The binding is of goatskin over boards, molded while wet and additionally adorned with repoussé work and coloring.[4] Another fine early example is the ninth-century Gospel Book of Fulda. In this binding a supremely satisfying effect is produced by triple fillets and diagonals producing four triangles in each of which is placed a three-pointed curved figure, roughly suggestive of a bird on the wing, the whole design being doubtless symbolic of the Trinity. Incised bindings, like their costly and bejeweled predecessors, also became overornate, especially in Germany, where there was a tendency to depict elaborate scenes: the background was often well differentiated by being darkened by punching all over.

Tooled bindings were also first known in the School of Fulda in the eighth century. From this time until the Renaissance these were always executed "in blind" in Western countries, that is, without gold or color. At and soon after the Conquest there were flourishing binderies in England in the monasteries of Durham and York and in Hyde Abbey, Winchester. The most noted surviving example of the last covers the Winchester Domesday

Book, which is in the possession of the Society of Antiquaries. The variety of tools used at Durham in the bindings of the twelfth and thirteenth centuries and the decorative sense in their disposition are remarkable. There are palmettes, roundels containing fantastic beasts, square and triangular designs, and especially dotted strips that when set together suggest rope work, and we find already the great variety of pattern obtained by combining simple elements, which is the pleasure of tooled binding.[5]

Unornamented bindings of the age of manuscript are often of vellum, stained to a red that must originally have been very gay. Although the exteriors are now always faded to pink, the doublures, protected from light, show the original tint. In such vellum-wrapped volumes the binding cords are carried through strips of horn or leather laid over the spine. Another plain style, which preceded and survived the invention of printing by no long period, was that of "half"-covering the boards with the leather back. More exactly it was nearer to quarter-covering, but it has always been known by the other title. A common English material for plain binding was soft, rough deerskin, with other countries using the most economically available substance, as will be explained further under "covering materials."

The covering material sometimes hung loose for a considerable length beyond the board of the book, either at the head or the tail. The material is plaited and worked into a form that enabled it to be tucked into a girdle or a saddle for the convenience of carrying. They can be traced to many European countries, frequently in leather or more "aristocratically" in velvet or other material. There is also an overhang on all boards in some instances to provide protection similar to yapp edges. Such bindings are usually referred to as "chemise," "pouch," or "wrapper" bindings.[6]

The larger volumes of the fifteenth century were provided with metal corner and center bosses, intended to protect the leather from rubbing on the desk. Books of the period also frequently had chains stapled to the lower cover and a brass frame with transparent talc or horn slip for the title on the upper cover. These metal excrescences have often been removed as making the books bad neighbors on the shelves.

By the time that the fifteenth century is reached, extant books in contemporary bindings are available in sufficient quantity for some real assessment to be attempted of trends in designs. At this time the field was generally divided into panels by fillets. Sometimes the fillets were diagonal and so created lozenges, which were also imitated in flamboyant style by curved tools. In each of the compartments so created was dotted a "semis," or sowing, of small tools, including ribbons bearing names of saints. These may occasionally indicate provenance; when the names were of places or people, which was a less frequent occurrence, then the assumption could be made more certainly. A method of creating compartments and design was by the continuing use of individual stamp tools as previously described. Increasingly they were used not primarily because of their own decoration, intricate though that was, but because of the overall pattern that they created. This was the style of binding design that G. D. Hobson called "romanesque," that is, built up by individually complete small tools. The late part of the fifteenth century, probably under the impact of the greater number of books requiring binding, introduced two new techniques. They were both effective in speeding up the binding operation and also permitting it to be done successfully by less highly skilled craftsmen.

The first of these was the roll stamp, a cylindrical tool cut in relief or engraved in intaglio so as to repeat its designs in rotation. These were used to create borders as the individual stamps had, but with greater certainty of a straight line. Roll stamps were very popular in Germany and the Netherlands, and to some extent also in France and England.

The regularity and continuity of the design is the factor that will usually indicate roll work as distinct from individual tool work. Points of juncture or of intersection will also help to distinguish the style of work. Rolls varied in their width, some with elaborate designs, some with simple line fillets.[7]

The second great innovation was the panel stamp. This was an engraved plate with an intaglio design that was placed over the dampened leather on the boards and the whole subjected to pressure. The design so imprinted in the leather became fixed and permanent as the leather dried. The normal procedure was for both boards to be so treated, and different panel-stamp designs would appear on each board. If the board sizes were fairly large, it was not uncommon for two small stamps to be used side by side on the same board. The great period of the panel-stamp binding was from 1470 until about 1550, and they are found particularly on bindings from northern France, southwestern Germany, the Netherlands, and England. The wide range of subjects usually found on binding stamps can be discovered here: representations of saints, or later the Reformers, coats of arms, and Biblical scenes. A strong local significance is often noticed, such as the Tudor Rose, or the portcullis appearing in English bindings of this style.[8]

Binding was a well-established trade long before the introduction of the printing press. Many binding establishments consequently remained as independent establishments, binding sheets for the individual book buyer. Alongside this were those printers and publishers who from the earliest days of their printing maintained their own binderies. This was especially so in the case of printing shops that were in a large way of business. The books, for example, that are attributed to "Caxton's binder" were, according to G. D. Hobson, the work of a Flemish binder who possibly accompanied Caxton to Westminster from Bruges or who traveled independently and set himself up near or possibly in association with Caxton's shop. No great number of bindings from this workshop has survived, owing to the misguided fashion that prevailed in the late eighteenth and early nineteenth centuries of having old books rebound; but enough are known to enable the tools to be identified. Thick boards beveled at the edges and lozenge spaces starred with small tools were characteristic of his shop.[9]

Meanwhile an entirely different style, heightened by the use of gold, was approaching. Gold-tooling, by means of heated tools, entered Europe from Morocco via Spain. The art was developed mainly in Italy, first in Naples at the bindery established there by the Aragonese kings. The earliest European gold-tooled bookbindings that can be surely dated, not earlier than 1480, originated in Naples. Other influences came from other centers. A number of excellent craftsmen, some of them Oriental leatherworkers, were at work in Venice, the natural meeting ground of West and East. The binders worked in the traditional Eastern manner, with arabesques and gilding and cut-out (*ajouré*) leather over a colored background. A simpler style, more natural to the West, that flourished in Italy and was combined with gold, is a variety of double fillets, which when placed together produced the effect of rope or knot work and are strongly suggestive of some of the blind-tooled bindings made at Durham three centuries earlier. Another characteristic of Venetian and Florentine binding of the first quarter of the sixteenth century is the fillet roll built up of a restrained arabesque flowing in a series of circles; this and an elaboration of the rope can be seen in a number of Florentine bindings of the period. By the mid–sixteenth century typical Italian binding had abandoned elaboration for a simple arrangement of fillets giving a plain border, sometimes with a little arabesque added, and an equally plain center panel, bearing the title of the book and sometimes the name of the owner. The leather was often morocco, a new importation into Europe. We find this style imitated (in calf) on books bound for Henry VIII, Edward VI, and Elizabeth I.

Just as German printers had gone abroad carrying their new art with them, so in the late fifteenth and early sixteenth centuries Italian binders crossed the Alps and worked for collectors in France and Central Europe. The most notable and perhaps the earliest of these patrons was Matthias Corvinus, King of Hungary from 1458 to 1490, the rare survivors of whose splendid collection confer outstanding distinction upon any library possessing one. At the time of the Walter's Art Gallery bookbinding exhibition in 1957 only one Corvinus binding was known in the United States (at the Yale University Library). Rarity alone, however, is not their sole distinction. Some of the earliest gold-toolings known are on books from the "Bibliotheca Corvina," which may be recognized by the King's rebus, a crow (*corvus*).

An Italian style of the early sixteenth century, of which fine examples are known, consisted of a fairly plainly tooled panel enclosing a sunken central cartouche impressed with a large cameo stamp. Thus the British Library possesses a Florentine binding (not before 1514) that shows in the cartouche a cameo portrait of Julius Caesar; the stamp itself (of course in intaglio) survives. The most notable collection of bindings in this style consists of those that are generically called "Canevari" bindings. The collection is now dispersed, but individual books may be recognized by a plaquette in which Apollo is driving his chariot toward a rock on which Pegasus stands. It is enclosed with a motto in Greek that translates as "straight and not crookedly." The plaquette was first recorded and described by Dibdin in his

The Bibliographical Decameron in 1817. The later nineteenth century assigned these bindings to a collector, Demetrio Canevari, physician to Pope Urban VII, hence the name by which they have been widely known. In 1926 G. D. Hobson reviewed the evidence and in place of Canevari advanced the claims of another collector, Pier Luigi Farnese.[10] In 1975 Farnese's claims were replaced in a study written by Anthony Hobson, the son of G. D. Hobson.[11] In this the books were assigned to Giovanni Battista Grimaldi. The earliest bindings made for the famous Jean Grolier were in a variety of this style, the center plaque being heightened with enamel.

Grolier (1479–1565) held the office of Treasurer of the French armies in Italy from 1510 to 1529, when he returned at the Peace of Cambrai, becoming Chancellor of France in 1545. There can be little doubt that the style named after him, since it first appeared in a fully developed state in the books bound for him, was due to his taste. This, the true Grolier style, which superseded the bindings with central plaquettes, depended for its effect on light and graceful geometrical "strapwork," i.e., interlaced double-fillets. Late in his career Grolier's binder employed color, painting the straps, or else substituted the arabesques, hitherto used only as subordinate decoration.[12] What may well be the original source of inspiration of this strapwork design can be seen in a large number of decorated Spanish bindings from the twelfth to the fifteenth centuries. Here the strapwork can be seen against the background of an interlacing Moorish design, and the tradition may well have entered Italy from Spain together with the art of gold-tooling and the introduction of morocco leather itself.[13] Grolier immortalized his name by having impressed on the covers of his books (after those in the earliest style, in which he merely wrote his name) the inscription IO GROLIERII ET AMICORVM, and also often PORTIO MEA DOMINE SIT IN TERRA VIVENTIVM. The words of the former were no idle sentiment, for Grolier made his library, containing many of the best books of his day, and notably those from the press of Aldus, accessible to scholars, for whom no public libraries were then available. He was imitated in this by another Italianate Frenchman, Thomas Mahieu, Secretary to Queen Catherine de Medici, whose books are inscribed THO. MAIOLI ET AMICORVM, whence his name was originally taken to be Tommaso Maioli. The tradition of using "et amicorum" was well established at this time as a manuscript mark of ownership, but Jean Grolier was the first to have it lettered on the boards of his books.[14]

Side by side with the influence of Grolier's workers on French, and so on northern, binding design, went that of Geofroy Tory, letter cutter and publisher. Tory used the arabesque style, working into it a broken pot, a device that is said to commemorate the loss of his young daughter. The binders of François I and Henri II show the same influences and were probably (particularly the former's) Italians. François I marked his books with a crowned F. Henri II and his mistress, Diane de Poitiers, had their books adorned not only with Grolieresque strapwork and other decorations, but also with the interlaced H and D and crescent moons, symbolic of the name Diana, which are found so freely used at Fontainebleau and Chantilly.

The Grolieresque style was imitated by other collectors with more or less success in other countries, but generally in a rather provincial fashion, notably by Thomas Wotton, in England. Wotton also adopted Grolier's form of ownership inscription. Because Wotton preferred Grolier's heavier style with colored strapwork, his bindings are only a poor shadow of what this graceful and lovely style could produce at its best.[15] The Grolieresque was directly or indirectly the ancestor of almost all ornate binding for two centuries. Grolier and his binders lay the foundation of that supremacy of French binders which lasted almost uninterrupted for two centuries and occasioned Ernest Thoinan's proud boast (only false in using the present tense), "La reliure est un art tout français." It branched down in two main lines of descent. The first was the Lyonnese style, showing either exaggerated painted or enameled strapwork, heavily and mechanically tooled, or else large sunken center and corner stamps with arabesques in relief on a background of gold, and the free space thickly covered with a semis. This, one of the ugliest of known styles of binding, was the destruction of the art in some countries, and especially in Central Europe. The opportunity of so large an expanse of gold was too great a temptation. In a simple form small Lyonnese stamps are found on late Elizabethan books, but luckily the richer book buyers in England never took to the style. The finer Elizabethan bindings are mostly of the simple Italian type, with gilt fillet and panel, with a coat of arms or crest, or else the book's title in the center.[16] Their Jacobean and Caroline successors adopted and adapted the other style descending from Grolier, which remains to be mentioned.

This was the "fanfare" (flourish), long but unfoundedly associated with the names of Nicolas and Clovis Eve, the former of whom bound for Henri III.[17] Bindings à la fanfare (the phrase is Nodier's) were richly covered, in defiance of an edict of Henri III forbidding costly decoration on books, with sprays of bay, worked into geometric strapwork. As usual, it is most beautiful when most restrained and when the leather has a chance to show, as in the examples bearing only the corner fleurons and the wreath surrounding the central cartouche for arms or book title. Too often the rest of the field is filled with a semis. Nicolas Eve used the latter style, but not the more elaborate. When viewing bindings, one should always bear in mind that the genius of the binder, and the French binder in particular, lies in the ability to suit the amount of decoration to the size of the board. An amount of decoration that can well look absurd on a book only eight and a half inches tall can be breathtaking on one twice that height. Binders were aware of this, and because of this fact it is impossible to make even an initial judgment on a binding from a photograph. Styles did certainly deteriorate and degenerate and frequently so because of too much decoration coarsely applied. This happened with "fanfare," which rapidly degenerated into wretchedly mechanical patterns, which look as though they were impressed with a single stamp on to the cover.

After the early sixteenth century we begin frequently to find decoration on the spines of books, a proof, incidentally, that books were now no longer kept lying on their sides but upright on shelves. The appearance of titles on the spines and the disappearance of titles written on the fore-edge, two later developments, are equally significant, as showing that books began to be placed with the spine instead of fore-edge outward.

Well into the seventeenth century the fanfare style was modified, possibly by a mysterious "Le Gascon," more probably by Florimund Badier. The strapwork is retained, and the enclosed spaces differentiated by inlaying leather of different colors; the sprays are lighter, not only in themselves but because impressed by pointillé tools, i.e., tools with a dotted surface. The use of the pointillé line is one of the most important at this period in helping to retain the lightness of the whole design when vast overall patterns were the common vogue.

The close relations between England and France immediately before and after the Civil War and Commonwealth produced in England a development of the fanfare and Le Gascon styles. At its best this is one of the most delightful of any styles and reigned for nearly a century. It is a style that is frequently, even if confusingly at certain times, named after Charles II's stationer and binder, Samuel Mearne.

Samuel Mearne has always been a rather elusive character. Even when little was known of him, either as binder or individual, he was regarded as the greatest English binder of the Restoration period. In 1918 G. D. Hobson reviewed the evidence and came to the conclusion that the traditional story was in fact a myth.[18] From that date onward it began increasingly to be doubted whether Mearne ever bound books himself or whether he merely contracted for binding. His output certainly seemed extremely prolific for a single binder. In 1956 Samuel Mearne and his family were restored to their full rightful place as binders and not simply contractors when H. M. Nixon dismissed the story of the "myth" as being itself a myth.[19] He showed that Mearne was in fact a binder, and, although he is still a rather shadowy figure, there is now no need to doubt his claims as a binder. A variety of designs has been connected with his name, some of which are among the best known of English bindings.

The fine series of books bound in red Turkey morocco that Mearne supplied to the Royal Library, for which the bills are still extant, show uniformly only a plain fillet with center and corner fleurons of Charles II's monogram, crossed Cs, crowned and flanked with palm wreaths. The main style associated with the name is one that was adopted by two generations. Charles Mearne, Samuel's son, signed (with "C. M. fecit") at least one binding in the style known by his father's name. "Mearne"—or, as they may perhaps be better named, "Restoration"—bindings, derive some of their charm from inlay of red in black but more from the astonishingly varied combinations of a comparatively few types of tool. These were (a) a curve, which being repeated could be built up into a fish-scale pattern; (b) the tulip; open or in bud, which was not, as might be expected, introduced in compliment to Dutch William after 1688 but is freely found in bindings of fifteen years earlier; in defiance of botany, but to a most excellent aesthetic effect, it frequently flowers on the ends of bay-twigs; and (c) the "drawer-handle," which has little beauty in itself, representing more probably the curved rocker of a cradle, or possibly a column capital, but which is extraordinarily fertile as a basis for the most varied designs. The center panel was often (not always happily) given a gable at head and foot, thus making what is called the "cottage," or "gable-end" pattern. It is possible that the Mearne bindings have been somewhat overestimated in England, because it is the first time that English binding was sufficiently closely connected with the best Continental binding to benefit fully. Mearne bindings are neither a pale adaptation of Le Gascon bindings nor a subservient copy of them. They stand as independent creations but with an unmistakable allegiance to the best French binding of the period.[20]

In the later seventeenth century in France there was a revolt against the overrich decoration of Le Gascon bindings, and we find in their place bindings of a severe simplicity, in which the excellent morocco is only decorated by a centerpiece (often armorial) and corner-fleurons. These are called the "Jansenist" bindings, and perhaps the most beautiful are those made for the Baron de Longepierre, in which the sole decoration is the quincunx thus formed by the repetition of his emblem of the Golden Fleece. Jansenist bindings have sometimes richly decorated *doublures* (linings), which belie their Quaker-like exteriors.

Two late–seventeenth- and eighteenth-century families of French binders were influential: the Padeloups, especially Antoine Michel le jeune, Royal binder from 1733 to 1758; and the Deromes, especially Nicolas Denis le jeune (d. 1788). Padeloup used many styles, and especially bold and free inlay; but the prevailing fashion was for a dentelle (lacework) border with a center field plain except for a (generally rather florid) coat of arms. In the hands of the masters the dentelle could be very beautiful, but less tasteful artists broadened the gold surfaces and ruined the effect; this happened especially in Germany and Italy. There were, however, in the later seventeenth and in the eighteenth centuries some excellent binders in Germany and Scandinavia, when the rather heavy portrait panel and Lyonnese styles of the sixteenth century had yielded to the Le Gascon influence; notable was the Court binder at Heidelberg between

1660 and 1710. The Derome dentelle was also delightfully varied in the 1770s by an Austrian binder who to the traditional bay added "rococo" clusters of grapes and flowering sprays. Italy, which had taught France the art of gold-tooling, in the seventeenth and eighteenth centuries mostly followed French fashion, at some distance in taste as well as in time.

In Britain the eighteenth century continued the run of excellent binding designs that had begun during the latter part of the seventeenth century. The Restoration style developed into:

(a) *The Harleian.* This style took its name from many of the bindings produced for Robert and Edward Harley, Earls of Oxford. The style consisted of a strongly marked center panel surrounded by a broad border. In these bindings, in common with a large number of those of this same century, the center of the board usually displayed a heraldic device. For a long time these bindings were regarded as the work of a firm named "Elliott and Chapman." In 1943 J. B. Oldham showed that this was incorrect. There was no such firm, and indeed Elliott and Chapman were rival binders and not partners.[21]

(b) *The Scottish.* This exists in two main styles. One, which more closely resembles the Harleian, is most easily recognized by its having for a centerpiece a straight stem. From this stem branch short sprays at regular intervals on either side. The Harleian influence is still marked particularly in the border, which has quite a separate entity from the main design on the boards. This style was particularly suited to a book that was high in proportion to its width. Consequently it was used especially on duodecimo volumes, which were in great production during the eighteenth century. The second style was one that was used more effectively on the proportionately wider board of a quarto. It is a later form than the stem design and is not by any means so well known. A trace of a border is still visible, but the most prominent feature is a large wheel pattern with a plenitude of radiating spokes. When delicately tooled, it is an extremely interesting and delightful design, but it often suffered due to poorly cut tools and haphazard workmanship.[22]

An interesting offshoot of these bindings can be found in some that were produced in America by Scottish bookbinders working in their native style.[23]

(c) *The Irish.* These eighteenth-century bindings have only begun to be fully investigated in recent years. Many of those still extant are rather stately folios, and they are usually distinguished by a slight border and, more particularly, a large center lozenge. This was on occasion solely a tooled design on the board but more usually an inlay of a variegated-color leather, most typically of fawn color.[24]

These styles flourished throughout most of the eighteenth century, yielding only toward its end to the classical movement.

The eighteenth century was above all else a period of sophisticated elegance in the decorative arts, and the end of the century brought the classical movement into all areas of the arts. Bookbindings were swept along in this tide and reflected the other arts in their own designs. Books that were to stand in cases made by Sheraton and in rooms designed by Adam and decorated with ornaments by Wedgwood had to be dressed in harmony with their surroundings. It is unfortunate for students that this important relationship is all too often not apparent as they seek out examples in modern libraries and museums. Inert in their glass cases, these books present very little of the harmony that their originators intended. Eighteenth-century bindings need to be viewed in an eighteenth-century room surrounded by contemporary furniture, fabrics, glassware, snuff boxes, and all the host of items that the designers of the bindings knew would be in juxtaposition with their handiwork. This same change in design is found in the bindings of Germany and Scandinavia, and also in France during the reign of "Empire" decoration.

In England the great binder of the period, probably indeed the country's greatest binder, was Roger Payne. He was fortunate in working for cultured collectors, such as Lord Spencer and the Reverend James Cracherode, who could appreciate his taste. Payne does not use classical detail much, though his swags, whether curved or vertical, are Roman in feeling; but he subtly adapted the dentelle to the new manner. If (as seems probable) he designed Cracherode's armorial stamp, he is to be credited with the one perfect example of the kind. It may have been based on that used in the late sixteenth century by the French historian and collector J. A. de Thou on the bindings made for him before his marriage. Unfortunately, however, Payne, like many of his contemporaries, used straight-grained morocco on his larger books, although it forms a less satisfactory background to the tooling than do the smooth moroccos used by the French binders; but he actually succeeded in finding a russia that has lasted very well. Neither he nor any other good binder used the atrocious calf popular in England for cheaper bindings at that period.[25]

One other feature in English eighteenth-century binding is worthy of comment, even though it had little direct influence on later stages. The Edwards family, originally of Halifax, Yorkshire, and later of London, introduced a number of decorative innovations.[26] In their so-called "Etruscan" bindings, with the use of terra-cotta stained medallions against the lighter brown calfskin, they sought to imitate the profiles of the coinage that was becoming known through archaeological expeditions. Combined with borders of the Greek key-pattern design, they reflected the same interest that was to affect English pottery of the period. Their other innovation was even more highly regarded in their own time. They perfected, and patented, a method of making vellum transparent. Thus any design, for example, a watercolor on paper, could be laid on the board and, when covered with the transparent vellum, would appear as painted vellum. Painted and enameled vellum bindings had been known from the earliest days of binding: their disadvantage had always been the wear to which the surface design was subjected. The Edwards brothers also popularized, but did not invent, the fore-edge painting.[27]

Nineteenth-century binding styles, in common with much decorative work of the period, were largely imitative and degenerate. Eighteenth-century influences were still strong but for the most part produced pale shadows of the originals. There were respectable names in plenty but no outstanding masters to rival the best of earlier periods. Nevertheless, since the bibliographer is concerned to ascertain and record facts rather than deal in aesthetic appreciation, there are styles and binders demanding recognition in this century as in earlier ones. Christian Kalthoeber, like many other London craftsmen of the period, was German by birth. He was active as a bookbinder during the last twenty or so years of the eighteenth and continued to trade in the first decade or so of the nineteenth. Charles Lewis, also of German descent, ran one of the largest binding shops in London, which following his death in 1836 was carried on by his foreman, Francis Bedford, on behalf of the widow. In due time Bedford himself became one of the leading practitioners. Two other less well-known binders also of German origin, L. Staggemeier and Samuel Welcher, settled in London in the 1790 period and were in partnership from 1799 until around 1810. They produced a large number of somewhat ornate designs of good-quality work. English provincial centers, such as Oxford, Southampton, Chichester, Manchester, Bath, and Northampton, all produced work of technical competence and of a style that suited the tastes of the book buyers of the period. Edinburgh and Dublin continued, even though diminished, the traditions of Scottish and Irish bindings that had flourished so markedly in the eighteenth century. In France the Romantic movement produced a short-lived and amusingly ugly "cathedral" style of elaborate Gothic architectural forms. Toward the latter part of the nineteenth century there were many experiments in appropriate pictorial design—such as a ship on a book of sea-voyages. For the most part they are bad enough to suggest that binding design should be formal.

In the United States of America hand-binding was established as a craft in the early colonial period and spread to all the major book-producing centers. By 1820 there were established binderies in Boston, Philadelphia, New York, Annapolis, Charleston, Worcester, and Salem. The immigrant binders were schooled in the styles of the areas from which they came, exhibiting adaptations that resulted from the local cutting of the tools.

Some large part of the decay of real binding in this century was due to the development of what was the nineteenth century's chief contribution to this art. In the 1820s the whole position was revolutionized by the use of book cloth as a covering material and the introduction of casing as distinct from binding. The trio of new influences was completed in about 1832 by the discovery of a method of gold-blocking on cloth. From these beginnings there grew a new range of materials and a new tradition of decoration. This soon became the established form of publishers' issue, and, although much of the work up to the present day has been uninspired and mechanical, it has shown itself capable of satisfactory work when well used. At any rate the nineteenth century cannot be considered as a fruitless period when it con-tributed so important a development to the art. Its limitation lay in the fact that the advance in technique was not rapidly fol-lowed by a corresponding advance in ideas of decoration on the new media.[28]

The real resurrection of leather bindings, however, came in the 1880s with the work of Cobden-Sanderson. Although all his bindings may not be of equal merit, he bound beautifully and was very influential. His work was carried on into the present century by Sarah Prideaux, Katharine Adams, and, above all, Douglas Cockerell. In the same manner the designs of Charles Ricketts, another notable designer, were the inspiration of the work of Sybil Pye. Although good binding is still being produced in Europe and in America, in the present economic position of the world there is no longer the same quantity of demand as pre-viously. Some of the most interesting of contemporary work is being produced in guild and trade schools. This of itself gives some measure of hope that the craftsmanship may be kept alive against the day when it might again serve the discriminating collector.

Methods of binding

The binder divides the processes of the craft into two series: "forwarding" and "finishing." Forwarding includes everything necessary to make a secure unit of book and cover; finishing, the last touches, such as lettering and decorating.

If the binder is concerned with a new book, which is being bound for the first time—that is, binding as opposed to rebinding—then the first task is to gather the sections of the book together in the correct order as determined by their signa-tures or back-marks or both. If, on the other hand, it is an instance of rebinding, then the initial steps will be more com-plex. The existing volume must be pulled into its constituent parts, collated, and made ready for resewing and rebinding. A wide variety of separate operations are comprised within the term "made ready for resewing." Torn leaves can be mended; bad confluences of wormholes can be filled; paper can be cleaned, washed, and resized. Books whose covers are broken or cracking can be rebacked, a strip of leather of the same color being substituted for the original back (which can be laid down over it) wide enough to be firmly glued down on to the covers, which are thus held in place. New leather can be glued onto boards and the original leather then replaced over it.

Within the field of binding conservation advances in modern techniques have brought about vast improvements in this area. It is highly skilled work, but unfortunately irreparable damage has been done by the ministrations of unqualified and inexperienced practitioners. Repair work in general and much rebinding in libraries have destroyed important bibliographical evidence. At the other end of the scale great binderies and repair centers have done much to preserve materials that would otherwise have been lost.

Contemporary bindings of old books are now, so far as possible, retained, even when rebacking, or complete rebinding, is necessary. Not only do flyleaves often bear owner's notes of value and margins that are cropped away bear annotations, but the binding itself may be dated and so help to date the book. An extraordinary example may be found in Gordon Duff's *Early Printed Books.* Writing of the earliest block-books, he says:

> The copies of the *Biblia Pauperum, Apocalypse and Ars Moriendi,* which belonged to Mr. Horn, were in their original binding, and it was stamped with a date. The books were separated and the binding destroyed. Mr. Horn asserted from memory that the first three figures of the date were certainly 142, and the last probably an 8. Mr. Conway very justly points out that the resemblance of a 5 of that date to our 2 was very strong, and that Mr. Horn's memory may have deceived him."[29]

An extensive literature has now grown up around the rebinding and care of bibliographically important materials. Some of the most important items are those that provide detailed descriptions of successful restorative binding.[30]

The sewing is the essence of the whole craft; of that alone it is true that if it fails, all fails, and the book falls to pieces. The earliest form of sewing books that consisted of multiple sections was to pass a sewing thread up the fold of each gathering and to leave a small tail of the thread protruding from a needlehole in the fold at the head and tail. These ends were then tied together in order to secure the sections to each other. It is a method that was used in Egypt and neighboring countries from around the seventh century. The method, known by reason of the region of its origin as "Coptic" sewing, spread widely throughout many parts of Europe. The earliest known extant English binding, the Stonyhurst Gospels, which is probably of the late seventh century, is on this "thongless" method. The development from this was to sew up and down the sections with a continuous thread and to enclose thongs or cords (*Fig.* 9 [ii]). This method of sewing, frequently referred to as raised-cord (or thong) became the common European practice from around the tenth century onward. In the second half of the nineteenth century tapes were used instead of cords in publisher's casings (*Fig* 9 [iv]), but there is little evidence of the use of tapes in original bindings before this time. By these means the pairs of conjugate leaves were secured to each other within the gathering and each gathering was in turn secured to its neighbors. There was also some part of the sewing, the thread in Coptic bindings or the cord or tapes in later bindings, that could be threaded into or inserted into the covering boards.

There were four to six cords, depending on the size of the book, with an additional pair at the head and tail. They were long, so as to lie about a third across the covers. The thread was carried through the fold of the first section and round the cords from head to tail, then across to the next section by means of a "kettle stitch," and up to its head. So it continued up and down across the entire back of the book. This is called "flexible allalong" sewing and is essentially a hand method. In medieval practice, when books were frequently heavy and great strength was required, double-cords were used and the sewing thread went between and round them (*Fig.* 9 [i]). The quality of the materials was at least as important as the methods used. The cords were normally of hemp and the sewing of best unbleached linen thread. Other materials were employed from time to time: vellum strips served occasionally instead of cords, and some binders, for example Roger Payne, sewed with silken thread.

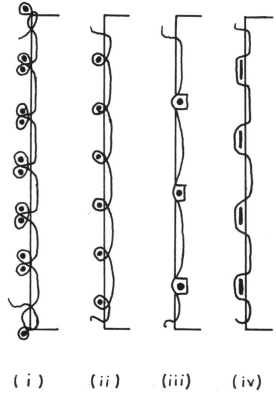

(i)   (ii)   (iii)   (iv)

FIG. 9. *Binder's sewings*

There have been important variations from this type of sewing over the years. Some of the methods are now little used while others occur with increasing frequency. Among the more important may be found the following:

(a) *Sewing two sheets on.* Also known as sewing "two-on" or "two-along." This is an alternative method to sewing "all-along." In all-along sewing the thread passes without interruption from end to end. When sheets are sewn "two-on," the thread passes from one section to its neighboring one each time the needle leaves the fold. The assumption has usually been that this method was adopted because it halved the elaboration of the sewing and prevented any swelling out of the spines of books that were composed of many thin sections. However, Bernard Middleton has said, "It is clear from the fact that even the thinnest books were thus sewn that the object was to save time and not to reduce swelling, the latter being the main reason for its use in hand binderies today."[31] The student needs to study diagrams of the sewing in order to see exactly how the object was achieved and is advised to consult the examples given by Middleton.[32]

(b) *Overcasting or oversewing.* This is a method of sewing in which the thread enters the gathering on the flat top of the gathering a short distance in from the spine. It is found in many eighteenth-century books, especially in the large plate books. Its advantage was in making a more solid and substantial hinge. Its disadvantage was in creating a false hinge to the section along the line of the sewing with a tendency, in some instances, to tear through the paper at this point. It was also relatively common, in the case of books that consisted of single leaves, such as some plate books, to oversew several leaves together and then to sew these groups with all-along sewing. This produced a tendency for the book to open at these points. During the nineteenth century it was used for large books although frequently only for the first few and the last few gatherings in order to strengthen the book at the hinges. This same kind of advantage was exploited by Cedric Chivers when he patented a method of oversewing in 1904 for his library bindings. Something similar to this method, or at least variations therefrom, has been the basis of much mass-produced sewn library binding during the twentieth century. The important element in Chivers's method was to pierce three rows of holes in each section so that the position of the thread alternated from section to section and so lessened the dangers from the pull and strain of the thread. It is a method of sewing that has distinct advantages when it is well done, but, as several examples will testify, it is liable to suffer through poor workmanship and error.

(c)   *Recessed cords or bands.* Sewing on cords in the normal manner produced ridges across the spine of the book, which the majority of binders were quick to incorporate as a part of their decoration. Other methods have been in use by binders of all periods that resulted in smooth spines. It is not apparent whether these methods were always employed with the main end in view of the smooth spine or whether it was not occasionally an accidental yet acceptable outcome. The methods of sewing in Coptic bindings produced this result, and others can be found at all periods. Some sixteenth-century books were sewn on flat strips of leather or vellum, which had practically the same effect.

      If, however, the book was sewn on cords, something more was necessary. Bernard Middleton quotes H. M. Nixon as saying that "in France in the mid–sixteenth century some books bound by Claude de Picques, and others bound for Thomas Mahieu, are sewn on raised cords and have the panels built up to make a smooth spine."[33] These would appear to be extreme cases. The more usual remedy was to saw a trench across the back of the sections in which the cords could lie and be enclosed by the thread (*Fig.* 9 [iii]).

(d)   *Stabbing.* Sewing not in the folds but by piercing the pile of sections from front to back. Stabbing is very cheap and quick, but the leaves will not open to the back, will not lie open, and if one tries to make them do so will tear at the sewings. Eighteenth-century pamphlets were generally issued stabbed, and the holes, often far out from the folds, can still be seen. Consequently they frequently provide important evidence in the case of such rebound pamphlets and must therefore not be neglected in bibliographical description. This method is now practically confined to stapling (see below), except in very ephemeral matter.

(e)   *Stapling.* Stabbing with wire clips or staples, either from the sides, or, less objectionably, in the place of the sewing thread through the folds. In the former method the evils of stabbing are intensified by the use of metal, which tears the paper; even in the latter the metal ultimately rusts and burns holes in it. A considerable number of these can be found in publishers' cased books from the 1880s. Some very reputable houses seem to have used them at this time, but later use is confined largely to ephemeral matter.

(f)   *Tipping-in.* Pasting the edge of a single leaf to the next leaf. Normally used for inserting plates but also sometimes for errata slips and single leaves of text—which ought incidentally never to exist, a "fold" (as the binder terms a pair of leaves) being the bindable unit. When such single leaves appear as text leaves, they demand careful examination in order to determine *why* they exist. Such an examination may reveal circumstances of major interest in the book's makeup. Where plates are printed on single leaves that are not wide enough to take the sewing, a fold can be made by laying to their edges flexible guards that will go round the fold of the nearest pair. Plates can also be guarded in this way in pairs.

(g)   *Spiral-backs.* This method of binding has been widely adopted for books that are required to open absolutely flat. Because of this it has been given considerable use for such utilitarian items as guidebooks, maps, cookbooks, data books, and, less frequently, bibliographical guides and library catalogs. Spirals of metal and the ubiquitous plastic have been used. While there are certain advantages in this method, the life of such bindings is not usually long and their ugliness is excessive.

(h)   *Unsewn bindings.* In 1836 William Hancock was granted a patent for a method of fixing single leaves to each other by means of a rubber solution. The leaves were brought together, the spine roughened and coated with india rubber. While the solution was still sticky, a backing was put on followed by the boards. The life of the binding was as long as the life of the rubber, which was a matter of months. After that period the book became, once again, a collection of loose leaves. These were widely known as "Caoutchouc" bindings and were in wide use up to the beginning of the Second World War for cheap book production. One of the most successful series in the 1920–1930 period was the "Reader's Library," which was marketed by F. W. Woolworth and which ran to hundreds of titles. For a long time it was common practice to condemn this type of binding for too general a use and to suggest that its use should be restricted to ephemeral publications, such as telephone directories. In the period since the Second World War the process has been resurrected with a great burst of publicity and a nomenclature of "perfect library binding," which can only be regarded as extremely misleading. The difference in the new form from its earlier experiments was that a plastic adhesive was used in place of rubber solution. Initial laboratory tests of the methods were most promising, and the supporters of the method were enthusiastic in its praise. It has been extensively used in the manufacture of paperbacks and increasingly so for more permanently designed publications. Constant testing has been taking place with regard to both the methods and the adhesives used with a view to improving the finished result. In the light of all the laboratory evidence it will seem illogical to continue to view unsewn bindings with any lingering suspicion. The reason says that they are adequate, the emotions recall the numerous instances of badly broken copies. The laboratory does not always know what happens in real life.

Following the completion of the sewing operations the edges of the leaves should be trimmed with the plough, but not more than is necessary to tidy them. Old or valuable books should be left "uncut." While the worship of the rough deckle-edge may be absurd, nothing is more hideous than merciless cutting down or cropping. One of the unfortunate results of this unnecessary cropping that the bibliographer has to face is a margin of manuscript annotations that have been crudely cut and rendered illegible. At this stage it is important that a clear distinction should be preserved between the terms "uncut" and "unopened." To repeat—the former term relates to binders and their shears, the latter to readers and their paper-knife.

It will be apparent that all these methods, in their various ways, result in the production of a compact unit of the sewn or attached sections. In the majority of cases throughout binding history, and certainly in the best instances, these sections will have been sewn on to cords, or thongs, or tapes.

The next stage is that of "gluing-up" and rounding. Glue is worked into the back or spine of the sewn gatherings. Early glues tended to dry hard and brittle, but during the course of the nineteenth century more flexible glues came into use. When the glue is dry but not yet hard, the sections are held in a clamp and then knocked outward and downward from the center on either side in order to produce a rounded back. If left flat, which has tended to be the habit in American books, the fore-edges will in time bulge. These stages are reached before the covers are attached. In the case of cords or thongs holes are punched in the boards so that they are on a level with the cords, which are then threaded through the board. They enter the board from the upper surface and then are frayed out on the underside so as to lie flat, placed in a small groove, glued, and hammered flat. In the case of tapes the board is split, or occasionally built up by means of two half-thickness boards, the tapes inserted between the boards, glued in position, and pressed.

For the best binding black board made from old rope is used; the old use of wooden boards has been revived for large and valuable books. It will be seen that, given good materials, the union between book and cover should be practically eternal. It is this fixture of the body of the book to the boards that is the essential part of binding and that most clearly differentiates it from casing. The book grows step by step as a sequence of operations, each one building on the previous.

Back-linings were then frequently glued down on to the spine of the book. In later days these are usually dull, uninteresting, but substantial pieces of brown paper. In earlier periods, however, they frequently consisted of binders' waste. Since these, especially in the early days of printing, included fragments of manuscripts and discarded sheets of printing, they can be of very considerable interest. Any paste-down that shakes out of a loose binding should be carefully preserved and duly noted with details of the provenance.[34]

The covering material is then stretched over the boards and the spine. When the material is glued directly on to the spine, it is said to be a "tight back." This will mean that the spine has added strength but also that, when the book is opened, the leather on the spine will assume a concave shape. The alternative to this is to create a "hollow back." This consisted of gluing the spine, placing on it a length of paper approximately twice the width of the spine so that one half will fold back upon itself. In this way a tube can be constructed, of more than the one double-fold of paper or material if required. The virtue of the hollow back was that the covering material on the spine did not fold in at each opening and so run the risk of damaging the tooled decoration. Additionally, if the paper of the book was somewhat on the thick side, it helped the book to open and lie flat. Additional strain was placed on the hinges of the book, and in the case of poor bindings this could be disastrous. Hollow backs can be found in French binding from about 1770 onward but are uncommon in English binding until after 1820.

The covering material is next mitered at the corners and the flange of the material folded down on the inside of the boards to create the doublure. The endpapers will then be pasted down on the inside of the boards.

The covering material does not necessarily stretch over the whole board. In many instances the spine and sometimes the spine and the corners are treated in a different manner from the boards. A common variation is leather for the spine and the corners with paper covering on the boards. If the covering material covers spine and boards completely, it is described as *full binding*. If the spine covering extends a considerable way across the board, approximately one-third, and the corners also extend approximately the same proportion, the description is *three-quarter binding*. If the proportion of the board covered by the spine and the corner material is significantly less than one-third, the description if *half-binding*. When the spine covering extends only a small way on the board, but the corners are not distinctly treated, the description is *quarter-binding*.

Headbands

When the covering leather was cut in order to fold down over the inside boards to form the doublure, special consideration was obviously necessary at the head and tail of the spine. The leather was not normally cut off sharp at these points but turned over on itself and sometimes strengthened by a narrow strip of vellum or board. In some cases the leather at head and tail was sewn and in other instances plaited. Any of these methods helped to strengthen the spine and prevented its breaking when the volume was taken off the shelf in an improper way by pulling it at the head. For the most part, however, headbands developed in an entirely decorative manner. Such headbands were usually silk sewn in two or three colors. A length of cord, thong, or vellum, cut slightly wider than the spine, was placed in position at the head of the spine. Lengths of decorative silk were wound around the cord and at frequent intervals stitched to the line of the kettle stitch. The headband was secured in place when the covering material was glued to the spine. It then appeared as a decorative strip inside the leather at the head of the spine. In modern books, when it is found at all, it has largely degenerated into an ornamental strip stuck onto the top of the leaves at the spine.

The general style of headbands has developed over the years and can provide a certain amount of evidence relating to the authenticity and dating of the binding.

Finishing

The volume, duly covered, now remains to be lettered with the author's name, title of work, occasionally the date, and perhaps also to be decorated.

Although in many examples of great binding the spine and the boards have been thought of, and decorated, as a unified surface, it is not unrealistic to consider the spine decoration separately. It has not always been, as we now commonly regard it, the most obvious place on which to find the name of the author and the title of the book. When books were stored flat on shelves, they were usually placed with the fore-edge outward. The title was then normally written in ink along the fore-edge or occasionally on the bottom edge of the leaves. This was a normal medieval practice, as was also the habit of affixing a small piece of vellum, bearing the title, to the board under a protective piece of horn. The increase in book collections in the sixteenth century caused books to be placed upright on shelves with their spines facing outward. Titling then was more conveniently placed on the spine.

Graham Pollard found that "the earliest titles tooled in gilt on the back seem to have been done in Venice or northern Italy about 1535."[35] "The earliest datable English bindings so lettered are three books bound by Williamson of Eton for Charles Somerset about 1604. But this is an isolated case; and it did not become general practice until after the Restoration."[36] Pollard also found examples of a lettering piece—that is, a small piece of leather bearing the title that is stuck on the spine—on bindings around 1680. The practice soon spread, and in Pollard's opinion "after 1700 lettering direct on to the leather is, I think, the exception rather than the rule."[37]

Apart from titling the spine treatment was largely decorative, although it is by no means uncommon to find marks of ownership in the form of heraldic device, rebus, initials, etc.

The treatment of the boards is again primarily decorative and is mainly considered in the section on the development of bookbinding styles. The boards have additionally been the place for titles of books and authors to be lettered, although this has never been an extensive practice. It is much more common to find the bibliographical interest of the boards limited to the evidence they afford as very common locations for marks of ownership, especially heraldic devices.

In the section on bookbinding styles reference was made to the introduction of gold-tooling. Two methods existed for applying gold to leather: one, the impression of the design in blind followed by the painting of this design with liquid gold; the other, the impression by heated tools through gold leaf. In this latter instance, which became the general method, the surface of the leather was prepared with glaire (egg-white), covered with gold, and subjected to heated tools, which impressed the design permanently. Dorothy Miner describes and illustrates a mid–thirteenth-century Qu'ran written at Marrakesh, which may be the earliest extant and datable piece of gold-tooled binding of this nature. The major European development of the art followed its introduction into Italy around 1470. Although gold-tooling is the most common form of this style of decoration, it was not the only one. Silver-tooling was also employed but only to a very limited extent, and even less frequent were examples of color work of the same nature.

When the decoration was applied by tools (normally heated) onto dampened leather but without any gold, silver, or color, it is described as "blind."

Whether the tooling was in gold or blind, the other main variation was in the size of the tools employed. The range was from very small tools that were used to create the intricacies of a large design, to larger blocks that were frequently used for corner ornaments and central cartouches, to large panel stamps that cover the whole board.

Treatment of edges

The final step in the finishing processes is the treatment of the edges. The following are the chief methods that have been employed.

(a) *Colored edges.* Coloring is a long-standing habit in bindings, the earliest known example being of the fourth century. Strickland Gibson recorded of Oxford bindings that "the colours most frequently used from the 15th to the 17th century to decorate the edges of a volume were red, yellow and ochre. . . . Some rare colours employed are olive green and violet. . . . Blue is also uncommon. . ."[38]

(b) *Sprinkled edges.* Sprinkling has long been a popular variation of solid-color edges; sometimes they are used in conjunction with each other. When sprinkling is used on its own, it is sometimes of one color and sometimes of two or three. It has been in widespread use since early in the sixteenth century.

In the case of both coloring and sprinkling it seems probable that further research may establish a relationship between certain colors and certain areas and periods of bookbinding. In the article already mentioned Graham Pollard wrote, "I have since examined several hundred books printed and bound in calf gilt between 1750 and 1800. Whereas the books printed in England

mostly have white or yellow edges, those printed in Ireland all
have rather vivid green or blue edges or a grey-green sprinkle. I
do not suppose that there can ever have been any absolute rule
about this; but I propound the provisional theory that green or
blue edges on calf books in the second half of the eighteenth
century are an indication of Irish binding."[39]

(c)   *Gilt edges.* The gilding of edges appears to be as old as the
use of gold-tooling on the bindings themselves and, country by country, was probably introduced at the same time.
A general short reference to this in catalogs is "g.e."
Around the middle of the nineteenth century the practice
developed of gilding the top edge only. The usual reference
in catalogs is "t.e.g."

(d)   *Gauffered edges.* Gauffering of the edges is found in conjunction with practically any type of edge—plain, gilt,
colored, sprinkled. The book is placed in a press and the
edge impressed with series of warm tools or rolls. The in-
dentation is long lasting. Gauffered edges can produce a
variety of effects apart from the design itself, including
multiple coloring. Gauffering is chiefly associated with gilt
edges and was introduced at the same time.

(e)   *Marbled edges.* Marble edging can be found on books back
to the late seventeenth century, but it was not in very
general use until late in the eighteenth century.

(f)   *Painted edges.* This term is used to distinguish a particular
style of edge decoration, other than the painting with a
solid color and with sprinkling as in (a) and (b) above. In
this instance the edge is painted with a design, some extremely simple but others of great elaboration. An advance
on this method was, according to H. M. Nixon, an English
contribution of the Commonwealth period.[40] The leaves
were fanned out and the design painted on the very edge of
the flat leaf, not on the edge of the leaf itself. When the
leaves were released after fanning they returned to their
normal position. The edge was then decorated in the normal
manner, usually by gilding, but coloring, sprinkling, or

marbling would serve equally well. If desired, the leaves could also be fanned in the other direction and decorated so that the gilding (or other covering) could conceal two decorations. The style enjoyed a great vogue during the last half of the eighteenth century and the first quarter of the nineteenth.

Covering materials

The covers that are stretched over the boards were not always part of the earliest bindings. The prime function of the covering material was to protect the cords and sewings at the back or spine, a part as vital in a book as in a person. In the fifteenth century books were still often only half-covered and had the wooden boards bare. It was in this tradition that Douglas Cockerell bound the Codex Sinaiticus, with white morocco spine and uncovered English oaken boards.

The materials for the covers consisted until very recently almost exclusively of skin, nor has any textile of equal flexibility, toughness, and durability yet been found to take its place. Over the centuries many fantastic hides have been used. The factor that affected the choice of leather in the past was primarily that of availability. Leathers used in one particular locality would not only be skins of native animals but they would be tanned and dressed in accordance with local usage. As the economics of a country or an area changed, so variations in binding materials can be discovered. For example, in the Middle Ages in England deer-skin was largely used. The only reason that can be attributed for its later entire disuse is the change in the country's economy, which resulted in the disappearance of the large herds of deer that had once roamed the country. Although economic considerations were the most important reasons for the change of leathers, there were others. A sense of humor and comic appropriateness motivated some binders in certain circumstances. Many large libraries can produce such examples as Charles James Fox's *History of the Early Part of the Reign of James the Second* bound in fox skin or Governor Phillip's *Voyage to Botany Bay* bound in kangaroo skin. There was also a natural urge for experimentation, which led binders to try practically anything, especially in times of restriction of normal supplies.[41] At the present day a comparatively few animals yield the leathers that bookbinders chiefly use; they are the pig, goat, calf, and sheep.

(a) *Pigskin* is a very strong, thick, and durable leather, but it needs special treatment in binding because it is rather stiff. One widely adopted method of dealing with thick skins, and especially so on the hinges, where they need maximum flexibility, is to pare the skin. This involves cutting the skin away on the underside or flesh side so as to make it thinner. No leather is improved by paring, but skins vary considerably in the extent of damage that can result. In the case of pigskin it is particularly harmful since so high a percentage of the strength of pigskin lies in the tough fibrous underpart of the skin. For this reason pigskin, and some other thick leathers, is bound with a French joint. The board is not pushed up close to the shoulder of the spine, but a gap of about one-eighth inch is left into which the leather can retract on opening the boards.[42]

Because of its great strength pigskin is excellent for binding very large, heavy books. It was widely used in the early days of printed-book bindings and particularly so by German binders of the fifteenth and sixteenth centuries. When, as was then so regularly the case, it was used over thick and heavy wooden boards, it makes a massive and impressive binding. It is frequently said that pigskin should not be dyed as the strength of the skin may be damaged. While this may be so, it is equally true that early bindings in dyed pigskin can be found still in excellent condition. The stronger argument against dyeing has probably been that, left in the natural color, pigskin takes on a very pleasant "cheesy" or oatmeal tone. It can also often be found in the form of "tawed" pigskin, for which purpose it was soaked in alum and common salt. This produced a somewhat bleached look to the skin, which appealed to certain binders.[43]

Pigskin is most often found with blind-tooling since the leather does not take gold-tooling well. Even blind-tooling can be difficult on so hard a surface, and it is often found with a minimum of tooling of any kind. It is among the most easily recognizable leathers because of the bristle-holes that appear in triads over the surface.

(b) Goatskin, otherwise generically called morocco, from the country whence it entered Europe in the sixteenth and seventeenth centuries, is, when properly prepared, perhaps the most generally trustworthy and suitable of all leathers for fine work. It has a strongly marked network grain that can be modified by stretching in one direction into "straight grain" (a series of parallel ridges) or in two directions into "cross-grain" or "pin-head." Morocco, in its better varieties, is frequently "crushed." The leather is dampened and then subjected to great pressure between polished metal plates. This has the effect of minimizing the grain of the leather and giving a pleasantly smooth appearance, which is ideal for tooling. This method was originally introduced for the purpose of preparing the surface to take, and show to advantage, really delicate gold-tooling. The rather burnished surface that was produced by crushing proved to be so attractive that in many cases it was left untooled, or with a minimum of tooling, as its own decoration.

The finest morocco is crushed levant, and no leather except vellum so well shows up gold-tooling. It is costly and is reserved for valuable books. This leather was originally imported from the eastern end of the Mediterranean, from which area it takes its name. Because of the strong trade links between the Levant and Italy, especially Venice, it is a leather that is found in much Italian bookbinding. As French binding styles in the early sixteenth century came to develop so much in the Italian fashion, it is found extensively there also. It differs from other morocco because of the basic difference in the skin itself, accentuated by the local methods of tanning and dressing.

For large and heavy books there is no leather better than niger morocco, which is thick and immensely strong. Once again the name suggests the area with which it has been most generally connected in the past, and again its qualities are dependent upon local usage. Its self-color is a light fawn, but it is generally seen in the dye given it by the native makers, a kind of yellowish terra-cotta that is very pleasing to the eye. Native-tanned (perhaps by sumach) and native-dyed niger is still nearly always free from the deleterious acids that have ruined so much leather. Some good binders import niger undyed and dye it themselves.

Although these two are the most widely known and used of the moroccos, they are not the only ones to which the name is applied. Some of these are genuine and reputable in that they are made from serviceable goatskins, such as Cape morocco. This is a perfectly good binding leather even though it has neither the strength nor the beauty of niger or levant. Other so-called moroccos are made from sheepskin, which is a much inferior skin, and many of them are useless as binding materials. Among the very worst is "Persian morocco," which has none of the sound qualities of real morocco and is valueless for long-term preservation. It is derived from Indian goat and sheep and is badly tanned.

Sheepskin is also met with in one other connection with morocco, although not a very worthy connection. The grain of morocco unfortunately lends itself to deceptions. Molds can be taken of it, since it is hard, and soft leathers, such as sheepskin, given the grain by pressure in these molds. The fraud can be detected both by testing the hardness of the surface with the fingernail and also by the price.

(c) *Calfskin,* once very widely used, has fallen into disfavor. Early in the eighteenth century English binders took to a lighter-tanned brown calf, from younger animals, which they shaved thin at the joints and often patterned with panel-stencils and powderings of green vitriol, producing elegant effects but losing strength. Few English calf-bound books between 1750 and the present day have not their joints either broken outright or at least (as the French put it) fatigued, and the sins of English calf have unjustly brought all English binding into condemnation abroad. Young calf has a perfectly smooth surface, without grain, and gives a pleasant polish, which was the reason for its popularity. The very qualities of its surface indeed have been the main reasons for its misuse. It has been subjected to a wide variety of decorative processes, such as tree calf, which, however attractive, contributed largely to its decay. In a tree-calf binding acid is poured over the leather in such a way that it takes stains somewhat resembling the growth of a tree. If the leather is allowed to become too dry and brittle, small areas of the stained leather tend to break away and the whole surface to become pitted.

Seventeenth-century and earlier dark calf is thick and has generally survived in fair state. Some of this is from the hides of yearling calves, that of the very young beasts having been used for making vellum. The virtues of calfskin are difficult to assess fairly, but it does not deserve the sweepingly bad reputation that is usually accorded it. When a good skin of full natural thickness is used, it can present an unusually attractive surface and one that takes gold- and blind-tooling extremely well. It can never be regarded as a particularly strong leather, however, and it has a tendency to rub and flake if care and precautions are not taken. But for attractiveness in use it is difficult to fault it.

(d) *Russia* leather is a form of calfskin that is soft-surfaced and, when kept in good condition, slightly scented. It is frequently met with dyed to a light reddish-brown color. It was a skin tanned by willow bark and dressed with the oil of the bark of the white birch. It is this latter that gives the leather its distinctive odor. Russia was popular in England during the late eighteenth and early nineteenth centuries but is all too rarely now met with in good condition. The leather was subject to red decay, in which the fibrous underlay of the skin powdered away and can frequently be seen in a red dust at the base of the spine. Roger Payne used it on a number of bindings, and in many cases these are still in a state of good preservation. This is probably due to two causes, first, that he had a source of supply of above-average leather, and second, that, since his bindings were highly expensive, they were well maintained from the outset.

(e) *Vellum* is calfskin, dressed with alum and polished. It has a beautiful, creamy-white surface when new that mellows pleasantly with age and repays gold-tooling as no other background does. It is, and always has been, an expensive material and, although not uncommon in older use, has never been used lightly or unadvisably. Even when new, it is not very flexible and will not give a tight flexible back. It was often used in the same manner as other covering skins, that is, drawn on over boards; but, unlike the other materials, it was frequently bound without boards in the style known as "limp vellum." Under extremes of heat and light it is inclined to contract and, when covering boards, to cause the boards to splay badly. Because of this vellum-bound books were frequently bound with metal clasps at the fore-edge and limp vellum often with ties. If extremes of heat are of long duration, with no counteracting remedy, the vellum can become brittle and is liable to crack. Except in this state it is unlikely to crack even when folded sharply at the corners of a flat-spined book.

Vellum is an easy surface to clean and maintain in good condition and repays every moment spent on it. Because of its expense and its lasting qualities it will often be found serving a second purpose. Vellum leaves from large service books were often used in the sixteenth century for binding books. In Italy vellum (or more often parchment) long remained a much-used material, as may be seen on any Italian secondhand bookstall. Both vellum and parchment, when prepared for binding, have their surface intact; when prepared for writing, it is scraped off.

(f) *Sheepskin*, if whole, is good enough for binding books for which, either by reason of use anticipated for them or of the paper on which they are printed, only a short life is required. It has little virtue for permanent preservation. In its split state, as "skiver" (having a pleasant, soft, suedelike surface), it is somewhat less durable than stout paper. "Basil" and "roan" denote various tannings, the latter by sumach.

Sheepskin has a rippling and somewhat pitted grain that is generally recognizable, and, as already observed, a soft loose texture.

Reddish-brown sheepskin was much used in England in the seventeenth and eighteenth centuries for account books, schoolbooks, and other cheap books, and it is sometimes in very fair preservation. All too often, however, if no care has been taken, sheepskin bindings can present an air of complete decay. The venerable odor of some old-fashioned lawyers' offices is partly compounded of this, and it bears recognizable kinship to the undertone of airs breathed on a Welsh hillside after the spring thaws.

(g) *Parchment* is a product similar to vellum but not so strong, being made of sheepskin, and recognizable by the grain, which is absent in vellum. It is usually found in circumstances in which the binder would have preferred vellum had the cost for it not been prohibitive. It will also make frequent appearance in those countries, such as Britain, where the economy was largely founded on the sheep.

(h) *Sealskin* is the hide not of the fur-bearing but of the Greenland seal, and is very strong. Unfortunately it is not cheap, the demand not making a moderate price possible. It has consequently never been widely used in the history of binding, but its qualities are so marked that it deserves study in order to understand the requirements of a good binding leather. Graham Pollard has noted the existence of two early sealskin bindings. "It has too long been the fashion to describe almost any leather not cured by tanning as doeskin or deerskin. A large glossed bible at Lincoln Cathedral and a book from Fountains Abbey are clearly bound in sealskin. We know this because the hair can still be seen on the skin."[44]

Seal has two great virtues. First, the hide, as it has to protect a warm-blooded creature from cold seawater, is full of oil, and this gives it a long-enduring life and flexibility. It is often said that oil may stain the endpapers and neighboring books on the shelf; but this does not in fact seem to be a major problem. Second, since the seal's hide is equally exposed all over to the water, it has, unlike the land animals, no sheltered or tender spots, and the hide is therefore good and strong throughout. There is a slight glister (no doubt a sign of oil) on the surface of seal, which otherwise has some resemblance to smooth morocco.

Decay and preservation of leather

If calf bindings of the last century and a half have for the most part failed to survive intact, this is because binders, in order to get a delicate surface, used the skins of animals slaughtered too young. But other leathers of the last half-century, and notably moroccos, have also shown lamentable signs of decay. In 1900 the Society of Arts in Great Britain appointed a Committee to investigate the subject, and their report appeared in 1901 and then was edited and reissued in 1905. They found that decay had become common since about 1830 and markedly so since 1860. They were able to show that the various forms of catechol tannin set up, under the action of light, the red powdery decay so noticeable in modern leathers, but that sumach was free from this objection. Gas fumes (this was soon after the days of naked gas jets) were proved to be highly injurious, as containing sulphuric and sulphurous acid, and sulphuric acid was equally condemned when used in dyeing. Light and heat were also discovered to be harmful.

Later research, much of it in England, especially by R. Faraday Innes, showed that the acid that is always found in rotted leathers may not have been due to the manufacturer, on whom the Society of Arts laid all the blame, but to subsequent infiltration from the atmosphere. It was also found that old and durable leathers contained sulphuric acid, but that their acidity was controlled by certain other chemicals in the leather. The result was that decay was found to be of two main kinds: *chemical decay* due to the leather rotting by the action of sulphuric acid that was formed in the leather because of absorption of sulphur dioxide from the atmosphere, and *mechanical decay*, which will be accelerated when chemical decay has already set in, due to the rubbing and pulling that the leather will receive in use. These disadvantages can be countered to some degree. Chemical decay can be guarded against by the use of 7-percent aqueous solution of potassium lactate, mechanical decay by the use of a good leather dressing. There are many such products on the market, and care must be taken in the selection of one for use. Some leather products were designed for leather in general and do not recognize the particular problems of gold-tooling.

Two separate and distinct things are therefore needed if leather bindings are to be given a chance of survival. First, the initial choice of the leather by the binder needs to be from those that are guaranteed by their manufacturers to be "acid-free." In Great Britain the Printing Industries Research Association evolved a test that would in the period of one week subject a leather to as much attack by acid as it might receive in years. If protective salts were present in the leather, there would be no deterioration. Leather manufacturers therefore stamp a leather on the flesh side with "guaranteed to withstand the P.I.R.A. test." If this is specified in a binding contract, it will, at least, ensure an initial standard. Second, leather bindings need regular overseeing to make certain that no decay is starting. Regular treatment with potassium lactate and leather dressing is necessary in order to maintain the volumes in good condition. It is impossible to generalize as to the frequency with which such treatment should be given since it will be dependent upon the impurity of the surrounding atmosphere. In 1932 the British Museum and the National Library of Wales each set up two control sets of books; one set of protected leathers and one of unprotected leathers. Initial experience during this intervening period demonstrated quite clearly that protection can be given even in an industrial atmosphere and equally, that in an atmosphere that is relatively free from impurities the problem is greatly lessened. By 1970, however, some reservations were beginning to creep in, and the controls as recommended in the 1930s might not provide the long-term preservation that had once been hoped.

The after-preservation of leather bindings consists, otherwise, mainly in their protection from atmospheric extremes—heat, light, damp, and drought. Books need much the same conditions that human beings need for health, one of them being fresh air. If dirt in the air makes glazed cases necessary, let holes be bored in the front or sides of the cases at top and bottom; and let the shelves not touch the back of the case, which in its turn should not touch an outer, or perhaps any, wall. Mere thieves can be countered by a sightly diaper of brass wires in place of glass in the case-doors.[45]

Publishers casings

So far the accent has been on fully bound, leather-covered books, but these are a tiny minority of the modern books being issued. Since the early part of the nineteenth century the average publishers' issue has been a cased book rather than a bound one.

Casing differs from binding in that the boards and their covering material are made up separately and usually in quantity. The sections are sewn in the normal way, sometimes on tapes but sometimes without tapes, and then a strip of mull is glued on to the back of the spines. The overhang of the mull is pasted down on the inside of the boards, where it can usually easily be seen inside a cased book since it is not inserted between split boards as in binding. This overhang is covered by the endpaper, which is pasted down over the inner board of the cover and the back edge of the outer section. This type of issue is frequently known as "edition binding" or "publishers' binding," although in the vast majority of instances the trade issue is cased and not bound. Until this revolutionary development hit the book trade, around 1825, there had previously been four common forms of issue.

(a) *Leather*, which was frequently used in a cheaper variety for a trade edition, but such books were bound in the full sense of the word.

(b) *In boards*, a style of issue that came into use late in the eighteenth century and was common in the first quarter of the nineteenth. These are sometimes referred to as boards-and-label books. The covers were simple board, usually uncovered and undecorated, with a paper spine entitled by means of paper label. This was designed by the publishers as being a temporary form of covering in order to transport the book safely from the publisher and bookseller to the owner, who would, it was assumed, then have it bound according to individual taste.

(c) *Issue in quires*, in those cases when books were issued with the sheets folded ready for binding but unsewn. This is a practice that has continued to the present day in some forms of deluxe book production, designed chiefly for the discriminating buyer who, as previously, wishes to have the book bound according to personal taste.

(d) *Issue in parts,* a form that became widespread in the nineteenth century and is best known as the form of issue of the majority of Victorian novels, was developed in the eighteenth century, chiefly as a method of publishing expensive books and making them readily available to a not-overaffluent buying public.

In one sense it is not incorrect to regard the introduction of the cased book as a direct development from the book issued in boards. It is probable that many of the earlier publishers concerned with this method regarded it as a somewhat temporary form of book covering. The steps by which it became a practical proposition occurred in fairly rapid succession. The first confirmed use of cloth in this respect was in 1823, followed two years later by the development of the case. The third development, which was delayed for a few years, was the knowledge of how to block onto cloth, not so much decoration but simply for titling on the spine. This was not successfully accomplished until about 1832. It is therefore not uncommon to find cased books in cloth bearing paper labels between 1823 and 1832. Some modern books have occasionally adopted this same practice, but this is a deliberate antiquarianism rather than a real necessity.

Although cloth was originally introduced for economy, being at that time a much cheaper material than leather, it has itself in modern times become too expensive for general use. A number of new preparations have come onto the market in the last few decades, many of them making great claims. Some are highly compressed paper, a material that has considerable strength and can be decorated in a variety of ways. Plastics have entered this field also; occasionally it has been a wholly plastic cover and occasionally a plastic-impregnated cloth. This is a covering that has been adopted in the majority of cases because of the virture that the books can be wiped with a damp cloth to remove dirt. It has an obvious advantage with car manuals and cookbooks but is of dubious benefit for the normal run of book production.

Over the century and a half since the introduction of the

cloth-cased book, styles and methods of decoration have varied considerably. Initially many of the books were blocked blind for decorative purposes with only the spine title distinguished by its gilding. As the nineteenth century wore on, advanced techniques for gold- and color-blocking onto boards became common, and a number of noteworthy artists turned their skills to casing decoration before the end of the nineteenth century. For a long time the methods remained the same; only the styles of decoration showed the passage of time and the fashions in the decorative arts. The wide use of dust jackets in the nineteenth, and above all the twentieth century, had a somewhat depressing effect upon the design of publishers' casings until it became possible to put lithographic designs onto cloth, so that once again a cloth-cased book could be as decorative as a binding had been in the old days or as a modern dust jacket had become in our own time. The mere fact, however, that so many reputable artists were concerned with designing publishers' casings means that they cannot be lightly overlooked or dismissed as a rather fanciful addition to the main development of the book trade.[46]

Description of binding styles

It is not an easy matter to produce a good description of a binding style, and not many first-rate examples exist of such descriptions in catalogs. There are several reasons why this should be so. Many bibliographers, including several who have defined bibliographical studies, have underplayed the importance of bookbinding as bibliographical evidence. This has been particularly so with regard to the historical aspects of bookbinding, which are widely regarded as peripheral to the mainstream of work. In many of the fields that have nurtured bibliography in its modern aspects it is true that considerations of binding have not played major roles. But in the concept of bibliography as a whole, rather than as applied to any one small segment, all kinds of evidence must be given equal weight in establishing the underlying theory of the discipline. Graham Pollard put the issue succinctly:

> Now it is important that we should be able to date and localize bindings, not only because it is a necessary part of the description

of books, but also because it may contribute to problems of text and authorship. This can only be done by selecting certain features that change and recording all that we can find out about them. The sort of features which I have here in mind are the use of new materials, such as russia or straight-grained morocco, the use of a lettering-piece, or the presence of a date tooled at the foot of the spine.

In a note to this paragraph Pollard added, "Though not very fully considered by the major bibliographical theoreticians, perhaps because they have been interested chiefly in English plays of the sixteenth and seventeenth centuries—a class of book which has been more extensively disbound than any other."[47] It must be assumed, until particular circumstances prove to the contrary, that attention to the binding is as vital a part of the description as is the collation. Binding description is also complicated by the fact that each binding is so essentially an individual production that it becomes difficult to think of general terms that are of wide application. What can, however, be done is to try and emphasize the elements within a binding that are the most worthy of record. This means, in essence, the features that will allow the individual copy to be most easily recognized and compared with other bindings.

The main elements that need to be covered are as follows:

(a) *Material.* The material in which the binding has been done is the most important. The variety can be enormous since it is difficult to think of any material that has not, at some stage of bookbinding history in some part of the world, been used as a covering material. Those that are in the widest and most general use are, however, comparatively few. The majority of them are the various leathers, and those most commonly met with have already been listed earlier in this chapter. Recognition of leathers is not always quite so easy as at first appears and is a matter in which assurance can only come with experience. In the last resort it is always possible for the leather to be subjected to analysis by a leather technologist, but this is an extreme measure that is not always warranted by the copy in hand.

(b)   *Color.* The problems of color description will also be discussed further in the section regarding the description of
casings. The problems here are many and the grounds for
assurance are few. There is one factor, however, in describing color in bindings that makes the problém a little easier
than with casings. The range of colors used and the range
of dyes that were suitable for leather meant a more restricted range than is found in the nineteenth-century book
cloths. There seems little purpose to be served in an over
elaboration of color in these instances, and it is for this
reason that the examples here given of binding descriptions
are those in which the pursuit of very fine terminology for
binding color was not pursued to inordinate lengths.

(c)   *The localization of the binding.* Under this heading it is assumed that it would be difficult to be more precise about a
binding than to say that it was bound by such and such a
binder, in such and such a place, at such and such a date.
This would be a precision to which it is unfortunately not
always possible to attain. It is for this reason that it is
common to find binding descriptions making suggestions as
to these categories rather than specific statements; for
example, it is common to find "probably by" a binder, or, a
binder who is identified solely by some of the tools that
were used—a definition such as "The Unicorn Binder." In
other cases a binder is known by categories of work that
were done, such as "The Queens' Binder B." These are all
indications of considerable importance when it is not possible to designate the binder in more specific terms. Similarly the place of binding may be as general as a statement
of country and not one specific binding center. The date
may be no closer than an "about 1525." In one sense these
can be regarded as interim statements awaiting further
identification. There are enough examples in the unraveling story of the history of binding to indicate that our
knowledge of binding styles and of binders themselves is
becoming more precise. It is also important to understand
the most usual places within the book where the binder will
frequently be declared by name. The doublure, on either
the front or the back board, and also the endpapers are

probable locations. The name is usually small and has to be looked for with great care. From the eighteenth century onward there was a habit among binders of putting in a small binder's ticket on the inner boards. These should be noted as they are of considerable importance not only in the identification of the bindery but also frequently in finding additional facts, such as addresses or occasionally other professions carried on by the binder at the same establishment.

(d) *The endpapers.* These, which as already stated in an earlier chapter, are not regarded, bibliographically, as a part of the book, are most usefully considered when the binding is being described. It is frequently of great importance that the endpapers should be described in detail since they may embody important evidence influencing the dating of the binding or, at least, in giving some indication whether the endpapers, and therefore most probably the binding, are original or not. A specific date can sometimes be determined with the help of endpapers if by chance an identifiable watermark is in the paper.

Some of the best descriptions in a volume that is easily available to most students are those in the *History of Bookbinding 525–1950 A.D.* catalog that was published by the Walters Art Gallery in Baltimore, Maryland, in 1957. This was the catalog of an exhibition held in the Baltimore Museum of Art from November 1957 to January 1958. The following examples of binding descriptions have been taken from that volume.[48]

193b. PUBLISHER'S DECORATED WRAPPERS
Germany (Augsburg), 1494

On: Obertus de Horto, *Kaiserliche Lehrenrecht...*, Augsburg, Lucas Zeissenmair, 1494. 270 × 192 mm.

The boards consist merely of two thicknesses of the same paper on which the book is printed, the woodcut being stamped upon the outermost one. The designs on the two covers are derived from the customary patterns of contemporary tooled leather bindings of southern Germany. The blocks measure approximately 180 × 115 mm. Upper cover: framed by a border of angular interlacing straps, a field of ogival frames around floral motifs. Lower: within a similar border (but reversed in color), a diaper of foliate lozenges.

In contrast to the binders' woodcut covers of Ferrara (no. 193a), covers such as these appear to have been issued by the publishers, as a means of making the unbound volume more convenient and attractive to the purchaser. As such, they seem to have been an experiment by several competing Augsburg printers, the earliest ones being issued by Schönsperger in 1482. These wrappers were intended simply to "sell the book" and not to serve as a usable binding (as were the later more substantial Ferrara woodcut bindings), and thus their survival is rare and accidental. The splendid preservation of both of these covers is due to the fact that in the sixteenth century or so the librarian of Klosterneuberg which possessed this volume, sheathed it in coarse pasteboard with a sheepskin spine, binding in the two temporary wrappers. Another example of the Zeissenmair woodcuts is in the Berlin Print Room, although on the copy of this book, only one cover is preserved.

Provenance: Klosterneuberg; F. Kreisler. Rosamund Loring.

Bibliography: Ludwig, *Klosterneuberg*, 5362 (this copy); Schreiber, V, 4482; Leo Baer, *Mit Holzschnitten verzierte Buchumschläge des XV und XVI Jahrh.*, Frankfurt/M, 1923, and ill. of back cover. Cf. also H. M. Nixon, *The Broxbourne Library*, London, 1956, pp. 14–17; W. A. Jackson in *Harvard Library Bulletin*, VI (1952), p. 314, pl. I.

THE HARVARD COLLEGE LIBRARY   PLATE XXXVIII

---

261. ARCHITECTURAL BINDING FOR GROLIER
France (Paris), about 1545

On: Iambilicus, *De Mysteriis Aegyptorum Chaldaeorum...*, Venice, Aldus, 1516. 325 × 212 mm. Back: 6 bands; the rich tooling and title added in 17th cent. Headbands: pink and green silk (damaged). Gilt edges. Vellum pastedowns.

Tan morocco, gold tooled on both covers with a design of a portico with acute pediment supported on corinthian columns, standing on a base furnished with mouldings. The door-area is used for lettering; on the upper cover, the author and title of the work, on the lower cover for Grolier's motto. His name appears on the stylobate on the upper cover: IO. GROLIERII ET AMICORVM./ The border of each cover is composed of square stamps gilt, displaying four flattened crescents in relief—the tool being very close to Venetian ones, such as used on no. 208, etc. It occurs on several other Grolier bindings.

This remarkable binding is one of four executed for Grolier showing architectural porticoes, in addition to one for Thomas Mahieu. This small group marks a significant departure from previous and contemporary French gold tooling, such as represented by nos. 249–260, in that, except for the border, no ornamental tools are used. The design is composed entirely of outlines constructed of straight and curved fillets. The idea of a representational pattern also was a novelty, but a short-lived one, it appears. Three of these bindings are clearly copied after the architectural design on the title-page of an edition of Sagredo printed in Paris in 1539. This particular example, however, does not relate at all closely to that model, and has no perspective features. It is probably the earliest of the group. The conception of an architectural design was revived briefly about twenty-five or thirty years later for a few luxurious bindings (cf. nos. 292, 312).

Provenance: Jean Grolier; Marquis de Menars (?); Renouard (?); G. Libri (sale, London, 1849; again in his sale, London, July 25, 1862); Stephen Whitney Phoenix, who bequeathed it to Columbia in 1881.

Bibliography: G. Libri, Monuments Inédits, London, 1862 and 1864, pl. XLIV; Le Roux de Lincy, 1907, no. 242; G. D. Hobson, Maioli, Canevari and Others, 1926, pp. 18–25, 32 no. II, pl. 20; Grolier Club, Catalogue of an Exhibition of

Renaissance Bookbindings... , New York, 1937, no. 32, pl.
V; E. Diehl. Bookbinding, Its Background and Technique,
New York, 1946, vol. I, pl. 32.

THE LIBRARY OF COLUMBIA UNIVERSITY   PLATE LXII

---

504. FOR RICHARD BULL BY EDWARDS OF
HALIFAX   England (Halifax), 1784

On: M. Annaeus Lucanus, Pharsalia, cum notis Hugonis
Grotii et Richard Bentleii ... , The Strawberry Hill Press,
1760. 307 × 232 mm. Flat back. Rose and white silk headbands. Blue silk doublures and endleaves; the vellum turn-
ins gilt with a floral arabesque on a green ground.

White vellum over pasteboard, the upper cover ornamented with a central vignette, painted under the vellum in grisaille, of cupids supporting the arms and crest of
Richard Bull, emblazoned in gold and colors and framed by
a wide Etruscan palmette border painted in black on pink.
Around the edge of the cover is the characteristic Edwards
"Doric entablature" roll sharply impressed in gold on green.
Lower cover: within the same ornamental borders is a central grisaille drawing of two women seated, one showing
gems from a casket on her knees, the other, Cornelia, indicating her son—all rendered in neo-classic fashion. The
back of the book is divided by the "Doric entablature" roll
into panels, the second one of which is filled with a green
leather label lettered LUCANUS. Other panels contain
grisaille vignettes under vellum: coins, military trophies,
the mourning Athena, and a view of Strawberry Hill.
Another view of Strawberry Hill is painted under the gold
on the fore-edge of the leaves. Besides being a fine specimen of an Edwards binding, this example contains a letter
signed J. Edwards (probably James, but possibly John),
which throws much light on the history of the firm. Dated
July 24, 1784, it is written to Horace Walpole's friend,
Richard Bull of Ongar in Essex, who had commissioned the
binding, and had not been too pleased at its cost. It is clear
that Edwards was very anxious to keep a good customer,

since the bill for the book—also preserved—has been altered from five guineas to four; in addition to which he enclosed a Prayer Book (no doubt in an Edwards binding) as a gift to Miss Bull. At this date, the patent for rendering the vellum transparent had not been obtained and the writer is somewhat guarded in discussing the process "As to the Drawing being perfectly fix'd, you need not be under any Apprehension—whenever the Book is soil'd, it may be clean'd with a wet cloth, without any Detriment, if it touches not the gilding—nothing can hurt the Drawing w'ch is not destructive to the vellum." The letter shows that the move to London had not yet taken place, although an important catalogue of antiquarian books had gone to the printers.

Provenance: Executed for Richard Bull; Lord Burgh (sale, Sotheby's, June 29, 1926, no. 66); Tregaskis, Cat. 425 (1927), no. 234; bequeathed to Yale by Dr. Fred T. Murphy of Detroit. Now deposited with Wilmarth S. Lewis at Farmington, Conn.

Bibliography: T. W. Hanson, "Edwards of Halifax Bookbinders" in *Book Handbook*, no. 6 (1948), pp. 329–38 and esp. p. 336; Ellic Howe, *A List of London Bookbinders 1648–1815*, London, The Bibliographical Society, 1950; *cf.* H. M. Nixon, *The Broxbourne Library*, p. 189.

THE YALE UNIVERSITY LIBRARY   PLATE XCV

Description of casings

The covering material for the majority of cased books since their introduction in the early nineteenth century has been cloth. Cloth has appeared in a wide variety of styles, and care must be taken to distinguish among the varieties as they appear. This is because fashion dictated the use of cloth at various periods of the nineteenth and twentieth centuries, and therefore a clear description of the type of material may help develop the chronological pattern.

For the most part the distinguishing feature between one

cloth-casing material and another is the design of the cloth itself. The description of these decorative patterns has always been difficult. This is partly because no two people will view each design and see precisely the same kind of pattern, and second, because even when the pattern is clear, it is not easy to decide in what particular manner it should be described. The first important attempt to provide the kind of description of cloth patterns that was both successful and influential was by Michael Sadleir in his *XIX Century Fiction*. Here Sadleir, with the aid of photographs, distinguished a number of patterns and gave them names that soon began to have a fairly wide acceptance. The system that Sadleir developed has been taken farther since 1951, and a useful survey is G. T. Tanselle's paper on "The Bibliographical Description of Patterns."[49] This article was also accompanied by photographs so that the main element in the pattern can be seen clearly for comparative purposes. No doubt the system that Tanselle advanced here, combined with Sadleir's initial study, will be refined as time goes by, but at the present moment it gives the best possible basis for the description of cloth patterns.

The second problem is that of the description of color. Here a number of problems arise. First and foremost is the problem of deciding exactly what the color was when the cloth was originally made. Most dyes used in book cloths are strongly susceptible to fading, and the spine in particular will normally have deteriorated severely. The boards have obviously been more protected but in many cases not sufficiently so as to enable the original color to be determined. The most useful procedure is to open the board and to view the color as it appears on the doublure, which is as close as anywhere in the book to the original coloring.

The next problem is that bibliographers are not necessarily noted for accurate color vision, and this can create a problem if too specific a notation is desirable. Once again a most useful basic article is by G. T. Tanselle: "System of Color Identification for Bibliographical Description."[50] A reading of these articles of Tanselle, together with other writings on the subject, will lead the reader to appreciate the crux of this problem. Variant casings are numerous, particularly in nineteenth-century bibliography. Because of this care has to be taken to differentiate each casing as accurately as possible in description since this may lead more readily to the identification of variant issues. On the other hand, if this pursuit of perfection is carried too far, difficulties can arise if the aspect being described can be viewed differently by individual bibliographers. There is thus a difference between the accuracy with which a casing pattern can be described as distinct from the accuracy with which a color can be described. The binding pattern is something that is capable of close verification with other models. If the color description is taken too far, too much subjective input can be a distraction and of disadvantage to the user—for example, the system recommended by Gaskell, using a system of nomenclature based on the United States National Bureau of Standards' *ISCC-NBS Method of Designating Colors.* [51] This system is based, in Gaskell's definition, "on ten names of hues and three names of neutral shades, with their adjectival forms; four adjectives indicating lightness; four adjectives indicating saturation; and three adjectives indicating combinations of lightness and saturation." This gives two hundred and sixty-seven possible colors for use in description. Although this may be the philosophy of perfection, it does seem in the light of the problems already stated to be overelaborate. A bibliographer might find it confusing to distinguish clearly among a variety of colors that come under the heading of greenish blue as being distinct from those that come under the general heading of bluish green.

The decoration on the boards, both typographical and decorative, must be described with considerable care since, again, this can be a distinguishing factor among variant issues. The boards will usually have been impressed with a stamp but can vary from being gilt or blind. The lettering on the spine, however, was frequently individually tooled and therefore often exhibits important differences.

REFERENCES

1. KENYON, Frederick G. *Books and Readers in Ancient Greece and Rome.* 2nd ed. 1951. p. 62.

2. The student needs to see as many examples of historical styles of binding as possible. Unfortunately good collections of them are

limited in any one country to a comparatively few great research libraries. It is also equally unfortunate that many examples that are of interest even if not of outstanding importance in lesser libraries are all too often shamefully neglected by their librarians. The consequence is that the students will frequently have to make their first acquaintance with some styles through photographs. In such cases it is important to remember that (a) such photographs are usually reduced in size from the original and (b) the color and texture of the leather are lost. These factors vitally affect the appreciation of the bindings. The following books give introductory surveys to the whole field and also include good photographs of important styles:

BODLEIAN LIBRARY. *Fine Bindings, 1500–1700, from Oxford Libraries*. 1968.
BODLEIAN LIBRARY. *Gold-tooled Bookbindings*. (Bodleian Picture Books, No. 2.) 1951.
BOOK COLLECTOR. Series on "English Bookbindings" by H. M. Nixon. (1952–   ). One hundred of these descriptions were collected and published as *Five Centuries of English Bookbinding*. 1978. Other series in the "Book Collector" are "English and Foreign Bookbindings," mainly by Mirjam M. Foot (1977–   ); "Foreign Bookbindings," by various contributors (1969–1976); and "Craft Binders at Work," by Dorothy M. Harrop (1972–   ).
BRITISH MUSEUM. *Royal English Bookbindings in the British Museum*. 1957.
GOLDSCHMIDT, E. P. *Gothic and Renaissance Bookbindings*. 2nd ed. 2v. 1966.
HOBSON, G. D. *Bindings in Cambridge Libraries*. 1929.
HOBSON, G. D. *English Bindings 1490–1940 in the Library of J. R. Abbey*. 1940.
HOBSON, G. D. *Thirty Bindings*. 1926.
LEHMANN-HAUPT, H.; FRENCH, Hannah D.; and ROGERS, Joseph W. *Bookbinding in America*. 1967.
MAGGS BROS. LTD. *Bookbinding in Great Britain*. (Catalogue 966.) 1975.
MINER, Dorothy, ed. *The History of Bookbinding 525 to 1950 A.D.* 1958.
NIXON, Howard M. *Broxbourne Library: Styles and Designs of Bookbindings from C12 to C20*. 1956.
NIXON, Howard M. *Twelve Books in Fine Bindings from the Library of J. W. Hely-Hutchinson*. 1953.

POLLARD, Graham. "Changes in the Style of Book Binding, 1550–1830." *The Library*. 5th Series. XI: 1956. pp. 71–94.
THOINAN, Ernest. *Les Reliures français, 1500–1800*. 1893.
VICTORIA AND ALBERT MUSEUM. *Bookbindings*. Introduction by John P. Harthan. 1950.

3. Good descriptions of a number of these treasure bindings can be found in Miner, *History of Bookbinding*.

4. The Stonyhurst Gospels will be found illustrated and discussed in:

BROWN, T. J. *The Stonyhurst Gospel of Saint John*. 1969.

and with other early bindings, in.

HOBSON, G. D. *English Binding Before 1500*. 1929.

5. The number of early bindings that can easily be seen are naturally very few. Some of the background to them, however, can be derived from such works as:

GRAY, G. J. *The Earlier Cambridge Stationers and Bookbinders*. 1904.
HOBSON, G. D. "Further Notes on Romanesque Bindings." *The Library*. 4th Series. XV: 1934–35. pp. 161–211.
HOBSON, G. D. "Some Early Bindings and Binders' Tools." *The Library*. 4th Series. XIX: 1938–39. pp. 202–249.
KER, Neil R. *Early Pastedowns in Oxford Bindings*. 1954.
POLLARD, Graham. "The Construction of English Twelfth-century Bindings." *The Library*. 5th Series. XVII: 1962. pp. 1–22.

6. Examples of these, which are not very common in libraries and museums, can be found in Miner, *History of Bookbinding* (Nos. 117, 118, 128–131) together with an illustration (Plate XXVIII).

7. For illustrations and discussion of these, especially the designs of the rolls, see:

GIBSON, Strickland. *Early Oxford Bindings*. 1903.

8. HOBSON, G. D. *Blind-stamped Panels in the English Book-trade. c1485–1555*. 1944.

OLDHAM, J. B. *Blind Panels of English Binders.* 1958.
OLDHAM, J. B. *English Blind-stamped Bindings.* 1952.

9. For the latest, easily available, comment on Caxton's binder see:

NIXON, Howard M. "William Caxton and Bookbinding." *Journal of the Printing Historical Society.* XI: 1975–76. pp. 92–113.

10. HOBSON, G. D. *Maioli, Canevari and Others.* 1926.

11. HOBSON, Anthony. *Apollo and Pegasus.* 1975.

Thirty-one of the known one hundred and twenty-eight Canevari bindings are in the Biblioteca Nazionale di Napoli. See:

GROLIER CLUB. *Iter Italicum.* 1963.

12. AUSTIN, Gabriel. *The Library of Jean Grolier.* 1971.
BRITISH MUSEUM. *Bookbindings from the Library of Jean Grolier.* 1965.
LEROUX DE LINCY, Antoine J. V. *Researches Concerning Jean Grolier.* Translated and revised by Carolyn Shipman. 1907.
NIXON, Howard M. "Grolier's Binders." *The Book Collector.* IX: 1960. pp. 45–51, 165–170. XI: 1962 pp. 79, 213–214.
NIXON, Howard M. "Grolier's 'Chrysostom.'" *The Book Collector.* XI: 1962. pp. 64–70.

Approximately five hundred and fifty Grolier bindings are known to be extant, of which the largest collections are in the Bibliothèque Nationale (sixty-one); the British Library (thirty); and the Pierpont Morgan Library (nine).

13. Descriptions and photographs of these Spanish bindings can most conveniently be seen in:

THOMAS, Henry. *Early Spanish Bookbindings XI–XV Centuries.* 1939.

14. HOBSON, G. D. "Et amicorum." *The Library.* 5th Series. IV: 1949–50. pp. 87–99.

15. DUFF, E. Gordon. "The Bindings of Thomas Wotton." *The Library.* 3rd Series. I: 1910. pp. 337–347.

MOSS, W. E. *The English Grolier. A Catalogue of Books from the Library of Thomas Wotton.* 1941.

16. GRAY, G. J. "Queen Elizabeth and Bookbinding." *The Library.* 3rd Series. VII: 1916. pp. 66–69.
      NIXON, Howard M. Elizabethan Gold-tooled Bindings," in *Essays in Honour of Victor Scholderer.* Edited by Dennis Rhodes. 1970. pp. 219–270.
      NIXON, Howard M. *Sixteenth-century Gold-tooled Bookbindings in the Pierpont Morgan Library.* 1971.

17. HOBSON, G. D. *Les Reliures à la fanfare: le problème de l'S fermé.* 2nd ed. 1967.

18. HOBSON, G. D. "The great Mearne Myth." *Papers of the Edinburgh Bibliographical Society.* XI: 1918.

19. NIXON, H. M. *Broxbourne Library, Styles and Designs of Book bindings.* 1956. pp. 150–151. Addendum, p. 240.

20. NIXON, Howard M. *English Restoration Bookbindings.* 1974.

21. OLDHAM, J. B. *Shrewsbury School Library Bindings.* 1943. pp. 112–116.

See also:

NIXON, Howard M. "Harleian Bindings," in *Studies in the Book Trade in Honour of Graham Pollard.* 1975. pp. 153–194.
WRIGHT, C. E., and RUTH, C. *The Diary of Humfry Wanley, 1715–1726.* 2v. 1966.

22. SOMMERLAD, M. J. *Scottish "Wheel" and "Herringbone" Bindings in the Bodleian Library.* 1967.

23. FRENCH, Hannah D. "The Amazing Career of Andrew Barclay, Scottish Bookbinder of Boston." *Studies in Bibliography.* XIV: 1961. pp. 145–162.

24. CRAIG, Maurice. *Irish Bookbindings, 1600–1800.* 1954.

25. Although Payne's life and career, and especially the elaborately documented bills that accompanied his bindings, have made him

a well-known and colorful figure, his life and work is not individually well documented. One of the more interesting writings about him to appear in recent years is the short account of his early career:

BIRLEY, Robert. "Roger and Thomas Payne: With Some Account of Their Earlier Bindings." *The Library*. 5th Series. XV: 1960. pp. 33–41.

26. The family consisted of William, the father, in partnership with his sons, James, John, and Thomas.

HANSON, T. W. "Edwards of Halifax. A Family of Booksellers, Collectors and Bookbinders." *Transactions of the Halifax Antiquarian Society*. V: 1912. pp. 141–200.
HANSON, T. W. "Edwards of Halifax, Bookbinders." *Book Handbook*. VI: 1948. pp. 329–338.

27. WEBER, Carl J. *Fore-edge Painting, A Historical Survey of a Curious Art in Book Decoration*. 1967.

28. CARTER, John. *Binding Variants in English Publishing, 1820–1900*. 1932.
CARTER, John. *Publisher's Cloth: An Outline History of Publisher's Binding in England, 1820–1900*. 1935.
HOWE, Ellic, and CHILD, John. *The Society of London Bookbinders, 1780–1951*. 1952.
LEIGHTON, Douglas. "Canvas and Bookcloth, An Essay on Beginnings." *The Library*. 5th Series. III: 1948–49. pp. 39–49.
McLEAN, Ruari. *Victorian Publishers' Bookbindings in Cloth and Leather*. 1974.
SADLEIR, Michael. *The Evolution of Publishers' Binding Styles, 1770–1900*. 1930.

29. DUFF, E. Gordon. *Early Printed Books*. 1893. pp. 9–10.

30. An account of first-class repair work and rebinding of a book of importance may be found, with illustrations, in:

POWELL, Roger. "The Lichfield St. Chad's Gospels: Repair and Rebinding, 1961–1962." *The Library*. 5th Series. XX: 1965. pp. 259–276.

A brief account of another famous work, *The Codex Sinaiticus,* rebound by Douglas Cockerell, in:

British Museum Quarterly. X: 1935–36. pp. 180–182.

31. MIDDLETON, Bernard C. *A History of English Craft Bookbinding Technique.* 1963. p. 20.

32. Middleton, pp. 20–24.

33. Middleton, p. 17, n. 2.

34. For examples of this see Ker, *Early Pastedowns.*

35. Pollard, "Changes," p. 83.

36. Pollard, "Changes," p. 84.

37. Pollard, "Changes," p. 85.

38. Gibson, *Early Oxford Bindings,* p. 42.

39. Pollard, "Changes," p. 90.

40. Nixon, *Broxbourne Library,* p. 118.

41. A short account of the range of skins can be found in:

    THOMPSON, Lawrence S. "Bibliopegia Fantastica," in *Bibliologia Comica.* 1968. Reprinted from the *Bulletin of the New York Public Library.* September 1944.

42. French joints are also referred to as "sunk joints." The opposite of this method, when the board is placed close up to the shoulder, is a "tight joint."

43. The correct name for the process is "Whittawing."

44. Pollard, "Construction," p. 13.

45. The best short summary of the problems, together with brief suggestions as to the steps to be taken for preservation, is:

PLENDERLEITH, H. J. The Preservation of Leather Book-bindings. 1947.

The student will soon realize that bindings constitute only one of the many kinds of material with whose preservation the librarian or bibliographer may become concerned. It is important at this stage also to take the opportunity to see:

PLENDERLEITH, H. J., and WERNER, A. E. A. The Conservation of Antiquities and Works of Art. 2nd ed. 1971.

In general, also see:

BELAYA, I. K. "Methods of Strengthening the Damaged Leather of Old Bindings." Restaurator. I: 1969. pp. 93–104.
GARDNER, Anthony. "The Ethics of Books Repair." The Library. 5th Series. IX: 1954. pp. 194–198.
HAINES, Betty M. "Deterioration in Leather Bookbindings: Our Present State of Knowledge." British Library Journal. III: 1977. pp. 59–70.
HORTON, Carolyn. Cleaning and Preserving Bindings and Related Materials. 1969.
MIDDLETON, Bernard C. The Restoration of Leather Bindings. 1972.

46. CARTER, John. Publishers' Cloth, 1820–1900. 1935.
Sadleir, Evolution.
SADLEIR, Michael. XIX Century Fiction: A Bibliographical Record. 2v. 1951.

47. Pollard, "Changes," p. 71 and n.

48. Miner, History.

Reference should also be made to the descriptions in:

FOOT, Mirjam M. A Collection of Bookbindings: The Henry Davis Gift. Vol. 1. 1978.
NEEDHAM, Paul. Twelve Centuries of Bookbindings. 400–1600. 1979.
Nixon, Sixteenth-century.

and to the discussion in:

POLLARD, Graham. "Describing Medieval Bookbindings," in *Medieval Learning and Literature.* Edited by J. G. G. Alexander and M. T. Gibson. 1976. pp. 50–65.

49. *Studies in Bibliography.* XXIII: 1970. pp. 71–102.

50. *Studies in Bibliography.* XX: 1967. pp. 203–234.

51. GASKELL, Philip. *A New Introduction to Bibliography.* 1972. pp. 237–239.

9.

THE COLLATION OF BOOKS

An understanding of the processes of book building, outlined in the preceding chapters, will enable books to be examined critically from a bibliographical perspective. From one viewpoint, even if it is something of an oversimplification, it can be said that bibliographical research is largely concerned with errors and imperfections in the various stages of production. If it could be assumed, however unlikely a proposition it may be, that a printing office received perfect copy of the author's work; that compositor, proofreader, and printer all combined to produce faultlessly printed sheets; that those sheets were all accurately folded, collated, and bound—then the resultant work would be singularly free from bibliographical problems. The whole process of the production of the book is therefore viewed in the light of identifying the steps that are capable of error, of understanding the nature of such errors as evidenced by the copy under examination, and of attempting to interpret such evidence as a step toward illuminating the development of the text. The description of the work, to which the following chapter is devoted, is better not regarded as a single operation that is carried out when the analysis of the book is completed but rather as a process concurrent with the examination. Each fact, or presumed fact, is noted at the moment of its detection (in Captain Cuttle's words, "When found, make a note of"), and these are later formalized into a description.

A book has to be examined for certain specific purposes. At the outset it may not always be easy to estimate how detailed an examination the book will demand; so much will depend upon the kind of problems that are met and the ultimate purpose for which the research is being conducted. Initially, however, there are three fundamental questions to be answered:

(a) What work, or works, does the volume contain?

(b) Of what recension and of what edition is it? That is, by whom was it edited, and where, when, and by whom was it printed?

(c) Is this a perfect copy?

The respective emphases on these three questions will vary from circumstance to circumstance, as will the amount of effort that will be necessary in order to answer them. Some broad areas of investigation will, however, emerge as being of general importance. The bibliographer must be prepared to seek for any kind of evidence that will shed light upon the search, both from within the book and without.

Identifying the work

The first matter to be addressed when faced with a book is the discovery as to exactly what it is that is in hand.

Care must be taken to distinguish between two or more works that are published in one issue or (as pamphlets often are) assembled in one binding for economy's sake. This latter practice, now generally abandoned in libraries in favor of separate preservation in file boxes or pamphlet covers, was once universal. "Tract-volumes" containing anything from half a dozen to fifty pieces abound on the shelves of old libraries. When two works printed in the same type, without distinctive headlines, pagination, signatures, or title pages, are bound together, as happened in the first days of printing, the resulting volume needs as careful analysis as one in manuscript. Generally, however, at least one of these guides is present (and the safest is the signatures) since if the second work were intended to be bound with the first, the printer would normally have given it a distinctive alphabet of signatures, either doubling the letters or using upper case (if the first book is signed in lower case), or a combination of upper case and lower case. If the division between two works occurs in the middle of a quire, it stands to reason that the two are of one edition and bibliographically inseparable. This fact has not always prevented owners from having such books cut in half and bound as two.

If there is sufficient evidence to suggest that the parts were intended to, or ever did, have a separate and individual existence, then they must be treated accordingly. If the parts have no more connection with each other than the accident of their being bound together by an owner, then this must be made clear.

Once there is certainty that the volume in hand was designed as a single work or that it consists of a random collection of two or more individual pieces, then the individual identities must be discovered. A combination of two facts is normally sufficient to establish the basic detail: the title of the work and the author's name.

The title of the work is usually found on the half-title page, the title page, the running title, or the colophon. The position will vary according to the place and date of the printing. These titles will frequently differ from each other, sometimes very considerably, and to them must be added another that so often provides an important variation: the binder's or spine title. Even though these variations exist, there should be little cause for confusion because the title-page title is the "official" one by which the book will always be known.

If the title proves to be completely elusive, the work can be described and known by the *incipit* and *explicit*. *Incipit* is the Latin for "here begins" and *explicit* for "here ends." The text should be quoted in sufficient detail to allow for identification.

The author's name will normally be found on the title page because there was usually more pride in publication than desire to hide the identity. In books without a title page the name together with the title can be expected in the colophon. There are nevertheless many exceptions to this common practice.

The author's name may be found only as a signature to the dedication, or sometimes half-concealed in an anagram, as in the famous example of the *Hypnerotomachia Poliphili* (Aldus, Venice, 1499), where Francesco Colonna's name, with that of his lady, Polia, appeared only in this way. Completely anonymous or pseudonymous books may be attributed to their true authors by the aid of several bibliographical dictionaries devoted to them, or sometimes, failing these and similar guides, by much original research. The great amount of anonymously published materials, for example, in nineteenth-century periodicals is only now beginning to yield identities as a result of much devoted bibliographical and literary detection. In its turn the twentieth century can provide interesting examples of pseudonymously published work. In some cases it was due to the reluctance of a writer, who had a reputation to establish or maintain, to acknowledge certain writings in which the prime, or even sole, interest had been monetary reward. Other instances come to mind of prolific authors who reserve pseudonyms for each of their different categories of writing. Therefore, although it is true that the author's correct name appears on the title page in the majority of cases, the exceptions are often of great interest. The reasons for the subterfuge are usually to be found in the history of the particular period.

An author's name, like that of a printer or a place-name, may be translated. Among authors the famous case of the Dutch humanist Desiderius Erasmus (1466–1536) stands alone. His real name was Gerard de Praet, and for the name Gerard (meaning "well beloved") he substituted the Latin and Greek equivalents, Desiderius Erasmus. The name of the German reforming theologian Philip Melanchthon (1497–1560) was arrived at by translating his real name, Schwarzard (meaning "black earth"), into Greek.[1]

When the title of the work and the name of the author have been established, a beginning has been made. In a few cases this may be sufficient—for example, in the case of one only printing of a work. Obviously there will be many more instances where this will not be of much help. The establishment of the identity of the work as Shakespeare's *Hamlet,* Walton's *Compleat Angler,* or Thackeray's *Vanity Fair* will not succeed in establishing very much identity in cases where total printings have run into hundreds. From this point onward the purpose of the whole investigation is to determine as closely as possible the individual identity of the book.

Identifying the edition

Following identification of author and title a number of other factors will add significantly to the basic knowledge of the book. Of these by far the most important will be identification of printer and place and date of publication. Although it may not help more than marginally to discover that the book is Walton's *Compleat Angler,* confusion is lessened considerably if it can be discovered that it is a copy of the edition printed by X at Y in the year Z.

Careful examination of the title page, colophon, and pre-liminaries (dedication, preface, ecclesiastical or secular licence to print) will normally reveal facts regarding the editing, translating, and printing of the work. Two circumstances can, however, arise: (a) that no details regarding these aspects of the book are included, or (b) that the true facts have in some way or another been deliberately disguised. In either event it means that the discovery of these facts must be attempted either within or without the book.

Printers' names were not infrequently translated, and the beginner must be prepared to recognize in Martinus Caesaris, or even in Martin Emperour, the Antwerp printer Martin de Keyser; and in Henricus Stephanus and also in Harry Stephens (an extreme example of the regular old practice of translating proper names) the scholar-printer Henri Estienne. Such changes were not usually designed to be misleading but were in the somewhat scholarly tradition of having details on the title page conform to the language of the book itself. Other variations from the true form of a printer's name could, however, be attempts at concealment. At times of political and religious turmoil, when seditious, heretical, or subversive writing tended to be rife, there were frequent occasions on which it was no more than reasonable caution to lay a false trail. Clandestine presses have flourished on many occasions in modern history, and examples are not difficult to locate. Some deliberate mystifications are easily recognized as such, as when a vehement Reformation tract is stated to be printed "before the Castell of Saint Angelo, at the sign of Saint Peter," or "not a mile from a bouncing priest," but experience is necessary to suspect the little books stating themselves as printed at the Sphere in Cologne to be really from Paris or the Low Countries.[2] Place-names, even when genuine, can appear strange to a modern eye. They were frequently printed in the Latin form and were occasionally somewhat fanciful in addition. A brief list of some of the place-names regularly met in imprints is given at the end of this chapter, and further listings can be located without undue difficulty.[3]

When the printer's name does not appear anywhere within the book or when there are reasons to suspect that the information given is incorrect, an analysis can sometimes be made based on the type designs, use of woodcuts or initial letters, markedly individual practices, and such like. Many printers used a number of fonts of type during their career and a variety of kinds of ornamentation. There is a growing body of published resources that can help by giving reproduction of type styles, initial letters, borders, woodcuts, etc. These can be of great use for purposes of comparison and identification. Yet in the final resort, there is a category of evidence that is of prime importance but never very easy to locate: a large collection of the books themselves. There are many occasions in bibliographical research when the need arises for, say, the works of a printer arranged in chronological order, the productions of a city or town in a given period of years, the printings of a given writer to be examined in sequence. Resources of this depth can be found in comparatively few libraries throughout the world, and it is in them that much bibliographical research must be concentrated. For the beginning student it is often enough to be able to say, at a particular point of difficulty, "This is what needs to be done now," even if local resources make it immediately impossible. But even the most detailed and lengthy research may not result in identifying a printer except in relation to other known works, for example, as "the printer of the 'Turkenkalender.'" This follows a well-established tradition in art history and is bibliographically common in connection with illustration and binding.

Apart from specific items of use, technical problems may also assist in locating the provenance of a work. All those working within the book trade exhibited signs of practices that were frequently peculiar to a small area and sometimes to a single workshop. This is akin to the way in which a binder may be recognized not only by the tools used but also by idiosyncracies of style, or an illustrator by an individual technique, or a medieval scribe by ineradicable personal habits. Many indications of this nature can be discovered in printings of a widely varied nature over a considerable span of years. For example, many English books printed in the Low Countries in the late seventeenth and early eighteenth centuries on account of the paper duty in England, which made it cheaper to import the book ready printed, can often be recognized by the tendency of the compositors, setting up a language they did not know, to set *ij* in place of *y*, a letter that did not occur in their language. It is regional, period, and personal habits of this nature that make it essential for any departure from what might be regarded as usual practice to be detected and recorded.

Dating the edition

Another precise form of identification is by date. Although the majority of printed books bear dates somewhere within themselves, these will frequently need to be checked; an attempt must also be made to ascribe dates to undated material. There are a number of ways of attempting to establish a date, and the beginner should look for examples of each of these. The general rules of evidence are not different from those that govern any other area of study. No conclusion can be based upon a single piece of evidence. Each piece that points in the same general direction strengthens the position, but reasonable certainty only comes when no contrary piece of evidence is unearthed. Then it is possible to evolve a theory that might be sustained and strengthened throughout the entire investigation. Of first concern will be those inquiries that can result in a reasonably specific date for the work in question. There can be no question of priority of these items according to any order of importance since they will vary from one investigation to another.

(a)   The first and most obvious action is to check the work in major bibliographies and the published catalogs of the great libraries. Although this may be regarded as arriving at a date by secondhand means, it would be absurd to neglect this step. A student is liable to learn of horrible examples of inaccuracies, from Wise's deliberate insertion of forgeries into the *Ashley Catalogue* to the unintentional, but celebrated, ghost entries in the *STC*. Because of these, and other such instances, caution is always necessary. Bibliographical investigation needs not only expertise but also access to great collections. The number of libraries, consequently, in which it can be undertaken are few and the results of such work correspondingly important. If, say, the British Museum, the Bodleian, Cambridge University Library, Harvard University, and the Folger Library had all agreed upon a date for an undated work, it would be presumptuous to ignore it. But all bibliographies and all catalogs are made by human beings and are liable to error.

(b) The dates of a printer's activity, where the name is known, will give the outside limits of date. Occasionally a deduction will have to be made from the dates of birth and death. In such cases it can be assumed that the printer would not have printed during the first fifteen or twenty years of life, and allowance must be made for books that might appear still bearing the printer's name for about two years after the date of death.

The deduction, when it is necessary to make one, is the easiest part of the procedure. Experience will show that it is far from easy to determine the exact dates of birth and death of many printers. The great ones are fairly well documented, but many books are printed by small, obscure printers. A few specialized dictionaries of the book trade have been compiled, such as the series published by the Bibliographical Society for Great Britain up to 1775.[4] General dictionaries of biographical information are of only limited use because of the relative unimportance of the printers. There is still a great deal of work to be done related to the establishment of dates of printers. Analyses of major bibliographical tools, such as the STC and Wing;[5] dictionaries of imprints;[6] as well as further developments along traditional lines, such as Todd's, are steps along the road.[7] There is a clear need, however, for investigations in newspapers, trade directories, and such like in order to clarify the situation. Much of this can only be done at a very local level, but it could add significantly to our knowledge.[8]

(c) The dates between which the printer is known to have printed, or the publisher to have published, at a particular address represents an extension of the previous form of dating. It follows that it needs an even more detailed knowledge of the printer's career. It also assumes that a printer has worked at more than one address and that the addresses are used in the printer's imprints. For instance, Wynkyn de Worde, conveniently for bibliographers, quitted Caxton's old shop at Westminster for the Sign of the Sun in Fleet Street, London, at the end of the year 1500. There are many examples of publications that bear the imprints of several publishers or booksellers who worked in conjunction with each other. Since such imprints frequently include addresses, a publication date can be narrowed to a short span of years during which they were all in existence at their specific locations.

(d)   The early printers were, at first, their own type cutters and type founders. Only as the distinct trade of the type foundry began to be established during the sixteenth century did this situation change. Perhaps it was this direct control over material that encouraged experimentation. Perhaps the early punches did not have the durability of those now used and so demanded frequent replacement. Whatever the reasons may have been, printers were constantly changing and recutting their fonts. Thus Caxton used eight text types in seventeen years. Even more importantly in his instance, he never returned to use an earlier type once he had begun on the later ones. By typographical analysis an estimate can frequently be made as to the date of a book. It was on just such typographical evidence that many of the early bibliographers, such as Bradshaw, Proctor, and Duff, worked. It was, and is, a logical step forward from palaeographic evidence where handwritings can be placed with astonishing accuracy as to provenance and date. As type designing and casting became more universal and less individual, such evidence lost some of its importance. By type analysis and comparison, undated books can, for some periods, be placed correctly into a sequence of dated works. While this may not produce a specific date, it does at least suggest the chronology. It is useful for the student to study the various kinds of typographical evidence in investigations, such as the Constance Missal or the T. J. Wise forgeries.

(f) Printers also often used, either in addition to their name or as a substitute for it, a woodcut device. These were changed from time to time, either because the block wore out or because its owner tired of it. The appearance of devices in dated books gives us a good foundation for dating those that are not.

It will be obvious that with so many hundreds of devices having been used only a small percentage of them have so far been recorded in the major bibliographical works. The best tools will always be the original books themselves in one of the major research libraries equipped for this purpose. In default of this several useful books have already been compiled, and the information available is being augmented steadily.[9]

The use of the evidence can be in several stages. It can serve solely to identify printers who used one device only. In that event much of the problem of dating remains. If a printer used more than one device, as Wynkyn de Worde used successively no fewer than seventeen, then they may help to establish sequence within printings and probably some relationship to dated works. Over and above this, devices may share the following evidence with other materials.

(g) Devices, borders, initial letters, ornaments, and all other forms of woodcut were liable to split from wear in the press or from being kept too dry. They might be attacked by worm and show the holes, though only the less careful or impecunious printer would use woodblocks in a badly worm-eaten state. Metal plates, and especially copper, owing to the softness of the metal, wear down in the course of printing and give inferior impressions. Progressive deterioration in all these ways may be used to arrange undated books, in which wood or metal blocks were used, in a chronological sequence. If, in copy B, the cracks are seen to have widened, the wormholes to have multiplied, or the engraving to have less definition than in copy A, then copy B is safely put down as the later of the two.

(h) Illustrations, and particularly plates, are frequently useful

in another way. There is a long-established habit or tradition for engravers, for example, to sign their plates. It may
be in the form of "by X after Y," in which the names
represent the engraver and the original artist respectively.
Or it may be in the form "pinxit: Y, sculpsit: X," with the
same relationship of letters to occupations. In whatever
form this information appears it provides other names that
are equally capable of being checked for dates. Plates will
frequently include names and addresses of the publishers of
the plates, which can be used as evidence in the same
manner as addresses in the book's imprint.

It was a widespread practice for the date of "publication"
to be given on the print itself. In certain countries the
procedures that led to the dating and including of imprint
details may be associated with a legal provision. In England, for example, the Engraving Copyright Act of 1734
conferred copyright on engravings for a period of fourteen
years. A date of publication consequently became essential. The reason why this first Act gave protection only to
plates where the engraver was also the designer is often
attributed to the fact that Hogarth, through whose influence the Act was introduced, invariably worked in both
capacities. Later Acts extended these provisions to other
forms of illustrative techniques. Under normal circumstances the date on the print must naturally be earlier than
the date of publication of the book itself, although the
period by which it precedes book publication may vary. If,
as may occasionally happen, the print dates are later than
the date on the title page, it is then reasonable to assume
that there was some unusual feature about the issue.

The illustration processes themselves may throw some
light on the problems, although they provide evidence that
can affect only a minority of instances. The dates of their
introduction into printing methods, developments in their
technique, and the periods of their chief use can provide,
at least, some indication of period or date. Even less certain, but not negligible, is dating by artistic style and influence. Book illustration is part of the whole history of art
and must, within limits, be subject to the same kind of
analytical historical approach.

Finally, the content of the illustration may assist. The events portrayed or the architecture, scenery, and other features can provide valuable clues. It must also be remembered that much of James Laver's expertise in costume came about through his work in dating prints at the Victoria and Albert Museum. Here he found an element in plate pictures that was most subject to continuous and rapid change and therefore most helpful in specifying a date with the minutest accuracy.

(i)   Dated manuscript notes of ownership may provide a date after which the book cannot have been printed. The most famous example is the copy in the Bibliothéque Nationale at Paris of the "Gutenburg" or "Mazarin" or "42-line" Bible. In this, Henricus Cremer, Vicar of St. Stephen's, Mainz, stated that he finished rubricating and binding this copy on 24 August 1456. Copies must therefore have been on sale before this date, and we are thus provided with a capital landmark in the history of printing. There is today no cause to worry unduly regarding the possibility of false or forged annotations, signatures, or dates in these cases. Apart from the fact that, at all periods, forgeries are rare, the possibilities of their detection by modern methods remove most of the anxieties.

In certain instances negative evidence of this kind is valuable. One of the tests applied by Carter and Pollard in the Wise forgeries was that in no case was there a contemporary date of acquisition; in one case only was there an author's presentation inscription, and that was dated thirty-two years after the alleged date of publication. This category is probably one of the best examples of the value of negative evidence.

(j)   There are many instances when it is not truly correct to say that a work is undated because in fact the date is concealed in a chronogram. They need to be dealt with here, however, because they are occasionally difficult to discover in the book and need a great deal of unraveling.

This tiresome device of the overingenious consists in embedding the roman figures of the date in a motto, so worded that these letters occur exactly often enough to add up to the required total, and distinguishing them by print-ing them in uppercase or a different font. They are in the process often tortured into almost unintelligible arrange-ments. The following is an easy example:

GUsta VUs aDoLphUs GLorIose pUgnans MorItUr

U	=	5
V	=	5
U	=	5
D	=	500
L	=	50
U	=	5
L	=	50
I	=	1
U	=	5
M	=	1000
I	=	1
U	=	5

1632, the year of Gustavus
Adolphus's death.

(k)   Another practice, common at certain times and among certain types of book, draws attention to the fact that there have been a variety of calendars in use throughout history, the use of which may create problems in immediate recog-nition. Dating in some books may naturally be in accor-dance with the Jewish calendar, the Moslem calendar, the Revolutionary calendar of late–eighteenth- and early–ninetenth-century France. Specific dates may be calculated according to the Roman calendar and appear as Ides and Kalends. A widespread European practice, and very com-mon in the manuscript and early printed-book era, was calculation by Saints' Days and Festivals. This necessitates recognition of such phrases as "the Vigil of the Feast of the Assumption" or "Saint Blasius' Day."

(1)   In every problem regarding the dating of books it must not

be forgotten that there have been two important adjustments to the calendar during the age of the printed book.

The present widespread method of beginning the calendar with the first of January ("new style," or "n.s.") was, in England throughout the seventeenth century, slowly superseding the "old style" (or "o.s.") calendar, which began on 25 March. The change was made gradually and without a general ordinance; for a time it was not uncommon for dates from 1 January to 24 March inclusive to be given in the double-form, e.g., $16\frac{69}{70}$. But this convenient form is exceedingly rare in imprints, and any date on a book may, unless there is evidence that it falls within the period 25 March to 31 December, stand for either of two years. A book printed at any time between 25 March 1670 and 31 December 1670 would be dated 1670 according to either style calendar; but if printed between 1 January and 24 March, it would be 1669 if the old-style calendar were in use and 1670 according to the new style. The possible range of a single year's date is therefore not twelve months but fifteen months all but seven days.

Now it is possible that the printer of a first edition appearing in the debatable three first months of the new-style used new style, and that the printer of the second edition still before 25 March used old-style, thus making it the close of the previous year, with the result that the first edition bears a date later by one year than that of the second. This fantastic result is found in the early editions of Milton's *Pro Populo Anglicano Defensio;* first edition (Londini, Typis Du-Gardianis), 1651, a handsomely printed quarto, and 3rd edition, (Londini, Typis Du-Gardianis) (but Utrecht), 1650, 12°; the true order was first pointed out by F. Madan.[10]

King Charles I was beheaded on 30 January 1649 (n.s.) or 1648 (o.s.). Within a few days there was rushed out the first edition of his prayers and meditations, entitled *Eikon Basilike.* No fewer than sixty editions and translations of this popular book appeared before the end of 1649 (o.s.) (i.e., 24 March 1650 n.s.); of these twenty-five are dated 1648, a date that has surprised later owners who had been brought up to believe that King Charles was beheaded in 1649 and who had no knowledge of the styles of dating with which to modify that belief.[11] These were of course (without deducting possible later unaltered reprints of 1648 imprints) produced in the two months before 25 March 16$\frac{48}{49}$, and so may have been some of those dated (if dated by new style) 1649. They are, at the lowest estimate of their number, remarkable evidence of the strength of the Royalist feeling roused in the country by the execution of the King. There were in fact so many copies on the market that only one edition (1662) was called for in the years following the Restoration, when everyone was eager to be thought Royalist, and how better than by buying "the King's Book"?

The other important change was the adjustment necessary on the introduction of the Gregorian calendar. The actual length of the solar year is a few hours more than three hundred and sixty-five days, and in 1582 Pope Gregory XIII canceled ten days from the old Julian calendar in order to bring the calendar into line with the seasons again. This reform was adopted by Roman Catholic countries, with the result that 4 October 1582 was followed immediately by 15 October 1582. In England the change was not made until 1752, by which time it was necessary to cancel eleven days, and 2 September 1752 was followed immediately by 14 September 1752.

Sequence of printings

Having now looked briefly at methods that hold out the possibility that a fairly firm date might be established, it is necessary to consider another kind of evidence. There will be occasions on which the best that a bibliographer is able to do is to place a book in the correct place in the sequence of printings, even when a firm date cannot be established. It is a question that frequently becomes a matter of special importance if two editions are rivals for the position of *editio princeps*, or first edition.

There is much general misunderstanding of the true value of

first editions. The value set on them in the market, often quite unintelligently, has led to an equally unintelligent contempt. In spite of certain notorious but quite occasional malpractices, most collecting is genuine and reputable with an honest regard for the author's text at its heart. At the present day proofs of every edition that appears in an author's lifetime are submitted to the author for corrections. The authentic definitive text of a book that future editors will have to reprint, and future scholars to study, is therefore most probably the last that the author ever saw. Even so the first will be of interest, and second only to the original manuscript as showing the writer's first thoughts and the process of corrections. The practice of submitting proofs to an author began long after the invention of printing; at first it took the form of permitting attendance at the press while the printing was in progress and only much later by sending proofs.

For the most part in the sixteenth and seventeenth centuries later editions are mere reprints of the first with the addition of fresh printer's errors; the first edition is therefore usually the nearest we can get to the author's own words. A noteworthy example is the First Folio Shakespeare of 1623, which is our prime authority for several of the plays for which no early separate quarto editions survive. The second, third, and fourth folios, which are purchased for large sums in order to make a set on the shelves of collectors, are merely inaccurate reprints, of interest as showing the dates at which the demand created a new edition, but intrinsically of no authority and textually unimportant.

The great exception to this simple hypothesis is in the case of an author who makes revisions to a text in the course of subsequent printings. It is for this reason that special attention is paid to all editions published during an author's lifetime. These can obviously have a special standing in that such textual changes can have authorial authority. The methods of an author are important in such an instance in order to try to establish an attitude to revision that might have been expressed in bibliographical terms. Some authors are known to have been constantly at work on revisions for new printings, others to have exhibited a remarkable indifference to the fate of their creation.

There will also be those instances in which the vitally important point of interest will not be simply the sequence of printings but in particular the complete relationship of two editions to each other, notably from the textual viewpoint. The 42-line Bible once more provides us with a palmary example. It used to be debated whether the other very early Bible printed in the still larger type associated with the first Mainz press, the 36-line Bible, were not the earlier of the two. But it was discovered that the printer of this had skipped a considerable passage in the text of the Old Testament and that the omitted matter corresponded exactly with a complete leaf of the 42-line Bible. The most likely explanation is that the copy that the compositor used lacked that leaf, in which case he must have set up from a copy of the 42-line Bible, and the later date of the 36-line Bible, suspected on other grounds, is amply proved. McKerrow has recorded another case of a reprint from an imperfect copy. The printer of the 1585 edition of *The Secrets and Wonders of the World,* working from a copy of *A Summarie of the Antiquities, and Wonders of the Worlde* (*c.* 1565), perceived the imperfection in his copy-text and filled in the hiatus from his own invention.[12] A more modern example can be found in connection with the Wise forgeries. One of the facts that helped to dismiss an early date for the forgeries was that some of them printed a text that embodied an authorial revision much later than the alleged date of the forged publication itself.

With such purposes as these in mind it is now time to view the kinds of evidence that will allow this sequence to be build up.

Printers of first editions normally start with the text, leaving the preliminaries to be printed last; the preface is probably not written until the text is all in type. They will sign the first quire of text as B and the Preliminaries A, following this up with a, b, etc., if the prefatory material overruns A. Alternatively, they may use A as the first signature for the text and allocate an arbitrary symbol, such as an asterisk, for the preliminary matter. Authors do, or at least did, not usually write a new preface for the second edition. There was therefore nothing to prevent printers from starting with the half-title or title and printing straight ahead. The break between preliminaries and text may often occur in the middle of a quire, proving that this has been the case. Where edition A collates with the preliminaries separate and edition B with the text following on without a break, A is usually the first edition. A good example is Dryden's *An Evening's Love,* in the first and second editions, both of 1671. The first edition collates, A⁴, a⁴, b²; A-L⁴, M² in fifty-six leaves; the second edition, A-N⁴, O² in fifty-four leaves.[13] It is worth noting that the preliminaries are often a half-sheet with the other half concluding the book; cases are known where the two halves have been left undivided by the binder.

There is a general rule that a first edition is printed in a larger and handsomer style, in a larger format, and with more leaves, than a later edition. Thus a folio will be followed by a quarto, a quarto by an octavo. This does not usually apply to special editions, such as collected editions; for example, the first *folio* edition of Shakespeare's plays came later in date than the *quarto* editions. Other exceptions are found, sometimes with no apparent reason.

In the early period of the art every printer made advances in technique that, once made, were not abandoned, and that can therefore be used as evidence of priority or vice versa. A book with a title page, or with foliation, or with signatures, or with perfect justification of the line-endings, will always be later than one from the same press without these signs of accomplishment. It need not be later than one from another press, since different printers, and printers in different centers, reached the same level of technique at different times. Caxton, for example, is to the end much more primitive than his contemporaries at Paris or Lyons or Venice. Conversely, two books representing the same level of technical advance and from the same press are necessarily close together in date. This is the case noticed in Chapter 1, the *Expositio S. Hieronymi in Symbolum Apostolorum* printed at Oxford by Theodoric Rood and bearing the date "1468." Certain associations of copy within the sequence of printings have come to be described by a widely used nomenclature. This would be of great advantage in bibliographical studies if the terms had ever been precisely defined and accurately used. Unfortunately the very existence of the phrases has caused confusion because they are loosely used in common speech and writing, often in publications that would otherwise seem to be reliable. Bibliographers have long recognized their obligation to employ them exactly if their descriptions of books are to be lucid and unambiguous. There have been many attempts in recent years to bring light into this area of the bibliographical jungle, but terms that should be capable of accurate definition are still the subject of debate. The following pages are no more than an introduction to a complicated subject.

(a) *Edition.* An edition of a book consists of all copies that are printed from a single setting-up of the text. If it is possible to imagine the ultimate absurdity of type that has been broken up and then, with perfect accuracy, reassembled in precisely the same order, then the resetting would still constitute a new edition. The reason for this insistence is that the bibliographer is interested not simply in change but always in any possibility of change. A "new edition" need not involve any revision of the text, though it is expected that any misprints observed will be corrected—and probably some new ones made. As soon as an admission of correction is made, then it can be argued that such corrections must of necessity involve some resetting, and consequently a new edition should be proclaimed.

The only guide is common sense applied to the habits of the printing shop. In McKerrow's words, "it depends upon the how much thereof." Allowance has to be made for the situations in which normal press operations result in variants. If a single—deliberate or accidental—resetting of a letter constituted a new edition, then the term could become, *reductio ad absurdum*, synonymous with copy. Unless the resetting is an attempt to produce a line-by-line reprint, and these are a small percentage of the whole, resetting in terms that would constitute an edition will be demonstrated much more readily by variations in length of line, lines per page, catchwords, relationship between running title and type page, as well as the text itself. There could not normally be a substantial resetting without something being apparent under one or more of these headings.

The obverse of this coin is that copies are technically of the same edition even when some external features might suggest the opposite. For example, the term will include all these copies printed from plates, even when this may extend over years. Discussion has also ranged around the question of copies printed from stored monotype spools and whether such reprintings, which may show variations in font used and number of lines per page, must be regarded as of the same edition or not. This would be quite logical because once the spool has been made the compositor's work is done. On the other hand, the type itself is reset each time the spool is placed in the caster. A new printing surface is created, and, although it should be identical with the previous setting, errors are not impossible. Also the matrix in the casting box can be changed although the spool is the same. The result would be that, from the same compositorial setting of the type, two very different products could emerge. There is some difference in the use of the term in publishing and bookselling circles. In 1898 the Publishers' Association put forward the following definition, which was endorsed by the trade a second time in 1929: "An edition is an impression in which the matter has undergone *some* change, or for which the type has been reset."

(b) *Impression; printing.* "Impression" (British) or "printing" (American) are the terms used to cover all those copies that were printed at any one time. This is normally interpreted as meaning without the type having been removed from the press and consequently without any very great possiblity of variation. In modern times there will frequently be several printings to an edition, but in many cases the information is of little bibliographical significance. "Six large impressions before publication" is largely a part of advertising and, without firm information regarding the size of each impression, has little meaning. Robert Lusty recorded the practice of one publisher of "stopping the run of certain titles after every five hundred copies and inserting the phrase 'second impression before publication,' and so on progressively. The total run might be modest, but the huge advertisements could proclaim 'Three Impressions Before Publication."[14] Nevertheless, a series of several completed runs from the same setting-up of type, which constitutes multiple impressions, is frequently of importance in clarifying the relationship between the impressions that exist within an edition. In earlier times impression and edition were usually synonymous because the type was broken down and redistributed when the form came off the bed of the press. A new impression is one that is taken from the same standing type or plates as the original. This would also constitute a *reprint*, or, more fully in the latter case, a *reprint from plates*.

Pocket editions are frequently produced by reprinting from plates on thinner and smaller paper. The resulting appearance is often so different that the inexperienced eye needs to see the two side by side to be convinced of their typographical identity.

The Publisher's Association defined "impression" as: "A number of copies printed at any one time. When a book is reprinted without change it shall be called a new impression to distinguish it from an edition."

(c) *Issue.* An issue similarly consists of all those copies of an edition that are put on the market at one time, if differentiated by some substituted, added, or subtracted matter from those copies of the same setting of the type that were put on the market at other times. A *separate issue* implies that the various forms of issue appear on the market simultaneously. The difference is specifically one of form, such as reimposition of type pages in order to produce a different format or amended title pages to meet different circumstances.

If the difference is one of time, such as a new title page, or an introduction or appendix added to the unsold original sheets, clearly establishing the copies containing such additions as later than those copies without them, then they form a *new issue* or a *reissue*.

(d) *Variant.* When the press was worked slowly and by hand, it was exceedingly easy and a common practice to stop it and to withdraw the form for the correction of any error that had been observed on the pulls already made. There is no reason to believe that, when completed sheets were stacked for the binder, any attempt was made to distinguish between the corrected and uncorrected pulls. Indeed it was quite possible for a further correction to be made while the form printing on the other side of the same sheet was in the press, and if in the work of perfecting (printing the second side) the printer chanced to start with the last printed copy, there would result sheets of which in some copies the outer form is in uncorrected and the inner in corrected state, and in others exactly the other way round. Manifestly neither of these could be called the earlier or the later issue, and the word "issue," dear to some booksellers, is therefore disallowed for these cases by bibliographers, who speak of them as variants.

An important example of the confusion between issue and variant, which cost the vendor of a book £1,500, was seen in the sale in 1926 of a copy of the first (1678) edition of Bunyan's *Pilgrim's Progress*, Part I. Ten copies of this edition are recorded, of which two have a small five-line errata printed below the Finis on the last page of text.[15] After the printer had printed off the forms containing the erring passages the errors were noticed. It was too late to correct any copies of those forms; nor was it worthwhile to reprint a whole leaf for each as a cancel (see below). The errors were not of the kind or of the magnitude that normally necessitated a cancelation or the reprinting of a whole sheet. But there was one chance left, and that was to utilize any blank space, which would otherwise be filled with quads and spaces, on the outer form (that containing the last page) of the last sheet; and this was done. The errata "slip," which is commonplace in modern times, was rarely if ever used then. Of course the printer did not issue the copies with the last form in this state separately from the others. The auctioneer's cataloger did not notice the errata, and simply (and correctly) described the copy as of the first edition. The purchaser actually returned the book as misdescribed; and, more surprisingly still, the auctioneer accepted its return. It was resold as a "second issue," which it was not, and its owner had to take £1,500 less. Yet it represented Bunyan's intentional first text, and what more does the collector of first editions desire?

In a letter written at the time Greg argued against calling the copies with the errata a second issue. "What the presence of the errata shows is that there are two states of the last sheet, not that there are two issues of the whole volume. Some pulls of the last sheet would have the errata, some would not, but the whole of the impression would be completed before any copies were 'gathered.' The sheets would then be sewn up indiscriminately, and the order in which the copies issued would be random."[16] Since the time of Greg's letter the status of these copies has become even more clear. Further investigation has demonstrated that other variants exist in other forms notably in gatherings B and L. It is in fact a typical example of corrected forms giving variant readings but undoubtedly within the same edition.

Variants are astonishingly numerous in books of the age of the handpress, but it is not worthwhile to stop the power-driven machine press for a correction; small corrections are therefore now reserved for an errata slip, while a large one would be dealt with by reprinting the sheet.

(e)   *Cancel.* If an error were discovered when the form had been printed off, and if it were of too great substance for uncorrected copies to go out into the world, a leaf could be reset and separately printed. The corrected copies of the leaf would then be substituted for the peccant original, which would be cut out by the binder, a scissor-slit in the tail being the signal to do so. The cutting out of the leaf would be done in such a way as to leave a stub to which the newly printed correct leaf could be attached.

Where the book would otherwise have a blank last leaf, and the last sheet had not been printed off when the cancel was decided on, it was obviously economical to set up the corrected version as part of the form for that sheet and to cut the leaf away afterward. In fact the reprinted leaf is sometimes found at the end, overlooked by the binder, and this is the bibliographer's delight because with both texts available the reason for the cancel will become clear and can be recorded.

The reasons for cancels are often among the most interesting and important elements in the history of a book. They involve conflicts of politicians, libels, seditions, heresies, and entertaining errors. Striking examples are given by McKerrow, and by Esdaile in his *Sources of English*

Literature. [17] The chief work devoted to the subject, and the best introduction to the problems, is by R. W. Chapman. [18] He first made it abundantly clear how frequent was the incidence of cancels, especially in the eighteenth century, where he estimated that at least one book in three will be found to contain one. The advent of machine printing in the nineteenth century changed the situation drastically, but it did not do away completely with the need for a cancel. Although they are comparatively rare in modern books, they can nevertheless be individually important. In a respectable percentage of such cases the cancel is no more than a title leaf reprinted for the sale of a book by a publisher other than the one for whom it was printed. In instances where the text proper is affected, as observed above in the case of variants, if an error be found deserving correction more drastic than can be administered in an errata slip, the publisher will probably instruct the printer to reprint the entire sheet. There still remains, however, a significant number of cancels in modern books that have a direct bearing on the text. John Wyllie's paper provided a good introduction to the nature and importance of a selection of these. [19] Somerset Maugham's *Painted Veil* (1925), which Wyllie described as "the standard twentieth-century example of the classical leaf-substitution cancel," had two complete gatherings canceled and fifteen single-leaf cancels. This extraordinarily high number was necessitated by a decision to change every reference to Hong Kong as the setting of the novel. [20] Another interesting modern example is D. H. Lawrence's *The White Peacock* (1911). Again the cancels are of textual importance since they result from the English publisher's request for the rewriting of an objectional paragraph. [21]

Both the original and the corrected leaves are indiscriminately called "cancels"; but it is more exact and preferable to call the former the *canceled leaf* or the *cancellandum*, even when it should have been, but has not been, canceled, and the latter the *canceling leaf* or the *cancellans*. There are several points for the detection of cancels: (1) A leaf-cancel will normally have the stub of the cancellandum showing, to which the cancellans is affixed. It must be remembered that there was no reason why a printer should take undue care to hide the fact that a cancel had been made. The important matter was the hiding of the offending text. Consequently, unless the printer was concerned with the appearance of the book, more important on some occasions than others, the stub is likely to be visible. (2) There would be many occasions when the quantity of the text removed was different from that which replaced it. Since the printer was normally limited to replacing the same number of leaves as were removed, this variation would have to be accommodated. A leaf with more or fewer lines to the page than average or a different length of lines raises suspicions of a cancel. (3) Any unusual break in the normal pattern of signatures within a book merits investigation. (4) A press figure that appears to run counter to accepted practice may suggest that a leaf was printed independently of the sheet of which it is now a "part." There can be no more than two press figures to a sheet, one on the outer and one on the inner form. (5) Indications may exist also in the paper itself; watermarks may appear, or not appear, in positions that are contrary to those suggested by the format of the work; chain lines may be in the "wrong" direction within the sheet, or in the right direction but not matching with those in the conjugate leaf. Work has also been done on the difference between the smooth and the indented sides of the paper.[22] Once again, there is a fifty-fifty chance that the cancellans will be affixed so that it does not match the leaf to which it is conjugate.

A cancel is normally described as a leaf or leaves or part of a leaf that is substituted or designed to be substituted for the corresponding part. The expression "part of a leaf" within the definition is necessary to meet the instances where the offending words were covered by a slip that could be pasted over them bearing the revised text. Many pasted-over cancels in modern books are limited to changes in imprint, but a surprisingly large number are concerned with textual matters. The surprise lies in that, since the slip can often be removed without undue difficulty, it is appropriate only when recovery of the original text is not a matter of great concern.

Two other forms of emendation have results that achieve, broadly speaking, the same purpose as cancels, and confusion can arise in their description. A comparatively rare occurrence is the complete removal of certain leaves at a stage when nothing can be done to mask their removal. The book is not "incomplete" or "imperfect," although pagination, signatures, and all other bibliographical indications will be awry. They do not constitute cancels because nothing replaces the excised text. They are best regarded as "suppressed leaves" since this most clearly indicates the authorized nature of their removal. Wyllie gives one example of a work of this nature, but it will be infrequently encountered.[23]

The other example is exactly the opposite and is met with far more often. Leaves are added to a gathering rather than being in substitution for anything. An example of this is Anthony Munday's edition of Stow's *Survey of London* (1618). Two leaves were inserted between C2 and C3 (pages 19/20 and 21/22) recording "The Speech at the Cefterne" at its opening on Michaelmas Day 1613. The first leaf bears a note on its recto page: "Let this halfe fheete be plac'd betweene Folio 20, and 21." It is extraneous to pagination, signatures, and catchwords.

(f) *Large- and fine-paper copies.* Special and more expensive copies are manufactured in various ways. One important form is the large-paper copy; this has varied in its purpose over the years from purely utilitarian to aesthetic. They are frequently designated in booksellers' catalogs as "L.P." to distinguish them from the "F.P." accorded to fine-paper copies. They are produced by printing the same type setting onto a larger sheet, following a reimposition of the type pages within the form. The reimposition is essential in formats other than folio, where, nevertheless, it is still usually done for aesthetic reasons and for convenience in use.

Early examples of large-paper copies, as in the Elizabethan law books printed by Richard Tottell, were sometimes intended for the utilitarian purpose of private annotation. This is a desirable characteristic in certain classes of book, and allowance has always been made for it. Wide margins are not the only attempt to answer the problem. Blank leaves at the end of a book, often designated by some phrase like "Personal Notes," and interleaving with plain paper have been utilized for the same purpose. In the nineteenth century, and particularly toward its close, there arose a fashion for excessive margins, bulking out (more agreeably, it must be said, than by means of featherweight paper) small books into important-looking tomes. One of these was once drastically described by a critic as "an epigram in one volume." Nor is the fashion purely modern. A century before the *Yellow Book* Richard Brinsley Sheridan had satirized such books as having "a rivulet of text meandering through wide meadows of margin," while the same thing may have been in the mind of Callimachus, the librarian of the great library at Alexandria, when he enunciated the opinion that a big book is a big evil.

The fine-paper copy is today more popular than the large-paper. From the beginning of printing there has been a tradition of printing some copies of a book on finer paper than the normal run. At times, as with the 42-line Bible and as revived by Morris at the Kelmscott Press and followed by some later private presses, a number of copies were printed on vellum. In general, however, the practice is for a limited number of copies. Some modern books, especially those illustrated by engravings, are frequently issued in two forms, the fine copies containing early pulls of the engravings, sometimes in more than one state. An example of this practice is given in Chapter 2 under "The statement of the number of copies printed."

There are also occasions on which the large-paper copy, because it is produced for aesthetic rather than utilitarian purposes, can be deemed to rank as the more sumptuous version.

Format

At this stage of the proceedings it should be possible to determine, with reasonable exactness, the basic identity of the book in hand. The next stage is to ascertain the format of the book, which is the first step toward the determination of its state of completeness. "Format" is the term used to describe it in accordance with the number of times and manner in which the original sheet was folded. Thus it follows that format is not size, because it gives no indication as to the size of the original sheet. Octavo, by itself, gives no idea of size whereas Crown octavo, stating exactly that the original sheet measured 20″ × 15″, will equally indicate that the untrimmed leaf size will be 7½″ × 5″. Knowledge of format also provides the opportunity to discover whether the book is complete and perfect or not. If it is so, then the whole of the original sheet will be present and the process of collation, against the background knowledge of the format, will enable this to be determined.

Just as bibliography is the biology of the book, collation is its bloodless anatomy. Anatomists must understand the structure they examine. The basis of the structure of the book is the folding of the sheets of paper to form the leaves.

The main formats that will be encountered, and with each of which a student should be familiar as soon as possible, are as follows:

Broadsheet (or Broadside)

In this case a book is made up of whole sheets of paper that have not been folded. They are usually, but not invariably, printed down the length of the sheet. The method also calls for unusual binding methods in that the single sheets have to be sewn down the edge by stabbing or oversewing. On occasions the sheet will be fixed to a guard strip that can be folded and sewn by normal methods accepting the disadvantage of a somewhat ungainly shaped volume. The format is found mainly in plate books, atlases, and such like where the maximum page size is necessary.

It is sometimes mistaken for a folio, probably because the term "folio" has come to be loosely associated with the idea of any large book. The same inaccuracy has crept into some descriptions of such books, necessitating the invention of terms such as "large folio" or more popularly "elephant folio." A book in broadsheet can normally be distinguished from a folio by the direction of the chain lines, horizontal in the former, vertical in the latter.

In certain circumstances, such as separate plates in a normal

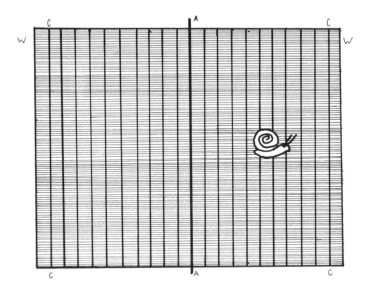

FIG. 10. *Two leaves of a sheet folded in folio (Watermark: Stras-bourg, France, 1478. Briquet 5975)*

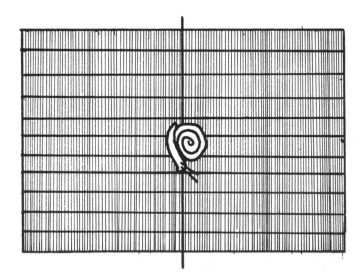

FIG. 11. *Two leaves of a sheet folded in quarto*

folio, half a sheet of paper was used unfolded. The most logical term to apply to this seems to be a half-sheet, although it has traditionally, but not very accurately, been called a single-sheet. Some writers urge that tradition has hallowed this nomenclature, but half-sheet is certainly to be preferred.

Outside book usage the broadsheet, or half-sheet, was used for proclamations, ballads, and the like. In these instances the text itself became known as a broadside.

Folio

In a broadsheet the watermark is usually to be found in the center of one half of the sheet, which is crossed breadthways by the spaced chain lines (C in *Fig.* 10) and lengthways by the close wirelines (W in *Fig.* 10). Fold the sheet once down line AA and we get a pair of leaves, or four pages, *in folio*. The watermark is in the middle of one leaf, the first or second according to how the printer places the sheet on the press, with the possibility of a countermark in the middle of the other, and the chain lines run perpendicularly.

Quarto

Fold it again across the first fold and we get a *quarto* folding of four leaves or eight pages. The watermark is divided by or close to the fold of one of the pairs of leaves, either the inner or the outer pair according to which way the fold is made. The chain lines run horizontally across the leaf, reversing their position in folio (*Fig.* 11).

Octavo

Fold it yet again across the last folding made, and there are eight leaves or sixteen pages, the commonest format since about 1700, when paper was first made in quantity in sheets of such dimensions as to yield a fair-sized page in this folding, which is called *octavo*. The proportions of the octavo leaf are not like the square quarto leaf, but are very much those of a folio; it is of course smaller, at least in the old handmade papers, which were not made in widely varying sizes. The chain lines run perpendicularly as in folio. The watermark is now (when the binder's shears allow it to be seen at all) in quarters in the top inner corner of either leaves 1, 4, 5, and 8 (the outer leaves of the quartet on either side of the sewing) or of leaves 2, 3, 6, and 7 (the inner). Illustrations do not show these multiple foldings easily, but by working them out with a sheet of paper one will have no difficulty understanding them.

Duodecimo

Another fairly common folding, especially in the eighteenth century, is the *duodecimo*, a folding in which there are twelve leaves or twenty-four pages.

There are many occasional but only two normal ways of folding. By one method, which was current in England in the late sixteenth, seventeenth, and eighteenth centuries, the sheet was cut into two-thirds and one-third. The larger part was folded as an octavo while the other was folded by two vertical folds, and the four leaves so formed were placed within the other folding. By the other method, common during the nineteenth century, the sheet was divided into three and then folded twice across. In both these cases the chain lines will be horizontal. By the first method the watermark will be toward the top outer corners of leaves 7 and 8 or 11 and 12; by the second method, toward the top outer corners of leaves 7 and 12 or the foot of leaves 9 and 10. In many instances the watermark will have disappeared in the process of binding, but there is still the shape of the leaf, which is rather narrower than in octavo, to distinguish it from the square leaf in sixteens. The distinctive shape of the duodecimo makes it difficult to reconcile this format with Austin Dobson's description of "the dear and the dumpy twelves."[24]

Doubling the duodecimo produces 24°; and a common variation in French books is eighteens. Half-sheets of this last achieve what bibliographers have denied the possibility of, and what one may be allowed to wish were really impossible, an intact section with an odd number of leaves, in this case, nine.

Other formats

Returning to the straightforward sequence of halving the previous folding, we see that the fold beyond the octavo brings the sheet to a sextodecimo or sixteens, a gathering of sixteen leaves or thirty-two pages; the chain lines are again horizontal as in quarto; the shape is again squarish but small in proportion. The watermark is to be found near the top of the fore-edges, and it is rare to find more than traces of it. The 16° has a fold at the foot of the leaf. Further doublings produce 32°, 64°, and 128°, but these are rare except in pocketbook diaries and in the book field in some volumes of private devotional manuals.

These terms are written in abbreviated forms:

Broadsheet	= 1° or bs.
Folio	= 2° or fol.
Quarto	= 4° or 4to or Q° or Q
Octavo	= 8° or 8vo.
Duodecimo	= 12° or 12mo
Sextodecimo	= 16° or 16mo.
Tricesimo-secundo	= 32° or 32mo.
Sexagesimo-quarto	= 64° or 64mo.

In every case the pronunciation should follow the full word.

Identification of format

One of the early steps of the bibliographer is to identify the format of the book under review, which in turn will lead to an appraisal of the degree of completeness of the work. There are frequently two early stumbling blocks for the student. One is to reckon the binder's flyleaves as part of the book. Bibliographically they are not a part of the book, in that they are not normally part of the sheets that have gone through the printing press. They are a part of the binding and will be treated as such. Modern eyes, accustomed to two endpapers only, have to readjust in order to recognize, in addition to the endpapers affixed to the inside of the boards, two or even three fly-endpapers. The second problem is the tendency to state that the format can

always be ascertained by simply counting the leaves from signature to signature. They who say this are less to blame in that
James Duff Brown in his *Manual of Practical Bibliography* makes
just this preposterous pronouncement, and he has been followed
by others in this error. One can only reply, *more Socratico,* by a
question, "Of what format, then, is a book with six leaves to a
section? Of what format one with fourteen? Still more, of what
format one in alternate eights and fours?"

The number of leaves to a gathering is of course only a secondary guide—of use when the shape, foldings, watermarks, and
laid marks have been duly noted. Each format had a range of
groupings and arrangements in order to create the gathering for
sewing.

Folios were frequently brought together three or four sheets at
a time, which when folded produced a gathering of six or eight
leaves. Only in the eighteenth century, and perhaps only in
England, has it been usual to make up folios in single-sheet
sections of two leaves; in the fifteenth century five sheets were
gathered, making a *quinternion,* or quire of ten leaves, often
alternating more or less regularly with *quaternions,* or quires of
eight.[25] There is at least one case of a folio quire of fourteen
leaves. In England in the sixteenth and seventeenth centuries
sixes were the rule for folios. The eighteenth-century practice of
making up in two is unexplained; it was immensely wasteful of
sewing, and avoidance of this is of course the motive for gathering several sheets into one quire.

Quartos are fairly often found in eights, i.e., the sheets
gathered in pairs; but preliminaries often show a sheet with a
half-sheet gathered into it (six leaves), and quarto books habitually end with half-sheets (two leaves).

In octavos the single-sheet section is the norm, and only an
experience limited to modern octavos could have occasioned
Brown's error. But even here half-sheet sections occur, notably
at the beginnings and ends of books.

Sixteens are now habitually so imposed as to be cut in half and
made up in half-sheets of eight leaves. These closely resemble
octavos, especially since modern machine-made paper does not
afford the old guides; if the bolt at the foot has been shorn away
in casing it is really indistinguishable from an octavo.

In the eighteenth century duodecimos were very often made

up in this way in half-sheet sections of six leaves. Variations of this practice gave, by cutting into two-thirds and one-third, alternate eights and fours (or else, by inserting the four leaves inside the eight, twelves); and by cutting into thirds, continuous fours.

Collation by watermarks

In addition to the evidence of the sheet folding and direction of chain lines, there will also be a need to collate by watermarks.

But first let it be observed that unwatermarked papers existed from the fifteenth century and were common in the eighteenth; and that modern machine-made paper does not give the regularly placed markings necessary to this method. The method does, however, work very well for the great mass of books up to 1700 at least and for a reasonable percentage of eighteenth-century books. Even in books that have apparently regular signatures, it is a method that can throw valuable additional light. The pattern of leaves that have whole or partial watermarks will, as has already been stated, vary from format to format. The procedure will be clear if examples are taken from two of the most common formats.

A *folio:* Look at the first leaf against the light, then the next, and so on, noting whether they have watermarks. Put down on a piece of paper an X or any other symbol for a watermarked leaf, and an O for an unmarked leaf. After four leaves begin to look for the sewing. If the book is tightly bound and the thread is invisible, restrain your impatience; the watermarks will in the end tell their tale, and the backs of books must not be broken, even in a good cause; collation is a *bloodless* anatomy. Let us say that you find your sewing. Mark it with a stroke and proceed with the search for watermarks. You have a notation: X O O X /.

As each complete sheet of paper has a watermark in one of its two halves and none in the other (see *Fig.* 10), the next leaf, which will be the pair of (or "conjugate with") that immediately preceding the sewing, must be without a watermark. Care must be exercised in considering the possibility of a countermark. The next two must have watermarks, since their pairs have none, and the fourth after the sewing will be unmarked. You now have X O

O X / O X X O, which should, if all is well, be a quire of eight leaves, a quaternio, followed by a visible division between it and the next; but only in original bindings can one see easily down to the back. Copies in the tightest late–eighteenth- and early–nineteenth-century morocco bindings, such as those made for King George III, Lord Spencer, Cracherode, the Duke of Devonshire, and others, were fortunately hot-pressed quire by quire, and the outside pages of the quires can be identified by the gloss. If the quire-ending does not appear after the eighth leaf, but clearly or doubtfully after the ninth, we have to make sure that there is not a leaf missing at the very beginning. It is true that it may be a blank; but, even if it is, it is a part of the book and must be accounted for. The best plan is to suspend judgment and to go on collating the watermarks for another quire, which will probably settle the matter. If neither the second nor the third quire explains the first, it is a hard case and will need much more detailed examination. At this stage it is sometimes necessary to remind oneself that this is not the sole evidence on which judgments will be made. It is evidence that must mesh with all other forms of evidence.

A *Quarto:* But suppose our book to be a quarto, a less common case in the earliest period. In the first leaf we may find either no watermark or half a watermark, divided by the sewing, and possibly not easy to see. It may have been placed a little out of the center and be complete in one leaf or the other: but, even so, it will be quite close to the sewing. Mark the unmarked leaf O and the marked X, as before, the X standing normally for half a watermark. We will, say, get before the sewing X O /. The leaf following the sewing must be the rest of the unmarked half of the sheet, and the next and last of the quire must bear the remaining half of the watermark, giving us the complete quire as X O / O X.

It is not surprising to realize that the paper maker or paper supplier did not pile or dispatch the sheets with the watermarked halves all at one end, nor did the pressman take them up and place them on the tympan of the press all in the same way. It is therefore most unlikely all the watermarked halves (in a folio) will be found before the sewing or all after it. They can, and usually do, run in any order. But one thing is certain, barring cancels, made-up copies, and such like sophistications, every watermarked half of a sheet is matched somewhere by an unwatermarked half. Exactly where the other half will be depends upon the format, the makeup of the particular format, and the position of the watermark within the sheet. The bibliographer, through an examination of the physical makeup of the book, attempts to discover the structure through the order of the folded sheets, to find out what there is and in what order it is presented.

Italian printers of the fifteenth and the first half of the sixteenth centuries had an admirable practice of printing at the end of the book, below the colophon, a *registrum*—whence the signatures are now sometimes spoken of as the "register"—setting out the quires of which the complete book should be made up. Before the days of signatures the first or identifying words of each recto before the sewing of each quire would be set out in due order. The invention of signatures simplified the registrum, since it was then only necessary to set out the series of signatures with a note of the number of leaves to be found in each, e.g.:

a-z, A-T

omnes sunt quaterniones praeter 1, duernionem;

or,

tutti sono fogli,

the latter meaning that, say in a quarto, all the quires are single and intact sheets, i.e., in fours. In such cases, unfortunately only a tiny percentage of all printing, the printer has provided what the bibliographer seeks to establish: the collation of the book.

As the bibliographer begins the process of collation there are a number of guiding lines that experience suggests are especially informative. They provide evidence that may assist in helping to determine minor differences between copies and from one printing to another. They will vary in importance from book to book, dependent upon a variety of circumstances, but in the vast majority of problems in bibliographical research they are too important ever to be ignored.

Gatherings, sections, quires, and signatures

In the simplest instances nothing is needed more than to discover and note the format of the sections, quires, or gatherings and then to run through the book as the binder does, checking their order and completeness by the signatures. Many modern books, especially those printed in North America, have discarded signatures in view of the presence of pagination and back marks. If the book were uncomplicated, the binder could collate by pagination by remembering that the first pages of the sections should read in an arithmetical progression, such as 1, 17, 33, 49, 65, and so on, though much higher numbers were probably not so ready to the mind. Even so, it was usually judged easier to fan the sections out and read the alphabet at the foot. If the structure of the book were in any way complicated, the work of the binder was still further multiplied for nothing. A multivolumed book without signatures compounded the problem in that sheets could appear in a wrong volume unless the text were checked by a binder and, moreover, one who at times might not be able to read the author's language. In other instances the arithmetical progression, inferior as it is at its best as a guide to the binder, may be thrown right out in two ways. First, the preliminary leaves may not be separately printed but may be given a separate roman pagination. For example, the text may begin with page 1 before the end of the first section, let us say after page xiv. Sections 2, 3, and 4 will then begin not on the easily remembered pages 17, 33, 49, but on pages 3, 19, 35. Second, if page 7, for example, in the second section and pages 21, 27, and 31 in the third section carry full-page illustrations that may not be reckoned in the pagination, then page 7 (as we should number it) being preceded by page 6 and followed by page 7, the sections would begin with pages 3, 18, and 31. It was in an attempt to simplify calculations and procedures of this nature that the signing of gatherings was begun and in many instances still continues.

In the manuscript book the scribe would write in the bottom outer corner of the margin of the first recto of a quire the letter *a* and the figure *1*, in the next *a 2*, and so on till the middle of the quire and the sewing was reached. Beyond this the scribe would continue for one recto, thus showing that nothing had dropped out, as could very easily occur unless the binder had lined the fold where the thread came with a strip of vellum to prevent it cutting the leaves. The remaining leaves formed integral parts of the signed leaves, and so when the book was unbound followed automatically in their proper places. It is therefore rare to find them also signed. The next quire would be lettered *b*, with leaf numbers as before; and so on. The binder, having obeyed the directions thus given, normally cut the signatures off with the plough, though sometimes the whole, or sufficient trace for our use, remains. It never entered his mind, good man, accustomed to medieval standards of workmanship, that a book once bound might need binding again.

The earliest printers followed the scribe in this, as in everything else, and left the signatures to be supplied in the traditional position in pen-and-ink. They also tended to follow the practice of signing a gathering up to and including the first leaf following the sewing. Then the habit developed of signing the first half of the gathering, up to the sewing and not beyond, so that by the eighteenth century Chapman could record this as the usual practice. [26] Prior to this it appears that only the small formats, such as 12° and 16°, normally had signatures up to the sewing only.

The earliest printers may have been deterred from setting up types for letters and figures at a distance from the type page since the page was surrounded and held tight by "furniture" consisting of bars of wood and metal. About 1470, however, in several centers of northern Italy experiments were made in stamping in typeset signatures by hand. They are found not in the old positions but irregularly near the fore-edge and generally near the head. This rather ugly device was of short vogue, for in 1472 Johann Koelhoff of Cologne showed the way to all subsequent printers by setting up a last line on the pages that needed signing, consisting of the necessary letter and number and, for the rest, of a row of quads or other spaces that left it blank in printing. The invention spread and in a dozen years was general. The presence or absence of signatures is one of the several aids to ascribing dates to undated books of that period.

The signature alphabet, being frequently the Latin, consisted not, like ours, of twenty-six letters but of twenty-three, having no *w*, and reckoning *i* and *j*, *u* and *v*, as alternative forms of but two letters. When the first alphabet was exhausted, printers went on with upper case if they had begun in lower, or by duplicating, triplicating, and multiplying to any number necessary the signature letters. A large book might then use, a-h (to cover the preliminaries) followed by A-Z, Aa-Zz, Aaa-Zzz, and so on. Within such sequences it is not unusual to find examples of individual practices of compositors. Thus one gathering may be an apparently random mixture of, for example, Bbb or 3B according to compositorial whim. In modern times Arabic figures are frequently used in place of letters, and it is also usual to sign not every recto before the sewing but only the first page of each gathering.

Whatever symbols are used, they must obviously be capable of being regarded as a sequence, hence alphabetical or numerical order. Arbitrary symbols would serve no purpose unless a key were provided. Care must therefore be taken to recognize symbols that appear arbitrary to modern eyes but that had an order in an earlier period. For example, the scribal abbreviations for *et*, *con*, and *-rum* are frequently found in that order in fifteenth-century books. Since they were commonly found on hornbooks following the alphabet they would have been recognized as an orderly sequence and have caused no confusion in use.

When two or more books, uniform in style, were being printed simultaneously in the same office, and also (as would doubtless be usual) bound in the same shop, it was very helpful to distinguish by the signature, which could be read on the standing type in the form as well as on the printed sheet, the book to which the form or sheet belonged. For want of this the binder could mix the sheets of two books that were outwardly similar, an annoying mistake but one that could be rectified. The printer could also print on two sides of the same sheet forms belonging to two different books, and this is incurable except by reprinting the sheet.[27]

The difficulty had been recognized and provided against in the fifteenth century, when, although the "publishers' series" did not exist under that name, certain Parisian presses specialized in books of Hours of the Virgin (the layman's prayer book) in general appearance all exactly the same, but differing in various parts according to the local "use."[28] To avoid the confusion that would inevitably have arisen it was the practice of these printers to add to the signature an abbreviated form of the name of the diocese of whose use the book was, such as "Sar." for "secundum usum Sarum," or "Par." for "secundum usum ecclesie Parisiensis." Similarly Wynkyn de Worde, who printed quantities of small quarto books of verse, employed the same device. Greg also found examples of this in a few early play printings; he called them "signature-titles" and recorded examples of them in his bibliography of Restoration drama.[29]

Another, not totally dissimilar, practice developed with part-issues especially in the last half of the eighteenth century. The indication, in the same signature line position, of "No 1," No 2," etc., clearly suggests this form of publication.

The risk of error in gathering the sections is not saved, if some trouble in composition may be, by the more recent device of using a small oblong block, called "a back mark." This is printed in the margin, where the outer fold of the first and last leaves of the sheet will come, in such a position that when the sheets are folded and piled for binding (or rather "casing") the black oblongs follow each other in a slanting sequence down the back of the book, thus showing at a glance an omission or a duplication.

Catchwords

A catchword is the first word of a page printed at the foot of the preceding page. In the manuscript these were most commonly found only at the foot of the last verso of a quire, and like the signatures were a guide to the binder. Later they appeared at the foot of every verso, and then commonly on every page. At this stage it would seem probable that they acted more as guides to the printer for imposition than to the binder. Practice from one country or printing center to another varied considerably between their first introduction in Italy in 1471 and their decay in the late eighteenth and very early nineteenth century.

Mismatching catchwords can frequently be a bibliographical indication of cancels, suppressed leaves, additional leaves, or, for a variety of reasons, errors in imposition.[30]

Press figures or press numbers

These provide an excellent example of the change in bibliographical attitudes in a comparatively short time. In 1927, when McKerrow first published his *Introduction,* he could state that press figures were "seldom of much bibliographical importance, as it relates solely to the organisation of the printing-house."[31] He could also say that attention had only recently been called to them.[32] Since that time, and increasingly in recent years, a great deal of attention has been paid to them.[33]

Press figures are small figures usually printed in the lower margin, on or close to the signature and catchword line. They are numbers that rarely, if ever, go beyond the 1–9 range. They are found very frequently in the eighteenth century and back into the last quarter of the seventeenth. In 1824 Johnson noted that the practice of "working with figures," as it was known, was then dead.[34] It seems clear that the figures were used within the printing house in order to record the quantity of work done by each press or pressman and therefore assist in the computation of wages. The exact method of operation and above all the bibliographical significance of the numbers are less certain. Few bibliographical descriptions until recent times have recorded them, and even now the practice is not invariable. Much more detailed evidence is necessary in order that their use may be more completely understood.

It is clear, however, that there could be one figure only to each form and consequently two only to each sheet. Any proven excess of this number would entail a clear reviewing of the evidence since it might, for example, be an indication of a cancel.

There is a faint chance that, on first meeting, press figures might be mistaken for signatures. Experience should soon guard against this possibility.

Foliation and pagination

Foliation and pagination must be checked in detail throughout the copy in the light of the practices obtaining at the period in question. In detail the process may not be very revealing. It is a part of the book-making process about which many printers were fairly cavalier in their attitudes, and a high percentage of accidentals will be found for which entirely logical explanations can be proposed. This covers instances when, for example, a sequence that runs 119, 120, 121, 212, 123, 124 can be easily

explained by the transposition of the first two figures of "122."
The numbering can provide more directly important information when new sequences of numbering help to distinguish what may be bibliographically separate entities within the work. A volume, for example, that consists of three "books" (in a literary sense, that is) and in which each book is separately paged can argue for its consideration as one in which each book was treated as a separate unit. If in addition each book had a separate sequence of signatures, the possibility would be further increased. Even though the volume in question may prove clearly to be a single unit, sections of separate paging may indicate that it had been planned for publication in separate books, had possibly been previously so issued, and was subsequently issued as a single volume. This is a common occurrence in nineteenth-century novels when the original printed sheets, designed for three-decker issue, were brought together and issued as a single volume, frequently as the first "cheap edition."

Headlines and running titles

A headline is the words that appear additional to the text at the head or top of each page; a running title—of the book, the chapter, or the section—is a headline that is repeated for several pages. It follows that they provide a part of the compositor's work that can be carried forward from one form to another without change. The earlier days of bibliographical investigation paid little attention to them as evidence, but the literature in the postwar years is already considerable.[35] The pattern of running titles should always be investigated in any analysis, and it is of equal concern that they should be recorded.

Plates

The plates as well as the text must be collated. Before the eighteenth century there is rarely a printed collation of plates beyond a numeration; a slip of directions to the binder was often printed, but has nearly always gone the way of all printed slips.

These are well named for they are the most elusive and evanescent of printed matters. In modern books the plates can usually be collated from the list in the preliminaries. These are not, however, always strictly accurate, and care must be taken to ensure that an apparently "missing" plate is not lurking in some unorthodox part of the book's makeup.

Blank leaves

Blank, or possibly blank, first and last leaves must be reckoned in collating, if only with a query. They are conjugate with printed leaves and are part of the book. Besides, they may not be blank. If their blankness is recorded, then the mind of the possessor of a copy that lacks them is set at rest. The first leaf may well bear a licence to print, the last leaf a device or a publisher's list. The modern publisher's list at the end of a book is normally a quite separate section or pamphlet, merely sewn in the casing, and is no part of the book it accompanies. Dryden's *Britannia Rediviva*, 1688, was reprinted by Jacob Tonson in 1691 to complete his collected set of the poet's works. The title page was reprinted unaltered from that of 1688, but on the spare last leaf Tonson added an advertisement that included the true date. Many copies of this textually valueless edition have been deprived, by accident or cunning, of their last leaf and have been passed off as the first edition.

Perfect or made perfect

In collating it is necessary to be sure that the book is perfect and has not merely been "made perfect." This latter process consists of supplying the place of a missing leaf by the appropriate leaf from another imperfect copy. Such leaves may be quite useful additions to an imperfect book to fit it to be a "working copy"; but they do not carry authority and in fact are not infrequently taken from wrong editions.

Many copies that have been "made perfect" in this way by the cannibalization of other copies have been done quite openly and with no intent to defraud. They are often admitted to be what they are and described accordingly. Such copies can never be regarded as bibliographically correct, but they may satisfy the acquisitive foibles of a collector. That madeup copies are not always as innocent as this is demonstrated by well-known examples of unscrupulous operators. An especially good example of this, well documented and providing clear indication of bibliographical proof, is that concerning T. J. Wise's depredations amid pre-Restoration drama.[36] Few cases are quite as remarkable as this, but it points clearly to the problems involved.

Great care must be taken to detect the insertion of leaves reproduced in facsimile. Many fine-book restorers and binders are capable of providing manuscript facsimiles of type pages, engravings, and other such fine detail that can defeat all but the most rigorous examination. In many more instances these days it is done photographically. As a rule the difference between a photographic facsimile and genuine leaves is clear from the paper, but it is not always so. Copies of complete modern photographic reprints are sometimes stained and passed off as originals. These can defy casual examination, but modern techniques now permit the most thorough examination of a book. One modern antiquarian bookseller has written:

> Every valuable book is subjected to the most rigorous examination. Page-by-page checking is done to determine if all leaves are original, in good condition, and if any are inserted from another copy. (An ultraviolet lamp is used to discover facsimiles and repairs.)[37]

A great deal of sophisticated technology is now available to libraries and book dealers in order to ensure a copy's authenticity.

Imprints

The following are a few of the more important and less easily recognized place-names found in imprints. They normally appear in the locative case, but often in adjectival or possessive forms, e.g., *in urbe Maguntina, in alma Parisiensium academia.*[38]

Abbatisvilla	Abbeville
Abredonia	Aberdeen
Andegavum	Angers
Andreapolis	St. Andrews
Aquisgranum	Aachen; Aix-la-Chapelle
Argentina, Argentoratum	Strassburg
Augusta (alone)	Augsburg or rarely London
Augusta Taurinorum, Taurinum	Turin
Augusta Trebocorum	Strassburg
Augusta Treverorum	Trèves; Trier
Augusta Trinobantum	London
Augusta Vangionum	Worms
Augusta Vindelicorum	Augsburg
Aurelia, Aureliacum	Orleans
Aurelia Allobrogum	Geneva
Avenio	Avignon
Babenberga	Bamberg
Barchino, Barcino	Barcelona
Basilea	Basle
Bisuntia, Vesuntio	Besançon
Bononia	Bologna
Borbetomagus	Worms
Brixia	Brescia
Cadomum	Caen
Caesaraugusta	Saragossa
Colonia	Cologne
Colonia Agrippina	Cologne
Colonia Allobrogum	Geneva
Colonia Claudia	Cologne
Colonia Munatiana	Basle
Colonia Ubiorum	Cologne
Complutum	Alcalà de Henares: famous for the "Complutensian" polyglot Bible, printed there in 1514–1517
Constantinople	almost always a fictitious imprint
Cosmopolis	always a fictitious imprint
Crisopolis	Parma
Daventria	Deventer
Divio	Dijon
Dordracum	Dordrecht
Duacum	Douai

Eblana	Dublin
Eboracum	York
Eleutheropolis	literally, "free city"; a fictitious imprint found on "free" books
Erfordia	Erfurt
Gandavum	Ghent
Gippeswicum	Ipswich
Gravionatium	Bamberg
Hafnia	Copenhagen
Herbipolis	Würzburg
Hispalis	Seville
Holmia	Stockholm
Leida	Leyden
Lipsia	Leipzig
Lovanium	Louvain
Lugdunum	Lyons
Lugdunum Batavorum	Leyden
Lutetia	Paris
Maguntia	Mainz; Mayence
Malborow ("in the land of Hessen")	Marburg. English books with this imprint were, however, probably printed at Cologne
Mancunium	Manchester
Mantua Carpetanorum	Madrid
Matritum	Madrid
Mediolanum	Milan
Moguntia	Mainz; Mayence
Monachium	Munich
Mounts	Mons
Mutina	Medina
Norica: Norimberga: Noriberga	Nuremberg; Nürnberg
Panormum	Palermo
Papia	Pavia
Parisius	a peculiar locative plural found regularly in the fifteenth century where Parisiis would be expected.
Parthenope (rarer than Neapolis)	Naples
Patavia	Passau
Roan; Roane; Rothomagum	Rouen
Salisburia	Salzburg

Salmantica	Salamanca
Sanctandrois	St. Andrews
Sarisburia; Sarum	Salisbury
Senae	Sienna
Spira	Speier; Speyer; Spires
Striveling	Stirling
Sublacense Monasterium	Subiaco
Taurinum; Augusta Taurinorum	Turin
Theatrum; Theatrum Sheldonianum	the first university press (late seventeenth century) at Oxford
Tigurum	Zurich
Trajectum Ad Rhenum	Utrecht
Treviri	Trèves; Trier
Tridentum	Trent
Ultrajectum	Utrecht
Ulyssipo	Lisbon
Venetiae	Venice
Vesuntio; Bisuntia	Besançon
Vienna	Vienne
Vindobona	Vienna
Vormatia	Worms
Vratislavia	Breslau
Wigornum	Worcester

REFERENCES

1. Examples of listings of anonymous and pseudonymous writings and of disguised imprints are:

   WELLER, Emil Lexicon Pseudonymorum: Wörterbuch der Pseudonymen aller Zeiten und Völker. 2nd ed. 1886.
   WELLER, Emil. Die falschen und fingierten Druckorte. 2nd ed. 2v. 1864.

   The chief one for English writings is:

HALKETT, Samuel, and LAING, John. *Dictionary of Anonymous and Pseudonymous English Literature.* Enlarged edition by James Kennedy, W. A. Smith, and A. F. Johnson. 7v. 1926–1934. Vol. 8 (covering 1900–1950). 1956. Vol. 9 (addenda and corrigenda). 1962. Both supplementary volumes edited by Dennis E. Rhodes and Anna E. C. Simoni.

A strong American element will be found in:

CUSHING, William. *Anonyms: A Dictionary of Revealed Authorship.* 1889.

and

CUSHING, William. *Initials and Pseudonyms: A Dictionary of Literary Disguises.* 2v. 1886–1888.

2. A number of studies have been published on surreptitious presses that indicate the complexity of their bibliography. For example:

ROSTENBERG, Leona. *The Minority Press and the English Crown, A Study in Repression 1558–1625.* 1971.
SOUTHERN, A. C. *Elizabeth Recusant Prose, 1559–1582.* 1950.
WOODFIELD, Denis B. *Surreptitious Printing in England, 1550–1640.* 1973.

3. Another list, with further suggestions, will be found in McKerrow's *Introduction to Bibliography.* Appendix 7.

4. Examples of such dictionaries are:

Handlists of Books Printed by London Printers, 1501–1556, by E. G. Duff, W. W. Greg, R. B. McKerrow, H. R. Plomer, A. W. Pollard, and R. Proctor. 4 parts in 1v. 1895–1913.
DUFF, E. Gordon. *A Century of the English Book Trade. Short Notices of All Printers, Stationers, Book-binders and Others Connected with It, 1475–1557.* 1905.
McKERROW, R. B. *A Dictionary of Printers and Book-sellers in England, Scotland and Ireland, and of Foreign Printers of English Books, 1557–1640.* 1910.
PLOMER, H. R. *A Dictionary of the Booksellers and Printers at Work in England, Scotland and Ireland from 1641–1667.* 1907

PLOMER, H. R. A Dictionary of the Printers and Booksellers Who Were at Work in England, Scotland and Ireland from 1668 to 1725. 1922.
PLOMER, H. R.; BUSHNELL, G. H.; and DIX, E. R. McC. A Dictionary of the Printers and Booksellers Who Were at Work in England, Scotland and Ireland from 1726 to 1775. 1932.

The Society has always had it in mind to carry these handlists beyond the limit of 1775 and also to produce new and revised editions of the earlier ones.

5. MORRISON, Paul G. Index of Printers, Publishers and Booksellers in . . .: Short-title Catalogue. 1950.
MORRISON, Paul G. Index of Printers, Publishers and Booksellers in Donald Wing's Short-title Cataglogue, 1641–1700. 1955.

6. Examples are:

McCORISON, Marcus A. Vermont Imprints, 1778–1820. 1963.
BELKNAP, George N. Oregon Imprints, 1845–1870. 1968.

7. TODD, William B. A Directory of Printers and Others in Allied Trades: London and Vicinity 1800–1840. 1972.

8. One of the interesting examples of local research activity is the work of the History of the Book Trade in the Northern Research Group at Newcastle upon Tyne.

9. DAVIES, H. W. Devices of the Early Printers, 1457–1560. 1935.
McKERROW, R. B. Printers' and Publishers' Devices in England and Scotland, 1485–1640. 1913
ROBERTS, W. Printers' Marks. 1893

10. MADAN, F. F. "Milton, Salmasius, and Dugard." The Library. 4th Series. IV: 1923–24. pp. 119–145.

11. MADAN, F. F. A New Bibliography of the "Eikon Basilike" of King Charles I. 1951.

12. McKERROW, R. B. Introduction to Bibliography. pp. 198–199.

13. Entries Nos. 75a and 75b in Hugh Macdonald's John Dryden; A Bibliography. 1939.

See also:

University of California. *The Works of John Dryden.* General editor, H. T. Swedenberg. Vol. 10. 1970. pp. 514–536.

14. LUSTY, Robert. *Bound to Be Read.* 1975. p. 37

15. A modern listing of copies is in the Clarendon Press edition of:

    The Pilgrim's Progress. Edited by J. B. Wharey and Roger Sharrock. 1967. pp. xxxvi–xliii.

16. *Times Literary Supplement.* 19 August 1926. p. 549.

17. ESDAILE, Arundell. *Sources of English Literature.* 1928.

18. CHAPMAN, R. W. *Cancels.* 1930.

19. WYLLIE, John C. "The Forms of Twentieth Century Cancels. *PBSA.* XLVII: 1953. pp. 95–112.

20. STOTT, Raymond Toole. *A Bibliography of the Works of W. Somerset Maugham.* 1973. Entries: A 33.

21. ROBERTS, Warren. *A Bibliography of D. H. Lawrence.* 1963. Entry: A 1.

22. STEVENSON, Allan. "Chain-indentations in Paper as Evidence." *Studies in Bibliography.* VI: 1954. pp. 181–195.

23. Wyllie, p. 98.

24. "My Books," in *At the Sign of the Lyre.*

25. This Latin *quaternio* is the true origin of our word "quire" and of the French *cahier.* The choir of a church, which has been absurdly held to be its origin (the leaves standing on either side of the sewing as do the singers), is of course from "chorus."

26. CHAPMAN, R. W. "Notes on Eighteenth-century Bookbuilding." *The Library.* 4th Series. IV: 1923–24. p. 169

27. Dr. Esdaile once found an example of this confusion when the

printer, having printed on one sheet forms from two books forming part of a series on games, one on bridge and one on lawn
tennis, produced a text that alternated in a manner bewildering
to the student of either of those pastimes.

28. The use prevalent over the larger, and particularly the southern,
     part of England, and also in Scotland, was that of Salisbury, or
     "Sarum." The York use was largely confined to the North. Sarum
     books were largely produced in Paris and Rouen.

29. GREG, W. W. *A Bibliography of the English Printed Drama to the
     Restoration.* 4v. 1939–1959. Vol. 4. p. 1i.

30. McKerrow, *Introduction to Bibliography*, pp. 82–84, especially his
     recording of different practices.

31. McKerrow, *Introduction to Bibliography*, p. 81.

32. CHAPMAN, R. W. "Printing with Figures." *The Library*. 4th
     Series. III: 1922–23. pp. 175–176.

33. A considerable literature has grown up on press figures in recent
     years. It is suggested that a student should start with:

     GASKELL, Philip. "Eighteenth-century Press Numbers, Their
     Use and Usefulness." *The Library*. 5th Series. IV: 1949–50. pp.
     249–261.
     POVEY, K. "A Century of Press-figures." *The Library*. 5th Series.
     XIV: 1959. pp. 251–273.
     TODD, W. B. "Observations on the Incidence and Interpreta-
     tion of Press Figures." *Studies in Bibliography*. III: 1950–51. pp.
     171–200.

34. JOHNSON, J. *Typographia*. Vol. 2. p. 489.

35. Much of the writing has been in relation to specific titles; some
     that will provide more general information are:

     BOWERS, Fredson. "Notes on Running Titles as Bibliographical
     Evidence." *The Library*. 4th Series. XIX: 1938–39. pp. 315–
     338.
     HINMAN, Charlton. "New Uses for Headlines as Bibliographi-
     cal Evidence." *English Institute Annual 1941*. 1942. pp. 207–
     222.

36. FOXON, D. F. *Thomas J. Wise and the Pre-Restoration Drama.* 1959

37. KRAUS, H. P. *A Rare Book Saga.* 1978.

38. Many other listings of various forms of place-names in imprints can be found to supplement this list. Examples are:

McKerrow, *Introduction to Bibliography,* Appendix 7.
PEDDIE, R. A. *Place Names in Imprints, an Index to the Latin and Other Forms Used on Title Pages.* 1932.

10.

THE DESCRIPTION OF BOOKS

After one has examined a book and learned all that it has to tell of its identity, its contents, and its history as shown by the condition in which it has survived, it will be necessary to record the knowledge so obtained, either for oneself or for others who do not have access to the volume. It is necessary, in other words, to describe the book.

Before the work of description can begin there are one or two basic questions to be answered, basic because the answers to the questions will have a very great effect upon the description itself. The fundamental point to be resolved is precisely what it is that the bibliographer is setting out to describe, and this means an unequivocal response to the issue of the difference between a catalog and a bibliography. That there is a very close connection between them is not capable of dispute, but, as Andrew Osborn wrote several years ago, "The relationship between cataloguing and bibliography has been a difficult one to define."[1] It has not become any easier with the passage of years, and a paper by Tanselle drew attention to a number of the varying viewpoints.[2] The situation is not made easier by the fact that many of the earlier bibliographers who were largely instrumental in forging the new bibliographical tools were themselves librarians. People like Bradshaw, Jenkinson, Sayle, Proctor, Duff, were initially drawn into the work by the need to apply themselves to the demands of their own collections. They belonged to the distinguished body of scholar-librarians, and their successors have worked along similar lines in the great research libraries ever since. We should not, consequently, hope or expect to find, or seek to establish, rigorously drawn dividing lines between the two areas.

The simplest and most basic division is that the catalog seeks to describe the individual copy or, as it may be in some instances, a set of individual copies, whereas the bibliography seeks to describe the "ideal copy." It must not be supposed from a very

342

general viewing of certain types of library catalog that a catalog is a tool with entries of very limited scope. It may be so in many instances in the same way that a bibliography will not necessarily produce a large amount of bibliographically significant information. Both types of tool serve different purposes at many different levels.

Every catalog entry is a description of the book cataloged. The purpose of the catalog is the main determining factor in the degree of elaboration of the description. At the lowest level the description must serve to identify the work. The simplest form of basic description is one that is illuminating even though blatantly unscientific: the Lindisfarne Gospel Book, the Aldus *Hypnerotomachia*, the Baskerville *Virgil*. For a certain number of purposes and for a very limited number of books such descriptive phrases are sufficient, but too wide an application could lead only to inaccuracy. Similarly, if a cataloger had to do no more than distinguish between two Bibles, one large and one small, it may well have been sufficient to say, "the big Bible." In somewhat similar manner a reference to the "42-line Bible" is sufficient to distinguish this Bible from all others. In each case the reference is to a bibliographical feature of the book and for certain basically simple purposes need not be elaborated.

At the other end of the scale a book can be described in such full and definite detail that a particular copy can be surely set apart from all other copies and described in the fullest possible detail. Here we reach the type of description that aims at providing information on a grand scale relating to the bibliographic nature of the book. This has been the role of a number of catalogs: for example, two that have already been referred to, the British Museum's fifteenth-century catalog and the Hunt Botanical Catalogue. Such catalogs are concerned to pursue and record the detailed specificity of the copy under review, the unique qualities of the copy. At one stage of bibliographical development this would have seemed absurd in relation to a printed book. Manuscripts were always set apart from printed books because of their status as unique items. Printed books were, on the other hand, known to have been multiplied in hundreds of copies at each printing, copies that for a long time were regarded and treated as being virtually identical to each other. Now we are increasingly conscious that many bibliographical features will set one copy of a printing apart from the others. The bibliographical catalog must pursue every such feature that establishes the identity of the copy being described.

Although the catalog is concerned with the individual copy, it would be unthinkable that it should not make reference to other copies of the same book that helped to illuminate the one being described. This would be particularly important if this copy were, for example, imperfect in any respect. A description that merely recorded "imperfect" would fall far short of any user's expectations if it did not explain such imperfections with reference to other copies. Fredson Bowers awarded high praise to W. A. Jackson's *Pforzheimer Catalogue* because of the detail that he recorded from his personal examination of copies outside the Pforzheimer collection.[3]

A bibliography, on the other hand, is an attempt to describe an edition in the terms of an ideally perfect copy of that edition rather than of one individual copy. Fredson Bowers described an ideal copy as

> a book which is complete in all its leaves as it ultimately left the printer's shop in perfect condition and in the complete state that he considered to represent the final and most perfect state of the book. An *ideal copy* contains not only all the blank leaves intended to be issued as integral parts of its gatherings but also all excisions and all cancellans leaves or insertions which represent the most perfect state of the book as the printer or publisher finally intended to issue it in the issue described.[4]

From this it follows that the description of an ideal copy might well not record the book in the state that is represented by any extant copy. All extant copies might well represent states that depart from that ideal. It must also follow that the description of one particular copy might well take the form of the description of the ideal copy with a record of every particular in which this copy differed from that ideal. It will also be appreciated that the description of the ideal copy cannot be attempted until multiple copies of the book have been collated and compared.

Within what may therefore be regarded in broad terms as bibliographical description it is apparent that considerable variations of detail and of emphasis can exist. The bibliographer must learn to adapt the general outline of description to the specific requirements of a particular book. This relates in particular to the actual amount of material that it is proposed to include.

In between what may appear to be the two far extremes the bibliographer is at complete liberty to decide exactly how much detail should be used and what respective balance should be made between the different parts of the description. The older tradition of descriptive work suggested a limitation by imposing distinct stages, such as "Short Description," "Short Standard Description," or "Full Standard Description." This approach is no longer valid, and the descriptive bibliographer needs more freedom than this would permit. A description should be as detailed as the purpose of the listing demands, and no longer, but it would be a wrong basis for the work if it were forced into a narrow and predetermined form. There is probably a minimum entry containing those elements without which the description can be said to contain no significant bibliographical detail. Even so, it would be wrong to suggest that anything less must always be wrong. The minimum entry usually contains the amount of basic information that can be found in the *Short-title Catalogue.* Author, title, printer, place of publication or printing, date, and, in the case of older or not readily accessible books, location of some copies; these are details that it would be difficult to envisage being excluded.

Equally, although any textbook, such as this one, must put the parts of a description into some logical and usually acceptable order, it is not a scheme that is sacrosanct. The bibliographer must know when to rearrange these items with advantage to the ultimate purpose of the list. The antiquarian bookseller, who is describing an individual copy of an important book with the intention of selling it, is reasonably likely to give more priority to facts about the copy than would a librarian in a catalog. Maggs Brothers in their catalog *Bookbinding in Great Britain* identified the books offered briefly and clearly but quite naturally devoted most of the descriptions and all the illustrations to the bindings.[5] Zeitlin and Ver Brugge in their catalog *Rare Books and Manuscripts in Medicine, Surgery, Physiology* devote most attention to notes on the importance of the work in relation to the history of the subject.[6] Bertram Rota's catalog *The Printer and the Artist* stressed the role of the artist especially in fine books of the period

1890 to the present.[7] This list could be multiplied many-fold with examples of catalogs from antiquarian bookshops that, by the emphasis within the entry and the arrangement of the catalog, adapt the formal outline of a description to the particular needs of the list.

It is important to remember that there are no "rules" in bibliographical description in the sense in which the library cataloger thinks of rules. This is perhaps another area where the cataloger and the bibliographer have shown increasing divergence in recent years. Cataloging has tended, with gathering emphasis on specific rules, to permit less freedom for personal interpretation. The development of cooperative schemes and machine applications have made this inevitable. Bibliography, on the other hand, encourages less adherence to specific rulings in an effort to mold the descriptions to the individual needs of the compilation in hand. Within a single catalog or bibliography there must obviously be uniformity; this is essential. It is equally essential that every fact, every transcript, should be set down with minute and absolute accuracy. If the user of a description receives from it a clear and accurate picture of the work, then it is a good description that has served its purpose.

In the first example of description now to be discussed, the parts are arranged in the formal order of a description, with the parts numbered here only for the purpose of reference. The relevance of each part and some of their particular problems will then be discussed in more detail. The example is reasonably typical of the average uncomplicated book of its period.

1. TASSO (TORQUATO) Aminta, *ed.* N. Ciangulo. Utrecht, 1725.

2. AMINTA/FAVOLA/BOSCA/RECCIA/DI/TORQUATO/ TASSO/ RISTAMPATA/ *Per uso degli Amatori della/Lingua Italiana,*/ DA/NICOLO CIANGULO/Maestro Italiano in questa/ celebre Università/ d'Utrecht./ [Ornament]/ Per Pietro Muntendam/ Stampator Italiano Utrecht/1725.

3. 12°.*,A-L⁴. pp. [1–8] + 9–96. pl. [Front] + I-VII. 28 lines + headline and signature and catchword line, 90 (95) × 57mm.

4. $*1^a$, title page; $*1^b$, blank; $*2^a$-3^b, Ciangulo's dedication to Sir Francis Head ("Fancesco [sic] Head Baronetto d'Inghilterra"), dated 26 Octob. 1725; $*4$, "In Lode del Medesmo. Ode", signed "Il suo N.C."; $A1^a$ (p. 9)-$L2^b$ (p. 92), text; $L3^a$-$L4^a$, tribute to Tasso by Trojano Boccalini; $L4^b$, another, from Louis Moreri's *Grand Dictionnaire Historique*.

5. Plates: line-engravings:
   (1) arms of Head, facing a conjugate leaf bearing
   (2) the engraved title, supported by angels holding a crown surmounting arms, numbered I;
   (3) numbered II. "Prologue fol. (*sic*. for pag.) 9";
   (4) -(8), numbered III-VII, heading the openings of Acts I-V, and facing pp. ("fol") 13, 37, 54, 66 and 81.

6. [Some note might perhaps be given here upon the dedica e and his travels, which are vaguely refered to in the dediction, and possibly amounted to no more than the Grand Tour. His Christian name is given as "Fancesco" both in the prose dedication and in the ode.]

7. 105 × 58 mm. Imperfect, wanting C2, 3. The last leaf mutilated. Contemporary mottled calf. Armorial bookplate of Thomas Philip, Earl de Grey, cut down to fit so small a volume.

(Library press mark)

Notes on the preceding description

1. The short-title entry with which this description is headed is provided in order to help the eye in turning over the leaves of a catalog or bibliography. In the case of modern books, say after 1700, when brief and concise title pages are more common than in earlier years, a very brief heading may well be sufficient. The heading should give prominence to whatever feature is the key to the arrangement. For example, in his *Bibliography of English Printed Drama to the Restoration* Greg gave as the order of his heading "in bold faced type. . . the serial number of the piece in the left margin, the title or other designation, and on the right the date accepted as that of printing or publication, on which the serial order depends."[8] A typical entry, consequently reads:

168. Much Ado about Nothing. 23 Aug. 1600.

Another kind of heading is provided by Allan Stevenson in his Hunt Botanical Catalogue. His version of the heading is as follows:

> The heading for each description is an abridged entry, made up mainly of author, short title, and facts of publication. As the descriptions are arranged chronologically and by serial numbers, the publication date appears also above each entry, centered, and the book number in the margin, where each can readily be found.[9]

This results in such headings as:

1729
477 BRADLEY, Richard (1688–1732), professor
of botany at Cambridge.
The Riches of a Hop-Garden Explain'd.
London 1729. Post 8°.

In both cases, although the actual information in the headings varies significantly, they share a common purpose in emphasizing the main features, which will be more fully developed in the transcription and in providing a satisfactory scheme for arrangement and identification.

2.(a) The title page should be transcribed exactly and in full. If the book has no title page but does have a colophon, then the colophon should be transcribed fully. If the book has both title page and colophon, both should usually be transcribed. An exception to this would be such instances as modern fine-press books in which that which can only be described as a colophon, and frequently so describes itself, often contains printing and publication details. This is valuable information that should be recorded, but not within the context of the title-page transcript. In the absence of a title page the incipit must be quoted, at sufficient length to allow for identification. If a formal colophon is absent, then any explicit should be quoted. In both instances references should indicate on which pages they occur.

Consideration also has to be given to the changing role of the imprint. As it normally appears on the title page the imprint is one of the most important features and a major source of information toward the problems of sorting out various printings. As the respective functions of printer, publisher, and bookseller diverged and separated over the years, the printer's imprint frequently became divorced from the title page. The verso of the title leaf and the end of the book became two common places for such information. Whenever the printer's imprint contains information, such as detailed address of the printer, that is not included on the title page, this should be recorded. Because it is somewhat accidental as to whether information relating to the printer is on the title page or elsewhere it is logical to record it immediately following the title-page transcript. For example:

> Printer's imprint: (verso of T/P):
> "London: Bradbury, Evans, and Co.,
> Printers, Whitefriars."

Many bibliographers recommend that excisions should be made in the transcript in cases of extreme verbosity. This is an option that should be exercised with extreme caution. Minor differences in wording, which could easily be regarded as "verbosity," can conceal indications of variant printings. If excisions are made they must be indicated by. . ., and, if more than a line be omitted, with the line-end stroke also (see below). Thus, supposing that the Tasso title page were very long, and that the words in italics were to be omitted, the passage would read,

> RISTAMPATA/. . ./. . ./ DA/NICOLO   etc.

Parts of a line omitted can be indicated similarly, as thus:

> Maestro Italiano. . . / . . . Università.[10]

(b) In a transcription of the title page upper-case letters must be reproduced by upper case. It is also necessary to distinguish, either in the transcription or by a note, between the three great divisions of type: roman, gothic, and italic.

It is usual in this connection to assume roman type unless

otherwise stated, with a well-established convention that small-capital letters are distinguished by double underlining and capitals by triple underlining. A single underlining will denote italic, but there is no widely accepted method for the designation of gothic type. It is preferable, therefore, to record this in a note.

In somewhat similar fashion color printing must be noted. Black will usually be assumed, but red, blue, and occasionally green are by no means uncommon. No satisfactory convention exists for recording these, and once again a note is necessary. This can be indicated within square brackets at the ending of the line, e.g.:   [red].   or, in a case of a number of lines, a note to the effect that "lines 2, 4, 5, and 8 are printed in blue."

The most difficult feature in this connection is the description of the type in terms of design and size. This is a general problem in the book whether the type is on the title page or in the text. A fuller discussion of this will be found below in this chapter with general problems of type classification and description.

(c) Contractions occur and must be represented either exactly or (since not all modern printers have them) by spelling out and italicizing supplied letters. These occur most frequently in early printed books and must be understood.[11] They were originally a device of the scribe for economizing in labor and writing material and, being largely conventional and of regular recurrence, were well understood. In technical books, e.g., of law and scholastic philosophy, they were much more drastic, and are very difficult for the nonexpert to decipher.

Printers inherited contractions with the rest of the outward aspect of the medieval book, but they were no saving to them, since every extra "sort" in a font meant an extra pigeonhole in the case and extra time in composition. Contractions gradually become less frequent (they are relatively sparse in the example chosen, printed in 1498), but survive in stray examples into the seventeenth century. The ampersand (& = et) is the only survivor of what was once a great army.[12]

Here is a typical highly contracted incipit of 1486:

Incipiūt titl'i p'ores d' duodecī ḡneralib' qd'lib ʒin ᵱhetas
scī Thome d' Aq'no ordīs frat ℞ p̄dicato 24 īp'ssi ᵱ Hānibalē
Parmēsem sociosqʒ ei⁹ āno dn̄i MCCCCLXXXVI die v'o
vltīo mēsis madij.

which being expanded reads:

Incipiunt tit*u*li priores de duodecim generalib*us* q*u*odlib*et* in prophetas *sancti* Thome de Aq*u*ino ordi*nis* fratr*um* pre- dicato*rum* im*pressi per* Hannibalem Parmensem sociosq*ue* ei*us* anno d*om*ini MCCCCLXXXVI die v*ero* vlti*mo* men- sis madij.

Three stock contractions:

ƺ = *et*
? = *con*
2‍4 = *rum*

are constantly used to follow the signature alphabet before a fresh alphabet is commenced. Almost any omitted letter, but mostly *m* or *n*, is represented by a stroke over the preceding letter, e.g., Incipiūt ordis. Other very common contractions are:

p̲ = *per* (or *par*)
p̓ = *pri*
p̄ = *prc* or *prae*
ꝑ = *pro*
9 = *us*
b' = *bus*

More elaborate contractions depend on the subject matter of the book and on the recurrent words that the original reader was expected to recognize in shorthand form. Thus in breviaries Omp̄s = Omnipotens; in scholastic treatises ph[9] = philosophus, i.e., (often) Aristotle, and ℞ = respondetur.

(d) Line endings are indicated by single upright strokes. Cau- tion has been advised regarding the use of a slanting stroke due to its employment by early printers as a mark of punctuation and, hence, liable to confusion. It can, on the other hand, be urged that in any but early printed books this printer's usage does not occur so that no confusion is likely. The only attraction of the sloping stroke is that it is a more common symbol to find on mod- ern typewriters.

The Oxford Bibliographical Society proposed a method of indicating the size of the interval between lines in books of the 1558–1800 period. This method would use a single line if the preceding interval were ½ inch or less, double-stroke if under 1 inch, and so on by ½ inches.[13] The method seems unnecessarily complicated without being really precise, and it has never been looked upon with much favor. Caution is also necessary in using other bibliographical tools in that a double-stroke can be used to denote other features than line endings. Greg, for example, used a double-stroke to indicate a rule across the page. The attempt to indicate distances between lines does nevertheless concentrate attention upon one of the purposes of transcription: namely, that it records the features of the title page that might help distinguish among various printings and also brings the title page's arrangement before the inward eye.

Another problem in line-by-line description arises when part of the text is arranged in columns. The simplest solution is probably the clearest, to record

[Two columns: Left transcribes four lines] . . .; [Right transcribes four lines] . . .

Each column then transcribes with normal line endings. Indication of the number of lines in each column makes it quite clear when full line length is resumed.

(e) In transcription from books printed before about 1640 difficulty will arise from the old use of *I* and *J* and of *U* and *V*.

In the upper case the tailed form (our *J*) was simply the gothic, and the short form (our *I*) simply the roman, form of one and the same letter. As a general rule, therefore, the printer will have used the form appropriate to the font that was being used. In lower case in English printing *j* was only used when following *i*, especially in roman numerals, as for example *xij* where we should write *xii*; otherwise *i* represents both our *i* and *j*. The simple rule is to follow the practice of the printer.

Similarly *U* and *V* were respectively the gothic and roman forms of the same letter. But the lower-case use was more complicated than that of *i* and *j*, for both occurred in roman. In initial positions *v* only was used, in medial and final positions *u* only. When this is grasped, the fact that "Juan" and "Ivan" are both forms of the name that we know as "John" becomes clear. Thus a sixteenth-century printer would set the Latin word that we write (or till recently wrote) "UVA" and "uva," if setting in upper case, "VVA," and if setting in lower case, "vua." Scholarly printers of the Renaissance, especially in Italy, often renounced *v* altogether in printing Latin and would have set up "uua." They could not have brought themselves to print "uva" or (Pollard's examples) "Qveene" or "Vniversitie." Yet so excellent a bibliographer as Charles Sayle did so in his catalog (1904–1907) of the early English books in the Cambridge University Library; and St. John Hornby, to an eye practiced in books of the period, did something to spoil his noble Ashendene Press edition of Spenser's *Faerie Queene*, in which an Elizabethan air was cultivated, by printing the title as "THE FAERIE QUEENE" when it should have read QVEENE. We have then . . .

Modern	Elizabethan
UVA	VVA
uva	vua (or uua)
QUEEN	QVEENE
queen	queene
UNIVERSITY	VNIVERSITIE
university	vniuersitie

When one is transcribing upper case in upper case or lower case in lower case, the simple rule again is to follow the practice of the printer. In transcription from upper case into lower case it is usual to adopt the form that would have been used had the printer been printing in lower case.

W and *w*, which also did not occur in the Latin alphabet, are at first, and freely in England till 1600, represented by VV and vv. It is well to retain this in transcribing. One exception is often made to this general rule. In the period just prior to the introduction of upper-case and lower-case *W* into the font, many printers anticipated the change by filing down the sides of the shank of two letter Vs so that they could be set closer together and so approximate to a *W*. In such instances it is common transcribing practice to recognize the printer's effort and intention and to transcribe it as a *W*. It is, however, a good example of the kind of practice that should be noted in the description. We have scant evidence as to exactly how widespread this practice was, over precisely what length of period it was done, and whether it was more common in some kinds of books than others. Full descriptions of books that represented this procedure would provide some of the answers.

A similar problem in transcription relates to the long s (ſ). Some bibliographers will argue that, at least in books before 1775, when ſ began to be discarded, it is not necessary to retain the long form in description. The justification that if the normal usage of the time would lead the reader to expect the long form, then it need not be mentioned. The same line of reasoning requires that if the long s appears in a book of much later date than this, it would merit a special note. The problem with this is the possibility of confusion over such questions as, "What is 'of much later date'?" If, however, the general principle is followed that the transcript should follow as close as is humanly possible to the printer's actual practice, then no confusion can arise, and, once again, our descriptions would provide the evidence from which deductions could be made. For these reasons the most accurate information will be produced by following the line of strict adherence to transcription.

It has always to be stressed that ſ is never to be confused with *f*. In the former case the crosspiece goes up to but not through the main stroke, whereas in the latter the crosspiece goes right through the upright.

(f) The title page is a common place on which to discover a printer's device. This should be described, within square brackets and enclosed by line-ending strokes. The overall measurement should be given, normally expressed in millimeters, and, if the device is an engraving, the measurements should be those of the plate line. The usual practice is to express the measurement in the order of width by height. The description of the device itself need not be elaborately detailed but sufficient for clear identification and, whenever possible, attributed to a particular printer. When a fuller description, with other instances of its use, is recorded in any acceptable listing of devices, such as McKerrow's, the reference to that work should be given.[14]

(g) Similar treatment, in terms of description and measurement, should be given to any other kind of ornament on the title page that is not a printer's device. These were usually employed for purely decorative purposes, and the overall description of the item can normally only be in terms of [Ornament: . . .].

(h) Lines across the page, produced by printer's rules, must be recorded. These also should be mentioned within square brackets within line-ending strokes. The length of the line should be recorded in millimeters. When two lines close together are used, the description should be "double-rule." Other descriptions, without involving too much elaboration, should be used, such as "swelling rule" or "spiral rule."

(i) At certain periods it was common for the text on the title page to be enclosed within a border. Such borders must be fully described. The simplest borders were rules, single or multiple. A more elaborate form was a line of printer's type ornaments at head and tail of the page. The most ornate was a large woodcut block (a "compartment"), which was frequently extremely elaborate. A close examination will sometimes reveal that the compartment actually consists of two or three separate blocks placed so as to act as a border. On other occasions the border enclosed a part of the title page text but not the whole of it. Whenever the description can include a reference to a bibliographical tool that records them in detail, such as McKerrow and Ferguson's work, this should be done.[15] One of the advantages of such references is that they will open up information relating to other appearances of the same block.

(j) So far the account has been on the traditional standards of a quasi-facsimile transcript. Instances not infrequently arise when the logical answer to some of the problems appears to be photographic reproduction of the title page. It is reasonably argued that only by this means can there be a resolution of such problems as recording the variant sizes of type, interline spacing, special type fonts, and any kind of pictorial matter. The strongest arguments against the use of photography are the uncertainty of the reliability of its basic operation and the problems of the publication of the finished result. The first of these objections can be countered by the undoubted truth that an accurate photograph can be made; the limitation is that the requisite amount of technical care and efficiency is all too rare. Minor imperfections in the negative can result in possible misreadings, and this risk is considered much too high by many bibliographers. The second objection is also a considerable one. If the photographic facsimile is to serve any purpose, it will need to be reproduced in a catalog or bibliography. The standards of accurate reproduction of the printing process must now be added to the basic photographic problems. Collotype is the most nearly accurate of all processes, but it is expensive and few modern printing establishments are equipped to use it. Photogravure and photolithography are both acceptable at their upper limits of sophistication, but neither is a cheap process over the size of printing that is usual for bibliographical tools. Finally, so far as a bibliography, as distinct from a catalog, is concerned, a photographic facsimile is restricted to a single copy instead of having the adaptability of a quasi-facsimile transcription.

Resolution of these varying viewpoints is most unlikely. There can be no generally accepted practice because the books themselves exhibit such a wide range of problems not susceptible to a general theory of description. It is obvious that in certain instances photography, in spite of all its risks, offers a better chance of conveying the detail of a title page than does a quasi-facsimile transcript. An engraved title page, for example, cannot easily be adequately represented by a transcript, nor one that is largely dependent for its effect upon some unusual typographical arrangement. In such instances it is not unreasonable to suggest that the photographic facsimile must be accompanied by the quasi-facsimile form. They will prove to be complementary and essential to each other.

3. The collational formulary is normally set immediately following the title-page transcript. It is in many senses the heart of the description. Current thinking, and practice, has been strongly influenced by Greg's article "A Formulary of Collation."[16] Even after this lapse of time little general or specific disagreement has been found with it. Although he based his

observations upon books of a limited chronological range, they remain true for books of more general categories.

(a) The format of the book, as described in the preceding chapter, must be stated. This applies to the basic description of the format itself. Thus a book that may be discussed as a folio in eights is rightly described as a folio. The fact that it is made up in gatherings of eight leaves is expressed by the succeeding part of the formulary.

(b) The signatures can most shortly and clearly be stated in the "algebraic" manner as shown. An older method was to say "* A-L in fours." But with a large book containing varying sequences of signatures this was very cumbrous. Such a sequence as

A–K^{8} L–N^{4} O–T$^{8/4}$ V–Z^{2} Aa^{4}

would have had to be stated thus:

> A–K in eights, L–N in fours, O–T in alternate eights and fours, V–Z in twos, Aa four leaves.

The designation for alternate eights and fours is also written as 8.4. The same principle is applied in more elaborate sequences of signatures, as when a part of the book runs in triads of eight leaves, six leaves, and six leaves; this, for brevity, is set down as 8.6.6. or 8/6/6.

The value of this algebraic expression of the collational formulary is less obvious in such cases as these than when the book is a mixture of very different patterns of groupings. This is a common occurrence in early printing, although it is not always easy to see the reason for the pattern. Three examples of fifteenth-century books in the British Library will illustrate the point.

(i) a–d^{8} e^{6} f–h^{8} i^{10} k–r^{8} s^{6} t–x^{8} y^{10} aa–cc^{8} a–k^{8} 1 m^{6} n^{8} o p^{6}.
(ii) a^{8} b^{10} c–e^{8} f^{10} g–l^{8} m^{6} mm^{6} n–p^{8} qr^{10} s–x^{8} y^{10} z ꝫ ? ꝝ^{10} A–D^{8} E^{10} F–K^{8} L LL^{6} M–Q^{8} R S^{6}.
(iii) A–H^{8} I^{6} a^{8} b^{6} cd^{8} L–Q$^{8.8.6.}$ R–V XYZ^{8} ꝫ ?^{8} ꝝ^{6} AA^{8} BB^{6}

It is difficult to imagine how a collection of this nature could be expressed more simply.

(c) A totally unsigned quire must be provided with a square-bracketed signature.

Various conventions have been adopted for a formula for a preliminary unsigned gathering. If the second gathering, the first signed, is B, then A is frequently given to the first; thus [A]⁴ B–F⁸. If two unsigned gatherings precede B then logic and clarity suggest [A]⁴ [a]² B–F⁸. Some have preferred to leave it in such instances as [ ]⁴ B–F⁸ and even [ ]⁴ [ ]² B–F⁸. When the first signature is A and the preceding one is unsigned, an asterisk has frequently been used because this is a symbol which had actual use in books in order to sign a gathering before A. This could lead, following the previous examples, to [∗]⁴ A–F⁸ and [∗]⁴ [∗∗]² A–F⁸ or [∗]⁴ [∗]² A–F⁸.

Another now generally accepted convention is to use the Greek letter pi (π) to indicate a preliminary unsigned gathering. This now enjoys so widespread a use as to be universally understood and is probably the most convenient way out of the dilemma.

An unsigned gathering that appears in the book other than as the preliminary gathering is now usually designated by the Greek letter chi (χ).

(d) The pagination should be shown exactly. In many books it does not cover the whole of the preliminaries and has to be explained thus:

pp. [8] + 87 + [1].

In many instances, especially in those of broken or confused collations, it may be preferable to intersperse the statement among the formulary of collation. For example:

A–K⁸ (pp. 1–160) L–N⁴ (pp. 161–184) etc.

(e) Leaves that have been removed and that may possibly appear elsewhere, must be indicated. Thus L⁸ (-L6) means that the sixth leaf of gathering L, which would otherwise appear normally in its folding of eight leaves, has been *intentionally* removed. Thus a book in which a section is so designated is complete in the sense that it includes all the text and material required and that it is as the printer or publisher intended it to be. This is quite different from a book of which the description would be, L^8 (L6 missing). In this latter instance it means that the sixth leaf should be there, and consequently the book so described is imperfect.

(f) Cancels are indicated as follows:

$A-K^8 (\pm G7)$

This means that the seventh leaf of signature G is a cancel, but it does not specify from which other part of the book the cancellans will have come. If it has been provided from one of the sheets of the same work, then the collation entry will somewhere bear record of this as in subparagraph (e) above.

(g) Additional leaves—that is, those that are not associated with a gathering by signatures—are dealt with according to their position in relation to the gathering. Each case is an extension of the use of χ as used in (c) for an unsigned gathering.

A single additional leaf, following the fifth leaf of a gathering in eights, would be indicated as:

$M^8 (M5 + \chi 1)$

Two nonconjugate leaves in a similar position as:

$M^8(M5 + \chi 1, 2)$

Two conjugate leaves as:

$M^8 (M5 + \chi 1.2)$

The conclusion of the formulary of collation is now generally indicated by a statement of the usual number of leaves signed in the book. The symbol is the dollar sign ($) followed by a number indicating the number of signed leaves in each gathering; $4 means that the first four leaves are signed in each gathering. Any variation from this is noted in parentheses after the statement. Thus +G5 would indicate that the fifth leaf of G is signed, and −S2 would indicate that the second leaf of S is not.

(i) The plates are similarly set out, so that the entire physical contents of the book are apparent. Details about them will, if it is justified, form a separate paragraph (see section 5 below)

Allan Stevenson has suggested and used a logical device for dealing with a problem frequently encountered in plate books. He used the Greek letter lambda (λ)

> to signify an unsigned, unpaged *leaf of letterpress* opposite (or associated with) a plate. The plate itself may have either a printed number or an assigned provisional number. Even when the letterpress carries the plate number, it is necessary to prefix the Greek letter in collation and reference. Thus λ 101 means the leaf or letterpress description just before or just after pl. 101, or otherwise closely associated with it.[17]

(j) The number of lines to an average page, whether in double-columns or long lines, whether with headlines, marginal notes, catchwords, etc., follow at the end of the collation entry.

The measurement of the type surface in millimeters (better than inches as being of international use) is the only measurement of old books that provides a norm, since binders will have cut down, more or less drastically, all surviving copies and no two will measure exactly the same. If the copy is uncut, this should be stated, and the measurement of the paper page given in this place in addition to the type-page measurement. As given here the type page is measured both with and without the headline and footline.

(k) It is occasionally the practice to record the first words of some selected page in the text, often page 11. These, called the "dictio probatoria," or "justificatory words," were a device of medieval catalogers for identifying the copy of a work belonging to a particular library. It is a practice that necessarily obtains in the description of manuscript works but has only limited use with printed books outside the realm of early printing. They serve some purpose in identifying very similar editions and indeed any edition where the searcher has only an imperfect copy. For this reason the page chosen should not be too near the beginning, where imperfections most often occur. But the justificatory words, though included in his model forms for Scottish books before 1700 by H. G. Aldis, are in most cases not worth including.[18]

4. The analysis of the contents shows the leaves and pages occupied by every part of the book, preliminaries and blank leaves and pages included. The name given to any part should be elaborated in sufficient detail to make identification as easy as possible. Thus "Dedication" would be less revealing than "Dedication: to Thomas Lord Parker, Baron of Macclesfield, Lord High Chancellor of Great Britain" and "Foreword" less revealing than "Foreword by author, dated from Litchfield, July 1739."

Blanks that are conjugate with printed leaves are a part of the book and must be reckoned; if not so conjugate, they are binder's flyleaves and of no consequence, except as carrying MS notes, which must be dealt with not here but in describing the copy (see section 7 below).

The usage adopted for a long time to denote blank leaves or pages was simply to write, for example; A1ª, blank. Allan Stevenson helped to popularize the convention of writing it thus: A1ª, □. It has certain advantages of condensation but in some circumstances presents problems for the compositor. Whether or not a bibliographer decides to use this symbol, there is no doubt that it is likely to grow sufficiently in popularity to make it important that it should be easily recognized. It is sufficiently important to emphasize here once again that it is absolutely necessary to be exact in the use of the words "leaf" and "page," which are much misused in common speech. A page is bibliographically not a piece of paper in a book but one of its sides. Utter confusion in calculating the makeup of a book results from any laxity in maintaining this distinction.

For this reason particular care is taken to ensure that the term "title leaf" is used when the leaf is intended instead of the page. "Title page" has become such a well-known term that it is frequently used incorrectly, such as "title page missing." Although this is true—it is missing—so is much more, and it needs a more accurate description.

"Sheet" is also a very confusing word, but one that it is difficult to avoid. It means the sheet as manufactured but also in some contexts the section as folded. This is especially common in those formats when the whole sheet is used. It is nevertheless confusing to use the term in such circumstances. "Section," "gathering," or "quire" are better terms for the latter meaning.

References to leaves and pages are best made by the signatures, as being generally more comprehensive than the pagination. A reference to the fourth leaf of quire C is given as C4, not as C^4, which is the form used to show in setting down the collation that quire C has four leaves. The later and unsigned leaves of a signed quire can be referred to without any brackets. In this context to describe the fifth leaf as C5 does not necessarily mean that it bears that signature. Recto and verso are differentiated as *a* and *b*. Some bibliographers use *r* and *v*, but these letters are so similar to handwriting that their use leads to misprints and misreadings, and *a* and *b* seem clearly preferable. Thus the recto of the last leaf in quire C is referred to as $C4^a$, the verso as $C4^b$.

5. Under the broad general heading of the "art collection" must be considered all those parts of the book that are not typographical. They will usually fall into the following categories, which need distinct treatment in the description.

Illustrations that are printed as part of the text page should be listed, with as much detail as can be established relating to method of illustration, names of artists, engravers, etc., identification of the design sufficiently detailed for recognition, sizes of outside measurement, and positions within the book. Woodcut borders, decorative initial letters, ornamental tailpieces, and other such "in-text" illustration are dealt with in the same way. The dividing line between this category of ornamental work and plates is that the former are printed on the same sheets as bear the text and consequently are bibliographically a part of the book.

Plates, on the other hand, are not bibliographically a part of the book. They are insertions and are frequently printed on different paper from the letterpress. From the standpoint of description the term "plates" must be understood to include similar insertions, such as maps, genealogical tables, and so on, as well as the more normal decorative kind. Because of the way in which such insertions are usually made it is clear that it is by no means unusual for there to be variations in position between one copy and another.

In the collation of the plates one common method in the past was to treat them in exactly the same manner as the then current practice of dealing with any inserted leaf:

B^8 (B5 + 1)

indicating a leaf, not specifically a plate, following B5.

Another method was that used in the Tasso example earlier in this chapter:

A-L⁴. Pl. [Front.] + 1–VII

The first had the advantage of precision so far as the position of the leaves was concerned, a strength not possessed by the second method, which nevertheless did specify clearly the fact that they were plates. In either case the collation depends upon the listing of the plates for full detail. In summary, the former method can be effective if the plates are few in number. When they are numerous, then the second method produces greater clarity. The barrier, always an arbitrary one, between effectiveness and confusion in this instance comes when more than one plate is included in each gathering. A finished description should always aim at an accurate simplicity whenever possible, and this factor, together with consistency, should always guide decisions.

The listing of the plates must be regarded as a corollary to the plate collation. The listing should be in the order in which they follow within the work and include details of process, color, artist, engraver, etc. The other important factor in plates, much more common than in any of the other forms of decorative work, is that of dating. Many artists embodied the date within the design area of the plate itself, frequently in association with their signature. The other common form of dating is outside the design area and frequently just below the caption line. It will frequently contain more than the date and will in fact constitute an "imprint" for the plate. An example would be in the form: "London Pub^d. July 1–1814, at 101, Strand, for R. Ackermann's History of Cambridge."

6. This section of the description is concerned with the recording of any facts that can be established regarding the work as a whole. It is material that may be gleaned from an examination of the book, especially from prefaces, dedications, forewords, and so forth, or from research outside the book itself. In the instance

of the Tasso book it might be worthy of record that the book was dedicated to an English baronet although published in Holland. The important thing is that they must be facts and not opinions. For example, it is *not* a fact that *Letters to a Patriot King* was written by Lord Bolingbroke; it *is* a fact that Halkett and Laing ascribes it to him. Also to be cited are references to unusual sources for biographical information on the author, printer, editor, illustrator; details of previous printings; references to suppression of the text; and so on.

7. The description of the individual copy follows. Up to this point the information given would equally be true of any perfect copy of this edition. What follows here is rigidly confined to those matters that concern the copy in hand and that copy only.

This is an important dividing line and raises again the issue, dealt with at the opening of this chapter, as to whether the description is being prepared for a bibliography or for a catalog. The former would call for a description that is true for many copies (or the "ideal copy"), the latter for one particular copy. This part of the description would have no place in a bibliography but is of vital importance in a catalog. On the other hand, it is not inconceivable that a description for a catalog might describe an "ideal copy" and then note the variations exhibited by an individual copy from that ideal. In the case of a very imperfect copy it would indeed be the logical thing to do.

Points that should be made under this heading include:

(a) *Imperfections.* This entry will be an expansion of some part of the collation entry if that collation was of an ideal copy. Missing leaves will be specified in more detail than in the collation, and minor imperfections that did not affect the collation will be detailed. This will include tears, stains, worming, foxing, etc.

(b) *Marks of ownership or any reconstruction of provenance.* Marks of ownership may be indicated in the book by signatures of owners, presentation notes, or bookplates. These should be established in as much detail as possible. More general provenance may be expressed by press marks. Any associated correspondence, snipped catalog entries, or press cuttings, which are not infrequently found in books, must be preserved as being of some assistance in establishing the book's pedigree.

(c) *Binding.* The description of the binding, as already dealt with in Chapter 8, must include description of the endpapers, which are associated with the binding rather than with the book.

(d) *Measurement of leaves*. In bound books there will be variations among copies due to the amount of trimming of the edges by the binder. In cased books there can be variations in size from one printing to another when type-page areas, settings, and format are identical. The actual size of the book, measured in terms of its leaves, can be a very individual characteristic.

The items dealt with so far have constituted part of the bibliographical description for a long time. As bibliographical studies have advanced, the importance of fresh areas of evidence has become apparent. Many of the bibliographies and catalogs published to date made no accommodation for these aspects. Now that their importance is unquestioned, they should be included if appropriate to the kind of book and its period.

8. *Paper:* Details of the paper as set out in Chapter 3.

9. *Press figures:* Although the exact use of press figures is not beyond any shadow of doubt, there is no way in which one can dispute the necessity of recording them in the description. Indeed, as the study of press figures is still at an experimental stage, it is of particular importance that they should be recorded in detail so that evidence may be garnered to help in the understanding of their use.

The need is to know which numbers are used and where they may be found within the book. Several methods have been suggested, but the simplest seems to be the listing of each press number followed by the page references to their appearances:

    1: B7^a, D8^a, F2^b, G7^b.
    2: B3^b, F3^b, H2^b.
    7: C7^b, E8^a.
    9: G4^b.
  10: H1^b.

10. *Typography*. It is almost a cliché to say that descriptive bibliography established itself and refined its techniques on early printed books. It is equally apparent that in early analytical bibliography and hence in early descriptions, typographical evidence was of fundamental importance. This stemmed at least

partially from the experience that the early bibliographers had had with palaeography. Typography was a natural extension of that interest.

As bibliographical work proceeded beyond the range of early printing, typographical evidence became of less interest, and in any event the problems of describing later typographical styles became too great. More recent work has swung the pendulum back somewhat, and new attempts at providing typographic description have gone along the lines suggested at the end of Chapter 4.

Last of all there should be a record of any reference to the same work, or indeed the same copy, in other bibliographies, catalogs, sale lists, and so on. The name of the library owning the copy, the date and source of acquisition (especially if by deed or bequest), and the press mark should be noted. It is always wise to put the date of the completion of the description. Changes in condition of books occur as time goes by, and it is helpful to know at what date the description was accurate.

In order to have an example of a description unlike the Tasso it is salutary to discuss the methods of describing incunabula. It is not only the especial concern with typography but other points of difference that also require attention.

In 1688, when after two centuries had elapsed the earliest products of the printing press began for the first time to be objects of interest in themselves, a Dutch bibliographer, Cornelius a Beughem, used the fanciful term *incunabula artis typographicae*, "swaddling clothes of the typographical art." The term did not pass into common use till it was revived late in the nineteenth century simply as "incunabula" (singular, incunabulum; *anglice*, incunable). In England this replaced the word "fifteener," which had sometimes been used, and came into general use in various vernacular forms. In Germany it was freely translated into *Wiegendrucke*, or "cradle-prints."

The cataloging of incunabula has now a technique of its own, strongly influenced by the so-called "natural-history method of bibliography" expounded by Henry Bradshaw. One of the great early practitioners of this descriptive art was Robert Proctor, whose method of arrangement of the entries was by country, town, printer, and date. This "Proctor Order," as it is now generally known, was strongly influenced by Bradshaw's work and obviously depended upon very precise dating of the material.[19] It was the intensive study of the types used before 1500 that has made it possible to use their evidence as a basis for dating and attributing to their presses the great mass of books of the period. It is not that an incunabulum needs a different kind of description but that additional information needs to be given to cover a number of specific points. One of the greatest bibliographies or catalogs of incunabula in existence is that of the British Museum. The following example is from that catalog, and the subsequent discussion will be related to it.[20] The book in question is a late Strassburg incunabulum, from the press of "the Printer of Jordanus de Quedlinburg," also called "the Printer of the Saints' Days," from his method of dating his books.

NICOLAUS DE BLONE   Sermones de
tempore et sanctis   23 August, 1498.

1ᵃ TITLE Sermones uenerabilis magistri Nicolai de ‖ blony decretorū doctoris. capellani episco‖pi Bosnoniensis ualde deseruientes popu⸗‖lo. ᶘ et clero utcūᶐ docto eos digne legenti ‖ predicāti. aut audienti. de tempore. et de scīs 384ᵇ. COLOPHON : Fiuiunt sermones venerabilis magistri ‖ Nicolai blony decretoᶙ doctoris de tem⸗‖pore : impꝑssi Argētine Anno dñi. Mcccc. ‖ xcviij. Finiti ī vigilia sancti Bartholomei. 385ᵃ. TITLE. Sermones Nicolai ‖ de Blony de sanctis. 477ᵃ. COLOPHON: Finiunt sermones ‖ magistri Nicolai de Blony decreto⸗‖rū doctorī. Capellani episcopi Bos⸗‖noniensis. de tempe et sanctī. Cōscri‖pti ab eodē Anno domini. M. cccc. ‖ xxxviij. vt videtur capi ex sermone. c⸗‖xiij. circa medium membri ꝑmi cius⸗‖dcm sermonis. Impressi Argentine. ‖ Anno domini. M cccc. xcviij. In vi‖gilia sancti Bartholomei.

Folio Part I: Aa⁸ Bb Cc⁶; a–c⁸ d–z A–D⁸⁶⁶ E⁶ F–V⁸⁶⁶ XY⁶ Z⁸ Aa⁶ Bb–Gg⁸⁶⁶ Hh⁸ Part II: [*]⁴ a–f⁸⁶⁶ g–n⁶ o⁸. 478 leaves, the last blank. 2 columns, with printed head-lines. 21ᵃ: 52 lines, 204 × 133 mm. Types: 160, title, head-lines, &c.; 80, text. Spaces left for capitals, with guide-letters. Hain * 3263.
   A reprint of the edition of 22 November 1495.
   This book contains three different heading types (Zf Bibl. 32 [1915]).

276 × 193 mm. Capitals and paragraph-marks supplied in red and blue alternately, initial strokes in red; the large capitals on 21ᵃ and 389ᵃ have border decoration in mauve, green, and gold. A slip containing a note of ownership has been torn away from the head of the first title-leaf, which has been mounted. On the first flyleaf is the signature of R. G. Mackintosh (1818). From the library of the Duke of Sussex, with his press-marked book-plate. Bought in November, 1844.   IB. 1975.

There is nothing fundamentally different between this description and the one already discussed. The chief points to be noticed are those where particular attention is paid to some matters of detail.

The exact date of printing, if in the colophon, should be mentioned. If given at all by the printer, it is often given either according to the ancient Roman calendar, by Nones and Ides, or as here (a habit of this printer) by the ecclesiastical year.[21]

The printer's name should be given if known, or, if not known (as here), the name given to the anonymous press to which the group of books being described is attributed. In the British Museum's fifteenth-century catalog this information is found in the heading to the series of descriptions of books from the press. In this particular instance, as in many others, much of the identification is based on type analysis, and all this is brought together in the heading, which reads as follows:

PRINTER OF THE 1483 JORDANUS DE QUEDLINBURG

DATE: Prior to the Sermons of Jordanus de Quedlinburg completed in 1483, this anonymous printer appears to have printed several books in types still retaining their original measurement of 99 mm., which were subsequently filed down to 91 mm. He was thus almost certainly at work in 1482, perhaps in 1481.

TYPES (see Plate XIII): 160 [P.1], title and head-line type, often leaded to 165, 170, and 180 mm. Used throughout.

99ᴬ, 99ᴮ, both by 1483 filed to 91 [P.2,P.3], text types with large and small face respectively. Both types are also used for lesser headings. Partly superseded after the later months of 1488 by type 80 [P.4]. Before 1483 Lombardic majuscules are used with 99ᴮ, chiefly for dictionary work.

80 [P.4,P.5], smaller text type used from the later months of 1488 onwards. The open U, used by Flach alone of the other Strassburg printers, is found unmixed with any other form from 1488 to 1490. In 1491 a crossed U, similar to that in 99ᴮ, comes in and gradually supplants the open, the displacement being complete by 1498. Mr. Proctor (followed by Dr. Haebler) divided this 89 type into two, in accordance with the preponderance of the crossed or open U, but the process is too gradual to permit of such a division. The 80 type was used with a few minute variations by many other printers, see Haebler, Typenrepertorium, I. p. 187, nos. 135–155. Besides the early use of the open U this variety may be distinguished from others by its more consistent use of an E with the centre stroke filed down for a C, and by the absence of paragraph-marks.

In the section on "Types" they are allotted to the purposes for which they are used in the book, e.g., whether for headlines, text, or commentary. They will be seen in this example to be differentiated by numbers. Thus the text type is entered as 80. This figure is that of twenty lines of type in millimeters, which is taken as the norm. If a type occurs only in single lines, it is difficult to estimate the figure for twenty lines at all exactly.

The types can be at least provisionally identified by the use of Dr. Haebler's work, which contains a table of one hundred forms of the gothic M (the letter most varying in design from font to font) that occur in fifteenth-century types. [22] Detailed descriptions of all the types are noted under each M, arranged by size and with information as to the presses and dates in which they were used.

Suppose, then, that the book under consideration was manifestly printed before 1501 in a gothic type. It is important to date and "place" the book, and the type provides the best evidence. In later periods, when the type founder was well established, types give way to ornaments as evidence of origin. The letter M in the text is compared with Haebler's table and is found to correspond most nearly to his M47. Twenty lines of solid-set type are measured in millimeters, and this, combined with its M-form reference number, becomes the notation by which the type is identified and to which reference is made. If twenty lines measure 80 mm., it is then described as M47 : 80. By running over Haebler's descriptions of the types of that measurement and with that M, which descriptions are all found together, one will be able to pick out the particular example. Comparison with other books or with facsimiles, such as those published by the Gesellschaft für Typenkunde or the Type Facsimile Society, or with the Woolley Photographs, made by George Dunn, will reveal the various sorts of the type as used by the printer indicated in Haebler's list. A more detailed comparison can then be made between the whole type design in the example and in the books or facsimiles. This is necessary because there will naturally be many points of necessary comparison in addition to the M that provided the initial spearhead. At this stage great care and discretion are needed, and hasty identification is a snare, particularly after 1480. But with that warning, the method is sound. It can of course only be practiced in a great library where a sufficiently wide range of books of a particular period may be found for identification. The similar method with roman types is much less satisfactory, as there is no letter so liable to variation in design as M in gothic; Qu (often a ligature) is the best.

We find then a statement in figures for twenty-line measurements of the type or types as part of the description.

If there are any ornamental woodcut *capitals* (again the distinction between capitals and upper case must be remembered), they should be noticed, and the dimensions given. They will identify the press even better than will types, since they could not, at that early period, be multiplied like type. The printer, however, very generally left a blank space for the rubrisher (or the illuminator) to fill the capitals in, and it is the practice to state this and to note whether "guide letters" have been printed in the spaces in order to save the rubrisher from making mistakes, which sometimes occurred. When we come to the description of the individual copy (and only then), we must note whether, and if so in what style, the capitals have been painted in by hand, for this will vary from copy to copy and in many copies will not have been done at all.

Any other points should be noted that show the printer's practice and stage of development; these may be useful, either to "place" this book or by its aid, if it is one that tells its own story, to place others that do not. Uneven line endings (long a thing of the past by 1498) are one of these points, since they are a mark of an early stage in technical skill.

It will now be apparent that, although the descriptions of the Strassburg incunabulum and the eighteenth-century Utrecht book follow a similar overall pattern, they exhibit several important differences. These are due not to any intrinsic difference in the importance of the books but rather that they are the products of different periods of book making. Similar important differences would be found between a mid–sixteenth-century polemical pamphlet and a late–eighteenth-century plate book. Consequently, although there would be basic resemblances, the nature of the books would result in very different descriptions in their detail. Even greater differences will be found when books pass beyond the very real watershed date of 1800.[23]

The revolution in nineteenth-century techniques brought about considerable differences in the book. Machine printed on machine-made paper, reprinted by stereoplate or electroplate, illustrated by photomechanical processes by the late part of the century and multicolored in their casings—they were a new kind of book. Designed with a new reading public in mind, they became increasingly the subject of the publisher rather than the printer and were increasingly influenced by the bookseller and the library. Because of these fundamental changes the bibliographer is interested in different kinds of facts from those that exercise the attention of the bibliographers of earlier books. No better bibliographical listing of nineteenth-century books has appeared than Michael Sadleir's *XIX Century Fiction*.[24] The following example is therefore taken from this work. It will serve to demonstrate once again the variety in the kind of information that the bibliographer is called upon to provide.

CAPTAIN MARRYAT.
[1582] LITTLE SAVAGE (The)

> Copy I: First Edition. 2 vols. Small 8vo. 'Part I', H. Hurst 1848; 'Part II', H. Hurst and Co. 1849. Dark green morocco cloth, blocked on front in gold and blind and gold-lettered with the words 'THE JUVENILE LIBRARY'; on back in blind; and gold-lettered on spine with title, author and 'PART I [11]'. Wood-engraved front. and 3 plates in each vol. Titles printed in red and green—inset leaves not on text paper nor reckoned in the collation—and printed with the words 'First Edition'.

Half-title in each vol.

'Part' I (iv) + (302) CC_6 CC_7 adverts., paged (1)–4. CC_7 is a single inset. The adverts. recommend 'The Juvenile Library'.

II (iv) + (284) BB_3 BB_4 adverts., paged (1)–4.

Binders' ticket: 'Weemys & Co.', at end of Vol. II. Ink signature: Anne H. Weston. 1848 (1849)', inside front cover of each vol. Bookseller's ticket: 'King, Brighton', inside front cover of Vol. 1. Very fine.

Note. The cloth on these volumes is not quite uniform. That on Vol. 1 is pebbly morocco, that on Vol. II coarse morocco. The end-papers also differ—Vol. I, yellow; Vol. II cream.

There can be no question of this being a mixed set. It is in perfect condition, with identical provenance, and was plainly sold on publication in its present form.

[1582a] Copy II: Another. 'Part I', First Edition; 'Part II', Second Edition. 2 vols. 1848/1849. Part I (H. Hurst) identical with Copy I, Part I. Part II: straight-grain coarse morocco cloth, blocked and lettered uniform with Copy I, Part II. Uniform end-papers. Plates as in Copy I. Title of Part II bears the words 'Second Edition, and imprint' H. Hurst and Co.'

Half-title in each vol.

'Part' I Identical with Copy I.
        II Leaf of adverts. precedes half-title. pp. (viii)+280. Page (v) carries a short new preface dated February 1849, signed by Frank Marryat and referring to his father's death and to the consequent delay in publication.

Binders' ticket: 'Westleys & Co.', at end of Vol. II. Ink signature: 'Philip Williams', inside front cover of each vol. Bookseller's stamp: '? Library, Cheltenham', in Vol. I and Bookseller's ticket: 'R. Davies, Birmingham', in Vol. II.

[1582b] Copy III: Another. 'Part I, Third Edition' (Hurst & Co. 1849); 'Part II, Fourth Edition' (Hurst & Co., 1850). Dark green fine-diaper cloth, blocked and lettered

uniform with foregoing; yellow end-papers. Plates as in Copy I. Titles in red and green.

Half-title in each vol.

'Part' I Identical with Copy I.
II Identical with Copy I.

Binders' ticket: 'Westleys and Co.', at end of Vol. I. Ink signature: 'Cecile Holford', on title of each vol.

To revert finally to a problem raised earlier in this chapter: although the foregoing descriptions can be taken as general models, they should not be copied slavishly. In the examples that follow it will be seen that they include the same kind of information but that each part of the entry is not entirely self-contained, and there is great variation in the emphasis on the various parts. They are taken from the book catalogs of two of the world's great antiquarian bookshops.

They treat different kinds of books, but, because of the nature of the catalogs in which the descriptions appeared, there is a concentration on the attributes and importance of one individual copy. This changes the emphasis in several important respects. Some of the best descriptive work at the present day is being done in such establishments, and they exhibit that impeccable standard of accuracy that so distinguishes our leading bookshops.

The first is from catalog No. 108, *The Illustrated Book*, of H. P. Kraus of New York, item No. 58.

THE ENGLISH EDITION OF THE MERCATOR-HONDIUS ATLAS
IN CONTEMPORARY BINDING AND COLOURING

MERCATOR, GERARD, and JODOCUS HONDIUS.— HENRY HEXHAM (trans.). Atlas or A Geographicke description of the Regions, Countries and Kingdomes of the world . . . Translated by Henry Hexham, Quarter-maister to the Regiment of Colonell Goring. 2 vols. 9 leaves, 222 pp. (misnumbered 216), 2 leaves; 1 leaf, pp. 223 (misn. 217)–478 (misn. 462). With two engraved titles, two-page double portrait of Mer-

cator and Hondius, and 196 double-page maps, all in fine contemporary colouring. With a few minor imperfections (see below). Folio. Contemporary English olive morocco, borders on the
sides formed of multiple gilt lines with pointillé ornamentation in
corners and midway on two of the vertical lines, central pointellé
ornaments, backs gilt-tooled in the compartments. (Corners of
binding skilfully mended.) Amsterdam, Henry Hondius and John
Johnson, 1636–1638.

THE FIRST EDITION of the Mercator-Hondius *Atlas* with
the English text of Hexham. As the present edition was issued by
the original publisher, and has the full size maps, it should be
carefully distinguished from the one with the translation by W.
Saltonstall, London, 1635, which had copies of the maps in
much reduced size.

Henry Hexham (c. 1585–c. 1650) was a noted English soldier
and author, who passed much of his life in Holland. He served
there under the adventurer, Col. George Goring.

The present copy is generally in excellent condition. Not present, however, is the Register leaf at the end of Vol. II. The
Register of Vol. I is present, with blank corners torn off. A few
maps are slightly torn or mended, mostly in the margins, and the
maps of the English Fens (I, p. 64 bis) and Osnabrück (I, 148)
have lost small pieces of the engraving. The bindings are in fine
condition. The copy has been carefully collated, as the work was
much used and is often in poor condition. Several of the extant
copies are, in fact, merely odd volumes.

Phillips, *Geographical Atlases*, I, no. 449 (incorrect collation,
calling for 492 pp; we have been informed by letter from the L.C.
that the pagination of their copy actually agrees with that of the
present one); Huntington Library *Checklist*, 287; STC 17827;
(for Hexham) DNB, Vol. 22, (Supplement), 843.

The second is from the Centenary Catalogue, 1947, of Bernard Quaritch of London, item No. 99.

HORAE. Horae, in laudem beatiss. semper virginis Mariae
secundum consuetudinem curiae Romanae... Parisiis Apud
Simonem Colinaeum. M.D.XXIIII. (*Colophon:*) ... M.D.XXV.
XVII. Cal. Febr.

Sm. 4to., *Roman letter, 152 leaves, printed in red and black; with
13 large woodcuts by* GEOFFROY TORY, *and every page sur-*

rounded by a border of Renaissance ornaments also by Tory; device of Simon de Colines (Silvestre 79) on the title; two or three minute holes in one leaf, but a fine copy of this beautiful book, in a sixteenth century Parisian binding of brown calf, in the centre of each side a large oval gilt stamp of the Crucifixion, gilt arabesque corner-pieces, rebacked but most of the original back with gilt ornaments in the panels preserved, a small repair to one side, gilt edges. Paris, Simon de Colines & Geoffroy Tory, 1524–25.

FIRST EDITION OF GEOFFROY TORY'S CELEBRATED BOOK OF HOURS. Tory and de Colines appear to have shared the impression between them, and three issues are recorded differing only in title-pages and colophons and in the arrangement of the almanac and privilege. Of this issue A. W. Pollard in his article in *Bibliographica* writes: "On the whole the little rabbits of Colines' device, with its dotted background, form a more attractive centre-piece to the delicate border than Tory's well-known 'pot cassé.'" The only copy known in France, that of the Bibliothèque de l'Arsenal, contains a folding plate of the Triumph of the Virgin, but it does not appear to be recorded in any other copy of any issue and is probably an insertion. Twelve of the thirteen large woodcuts bear Tory's mark of a Cross of Lorraine, the exception being one of the pair, facing each other on opposite pages, representing the Annunciation. The treatment of this subject in two woodcuts is most unusual. Many of the borders also bear Tory's mark.

"The volume, containing sixteen full-page borders (often repeated) and thirteen large woodcuts, has long since become one of the most famous of all books of hours. Not only did it break with tradition, but it set new standards of beautiful bookmaking, forming a precedent to which even to-day the greatest designers of beautiful books return again and again to gather strength... The revolution it worked can be compared only to that produced by the first italic volume from the Aldine press, for it meant suddenly that the day of the gothic book in France was over, attacked and killed in its deepest citadel, the prayer book... The cuts and decorations present the sharpest possible divergence from the illustrations full of that German influence, which like some plague had overrun the true French Horae such as those which Vérard and Vostre had published towards the end of the fifteenth century. Where they represent the culmination of the gothic in French printing, this is fully modern in its every important detail... the illustrations and borders harmonize perfectly with the lovely roman type in which it is printed... the decoration and mise en page have been most conscientiously and beautifully considered.

Many of the earlier Parisian illustrated books had beauty and charm and much character, but here, it is possibly not too much to say, was the first French book which from beginning to end was a highly conscious and deliberate work of art. Seldom in the long history of book making has anything more refined and delicate been made, and it is small wonder that its reputation has grown with the years."

—IVINS, Prints and Books.

** See illustrations facing pp. 39 and 41.

REFERENCES

1. OSBORN, Andrew D. "The Crisis in Cataloguing." *Library Quarterly.* XI: 1941. p. 400.

2. TANSELLE, G. Thomas. "Descriptive Bibliography and Library Cataloguing." *Studies in Bibliography.* XXX: 1977. pp. 1–56.

3. BOWERS, Fredson. *Principles of Bibliographical Description.* 1949. p. 6.

4. Bowers, p. 113

   See also:

   POUNCEY, Lorene. "The Fallacy of the Ideal Copy." *The Library.* 5th Series. XXXIII: 1978. pp. 108–118.

5. Maggs Catalogue, No. 966. 1975.

6. Zeitlin & Ver Brugge Catalogue, No. 221. 1969.

7. Bertram Rota Catalogue, No. 192. 1974.

8. GREG, W. W. *A Bibliography of the English Printed Drama to the Restoration.* 4v. 1939–1959. Vol. 4. pp. xliii–xliv.

9. STEVENSON, Allan. *A Bibliographical Method for the Description of Botanical Books,* in *Catalogue of Botanical Books in the Collection of Rachel McMasters Miller Hunt,* Vol. II, Part 1, 1961. p. clii.

10. This does not maintain grammar, as omissions should, but will serve to illustrate the principle.

11. Fuller information on these must be sought in the textbooks on palaeography. A good introduction to their use in early printing may be found in "Appendix Four" of McKerrow's *Introduction to Bibliography*.

12. It is difficult to believe that "poetaz" in the phrase "narcissus poetaz" is not a nurseryman's version of a medievalist gardener's "poetarum," written "poeta 2⌊".

13. MADAN, F.; DUFF, E.G.; and GIBSON, S. *Standard descriptions of printed books, Oxford Bibliographical Society. Proceedings & Papers.* Vol. I, Part 1. 1923. pp. 55–64.

14. McKERROW, R.B. *Printers' and Publishers' Devices in England and Scotland, 1485–1640.* 1913.
    DAVIES, H. W. *Devices of the Early Printers:. 1457–1560.* 1935.

15. McKERROW, R. B., and FERGUSON, F. S. *Title-page Borders Used in England & Scotland 1485–1640.* 1932.

16. *The Library.* 4th Series. XIV: 1933–34. pp. 365–382.

17. Stevenson, pp. cxlvii cxlviii.

18. ALDIS, H. G. *A List of Books Printed in Scotland Before 1700. . . .* 1904.

19. Proctor's is one of several important bibliographical tools relating to incunabula that should be studied in order to compare the varying styles and details of treatment.

The ideal of a complete bibliography has been approached for one period only, and that is the pioneer period of printing, reckoned for convenience as ending at the end of the fifteenth century. As early as the end of the eighteenth century Georg Panzer produced his annals of the presses of this and the next generation.

PANZER, Georg W. F. *Annales Typographici ad Annum 1536.* 11v. 1793–1803.

In 1812–1815, T. F. Dibdin, with much enthusiasm and splendor of printing, cataloged the fine library of early books collected by Earl Spencer. This, the Althorp, library passed in 1897 into the John Rylands Library, Manchester. It is in the catalog of books of this library, compiled by Gordon Duff, then librarian there, rather than in Dibdin, that instructed information as to presses and dates must be sought.

A quarter of a century later than Panzer followed the famous work of Ludwig Hain:

HAIN, Ludwig F. T. *Repertorium Bibliographicum ad Annum MD.* 2v. in 4. 1826–1838.

to which can be added a series of supplements:

BURGER, K. *Register. Die Drucker des XV Jahrhunderts.* 1891.
COPINGER, W. A. *Supplement.* 2v. in 3. 1895–1902.
BURGER, K. *Supplement zu Hain und Panzer.* 1908.
REICHLING, D. *Supplement.* 7v. 1905–1911.
REICHLING, D. *Supplement and General Index of Authors.* 1914.

Based largely on the collections of the Munich Hofbibliotek, then greatly enriched by books from the Bavarian monasteries, Hain's is an author list. It is noted for its extreme accuracy, at least in the entries that he distinguished with an asterisk as of books seen by himself. He gives the number of leaves, and some other typographical notes, in a code of abbreviations that needs some practice to decipher; but, though he mentions the presence of signatures, he does not collate by them. Nor does he attempt to attribute books to their printers. His descriptions of some sixteen thousand incunabula, however, put the knowledge of early printing on a new basis, and Burger's index of printers paved the way for Proctor. The Supplements to Hain by Copinger and Reichling are unfortunately not nearly as accurate as their original.

The work of Henry Bradshaw, Holtrop, and Campbell on the early productions of the Low Country presses gave a new method of study of these monuments. As a consequence, the catalog of the incunabula in the public libraries of France made for the Ministry of Public Instruction is, though an author list like Hain's, much more expert on the typographical side.

PELLECHET, Marie L. C. *Catalogue général des incunables des bibliothèques publiques de France* (continued by Louis Polain). 3v. 1897–1909.

This was for a long time left unfinished at "Gregorius Magnus," but was completed in 1970 by the publication (Vols. 4–26) of a photolithographic reprint of the remainder of the work in Louis Polain's manuscript. But the full fruits of the "natural history method," taught by Bradshaw, appeared in:

PROCTOR, Robert. *Index to the Early Printed Books in the British Museum . . . to 1500, with Notes of those in the Bodleian Library.* 4v. 1898–1899.

This was a marvelous piece of work, achieved in ten years by a near-sighted man with other duties, in which not far short of ten thousand books (perhaps a third of them bearing no printer's name) are sorted out on typographical evidence under their countries, towns, presses and dates—an arrangement that has ever since been spoken of as "Proctor Order." Indexes of authors are of course provided. Part II of Proctor's work was designed to take the work down from 1501 to 1520, a period in which woodcut illustrations and ornaments are more salient features than types, since types were by now being made wholesale by type founders and therefore used at unconnected presses. The date 1520 was chosen as stopping short of the flood of Lutheran pamphlets. Proctor lived to complete only Section 1, covering Germany, of this second part. Sections 2 and 3, covering Italy, Switzerland, and Eastern Europe, were completed by Frank Isaac and published in 1938.

Proctor's short-title Index is expanded and worked over, and his method carried further, in:

BRITISH MUSEUM. *Catalogue of Books Printed in XVth Century Now in the British Museum.* 1908–.

This is fully illustrated with facsimiles of types. German and Italian printing was finished in the first seven volumes. France and French-speaking Switzerland were covered in the eighth volume, which was published in 1949. Holland and Belgium were covered in the ninth volume, published in 1962. Spain, Austria, England, and Scandinavia remain for later volumes. A photolitho reprint of the first eight parts was issued in 1963. This was photographed from the B.M. copy and so reproduced manuscript amendments to that copy up to the date of issue of the reprint.

In 1912 the Prussian government projected a definitive author

catalog of incunabula. The Commission then formed for the purpose under Konrad Haebler later became independent of the
state. The result of their exhaustive census of the surviving copies
of known incunabula was *Gesamtkatalog der Wiegendrucke.* Publication of the parts began in 1925, and the last to appear was Part I
of Volume 8 in 1940, covering up to "Fredericus." Although it
was discovered, after the Second World War, that much of the
material gathered by the Commission, together with the slips
ready for printing, was still in existence, it now seems improbable
that any further progress can be expected with this great project.

Another library that has an outstanding collection of incunabula
and has published a catalog of equal merit is:

OATES, J. C. T. *A Catalogue of the Fifteenth-century Printed
Books in the University Library, Cambridge.* 1954.

For ordinary purposes the whole output of English presses to 1500
(except for stray later discoveries) has been adequately described
by:

DUFF, E. Gordon. *Fifteenth Century English Books.* 1917.

20. Part 1. 1963 reprint. p. 146.

21. Reference in any case of doubt should be made to such works as:

CAPPELLI, A. *Chronologia e calendario perpetuo.* 1906.

22. HAEBLER, Konrad. *Typenrepertorium der Wiegendrucke.* 1905–
1924.

23. The particular problems of post-1800 books are dealt with in
varying ways by a number of books:

BOWERS, Fredson. *Principles of Bibliographical Description.* 1962.
Chapters on "The Nineteenth and Twentieth Centuries."
RAY, Gordon N.; WEBER, Carl J.; and CARTER, John.
Nineteenth Century English Books. 1952.
SADLEIR, Michael. *Excursions in Victorian Bibliography.* 1922.
SUTHERLAND, J. A. *Victorian Novelists & Publishers.* 1976.
TILLOTSON, Kathleen. *Novels of the Eighteen-forties.* 1954.

15. SADLEIR, Michael. *XIX Century Fiction.* 1951.

This is of paramount importance to bibliographical work on nineteenth-century books not solely because of the information related to the specific titles in the collection but for its total absorbtion with that period's special problems. It should be read in conjunction with Sadleir's essay in the Bibliographical Society's *Studies in Retrospect.* 1945. pp. 146–158.

In addition to works already quoted as specific references, the following should be read for general background:

BÜHLER, Curt F., and others. *Standards of Bibliographical Description.* 1949.

COWLEY, J. D. *Bibliographical Description and Cataloguing.* 1939.

DE MORGAN, Augustus. *On the Difficulty of the Correct Description of Books.* 1853. Reprinted with an introduction by Henry Guppy, 1902.

DUNKIN, Paul S. *How to Catalog a Rare Book.* 1951.

FOXON, D. F. *Thoughts on the History and Future of Bibliographical Description.* 1970.

GREG, W. W. Introduction to Volume IV of *A Bibliography of the English Printed Drama to the Restoration.* 1959.

GUPPY, Henry. *Rules for the Cataloguing of Incunabula.* 2nd ed. 1932.

JONES, J. B., ed. *Readings in Descriptive Bibliography.* 1974.

MADAN, Falconer; DUFF, E. G.; and GIBSON, S. "Standard Descriptions of Printed Books." *Oxford Bibliographical Society: Proceedings and Papers.* Vol. I, Part 1. 1923. pp. 56–64.

POLLARD, A. W. "The Object and Methods of Bibliographical Collations and Descriptions." *The Library.* 2nd Series. VIII: 1907. pp. 193–217.

POLLARD, A. W., and GREG, W. W. "Some Points in Bibliographical Description." *Transactions of the Bibliographical Society.* IX: 1908. pp. 31–52.

to be read with:

MADAN, Falconer. "Degressive Bibliography: A Memorandum." *Ibid.* pp. 53–65.

STEVENSON, Allan. "A Bibliographical Method for the Description of Botanical Books," in Vol. 2 of *Catalogue of Botanical Books in the Collection of Rachel McMasters Miller Hunt.* 1961.

TANSELLE, G. T. "Some Remarks on Bibliographical Nonproliferation." *Proof.* I: 1971. pp. 169–179.

GLOSSARY

The brief definitions listed below should be used in conjunction with fuller descriptions of many of them included in the text.

The largest glossary currently available of terms associated primarily with book production rather than bibliography is: GLAISTER, Geoffrey Ashall. *Glaister's Glossary of the Book.* 2nd ed. Berkeley and Los Angeles: University of California Press. 1979.

ANOPISTHOGRAPH. Manuscript or book having writing on one side only of the leaf or sheet.

BLACK LETTER. A general description of the type designs also known as *gothic.* The term is used for a group of types in contradistinction to the other main groups of *roman* and *italic.*

BOARDS. In general, the wood or other base used in a bound or cased book. It is found in such terms as "front board," "back board," "marbled boards," etc. Also applied specifically to a method of issuing books in the 1770–1830 period. Light boards and a paper spine created the "boards-and-label period."

CANCEL. "A cancel is any part of a book substituted for what was originally printed. It may be of any size from a tiny scrap of paper bearing one or two letters, pasted on over those first printed, to several sheets replacing the original ones. The most common form of cancel is perhaps a single leaf inserted in place of the original leaf" (McKerrow).

CASING. In cased books, as opposed to bound books, the boards and their covering material are manufactured separately from the book itself. The sewn gatherings are attached to a strip of backing material, of varying strengths, the overhang of which is glued to the inside of the boards.

CATCHWORD. The printing, below the last line of a page, of the first word of the succeeding page.

CHAIN LINES. Lines produced in the sheet of paper by the mesh of the paper maker's frame. They are normally widely spaced, as distinct from the wire lines, which are close together. Chain lines normally run across the width of the full sheet.

CHASE. The metal frame in which type pages are arranged and locked up in readiness for printing.

CODEX. (*Latin* [older form *caudex*]: trunk of a tree.) Book made up of hinged wooden tablets; later, book of hinged form as distinct from the roll. Also, a manuscript volume, especially one of the ancient Biblical manuscripts, such as the Codex Sinaiticus.

COLLATE (To). To examine a book in order to establish all the bibliographical details related to its present makeup. It is a process that aims at a knowledge of the item that would enable a detailed comparison of copies to be made.

COLLATION. A record of the bibliographical details of a book expressed in a standardized formula.

COLOPHON. An inscription, sometimes with a device, at the end of a text giving scribe's or printer's name, title of work, date, and place of writing or printing.

CONJUGATE. Joined together, a pair. Applied especially to "conjugate leaves."

COPY TEXT. The text that the editor selects as the basis for an edition. Opinion and practice vary as to the extent to which it is permissible to depart from the copy text.

COUNTERMARK. A second watermark in paper, often incorporating name or initials of a paper manufacturer.

DEVICES, PRINTERS'. Distinguishing design, virtually a trademark, placed by printers usually on the title page or colophon. Their modern descendants are publishers' devices, which serve the same purpose of easy recognition.

DUODECIMO. The name given to the format of a book when the sheet has been folded, in a number of possible ways, with the result of producing twelve leaves or twenty-four pages.

EDITION. Term used to comprise all those copies of a work printed from the same setting up of type.

ENDPAPERS. Double-leaves added at front and back of a book. One leaf is pasted to the inside of the board, the others form the first and last leaves within the bound or cased book. Bibliographically, the endpapers do not form part of the book.

FACTOTUM. In printing, an ornamental block with a hollow center into which a piece of type is inserted in order to create the appearance of a decorated initial letter.

FOLIATION. The numbering of leaves as distinct from the numbering of pages, "pagination." Foliation was the normal practice in manuscripts and in early printed books. It was unusual in printed books after 1600.

FOLIO. The name given to the format of a book when the sheet has been folded once, to make two leaves or four pages.

FONT (also FOUNT). A complete set of one size of one design of type. For example, a font of 12-point Centaur.

FORE-EDGE. The edge of the leaves of a book opposite the spine.

FORE-EDGE PAINTING. Painting that is executed on the fore-edge of a book. Of especial interest when it has been done on a minute flat edge of the pages so that the decoration appears only when the leaves are fanned.

FORM (also FORME). Type pages that have been locked up in the chase in readiness for printing. The actual typographical unit that lies on the bed of the press.

FORMAT. A term used to describe a book according to the manner and number of times the full sheet had been folded. For example, folio, quarto, octavo, duodecimo. Format does not indicate size unless it is used in conjunction with a statement of the size of the sheet. For example, "octavo" is *not* size; "crown octavo" is.

FOUL PAPERS. A phrase, largely popularized by Greg, to denote all the early drafts of a work by an author up to the final "clean" manuscript.

FOXING. The discoloration in paper caused by microorganisms as the paper ages. It usually takes the form of light brown spots.

FURNITURE. Pieces of metal or wood, less than type height, that are placed around type in the chase in order to secure them.

GALLEY. A shallow metal tray, open on one side only, used for holding composed type matter.

GALLEY PROOF. A proof taken from type while it is still in the galley and before it has been made into pages.

GATHERING. The group of leaves that results from the folding of a whole sheet, part of a sheet, or more than one sheet to form the sewing unit of a book. Each gathering is normally differentiated by a *signature*.

GRANGERIZED. Between 1769 and 1774 James Granger published his five-volume *Biographical History of England*, with blank leaves on which the owner could add such portraits or other illustrative material as desired. The term is now applied to a copy in which this has been done. It is also known as "extra-illustrated."

GUARDS. A leaf or plate that is guarded is one that has been pasted to a stub rather than sewn in as one of a pair of conjugate leaves. It is particularly common when the plate is of the size of two leaves and so can be fixed into the book with no sewing in its fold and can then more easily open flat.

HALF-TITLE. The half-title leaf precedes the title leaf. Originally designed solely for the protection of the title page, it now usually bears on its recto a shortened version of the title.

HEADLINE. "A line of type at the top of a page, above the text, is called a 'head-line'; or, if it consists of the title of the book (or of the section of the book) on every page or every 'opening' (i.e., two pages facing one another), sometimes a 'running-title' or 'running-head'" (McKerrow).

IDEAL COPY. A bibliographical concept that postulates the bibliographical nature of the book as the printer/publisher intended it to be at the moment of issue.

IMPOSITION. The arrangement of type pages within the form so that, when the sheet is folded, the pages will read in the correct order.

IMPRESSION. All those copies printed from the same type at any one time. There can thus be several impressions within an edition, and it is in this connection that the term is most often found ("third impression of the second edition"). Also referred to as a "printing."

IMPRIMATUR. (*Latin:* "let it be printed.") A formula whereby an organization grants permission to one of its members to print a text. Especially, when the Roman Catholic Church grants such permission, designed to assure the reader that the text adheres strictly to the Church's teaching.

IMPRINT. A statement, now usually on the title page, that records the names of those associated with the printing and publication of the book. For example, "Printed by A for B and to be sold by C and D." In manuscript and early printed books such information was usually provided in the colophon.

INCUNABULA. (*Latin:* "swaddling-clothes," thus "infancy.") Books printed in the fifteenth century. Singular "incunabulum." Sometimes anglicized as "incunable" and "incunables."

INTERLEAVING. The insertion of leaves, usually blank, between the leaves of the text. Occasionally provided as part of the work as issued, more frequently done by an individual owner.

ISSUE. "Some special form of the book in which, for the most part, the original printed sheets are used but which differs from the earlier or normal form by the addition of new matter or by some difference in arrangement" (McKerrow).

LEADING. A strip of metal, less than type height, placed in order to separate two lines of type in the composition process. The same effect is achieved more easily with type cast on a larger body; e.g., ten-point type cast on a twelve-point body.

LEAF. The basic bibliographical unit of a book, consisting of two pages, one on the recto of a leaf and one on the verso. There is thus an important distinction between information that is on the title page or that which is on the title leaf. A leaf can be missing from a copy, a page cannot be.

OCTAVO. The name given to the format of a book when the sheet has been folded three times, the second and third folds being at right angles to the previous fold. This produces eight leaves, or sixteen pages.

OPISTHOGRAPH. Manuscript or book having writing or printing on both sides of the leaf or sheet.

PROVENANCE. The origin and history of the material. Used chiefly in the phrase "the provenance of a copy," which indicates the history of the ownership and location of an individual work.

QUARTO. The name given to the format of a book when the sheet has been folded twice, the second fold being at right angles to the first. This produces four leaves, or eight pages.

QUOINS. Wedges that are driven between the furniture in the chase in order to make a secure unit.

RECENSION. A revised or distinct form of anything (*O.E.D.*). A particular version of a text.

RECTO. The righthand page of an open book. The other side of the leaf is the "verso."

RULE. Strip of type-high metal used to print a line, either continuous or patterned—such as swelling, spiral, etc.

SCRIVENER. A scribe or copyist.

SHEET. The unit of paper that comes off the paper maker's frame or mold and that goes on to the printing press. The folding of the sheet produces the gatherings that will be sewn together to create the book.

SIGNATURES. The series of letters that are found, normally below the last line of text, on at least the first page of each gathering. The "alphabet" normally consisted of twenty-three letters, since I and J, U and V were respectively each represented by one letter and W was not used. They were provided to enable the binder to arrange the gatherings in the correct order. In some modern books (i.e., post-1800) letters are replaced by numbers.

STEMMA. A genealogical tree. Used bibliographically to record and clarify the relationships between groups of manuscripts and printed books.

SUBSCRIPTION LISTS. Publication by subscription in England began at least as early as 1617. Lists of the names, sometimes with addresses and occasionally with occupations, appear in the publications.

SWASH LETTERS. Ornamental upper-case letters associated with some fonts of italic type.

TITLE PAGE. The recto of an early leaf in a book that carries, normally, the official title of the book and name of author. Other details of publication—printer, publisher, and place and date of publication are usually included. Occasionally, especially in modern books, some important detail of this nature is included on the verso, making it important to realize the distinction between information on the title page or on the title leaf.

UNCUT. The term used to describe a copy in which the edges of the leaves have not been cut or trimmed in rebinding. In such instances the margins have been left as full as was intended by the original printer and binder.

UNOPENED. When the sheet is folded to create any format other than a folio, the edges—especially the head and the fore-edge—will be joined ("the bolts"). An unopened book is one in which the bolts have not been cut, and therefore the book cannot be read.

VARIANTS. In general, differences between copies that might be supposed to be identical. Thus there can be variant casings, variant title pages, textual variants, and so on.

VERSO. The lefthand page of an open book. The other side of the leaf is the "recto."

VOLUMEN. Originally, anything that was rolled. Thus applied to the book in its early roll form and so eventually to what could be contained on a roll—a volume.

WATERMARK. A device made in the paper by a wire design in the mesh of the paper maker's frame.

WIRE LINES. Lines produced in the sheet of paper by the mesh of the paper maker's frame. They are very close together, as distinct from the chain lines.

XYLOGRAPHY. The general term that covers all the aspects of using wood blocks for printing. It is a convenience to have one word that covers both wood-cutting and wood-engraving.

INDEX